ALSO AVAILABLE FROM HANS BEUMER

----------TRAVEL----------

Swiss Camino – Volume I: North-East Switzerland

Swiss Camino – Volume III: South-West Switzerland

Kumano Kodo Pilgrimage

Japan's Travel Culture

20'000 km by Train

----------SELF-HELP----------

Success for Everyone

Happiness for Everyone

Travel Guide to Self-actualization

----------INTERNAL AUDIT----------

The Leadership & Managerial Habits of Highly Effective CAEs

The 7 Leadership Habits of Highly Effective CAEs

The 7 Managerial Habits of Highly Effective CAEs

The Internal Audit Handbook

Audit Function Strategy

Audit Engagement Strategy

Audit Risk Management

Visit www.hansbeumer.com

Swiss Camino – Volume I: North-East Switzerland

GENERAL INTRODUCTION
Organizational Tips, Religious Context, Church Terminology, Hiking Routes, Raising Expectations

KONSTANZ TO EINSIEDELN

Stage K1:	Konstanz to Märstetten	16 km
Stage K2:	Märstetten to Fischingen	35 km
Stage K3:	Fischingen to Rapperswil	33 km
Stage 4:	Rapperswil to Einsiedeln	18 km

RORSCHACH TO EINSIEDELN

Stage R1a:	Rorschach to St. Gallen	18 km
Stage R1b:	St. Gallen to Herisau	11 km
Stage R2:	Herisau to Wattwil	26 km
	via Rapperswil:	
Stage R3:	Wattwil to Rapperswil	29 km
Stage 4:	Rapperswil to Einsiedeln	18 km
	via Siebnen:	
Stage S1:	Wattwil to Siebnen	31 km
Stage S2:	Siebnen to Einsiedeln	19 km

Available as
- Hiking edition: ISBN 978-3-906861-32-6
- Luxury edition: ISBN 978-3-906861-33-3
- eBook edition: ISBN 978-3-906861-34-0

Swiss Camino – Volume III: South-West Switzerland

FRIBOURG TO MOUDON

	via Romont:	
Stage 14:	Fribourg to Romont	30 km
Stage 15:	Romont to Moudon	17 km
	via Payerne:	
Stage P1:	Fribourg to Payerne	25 km
Stage P2:	Payerne to Moudon	29 km

MOUDON TO GENEVA

Stage 16:	Moudon to Lausanne	30 km
Stage 17:	Lausanne to Rolle	33 km
Stage 18:	Rolle to Coppet	32 km
Stage 19:	Coppet to Geneva	19 km
Stage 20:	Geneva to French border	8 km

Available as
- Hiking edition: ISBN 978-3-906861-38-8
- Luxury edition: ISBN 978-3-906861-39-5
- eBook edition: ISBN 978-3-906861-40-1

SWISS CAMINO

Volume II: Central Switzerland

300 Churches
800 km Hiking
1'000 yrs History
on
the Way of St. James
through Switzerland

HANS BEUMER

HB Publications
Unterägeri, Switzerland
www.hansbeumer.com

First edition published in September 2019

This book is available as:
- Hiking edition (B/W): ISBN 978-3-906861-35-7
- Luxury edition (Color): ISBN 978-3-906861-36-4
- eBook edition (EPUB): ISBN 978-3-906861-37-1

Printed and distributed by Lulu Press, Inc.

CONTENTS

CENTRAL SWITZERLAND
to Saint Canisius of Fribourg

ALTERNATIVE VIA LUZERN/BERN 285

APPENDICES 409

Foreword

Liber Sancti Jacobi Helvetia

The first Way of St. James Pilgrim's Handbook was handwritten around 1130. The Latin manuscript was called the 'Liber Sancti Jacobi' (also Codex Callixtus – attributed to Pope Callixtus II) and consisted of five parts. Two parts related to stories, miracles, and legends of St. James. The fifth part described four French Ways to the Pyrenees and Santiago de Compostela. These route descriptions included all important churches the pilgrim was to visit along the way.

Nearly 900 years after the Liber Sancti Jacobi for France, my book describes the Way of Saint James for Switzerland in a comparable manner. The 'Swiss Camino' is the definitive guide for the 21st century pilgrim on the Swiss routes. Hence its Latin title: *Liber Sancti Jacobi Helvetia.*

Three Volumes

The Swiss Camino pilgrim's guide is split into three volumes:

Volume I consists of two main sections:

1. A general introduction to the 18- to 21-day pilgrimage on the Way of St. James through Switzerland, including:
    - Organizational tips for a successful pilgrimage at a low cost in this high-cost country.
    - Religious context of St. James, Roman catacomb relics, saints, monastic Orders, and the Swiss religious Reformation in the 1520s-30s.
    - Church terminology, designations, architecture, interiors, and monastic Order terminology.
    - Route decisions, route possibilities, stages, and route signaling.
    - Raising expectations of the routes, churches, monasteries, and points of interest.
2. A complete coverage of the pilgrimage routes with details of the trails, churches, saints, catacomb relics, monasteries, castles, cities, and other points of interest in German-speaking North-East Switzerland:
    - From Konstanz to Einsiedeln, via Rapperswil (101 km in 4 stages); and
    - From Rorschach to Einsiedeln, via Rapperswil (101 km in 4 or 5 stages) and via Siebnen (105 km in 4 or 5 stages).

Volume II (this book) provides a complete coverage of the pilgrimage routes with details of the trails, churches, saints, catacomb relics, monasteries, castles, cities, and other points of interest in German-speaking Central Switzerland:

- From Einsiedeln to Fribourg, via Alpine Lakes (224 km in 9 stages); and
- From Einsiedeln to Fribourg, via Luzern/Bern (200 km in 7 stages).

Volume III provides a complete coverage of the pilgrimage routes with details of the trails, churches, saints, catacomb relics, monasteries, castles, chateaus, cities, and other points of interest in French-speaking South-West Switzerland:

- From Fribourg to Moudon, via Romont (47 km in 2 stages) and via Payerne (54 km in 2 stages);
  and onwards
- From Moudon to Geneva, and French border (123 km in 5 stages).

The 54-page General Introduction to the Swiss Way of St. James of Volume I is not copied in the other two volumes. This prevents a repetition of many pages, even though its content equally applies to Volumes II and III. Therefore, for the General Introduction to the Swiss Camino please refer to Volume I.

This foreword to Volume II is kept short. Please see Volume I for the extensive introductory foreword.

Thank you for using this book as your guide on the Swiss Way of St. James.

Bon Camino!
drs. Hans Beumer
September 2019

CENTRAL SWITZERLAND

TO SAINT CANISIUS OF FRIBOURG

Overview of Routes

The Way of St. James in Central Switzerland

Central Switzerland routes

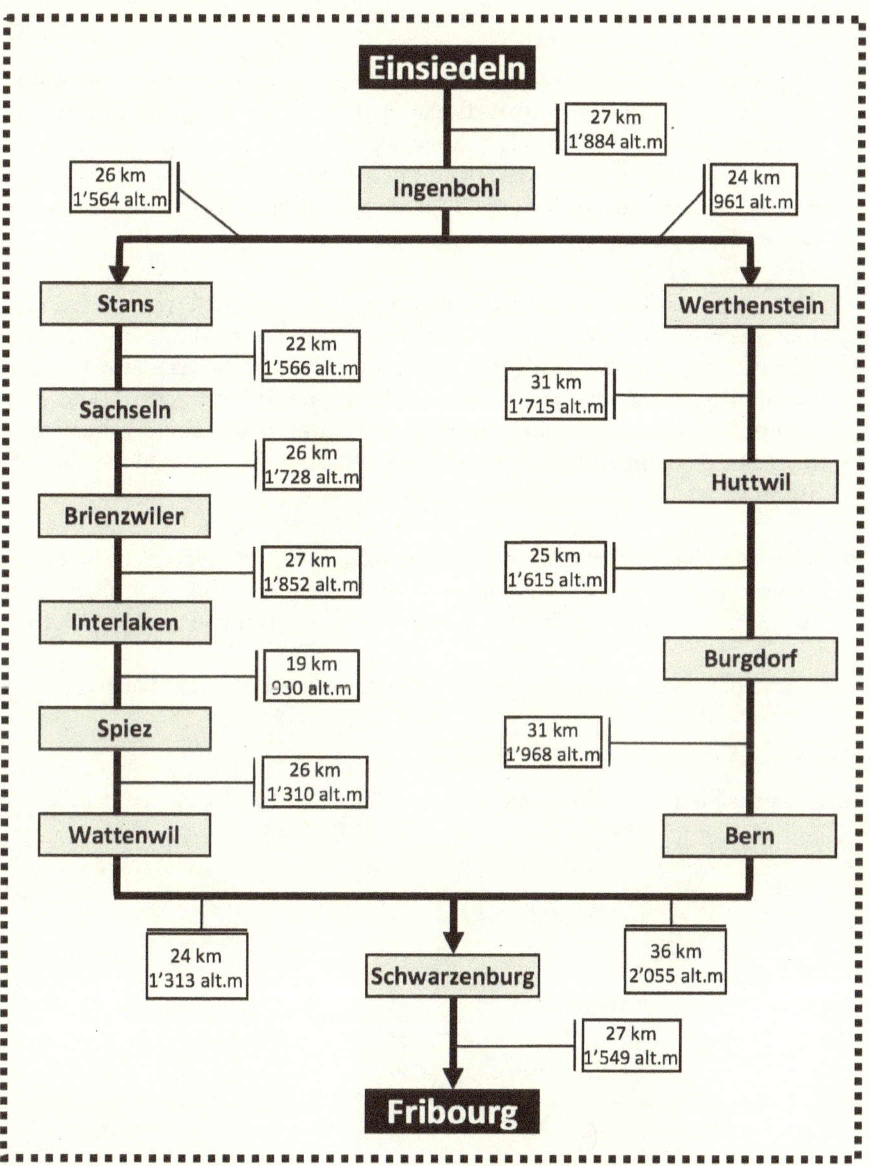

Route choices

For the choice of the route via Alpine Lakes (Interlaken) or Luzern/Bern, consider the following for your decision:

- The route via Interlaken passes by turquoise alpine lakes with snow-capped Alps in the distance. This is a unique scenery and probably the main reason you came to Switzerland. Such scenery and landscapes are not available on the route via Luzern/Bern. The route via Interlaken goes through alpine and agricultural rural areas, whereas the trails via Luzern/Bern are through agricultural rural areas over rolling foothills.

- The route via Interlaken passes through three catholic Cantons (Nidwalden, Obwalden, and Fribourg) that display many religious artefacts and treasures in their churches and chapels. Above all, this route passes by the birthplace, hermit cell, and grave of Switzerland's patron Saint, Nicholas of Flüe (Brother Klaus). The route via Luzern/Bern passes through two catholic Cantons (Luzern and Fribourg).

- The route via Luzern/Bern passes through two major Swiss tourist cities: Luzern and Bern. Both have a significant number of medieval historical sites that are unique for Switzerland. Luzern was a catholic powerhouse during the Counter-Reformation, while Bern is the capital of Switzerland and had a significant influence on the history of the country. The route via Interlaken does not pass through comparable power-cities; the towns along the route are small.

- The Interlaken route is 23 km longer, has 1'949 (23 percent) more altitude meters, and takes 2 days longer to hike. On average the daily hikes on the route via Interlaken are 5 km shorter than on the route via Luzern/Bern.

My recommendation: choose the route via Interlaken, the Alpine Lakes.

Route stats

The two possible routes (with overlapping stages 5 and 13) compare as follows:

	#	From	To	Km	Alt. m	Churches
1	5	Einsiedeln	Ingenbohl	27	1'884	24
2	6	Ingenbohl	Stans	26	1'564	25
3	7	Stans	Sachseln	22	1'566	14
4	8	Sachseln	Brienzwiler	26	1'728	7
5	9	Brienzwiler	Interlaken	27	1'852	8
6	10	Interlaken	Spiez	19	930	7
7	11	Spiez	Wattenwil	26	1'310	4
8	12	Wattenwil	Schwarzenburg	24	1'313	5
9	13	Schwarzenburg	Fribourg	27	1'549	24
	From Einsiedeln to Fribourg, via Alpine Lakes			**224**	**13'696**	**118**
1	5	Einsiedeln	Ingenbohl	27	1'884	24
2	L1	Ingenbohl	Werthenstein	24	961	16
3	L2	Werthenstein	Huttwil	31	1'715	10
4	L3	Huttwil	Burgdorf	25	1'615	5
5	L4	Burgdorf	Bern	31	1'968	6
6	L5	Bern	Schwarzenburg	36	2'055	7
7	13	Schwarzenburg	Fribourg	27	1'549	24
	From Einsiedeln to Fribourg, via Luzern/Bern			**200**	**11'747**	**92**

Route summaries

From Einsiedeln to Fribourg, via Alpine Lakes (Interlaken)

Stage 5 (Einsiedeln to Ingenbohl) guides you through the Einsiedeln highland valley, up the Haggenegg Pass, and down to Lake Lucerne. The first 10 km are an easy hike on a broad gravel pathway sloping up very gradually. The hike through the valley, towards the Mythen peaks, provides panoramic views of these mountains. What follows is a relatively short but steep ascent (over 3 km) to the Haggenegg Pass. This pass marks the highest altitude of the Swiss Way of St. James at 1'414 meters. From the pass level it is one long descent until the route reaches Ingenbohl. The first 3 km descent from the pass level are extremely steep. From km 17 to 27 most of the underground is tarmac, making it an easy pathway through the towns Schwyz and Ibach, until the route reaches the convent and pilgrim inn in Ingenbohl. The route is in catholic Canton Schwyz and passes by 24 churches and chapels, and five monasteries.

Stage 6 (Ingenbohl to Stans) guides you across Lake Lucerne, up to the highlands of Emmetten and down again, and along the southern side of Lake Lucerne. The stage starts with an easy walk through Brunnen to the boat pier. You will have to take an 8-minute boat ride to get across Lake Lucerne from Brunnen to Treib. From Treib the route climbs to the highest point of the day at 788 meters over 6 km. The 500 meters before this high point resemble alpine hiking: it is a forested mountain trail, along cliffs, hewn into the rocks to pass by a very steep area on the cliff side of the Stützberg. After about 4 km on the highlands the route descends again to the southern shore of Lake Lucerne and closely follows the shore line, providing panoramic views over the lake. The route goes over the northwestern foothills of the Buochserhorn mountain and descends into Stans, the capital of Canton Nidwalden. The route starts in Canton Schwyz, but after crossing Lake Lucerne changes to catholic Canton Nidwalden. Stage 6 has the highest number of churches and chapels (25) of all the stages of the Swiss Way of St. James. It promises to be a very spiritual day, with many interesting churches and chapels along the route. Two monasteries and the Rose Castle of Stans end stage 6.

Stage 7 (Stans to Sachseln) guides you out of the Lake Lucerne basin, over the western foothills of the Stanserhorn and Gräfimattstand mountains, across the Melchaa gorge, and down to the Lake Sarnen basin. Similar to the two previous stages, it is marked by the high number of churches and chapels (14) along the route. After 7.6 km in catholic Canton Nidwalden, the route enters catholic Canton Obwalden. The relatively short distance (22 km) leaves enough time to immerse in the religious significance of the churches and chapels, particularly those in the last 6 km in St. Niklausen, Flüeli-Ranft, and Sachseln. The four chapels in Flüeli-Ranft and the church in Sachseln relate to the Swiss Saint Nicholas of Flüe, and are one of the spiritual highlights along the Swiss Way of St. James. Visit the Saint's cell where he retreated for 20 years, his birth house, and the house where he lived with his family, to gain insight in the rural living conditions of the 15th century. Most of the route between Stans and Sachseln follows the so-called 'Way to Brother Klaus' (*Bruderklausenweg*). The route passes by a Dominican convent that offers low-cost pilgrim accommodations.

Stage 8 (Sachseln to Brienzwiler) guides you along Lake Sarnen and after a forested ascent along Lake Lungern. After another forested ascent to the Brünig Pass, the route passes over the third-highest altitude (1'083 meters) of the Swiss Way of St. James and descends through the forest to the highland plateau of Brienzwiler. Stage 8 is a tough hiking day with only seven churches along the route, but with multiple points of interest (former castles and a waterfall). The first 9 km are an easy hike on gravel footpaths, without altitude meters. While hiking km 10 and 11 the trail ascends through a forest from the Lake Sarnen level (at 470 meters) to the Lake Lungern level (at 700 meters). Lake Lungern is the most beautiful turquoise colored lake against the background of snow-capped mountain peaks glistering in the sun; one of the most beautiful views along the Swiss Way of St. James. The 6 km along the lake are on easy pathways, with some gradual ascents and descents. At km 18 the real climbing starts. It takes 4 km to ascend the Brünig Pass at 1'008 meters, where the route changes from catholic Canton Obwalden to protestant Canton Bern. After another ascent over 1 km to the highest point of the day (1'083 meters), the last 2 km descend through the forest to the highland plateau of Brienzwiler. Brienzwiler has a low-cost pilgrim inn.

Stage 9 (Brienzwiler to Interlaken) guides you from the highland plateau down to Lake Brienz and, over the lower flanks of both the Tannhorn and Augstmatthorn along the western side of Lake Brienz, to Interlaken. The route follows the full length of Lake Brienz along its western shore in a southwestern direction. The routes alongside Lake Sarnen and Lake Lungern may have been flat, but this is not the case for the route along Lake Brienz; stage 9 has a high number of altitude meters. From Brienzwiler the first 4 km of the route are on the highland plateau. After a gradual descent over 1 km to Brienz, the route stays along the lake for about 3 km. The following 5 km the trail goes up and down the flanks of the Tannhorn mountain. The trail descends into Oberried, where it stays at the lake level for about 2 km. The following 4 km the trail goes up and down the flanks of the Augstmatthorn mountain. At km 24 the route reaches the end of Lake Brienz. The lake flows into the Aare River, where the route enters Interlaken and ends at the former Augustinian monastery. The hiking trails are easy, the ascents and descents not steep, and the higher locations provide panoramic views of Lake Brienz and the mountains. The stage is in protestant Canton Bern; only eight churches are passed. The 80-meter suspension footbridge at km 11.7 is the adventurous highlight of the day. Several 13th century castle ruins stand on the western shore of Lake Brienz, demonstrating the medieval significance of the trade and travel route the pilgrimage trail is following. Interlaken is an international tourist hotspot offering beautiful views of the 4'000-meter-high snow-capped peaks of the Eiger, Mönch, and Jungfrau.

Stage 10 (Interlaken to Spiez) guides you across the bödeli between Lake Brienz and Lake Thun, over the southern flanks of the Beatenberg, along the northern shore of Lake Thun, and across the lake to Spiez. Similar to the two previous stages, the route guarantees wonderful views of a turquoise lake and is marked by a low number (seven) of churches and chapels. Different from the two previous stages, the distance is relatively short with 19 km only. There are two reasons why it is short: you may need time to explore the St. Beatus caves and the boat from Merligen across Lake Thun to Spiez goes infrequently, so that you may incur waiting time of up to two hours. Leaving Interlaken, you have panoramic views of the Eiger, Mönch, and Jungfrau peaks in the south. After 7 km the route leaves the flat area between Lake Brienz and Lake Thun, and follows the northern shore of Lake Thun for 8 km. The route along the northern shore is mountainous, trailing on the lower flanks of the Beatenberg. The St. Beatus caves and the grave of Swiss Saint Beatus (at km 10) are the highlight of the day, providing a unique experience along the Way of St. James through Switzerland. From the town Merligen (northern shore) the route crosses the lake by boat (27 minutes) to Spiez (southern shore). Since Spiez is built against a hill, the visit of the last churches involves some gradual ascending. Spiez's 800-year-old castle and 1'000-year-old church at the small bay provide a perfect ending of the day.

Stage 11 (Spiez to Wattenwil) guides you along the southern shore of Lake Thun to the eastern highland valleys of the Gantrisch mountain range. The trails are easy, the distance is moderate. Only four churches are passed by (you are still in Canton Bern). The stage has many gradual short ascents and descents, as the trail passes through highland valleys and follows small streams. Most of the time the route offers panoramic views of the Bernese Alps in the east, behind Lake Thun. It is worthwhile to regularly look back, as these views are one of the most beautiful along the Swiss Way of St. James. The route passes by two 1'000-year-old churches and the former Strättligen Castle. Because the church of Blumenstein is outside the village, a 3.3 km detour away from the signposted route is required to visit this church, in one of the most beautiful nature settings.

Stage 12 (Wattenwil to Schwarzenburg) guides you over the eastern and northern foothills that half-circle the Gantrisch mountain range in Canton Bern. The route immediately enters the foothills and starts with a steep climb over 1 km to reach the first highland plateau. The route stays on this highland plateau, with many short ascents and descents, for 6 km. From Riggisberg the route turns west, crossing the northern Gantrisch foothills. Over 3 km the route gradually ascends on farm roads through meadows to Mättiwil, where the Way of St. James route via Luzern/Bern (coming from the north) converges with stage 12. In the village Rüeggisberg the highest point of the day at 930 meters is reached about 1 km later. In Rüeggisberg the route passes by the 950-year-old Cluniac monastery ruins. From the ruins the route follows a historical pilgrimage path in a southwestern direction, descending to the Schwarzwasser River. The route briefly follows the left bank of the Schwarzwasser River, after which it climbs out of the valley on a steep forest trail to reach the second highland plateau. The route crosses this highland plateau on easy and nearly flat roads, and subsequently descends into Schwarzenburg. At around km 22 you reach the chapel in the town's center. The main church is, however, on a hill outside Schwarzenburg. At km 24 the church on the hill in Wahlern marks the end of the stage.

Stage 13 (Schwarzenburg to Fribourg) guides you over two highland plateaus between the Sense and Sarine rivers to the city of Fribourg. After 5.3 km the Way of St. James crosses the Sense River, which is the border between Canton Bern and Canton Fribourg. In the previous stages in protestant Canton Bern the number of churches and chapels was limited. This number significantly increases in stage 13, when the Way of St. James enters Canton Fribourg, a historical catholic stronghold. At the end of the descent to the Sarine River in Fribourg, the route passes through 13th century city fortifications (city walls, watchtowers, access gate, wooden bridge) providing the most beautiful medieval city scenery along the Swiss Way of St. James. The final 3 km in Fribourg the route passes by 10 churches/chapels and six monasteries, requiring significant time for the sightseeing of the many religious arts and treasures. Fribourg has a low-cost pilgrim inn at the Franciscan monastery.

From Einsiedeln to Fribourg, via Luzern/Bern

Stage 5 from Einsiedeln to Ingenbohl is the same as described on page 15.

Stage L1 (Ingenbohl to Werthenstein) guides you across Lake Lucerne, through the medieval city of Luzern, over a northern foothill of the Pilatus mountain, and along the Small Emme River to the Werthenstein monastery. The main challenge of this stage is not the hiking distance (24 km), but the time needed both for the boat from Brunnen to Luzern and for sightseeing in the historical city of Luzern. The relatively short hiking distance should provide some flexibility. The boat crossing of Lake Lucerne is one of the most scenic lake tours of Switzerland; very worthwhile to do, and a relaxing and enjoyable start of the day. Several detours from the signposted route nr. 4 are necessary to visit the 16 churches and several points of interest in close vicinity of the route in catholic Canton Luzern. Stage L1 ends at the monastery of Werthenstein. Together with Einsiedeln, the monastery's church was one of the most frequented pilgrimage destinations in Switzerland during the 17th and 18th centuries. The monastery has a low-cost pilgrim inn.

Stage L2 (Werthenstein to Huttwil) guides you over rolling hills to the medieval city of Willisau and across the northern foothills of the Napf mountain to the town Huttwil. These foothills result in a significant number of altitude meters: more than 1'700. The highest point of the day is a mere 740 meters; the high number of altitude meters is caused by the many ascents and descents – seven 'peaks' between 640 and 740 meters are reached. Combined with the distance of 31 km, this is a tough hiking day. Most of the route is on farm roads, grasslands, and forest/dirt trails. Shortly before the end of the stage the route changes from catholic Canton Luzern to protestant Canton Bern. Only three small towns (Geiss, Willisau, and Ufhusen) are passed before reaching Huttwil. Apart from in Buholz, there are no chapels or churches in between the towns, making it seem like stage L2 is mostly a hiking day. The highlight of the day is the historical city of Willisau (about halfway).

Stage L3 (Huttwil to Burgdorf) guides you across the northwestern foothills of the Napf mountain to the medieval city of Burgdorf in the Emme River valley. These foothills result in a significant number of altitude meters: more than 1'600. The highest point of the day is 887 meters; the many altitude meters are caused by two ascents and one long descent from the highest point to the city of Burgdorf. Most of the route is on farm roads, grasslands, and dirt trails. Only one small town (Dürrenroth) is passed before reaching Burgdorf. Other than in Dürrenroth, no chapels or churches are passed, making it seem like stage L3 is mostly a hiking day (similar to stage L2 – only a bit shorter). The stage, in protestant Canton Bern, has only five churches along the route (of which four at the end in Burgdorf). Burgdorf has a magnificent 11th century castle that is under renovation until May 2020. When it opens again, it will have a museum, a restaurant, and a youth hostel that will also serve as a pilgrim inn. A unique possibility to spend the night in a medieval castle.

Stage L4 (Burgdorf to Bern) guides you across the northwestern foothills of the Emmental mountains to the medieval city of Bern in the Aare River valley. Stage L4 goes over four mountains in protestant Canton Bern. Though these mountains are not very high (623, 729, 854, and 722 meters), they do lead to nearly 2'000 altitude meters. In combination with a length of 31 km this is a tough hiking day. A significant part of the route is through forests. Farm roads through agricultural fields connect the routes between the forests. The route passes through only two towns that are situated in valleys: Krauchthal after the second mountain and Boll after the third mountain (Bern lies after the fourth mountain). The last 5 km the route goes through the urban agglomerations of Bern. Upon arrival in Bern you will notice that the signposted route nr. 4 does not pass through the city. It circumvents the historical city of Bern by staying in the Aare River valley and following the eastern bank to the southern suburbs. Because the historical city of

Bern has been designated a UNESCO World Cultural Heritage, the route described in this book does enter the town (only 1.6 km deviation from the signposted route nr. 4). Two cathedrals, two churches, a former castle, medieval figured fountains, and several other points of interest make the visit to Bern a highlight of the Luzern/Bern route.

Stage L5 (Bern to Schwarzenburg) guides you out of the Aare River valley to the northern highlands of the Gantrisch mountain range. This stage is the longest (36 km) and has the highest number of altitude meters (2'055) of all stages of the Swiss Way of St. James. The route passes by only seven churches (in protestant Canton Bern), making it a long and strenuous hiking day. From Bern the route climbs in a southern direction to the agricultural and forested highlands, high above the Aare/Gürbe River valley. The route reaches three high points (692 m, 921 m, and 980 m) before converging with stage 12 (Wattenwil to Schwarzenburg) in Mättiwil at km 22. After Mättiwil the route passes by the 950-year-old Cluniac monastery ruins in Rüeggisberg. The route follows a historical pilgrimage path in a southwestern direction, descending to the Schwarzwasser River. The route briefly follows the left bank of the Schwarzwasser River, after which it climbs out of the valley on a steep forest trail to reach another highland plateau. The route crosses this highland plateau on easy and nearly flat roads, and descends into Schwarzenburg. The main church is, however, on a hill outside Schwarzenburg, in Wahlern.

Stage 13 from Schwarzenburg to Fribourg is the same as described on page 18.

Route Map and Profile

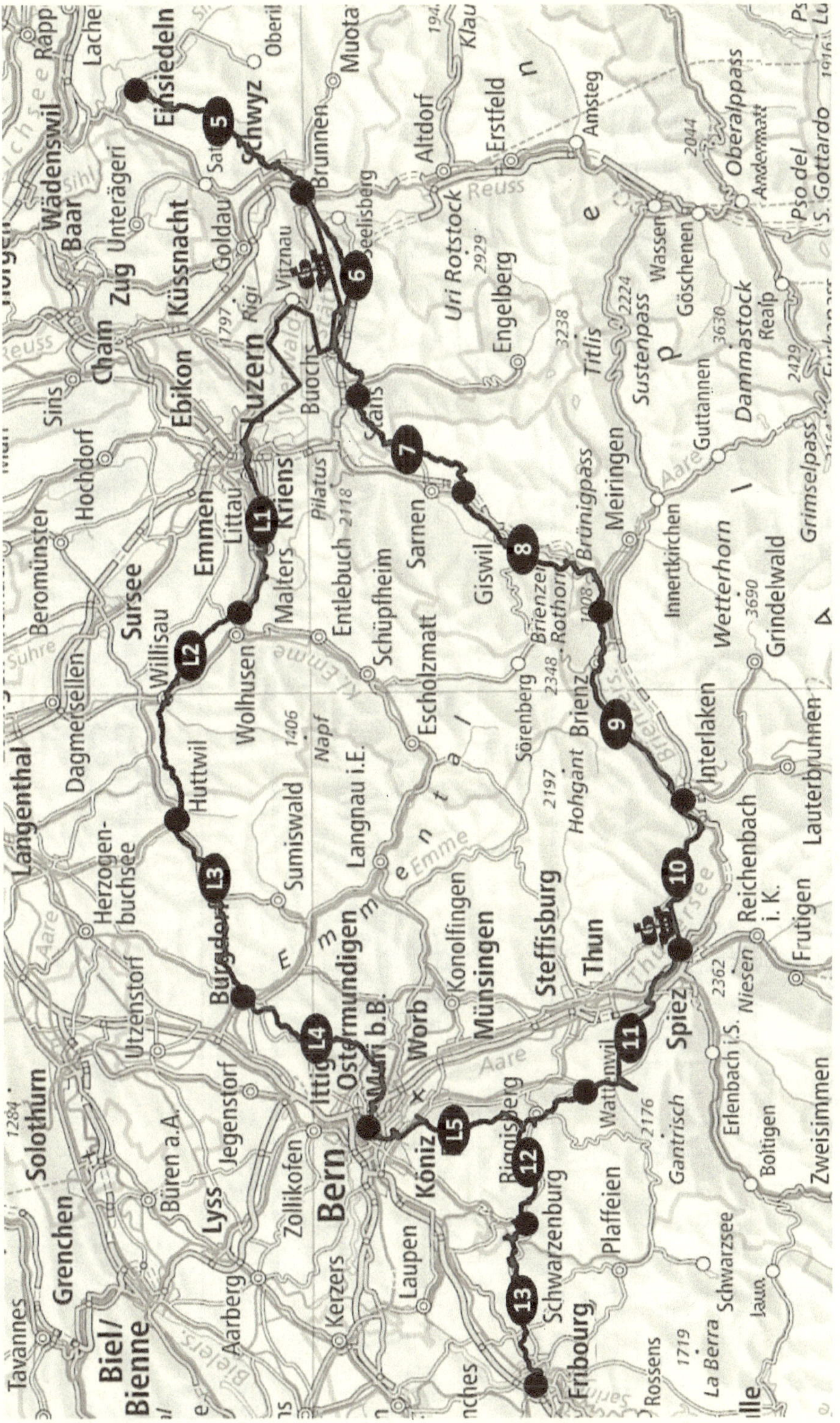
Biel/
Bienne
Grenchen
Solothurn
Tavannes
Lyss
Aarberg
Büren a.A.
Jegenstorf
Utzenstorf
Herzogen-
buchsee
Langenthal
Dagmersellen
Beromünster
Hochdorf
Sins
Wädenswil
Baar
Zug
Cham
Küssnacht
Unterägeri
Goldau
Einsiedeln
Schwyz
Brunnen
Muotatal
Seelisberg
Vitznau
Rigi
Luzern
Ebikon
Emmen
Sursee
Willisau
Wolhusen
Malters
Littau
Kriens
Pilatus
Buochs
Stans
Altdorf
Erstfeld
Amsteg
Uri Rotstock
Engelberg
Titlis
Sarnen
Giswil
Entlebuch
Schüpfheim
Escholzmatt
Sörenberg
Brienzer Rothorn
Brünigpass
Meiringen
Innertkirchen
Guttannen
Sustenpass
Wassen
Göschenen
Andermatt
Oberalppass
Dammastock
Realp
Grimselpass
Wetterhorn
Grindelwald
Brienz
Interlaken
Lauterbrunnen
Reichenbach i. K.
Frutigen
Spiez
Thun
Steffisburg
Münsingen
Konolfingen
Worb
Ostermundigen
Ittigen
Muri b.B.
Bern
Köniz
Zollikofen
Laupen
Kerzers
Riggisberg
Wattenwil
Gantrisch
Schwarzenburg
Plaffeien
Fribourg
Rossens
La Berra
Schwarzsee
Jaun
Boltigen
Zweisimmen
Erlenbach i.S.
Niesen
Burgdorf
Huttwil
Sumiswald
Langnau i.E.
Napf
Hohgant
Emme
Aare
Reuss
5
6
7
8
9
10
11
12
13
L1
L2
L3
L4
L5

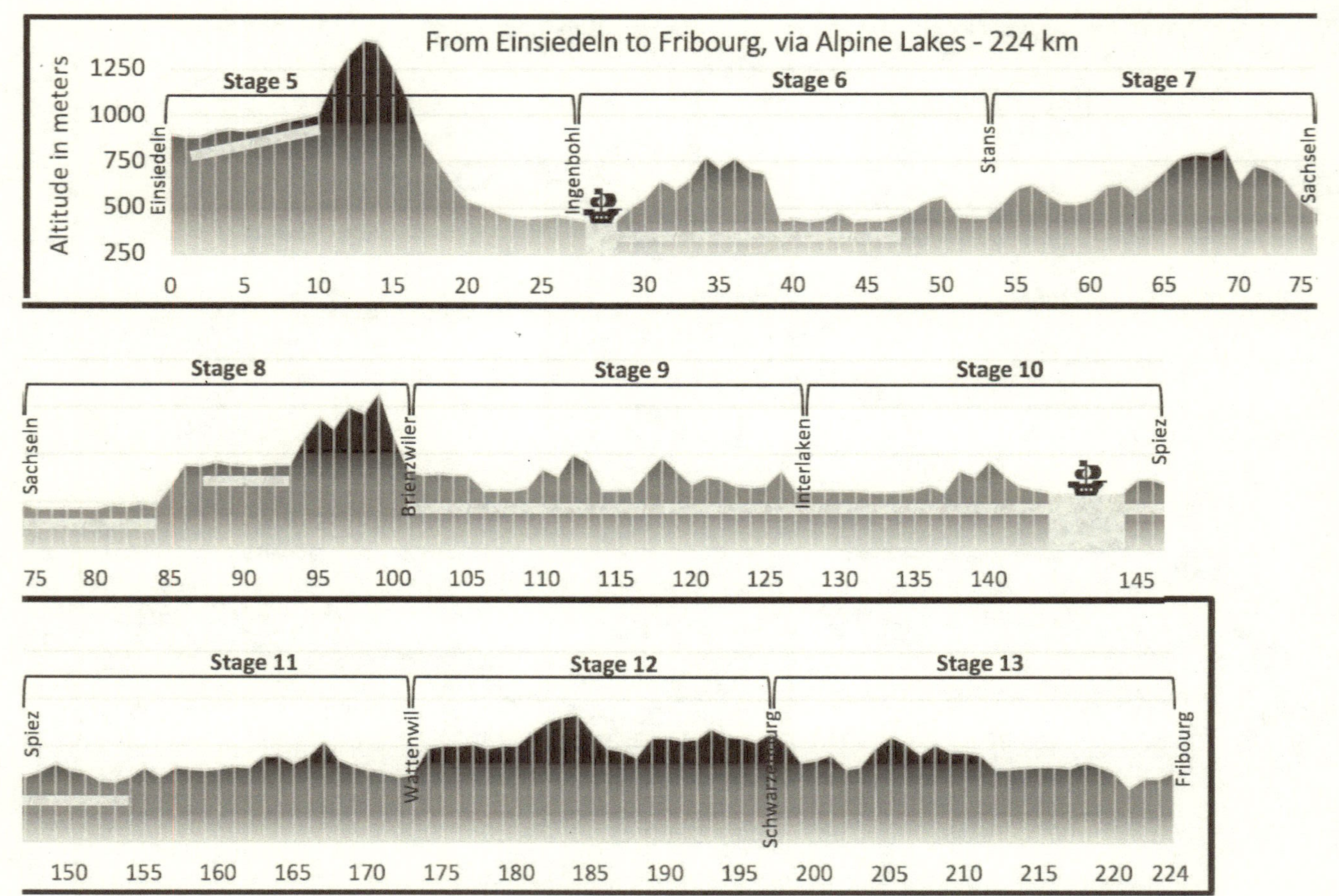
From Einsiedeln to Fribourg, via Alpine Lakes - 224 km
Altitude in meters
1250
1000
750
500
250
Stage 5
Stage 6
Stage 7
Einsiedeln
Ingenbohl
Stans
Sachseln
0
5
10
15
20
25
30
35
40
45
50
55
60
65
70
75
Stage 8
Stage 9
Stage 10
Sachseln
Brienzwiler
Interlaken
Spiez
75
80
85
90
95
100
105
110
115
120
125
130
135
140
145
Stage 11
Stage 12
Stage 13
Spiez
Wattenwil
Schwarzenburg
Fribourg
150
155
160
165
170
175
180
185
190
195
200
205
210
215
220
224

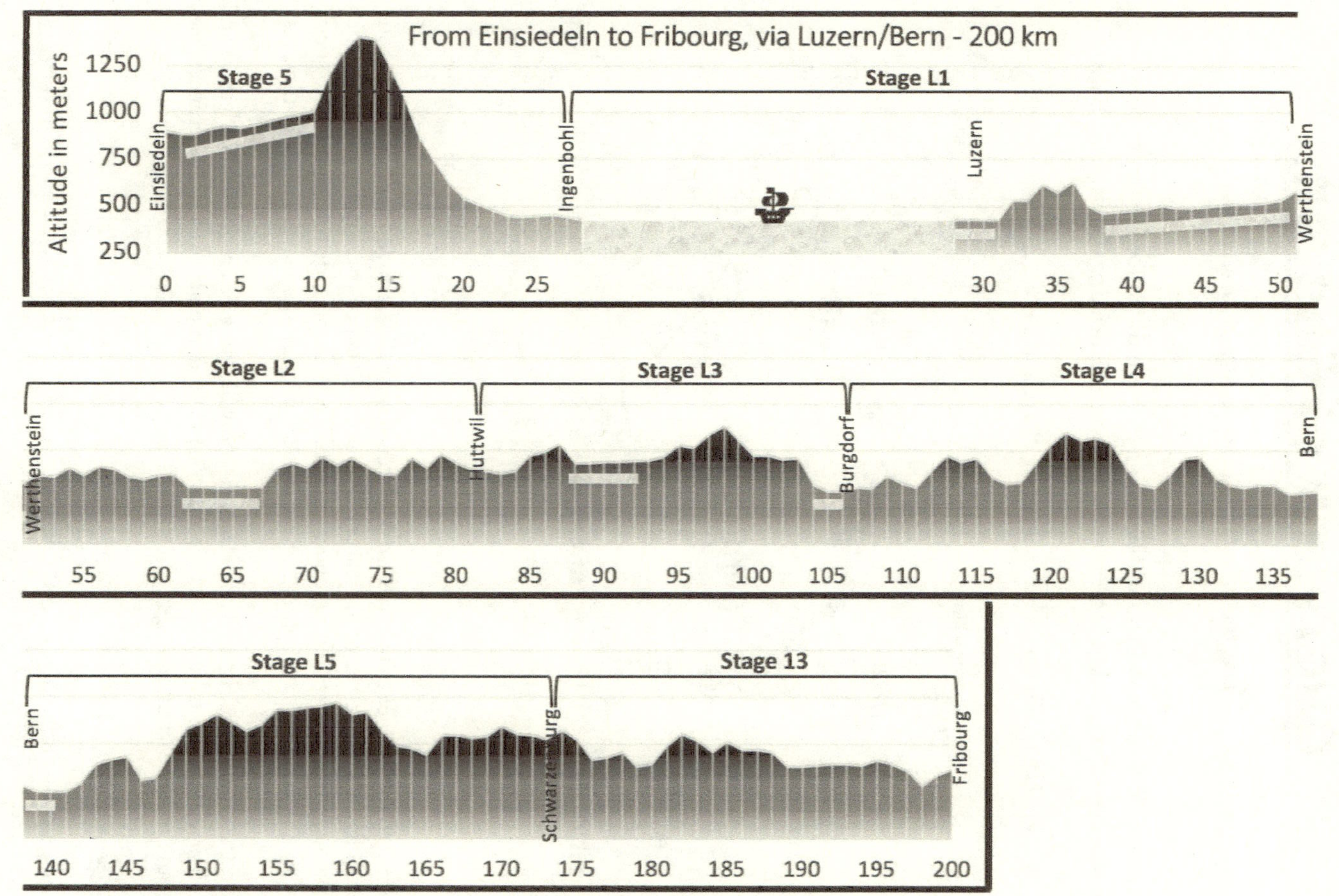
From Einsiedeln to Fribourg, via Luzern/Bern - 200 km
Altitude in meters
1250
1000
750
500
250
Stage 5
Stage L1
Einsiedeln
Ingenbohl
Luzern
Werthenstein
0 5 10 15 20 25 30 35 40 45 50
Stage L2
Stage L3
Stage L4
Werthenstein
Huttwil
Burgdorf
Bern
55 60 65 70 75 80 85 90 95 100 105 110 115 120 125 130 135
Stage L5
Stage 13
Bern
Fribourg
140 145 150 155 160 165 170 175 180 185 190 195 200

Overview of Cantons

Understanding the relevant history of the Cantons

In Central Switzerland you will be hiking through the following Cantons:

- Via Alpine Lakes (Interlaken): Schwyz, Nidwalden, Obwalden, Bern, and Fribourg
- Via Luzern/Bern: Schwyz, Luzern, Bern, and Fribourg

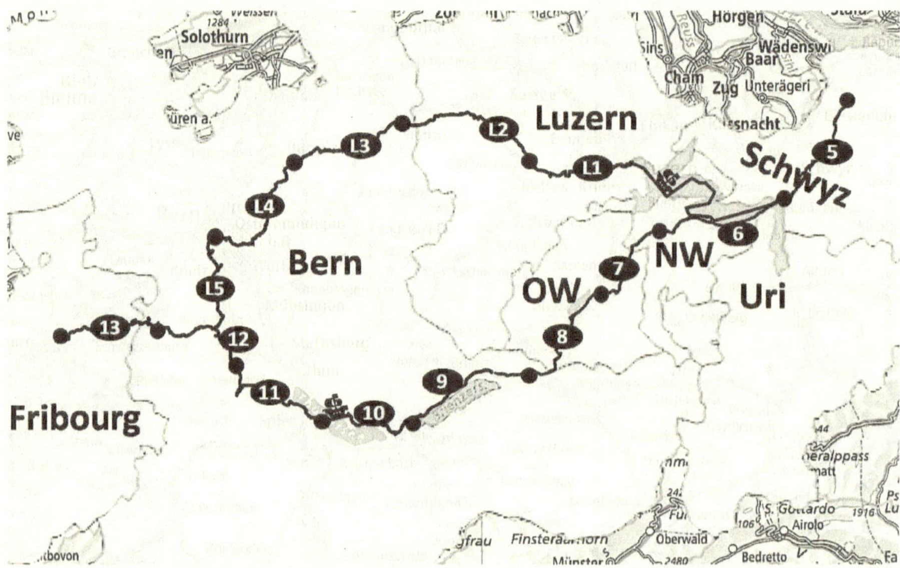

The following sections provide an overview of the above-mentioned Cantons, highlighting their religious history. Read the background information provided below, whenever you enter a new Canton. This will provide the appropriate social, cultural, and religious context of the churches, monasteries, and points of interest.

In the chapters of the individual stages you will find a reference to the Canton and changes from one Canton to the other. As you come across such references, you can flip back to these pages.

Canton Schwyz

Stage 5 is completely in catholic Canton Schwyz, as is the first kilometer of stages 6 and L1.

In Canton Schwyz the car license plates start with SZ and the people speak Swiss-German (greeting with *Grüezi*). The Canton was formed in 1291 and was named after its capital city, Schwyz. Together with the Cantons Uri and Unterwalden (nowadays split in Nidwalden and Obwalden) the Canton founded the first Swiss Confederation (a defensive alliance) in 1291. For this reason, these Cantons are called the original Cantons or Ur-Cantons. Its coat-of-arms dates from 1240, when it was a fully red war-flag. The small white cross was added in 1815. The Canton has around 160'000 inhabitants (2 percent) and covers about 2 percent of Switzerland's land area.

At the time of the religious Reformation in the 1520s-30s, Canton Schwyz, being conservative catholic, strongly rejected the Protestantism coming from Zurich. Canton Schwyz remained catholic and forbade Protestantism. By 1650 the Canton was pursuing and imprisoning Protestants on its territory and confiscating their assets when they fled to Canton Zurich.

The Canton's strive for independence from the protestant Cantons of the Swiss Confederation culminated in the formation of an alliance with six other catholic Cantons (*Sonderbund*) in 1845. This caused a civil war (***Sonderbund*** **War**) based on a religious dispute. The *Sonderbund* wanted to defend their catholic autonomy against a centralization of authority by the liberal Swiss Confederation, mainly consisting of protestant progressive Cantons led by Bern. Fifteen Confederate Cantons put together an army and defeated the *Sonderbund* alliance in 1847 (in a battle with only very few casualties). Up to that time Switzerland as a country consisted of loosely organized and independent Cantons. The victory resulted in the Confederates solidifying their power through a new Federal Constitution in 1848, limiting the autonomy of the Cantons and bringing them under one modern roof; the Swiss Federal State was born.

At the formation of the Swiss Confederation freedom of religion for the whole of Switzerland was declared in the country's constitution. Still, Canton Schwyz remained conservative catholic: you will come across many catholic chapels and churches, but hardly any protestant ones on its territory.

Canton Nidwalden

Most of stage 6 and the beginning of stage 7 are in catholic Canton Nidwalden.

In Canton Nidwalden the car license plates start with NW and the people speak Swiss-German (greeting with *Grüezi*). The name Nidwalden means 'low forests', referring to the forests in the valleys south of Lake Lucerne. The Canton was half of Canton Unterwalden that was formed in 1291 (Obwalden formed the other half). The name Unterwalden means 'between the forests'. After the Abbey of Murbach (Alsace, France) sold the lands of Unterwalden to the House of Habsburg in 1291, Canton Unterwalden was established and together with the Cantons Uri and Schwyz formed a defensive alliance to protect their independence from the House of Habsburg. In effect they founded the first Swiss Confederation in 1291. For this reason, these Cantons are called the original Cantons or Ur-Cantons. At the establishment of the Helvetic Republic in 1798, Nidwalden became a separate Canton.

The Canton's capital city is Stans, with a population of around 8'200. The coat-of-arms dates from 1512, though during its earlier time as part of Canton Unterwalden a version of this emblem had already been in use. The double keys represent St. Peter's keys to the Kingdom of Heaven (the coat-of-arms of the Holy See and Vatican City display the same two keys, only crossed). The Pope officially approved the use of the two keys in 1512. The Canton has around 45'000 inhabitants (0.5 percent) and covers about 0.7 percent of Switzerland's land area. It is the fifth-smallest in terms of population of the 26 Cantons.

At the time of the religious Reformation in the 1520s-30s, Canton Nidwalden, being conservative catholic, strongly rejected the Protestantism coming from both Zurich and Bern, and remained catholic. It was not until 1934 that the first protestant church was built in the Canton.

Canton Obwalden

Most of stages 7 and 8 are in catholic Canton Obwalden.

In Canton Obwalden the car license plates start with OW and the people speak Swiss-German (greeting with *Grüezi*). The name Obwalden means 'upper forests', referring to the forests in the higher valleys south of Canton Nidwalden. The Canton was half of Canton Unterwalden that was formed in 1291 (Nidwalden formed the other half). For its history, see the description under Canton Nidwalden. At the establishment of the Helvetic Republic in 1798, Obwalden became a separate Canton.

The Canton's capital city is Sarnen, with a population of around 6'000. The coat-of-arms dates from 1816, though during its earlier time as part of Canton Unterwalden a version of this emblem had already been in use. The single key represents one of St. Peter's keys to the Kingdom of Heaven. The Canton has around 40'000 inhabitants (0.4 percent) and covers about 1.2 percent of Switzerland's land area (most of their lands are uninhabitable alpine mountains). It is the third-smallest in terms of population of the 26 Cantons.

At the time of the religious Reformation in the 1520s-30s, Canton Obwalden, being conservative catholic, strongly rejected the Protestantism coming from both Zurich and Bern, and remained catholic. It was not until 1872 that the first protestant church was built in the Canton.

Canton Luzern

Stages L1 and L2 are in catholic Canton Luzern.

In Canton Luzern the car license plates start with LU and the people speak Swiss-German (greeting with *Grüezi*). The Canton was formed in 1332 and was named after its capital city, Luzern. It was the fourth Canton established after the three Ur-Cantons (Schwyz, Unterwalden, Uri – 1291) and is one of the Cantons of Central Switzerland (*Zentral Schweiz*). Its blue/white coat-of-arms dates from 1386. The Canton has around 406'000 inhabitants (5 percent) and covers about 4 percent of Switzerland's land area.

At the time of the religious Reformation in the 1520s-30s, Canton Luzern rejected the Protestantism coming from Zurich, despite its population being sympathetic to the new ideas. The main reason for this rejection was of economical/political nature. The City of Luzern's main source of income was its business with Swiss mercenaries (the hiring out of professional soldiers to foreign armies). This business was in the hands of a few patriarchal families and the politicians of the City. To protect the source that had made them and the City wealthy, they rejected the Protestantism (as acceptance would have led to the abolishment of their mercenary business). In 1524 Canton Luzern imposed Catholicism on its population, and subsequently persecuted and exiled those who had converted to Protestantism. For 275 years protestant services were forbidden, until the establishment of the Helvetic Republic in 1798, after Napoleon's armies had conquered Switzerland. It was not until 1848, at the formation of the Swiss Confederate Republic, that the country's constitution declared religious freedom for the whole of Switzerland. Still, Canton Luzern remained conservative catholic: you will come across many catholic churches and chapels, but hardly any protestant churches (built after 1860) on its territory.

During the late middle ages **Swiss Mercenaries** were well-known and had a good reputation on the battlefield; they were feared and had an excellent track-record of victories. Usually they were hired as a contingent of highly skilled soldiers, who came battle-ready with their armory of long spears, pikes, and halberds. Foreign armies could simply contract them from Cantonal governments, who trained these professional soldiers. It is estimated that between one and two million of such Swiss mercenaries fought in foreign battles in the 15th to 18th centuries. Most of these men escaped poverty at home for a well-paid job as a hired soldier. Such mercenary contingents fought all over the continent, mainly for the armies of the French and Spanish Kings.

The last remaining mercenaries are the **Swiss Guard at the Vatican**; after the new Federal constitution of 1848, all mercenary activities were prohibited except for the Swiss Guards hired by the Pope. The Vatican has already been contracting these Swiss mercenaries for the protection of the Pope since 1506 – for more than 500 years. Nowadays the Swiss Guard consists of 135 foot-soldiers, still in their traditional outfits with halberd (as well as small modern weapons). They are the sole (hired) military of the Vatican State. Only unmarried Swiss catholic men between 19 and 30 years, who trained in the Swiss army, can qualify for service in the Pontifical Swiss Guard.

Canton Bern

Stages 9, 10, 11, and 12 (via Alpine Lakes/Interlaken) and stages L3, L4, L5 (via Luzern/Bern) are in protestant Canton Bern.

In Canton Bern the car license plates start with BE. The Canton has two official languages: German and French. Swiss-German is spoken north and east of Bern, where the Canton borders other German-speaking Cantons; Swiss-French is spoken west and south of Bern, where the Canton borders other French-speaking Cantons. The Swiss Way of St. James passes through only the Swiss-German speaking territories of the Canton (greeting with *Grüessich*).

The Canton was formed in 1353 and was named after its capital city, Bern. This city is also the capital of the Swiss Confederation, housing the Parliament, Cabinet, and President. The Canton's coat-of-arms with the red/yellow colors and bear was designed in 1289. The male bear was taken from the coat-of-arms of the City of Bern. According to folklore it was the Duke of Zähringen, founder of the City of Bern in 1191, who gave rise to the bear emblem. According to legend, he would name the new town after the first animal he would kill during a hunt. This first animal was supposedly a bear; hence, the name Bern was derived from bear. The Canton has about 1.0 million inhabitants (12 percent) and covers about 14 percent of Switzerland's land area. After Canton Zurich it has the second-largest population. After Canton Grisons (*Graubünden*) it has the second-largest land area.

The religious Reformation, which started in the 1520s in Zurich, had a significant influence on Canton Bern. The Canton's clergy and authorities in Bern became strong proponents of Protestantism. From 1528 all catholic worship was legally forbidden in the whole Canton. Protestantism was enforced, resulting in the destruction of nearly all catholic religious icons (statues, altars, paintings, frescos, crucifixes, and so forth) in many churches. All monasteries were secularized and their buildings either demolished or utilized for a different purpose. All churches and chapels that were not needed as a parish church were demolished or received a different purpose. This caused a significant loss of medieval religious art, without any consideration for their value and importance over the many preceding centuries.

For 270 years only protestant worship was allowed (Catholics were pursued, imprisoned, or fined when practicing their worship). This changed when Napoleon conquered Switzerland in 1798 and founded the Helvetic Republic, which declared freedom of religion. However, after the Republic Government stepped down in 1803, Canton Bern limited this freedom again. It was not until 1848, at the formation of the Swiss Confederate Republic, that the country's constitution declared religious freedom for the whole of Switzerland. The first new catholic church (since 1528) in Canton Bern was built in 1860. For these reasons, the churches you will pass in Canton Bern are reformed and few: they are limited to the former parish churches (all others having been destroyed or reutilized in 1528) and a few new catholic churches built after 1860.

Canton Fribourg

Stage 13 is in catholic Canton Fribourg.

In Canton Fribourg the car license plates start with FR. The Canton has two official languages: German and French. Swiss-German is spoken in the region northeast of Fribourg, called the Sense District (between the Sense and Sarine rivers), where the Canton borders German-speaking Cantons (greeting with *Grüessich*). Swiss-French is spoken in the much larger region southwest of Fribourg, where the Canton borders French-speaking Cantons (greeting with *Bonjour*). The City of Fribourg itself officially has two languages, though most of its population speaks French (but will also understand German). In the city most signs and information are both in French and German. The historical explanation for the two languages in the city and Canton is that the areas were divided between French-speaking rulers and German-speaking rulers. In medieval times the Kingdom of Burgundy/Duchy of Savoy (French) occupied the southwestern area (west of the Sarine River) that nowadays makes up the French-speaking part of Switzerland. At the same time the House of Habsburg (German) occupied the northeastern area (east of the Sarine River) that nowadays makes up the German-speaking part of Switzerland.

The Canton was formed in 1481 (the year it joined the Swiss Confederation), after it became independent from the House of Savoy in 1477. From 1478 until 1798 the City of Fribourg was an independent City-State (Republic) and the political powerhouse of the region, ruled by a few patrician families. With military force they expanded their landownership to what became Canton Fribourg, named after its capital city, Fribourg (Freiburg in German, meaning 'Free Castle'). The black/white coat-of-arms dates from 1478 and was the banner of the City-Republic of Fribourg, from the time it became independent from the House of Savoy. The Canton has about 315'000 inhabitants (4 percent) and covers about 4 percent of Switzerland's land area.

At the time of the religious Reformation in the 1520s-30s, Canton Fribourg, being conservative catholic, strongly rejected the Protestantism coming from Bern. In 1524 Canton Fribourg imposed Catholicism on its population, and subsequently persecuted and exiled those who had converted to Protestantism. When Canton Bern used military force to expand Protestantism to the lands of Vaud in 1536, Canton Fribourg did the same to establish Catholicism in the regions south of its city (thereby expanding its Canton). The Canton's opposition against the Reformation frequently resulted in military conflicts in the border regions with

Canton Bern. The City of Fribourg became a major force in the Counter-Reformation; it was a catholic island surrounded by protestant Cantons (Bern and Vaud). As part of the Counter-Reformation many monastic Orders settled in the city of Fribourg and the Bishopric of Lausanne relocated to the city.

Fribourg was part of the catholic *Sonderbund* that lost the civil war against the protestant Confederate Cantons. For more details, please see the description on page 25.

At the formation of the Swiss Confederation freedom of religion for the whole of Switzerland was declared in the country's constitution. Still, Canton Fribourg remained conservative catholic: you will come across many catholic chapels and churches, but hardly any protestant churches on its territory.

EINSIEDELN TO FRIBOURG: VIA ALPINE LAKES

Stage 5: Einsiedeln to Ingenbohl 27 km

The Way over the highest altitude

Route stats

	Distance in km	*Time in hrs:min*
Signposted route nr. 4	23.5	5:30
Churches/chapels	3.4	3:00
Points of interest	0.1	0:10
Rest/lunch		1:00
Stage 5	27.0	9:40

In case you hike this stage as a daytrip, you need to add 600 meters in Einsiedeln and 400 meters in Ingenbohl (from and to the train stations).

Ascent/descent/total	+714 / -1'170 / 1'884 altitude meters
Lowest/highest altitude	439 / 1'414 meters
Pathway/condition	moderate / difficult
Churches/chapels	Einsiedeln, Au, Trachslau, Alpthal, Haggenegg Pass (2), Ried, Schwyz (8), Ibach (3), Unterschönenbuch (2), Ingenbohl (4)
Monasteries	Benedictine Convent Au, Former Jesuit Collegium Schwyz, Dominican Convent Schwyz, Capuchin Monastery Schwyz, Merciful Sisters of the Holy Cross Ingenbohl
Points of interest	Archive Tower

Route summary

Stage 5 continues in catholic **Canton Schwyz**.

Stage 5 guides you through the Einsiedeln highland valley, up the Haggenegg Pass, and down to Lake Lucerne.

The pilgrim-statue's viewpoint of the previous stage, shortly before arriving in Einsiedeln, offers a good perspective of the first half of stage 5: the town Einsiedeln with the abbey on the left and the Alp valley on the right, with in the distance the 'big' (left) and 'small' (right) Mythen mountains, peaking at 1'898 and

1'811 meters respectively. The first half of stage 5 leads through Einsiedeln, via the Alp highland valley, up the Haggenegg Pass to 1'414 meters (west of the small Mythen).

The first 10 km are a relatively easy hike. After leaving Einsiedeln the route is on a broad gravel pathway (watch out for mountain bikers). The trail slopes up very gradually. The gravel path follows the Alp stream, alternating between its left and right bank. As the valley narrows the stream, the trail, and the road come closer together. The hike through the valley, towards the Mythen peaks, offers great panoramic views of these mountains; they come closer and grow higher with every step. What follows is a relatively short (3 km) but steep ascent to the Haggenegg Pass at 1'414 meters. This marks the highest altitude of the Swiss Way of St. James and the closest location to the two Mythen peaks. It is certainly an alpine highlight. Hopefully the weather is clear, offering great views. From the pass level it is one long descent until Ingenbohl. The first 3 km descent from the pass level is extremely steep. The loose gravel makes this part dangerous; be careful. From km 17 to 27 most of the underground is tarmac, making it an easy pathway through the towns Schwyz and Ibach, until the convent and pilgrim inn in Ingenbohl.

Getting to the starting point

The starting point in Einsiedeln is in front of the abbey. In case you spent the night at the guest rooms of the abbey, or at a hotel around the square, you are already at the right location to start stage 5. In case you stayed at the Eremita Zen Temple, you need to walk 1.3 km to the abbey.

In case you hike stage 5 as a daytrip, you need to walk 600 meters from the Einsiedeln train station to the abbey.

Route Map and Profile

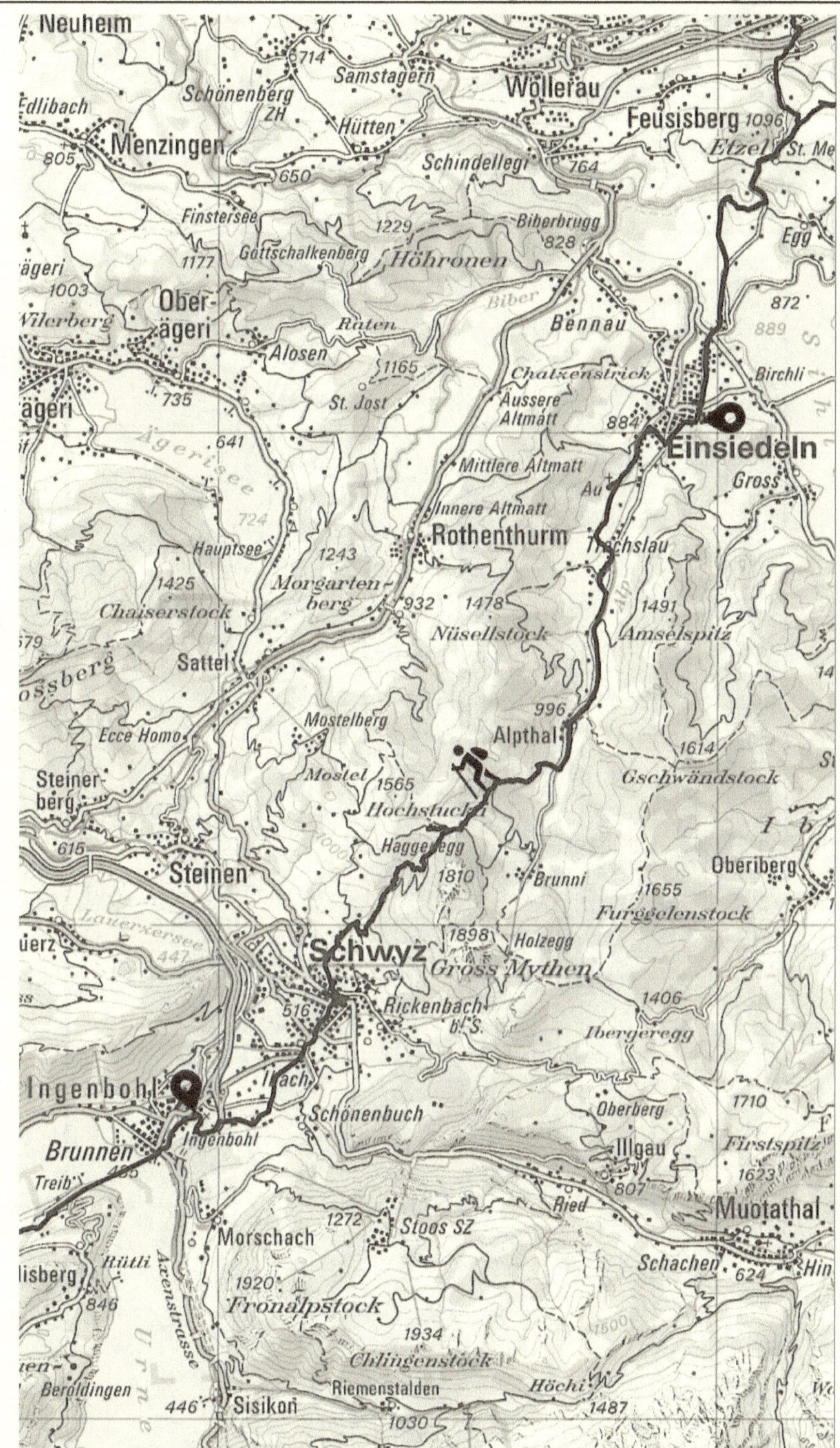
Neuheim
714
Samstagern
Wollerau
Schönenberg ZH
Feusisberg
1096
Edlibach
Hütten
Menzingen
Etzel
805
650
Schindellegi
764
Finstersee
1229
Biberbrugg
828
Egg
Gottschalkenberg
Höhronen
1177
1003
Ober-ägeri
Biber
872
889
Wilerberg
Raten
Bennau
Alosen
1165
Chatzenstrick
Birchli
735
St. Jost
Äussere Altmatt
884
Einsiedeln
641
Mittlere Altmatt
Gross
Ägerisee
Au
724
Innere Altmatt
Rothenthurm
Hauptsee
1243
1425
Morgartenberg
932
1478
1491
Chaiserstock
Nüsellstock
Amselspitz
Sattel
996
Mostelberg
Alpthal
Ecce Homo
1614
Steinerberg
Mostel
1565
Gschwändstock
Hochstuckli
Haggenegg
615
Steinen
1810
Brunni
1655
Oberiberg
Lauerzersee
Furggelenstock
447
1898
Holzegg
Schwyz
Gross Mythen
1406
516
Rickenbach b. S.
Ibergeregg
Ingenbohl
Ibach
Schönenbuch
Oberberg
1710
Brunnen
Ingenbohl
Illgau
Firstspitz
1623
807
Ried
Muotathal
1272
Stoos SZ
Morschach
Rütli
Schachen
624
1920
Fronalpstock
846
Axenstrasse
1934
Chlingenstöck
Beroldingen
Höchi
Riemenstalden
446
Sisikon
1487
1030

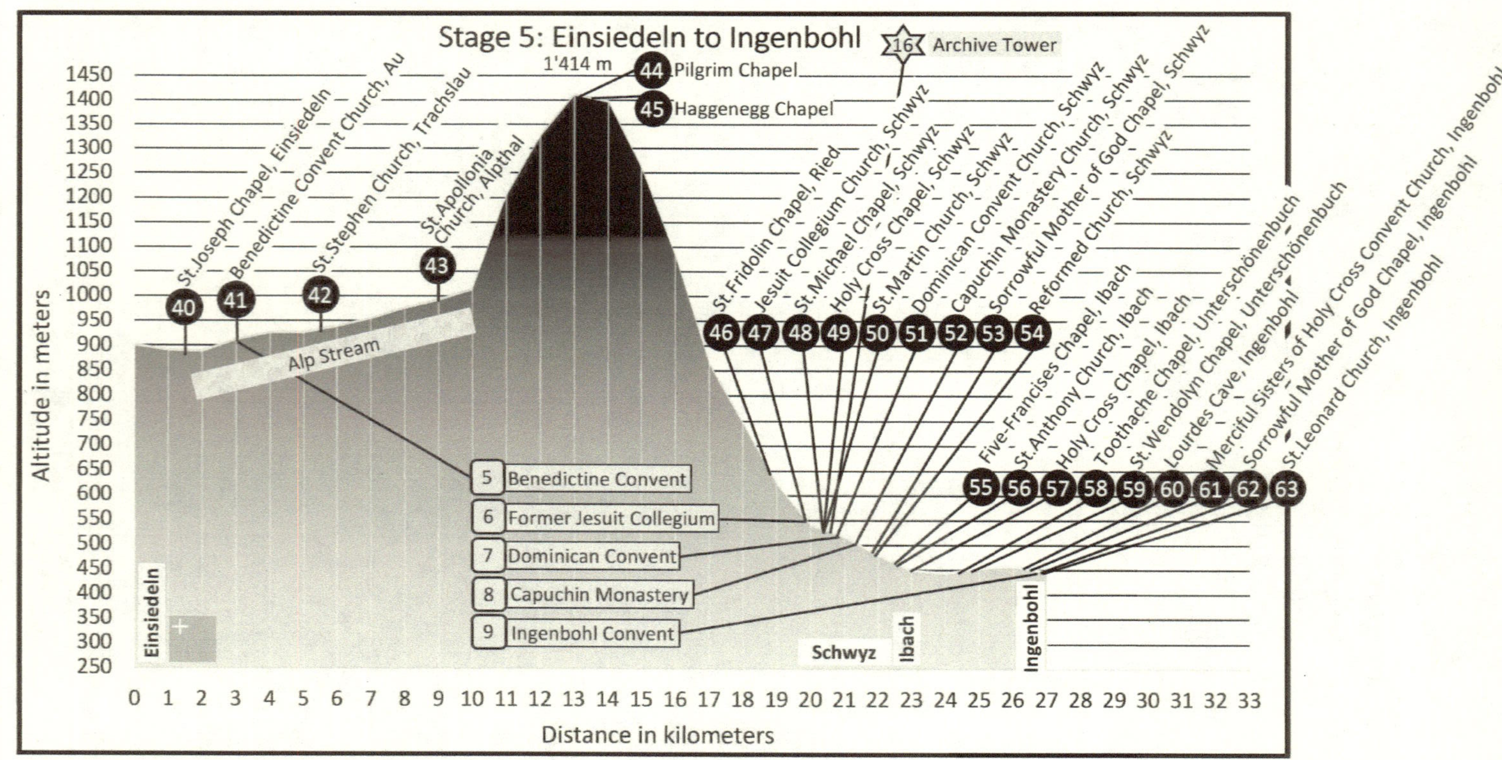
Stage 5: Einsiedeln to Ingenbohl
16 Archive Tower
1'414 m
44 Pilgrim Chapel
45 Haggenegg Chapel
40 St.Joseph Chapel, Einsiedeln
41 Benedictine Convent Church, Au
42 St.Stephen Church, Trachslau
43 St.Apollonia Church, Alpthal
46 St.Fridolin Chapel, Ried
47 Jesuit Collegium Church, Schwyz
48 St.Michael Chapel, Schwyz
49 Holy Cross Chapel, Schwyz
50 St.Martin Church, Schwyz
51 Dominican Convent Church, Schwyz
52 Capuchin Monastery Church, Schwyz
53 Sorrowful Mother of God Chapel, Schwyz
54 Reformed Church, Schwyz
55 Five-Francises Chapel, Ibach
56 St.Anthony Church, Ibach
57 Holy Cross Chapel, Ibach
58 Toothache Chapel, Ibach
59 St.Wendolyn Chapel, Unterschönenbuch
60 Lourdes Cave, Ingenbohl
61 Merciful Sisters of Holy Cross Convent Church, Ingenbohl
62 Sorrowful Mother of God Chapel, Ingenbohl
63 St.Leonard Church, Ingenbohl
Alp Stream
5 Benedictine Convent
6 Former Jesuit Collegium
7 Dominican Convent
8 Capuchin Monastery
9 Ingenbohl Convent
Einsiedeln
Schwyz
Ibach
Ingenbohl
Altitude in meters
1450 1400 1350 1300 1250 1200 1150 1100 1050 1000 950 900 850 800 750 700 650 600 550 500 450 400 350 300 250
0 1 2 3 4 5 6 7 8 9 10 11 12 13 14 15 16 17 18 19 20 21 22 23 24 25 26 27 28 29 30 31 32 33
Distance in kilometers

Hiking the Route

Since the starting point of stage 5 is in front of the abbey, go to the Our Lady Fountain and fill your drinking bottles with its fresh water.

The number 4 signs guide you through the streets of Einsiedeln towards the Alp valley. First you walk around a forested and grassland hill (on your left) and pass by a sawmill and its timber yard, where you take a right (cross road nr. 386) and a left to the *Allmeindstrasse* towards the Alp stream.

You pass by a soccer field, industrial buildings, and at a roundabout you see the St. Joseph Chapel (at km 1.4) on your left, next to a bus stop and playground.

St. Joseph Chapel, Einsiedeln (St. Josef Kapelle) **40**

- Kornhausstrasse 48, 8840 Einsiedeln
- St. Joseph, Holy Family
- The catholic chapel belongs to the Benedictine Convent of Au (see below). During the middle ages a small wooden roadside chapel already stood on this site, where Mother Ochsner from the convent had a vision of St. Joseph as a beggar (1653). The convent purchased the meadow on which the small chapel stood and built a new one in stone, dedicated to St. Joseph (1654).

  The chapel was reconstructed and redecorated in a neo-Gothic style in 1895, determining its present-day appearance.
- It has a most beautiful sculpted altar scene, unique along the Swiss Way of St. James. It contains three statues representing the Holy Family: Joseph on his deathbed, with Jesus on the left and Mary on the right. They are underneath an elaborately wood-carved and gold-colored canopy with spires reaching to the heavens (1895).

  The chapel is only open on Sundays for rosary prayers and on special occasions.

From the chapel you reach the Alp stream in about 50 meters. The route crosses the stream and turns left on a gravel path. The path takes you into the highland valley in a southern direction, where you arrive at the Benedictine Convent at km 3.0.

5 Benedictine Convent, Au (Benediktinerinnen Kloster)

Austrasse 8, 8840 Trachslau bei Einsiedeln

Benedictine Order

The convent has its roots in the 12th century. The existence of four wooden houses of the Forest Sisters (*Waldschwestern*) was first mentioned in official documents in 1359. By 1400 around 40 religious women lived in these houses, in what was at that time the dark and isolated forest of the Alp valley, south of the Abbey of Einsiedeln. They did not belong to an Order but lived by their own rules of poverty, dedication, and celibacy. After the Reformation in the 1520s-30s they set up a community, with a small chapel, at the northern end of the valley. Around 1600 their accommodation was rebuilt into a small convent with a chapel. Because they were not part of an Order, they still had to attend services at the church of the (male) Benedictine Abbey of Einsiedeln.

Their Benedictine convent was founded in 1617, when the abbot of the Benedictine Abbey of Einsiedeln established the statutes of the convent of the Forest Sisters, where his sister was the Mother Abbess. The first convent building was completed soon afterwards (1619). A large fire burned down their convent buildings in 1684. Based on donations the convent could be rebuilt three years later (1687).

The second disaster occurred in 1798, when French troops plundered the convent and destroyed many of its religious icons, weaving materials and equipment. The convent met the same fate as the Abbey of Einsiedeln; during the time of the Helvetic Republic it was closed for about four years (1799-1803).

Upon reinstatement of the convent in 1803, the sisters returned and restarted their weaving business. By 1881 the convent expanded their weaving activities and increased the number of resident nuns. The convent was successively reconstructed and expanded to the rectangular building with a central courtyard, as you see it today.

The convent has a history of more than 600 years of weaving and decorating textiles used in catholic worship, called paraments. They operated several weaving machines on which they produced specialized paraments, with gold, silver, and silk threads, decorated with precious stones and pearls. The skilled sisters made the 27 outfits of the Black Madonna of the Our Lady Chapel in Einsiedeln. For many centuries they have maintained the unique expertise in preparing, repairing, and decorating relics and catacomb saints (bones, skulls, skeletons) in cloth and precious stones. For example, the decorated relics at the castle chapel in Pfäffikon and the St. Meinrad chapel at the Etzel Pass were prepared in their workshop.

The convent has two treasures (not on public display) that survived the centuries: a tree-root in the shape of a cross (laid in a gold-framed casing of a cross) dating from around 1277; and six statues of boys in Roman dress (1602) that represent the Innocent Children, who were murdered by order of King Herod after Jesus was born (they are displayed at their Christmas manger every year).

Nowadays around 13 nuns live and work at the convent. Apart from weaving and decorating paraments, they derive their income from a small shop where they sell products from their herb garden (such as tea), honey from the beehives, and handicraft work (handwoven cloth, knitwear, cards, and candles).

Benedictine Convent Church, Au (Benediktinerinnen Kloster Kirche) **41**

Austrasse 8, 8840 Trachslau bei Einsiedeln

Ring the doorbell of the office (*Pforte*), which is the door left of the church entrance, where you also find the shop.

🏛 The church was built as a new construction of a previous church in 1972-74. Its interior has the typical 1970s modern designs, colorful frescos on the walls, a non-traditional footprint, and undecorated concrete.

📷 On the right is an elevated space used as a side-chapel, with the organ (2001) at its back wall. This is where the nuns perform their Eternal Worship, facing the round tabernacle. This day and night worship has been practiced for more than 170 years (since 1845). The round tabernacle at the front-right represents the Burning Thornbush. Apart from the Eternal Worship, the sisters conduct services five times, and read a passage from the Rule of St. Benedict, every day.

The gravel path of the Way of St. James continues through the Trachslau moors with forested hills on the right. The route passes by a stone quarry and processing plant that has served the Abbey of Einsiedeln since the 17th century. The marble of the Our Lady Chapel comes from there. In the village Trachslau you get to road nr. 386. After 100 meters on this road the signpost directs you to the left, onto a gravel path directly alongside the Alp stream. From there you will see the St. Stephen church on a hill (to the right).

Since there is no direct path from the signposted route nr. 4 to the St. Stephen church, you need to make a small detour away from the route. Instead of turning left towards the Alp stream, turn right into a small street that goes up the hill towards Ober Trachslau. After 350 meters you arrive at the St. Stephen Church (at km 5.5).

St. Stephen Church, Trachslau (St. Stefans Kirche) 42

Eigenstrasse 1, 8840 Trachslau

St. Stephen

On a table left of the entrance

The catholic church was built in 1875-78, to serve the parishioners of the small village. Given the importance of the stone quarry to the village, it is logical that the church was dedicated to the patron St. Stephen. It is strange to see a medieval battle instrument (called Morningstar) on the stamp of the church; it was copied from the coat-of-arms of the municipality of Trachslau. The Morningstar refers to the battles over the ownership of the valley, which occurred between the Abbey of Einsiedeln and City of Schwyz around 1308.

The interior is austere. Natural wood dominates the appearance. The painting at the high-altar depicts St. Stephen.

From the church turn left (south) and left again onto a grass trail. Pass by the farmhouse and 460 meters from the church you are back on road nr. 368 and the gravel trail directly alongside the Alp stream. Along the stream you have panoramic views of the Mythen. You cross a small bridge to the left bank of the stream and continue for 2.3 km through narrow patches of forest and along open grasslands, until you switch again to the other side of the stream in the village Alpthal. From the bridge crossing the Alp stream you have a beautiful view of the church with the Mythen in the background. At km 9.0 you arrive at the St. Apollonia Church.

43 St. Apollonia Church, Alpthal (St. Apollonia Kirche)

- Dorfstrasse 17, 8849 Alpthal
- St. Apollonia
- At the municipal office, about 50 meters to the back-right (follow the sign to the toilets). Ask for the pilgrim stamp at the counter right of the entrance.
- A small chapel on this site was first mentioned in 1690. It was replaced by a church in 1787. The present neo-Gothic church was built in 1885-87.
- Compared to the church in Trachslau (built 10 years earlier), the church's interior is styled completely different. The use of pastel colors on the walls and ceiling make the interior very light. The long spires of the neo-Gothic decorations of the pulpit, altars, and crucifixion way stations are eye-catchers. The vaulted ceiling and wall frescos accentuate the interior, which one would not expect given the dull exterior of the church. The color-scheme and decorations share many similarities with the St. Joseph chapel in Einsiedeln, dating from the same period (end of the 19th century).

The pathway switches back to the left side of the stream as the valley becomes narrower. A kilometer later you cross the stream and road nr. 368 for the last time. The signpost directs you across the road to start the steep ascent over 3 km to the Haggenegg Pass, the highest point of the Way of St. James through Switzerland. After 10 km you leave the valley and start the strenuous part of stage 5.

The ascent is not so long, but extremely steep throughout the first kilometer. It starts through the forest with a difficult under-footing: fixed and loose, small and large, stones and rocks. A kilometer into the ascent you leave the forest with the difficult under-footing and come to a patch of grassland. There you pass by a small roadside chapel (*Wegkapelle*), fenced off from the cows.

The trail continues steeply up until you reach a broad gravel road, where you turn left towards the Mythen mountains. From there it becomes less steep. Keep following the route through patches of forest, meadows, and moors.

You pass by a shelter, a ski lift, and a small farm where they make cheese (*Alpkäserei Gummen*), all the while enjoying magnificent views of the two Mythen peaks (weather permitting). The last part of the ascent is on concrete and tarmac roads.

The **Haggenegg Pass** has a long history as a transit pass between north and central Switzerland. It has been the shortest route between Einsiedeln and Schwyz for many centuries. Already in medieval times the Way of St. James guided the pilgrims from the north over this pass; there was already mention of a pilgrim inn at the pass in 1483. Famous people crossed this pass, such as Johann Wolfgang von Goethe (1775 and 1779), Felix Mendelssohn (1809), and according to legend also Saint Nicholas of Flüe and Saint Borromeo. At the time of the French Revolution in 1798, soldiers from Schwyz defended the pass and tried to stop the advancing French troops that came from Einsiedeln (on the same route as you hiked). At 1'414 meters above sea level it is not only the highest altitude of the Way of St. James through Switzerland, but also the highest altitude of the Way of St. James north of the Pyrenees.

The Pilgrim Chapel is a few meters over the pass (at km 13.4).

44 Pilgrim Chapel, Haggenegg Pass (Pilgerkapelle Haggenegg)

- Haggenegg Pass, 6430 Schwyz
- On the windowsill to the left, together with The Bible and a guestbook.
- The chapel was originally built in 1700, most recently restored in 2010, and stands on the site of a medieval stone cross. The top part of this small sandstone cross (from around 1500) now stands on the wooden pillar.
- This is the highest-elevation chapel (1'412 meters) of the Way of St. James, not only through Switzerland, but also north of the Pyrenees. Its interior is small and ascetic; it is more like a shelter.

  The bell in the metal frame, made in 2010, is unique. Try to toll the bell: you cannot, as the rope is locked. Look inside the bell: it has a Latin/German inscription "*Ultreia – Der Weg ist das Ziel – Iter para tutum – 2010 A.D*". "*Ultreia*" is Latin for beyond. It is an old greeting of pilgrims on the Way of St. James, which says keep going and go beyond the horizon to reach Santiago de Compostela. This phrase was already used in the first pilgrim's guide Liber Sancti Jacobi, dating from around 1130. "*Der Weg ist das Ziel*" is German for the journey is the goal. "*Iter para tutum*" is a Latin prayer to Mary for a safe journey. The phrases encourage the pilgrim to keep going, to be safe on their way, and to enjoy the journey as the goal.

The views of Lake Lucerne and the Alps are spectacular (weather permitting). A few meters from the chapel is the Haggenegg Inn, standing on the site of the historical pilgrim inn. A winding tarmac road for motorized vehicles provides access from Schwyz to the southern side of Haggenegg Pass. From the northern side only the hiking trail leads to the pass.

From the Pilgrim Chapel you need to briefly leave the signposted route to go to another chapel, slightly below the pass level. Follow the gradually descending tarmac road past the inn for about 400 meters. The chapel is at a unique location, against the background of the two Mythen peaks and the valley to the south. This is the second-highest chapel of the Way of St. James north of the Pyrenees, at 1'382 meters. You reach the Haggenegg Chapel at km 13.8.

45 Haggenegg Chapel, Haggenegg Pass (Haggenegg Kapelle)

Haggenegg Pass, 6430 Schwyz

Our Lady, St. Anne, St. Joachim, St. Meinrad

The chapel was built in 1920-21, to commemorate the nearby location where the Black Madonna statue had been buried. In 1798 the Benedictine Abbey of Einsiedeln had temporarily (three months) buried the Black Madonna statue to protect it from the plundering French troops. After the statue was taken to Austria, local people built a small roadside chapel (1848) at its former hiding location. As more people came to worship at the former hiding place of the Black Madonna, a small chapel was erected in 1877, which was replaced by the present larger chapel in 1920-21.

The chapel is made completely of wood and radiates warmth. Special features are the Black Madonna statue, a Virgin Mary painting, the small stained-glass frames in the windows, and the votives.

The Black Madonna statue at the altar is a replica of the one in Einsiedeln (117 cm), including a dress that is regularly changed. From the chancel look back towards the entrance to see a painting depicting the Virgin Mary with baby Jesus, accompanied by her mother, St. Anne, and her father, St. Joachim.

The small stained-glass centerpieces in the windows have beautifully colored scenes depicting Saints. St. Meinrad with two ravens and the Abbey of Einsiedeln is one of them.

The many small votive frames at the entrance portal were left by worshippers of the Black Madonna, in fulfilment of a vow or as appreciation for a healing after praying to Mary. They are self-made and very artistic. Notice how some date back to 1920, when the chapel was built. Read them; they are faith inspiring.

From the chapel trace back the same 400 meters to the inn. Behind the inn the descent starts. The next 2 km descend extremely steep on a gravel path through the forest. Some parts are so steep that you need a walking stick (or hiking poles) to prevent from slipping on the gravel. When it is wet from rain, snow, or fog it will be dangerous. If you can, plan this stage according to the weather forecast and try to walk on the grassy sides of the path.

The gravel turns into a tarmac road that zigzags down the mountain. You pass by isolated houses and farms. The forest makes room for meadows and grasslands of the local farms, providing wide and far views. You can see the Alps, Lake Lucerne (*Vierwaldstättersee*), the Rigi mountain, Lake Lauerz, and Ingenbohl, the destination of stage 5, in the distance. At km 18.7 you arrive at the St. Fridolin Chapel.

St. Fridolin Chapel, Ried (Fridolinskapelle) 46

- Ried, 6430 Schwyz
- St. Fridolin, St. Joseph, St. Anthony of Padua
- In the chancel, on a small shelf attached to the wall, above the stone jug containing holy water.
- The chapel was built in 1780 and was renovated several times over the centuries. This chapel replaced an earlier chapel from 1691, which stood near the Nietenbach stream, but was endangered by floods and had become too small.
- The baroque altar has a painting depicting the Virgin Mary with baby Jesus. The left statue represents St. Joseph, the right statue St. Anthony.

After 500 meters along the road (past a soccer field) the route turns left and enters the outskirts of Schwyz. You keep descending on a road while passing by a large building (yellowish with a brown roof) on your left. That building looks like a monastery (it was) but (nowadays) houses the Cantonal High School (*Gymnasium*).

6 Former Jesuit Collegium, Schwyz (Jesuit Kollegium)

Kollegiumstrasse 24, 6431 Schwyz

Jesuit Order

Until 1627 the town Schwyz did not have a secondary school; students had to attend, for example, the abbey's school in Einsiedeln. From 1627 the town established its own gymnasium. During the Helvetic Republic (1798-1803) this school was closed; it was reopened under management of the Abbey of Einsiedeln in 1804. Several decades later the town Schwyz gave the Jesuit Order the assignment to build a new catholic boys' gymnasium.

The Jesuits built their collegium in 1841-44. As is normal for a Jesuit Collegium, it consisted of a monastery, church, and school, within one large building complex.

Only three years later the collegium was destroyed and the Jesuits were expelled, as a result of the Sonderbund War (1847). Troops of the protestant Cantons marched into Schwyz and destroyed many of the buildings. For several years the collegium lay in ruins.

In 1855 Capuchin friar Florentini rebuilt the complex, financed by the Bishops of Basel, Chur, and St. Gallen. The school was reopened as the first catholic boys' boarding school in Schwyz, named Mary-Help (*Maria Hilf*), in 1856. The buildings were destroyed by a devastating fire in 1910, but rebuilt again and expanded in 1911.

In 1972 ownership changed to the Canton, the school became public, and allowed girls for the first time. Until that time, girls attended the girls' school in Ingenbohl (the Theresianum, which you will pass by at the end of the stage). During renovations another large fire destroyed part of the buildings in 1979. The boarding facilities were discontinued in 2001 and in 2008-11 the complex was closed, because of extensive renovations.

Nowadays about half of the complex is used for the Cantonal school and the other half for Cantonal administration offices and archives.

To reach the church, you need to briefly leave the signposted route. To access it, turn left in front of the building and go up the steps in the middle (the church is open during school times). At km 19.9 you arrive at the Jesuit Collegium Church Mary-Help.

Jesuit Collegium Church Mary-Help, Schwyz (Kollegium Kirche Maria-Hilf) 47

Kollegiumstrasse 24, 6431 Schwyz

St. Mary

The church has the same history as the collegium complex: it was built by the Jesuits in 1841-44, destroyed by Confederate troops during the Sonderbund War in 1847, rebuilt in 1856, and destroyed by fire and rebuilt in 1910 and 1979.

The interior of the church originates from the extensive renovations in 2008-11, when the church was restored to its original late-baroque style.

The Jesuits used the church for their monastery as well as for the school. Nowadays the church is used for events, concerts, and school celebrations. The church has beautiful rococo plastering on the nave's side galleries.

Special features of the church are: the six side-altars along the nave; the stained-glass ceiling of the chancel; the side-galleries resembling a theater; the high-altar with its gold colored decorations and one of the tallest altar paintings along the Swiss Way of St. James.

This oil painting (1913) depicts Mary-Help, the patroness Saint of the church, with two angels who spread her cape over eight Saints (Nicholas of Flüe, Florentini, Catherine, Maurice, and several Popes).

From the collegium walk back to the signposted route. Keep looking back to the Mythen; they look impressive from this location. A bit later you follow the signs through the streets of the town Schwyz, the capital city of the Canton with the same name. You already see the bell tower of the St. Martin church in the distance. Through a narrow street you arrive at the St. Martin Church at km 20.3.

You first pass by two chapels located north of the church: the two-storied ossuary with the St. Michael Chapel up the stairs and the Holy Cross Chapel. The door of the ossuary will be locked, unless there is a service. The door of the Holy Cross Chapel is open during the day.

48 St. Michael Chapel, Schwyz (Michaelskapelle)

Schulgasse, 6430 Schwyz

St. Michael

The chapel was built as a replacement of a smaller ossuary in 1512-18. It is situated at the former cemetery that was moved to a different location in 1857. The upper St. Michael chapel was used for services, whereas the lower ossuary was used for the storage of bodies and bones. The two-storied chapel was last renovated in 1976-77.

The upper chapel has a vaulted ceiling and wall frescos from the time of construction in 1518. The St. Michael statue at the altar dates from 1740.

The vaulted lower ossuary contains a beautiful wood-carved two-winged Gothic relief Pietà dating from the 15th century (behind the pillars at the back wall).

Holy Cross Chapel, Schwyz (Heiligkreuz Kapelle) 49

Schulgasse, 6430 Schwyz

St. Mary, St. John the Baptist, St. Mary Magdalene

The chapel stands on the site of the former cemetery. At the cemetery the crucifix stood underneath a small roof. After a fire destroyed much of the village in 1642, it was considered a miracle that the crucifix was not damaged. To commemorate this miracle, the local military director built a new chapel to replace the small wooden roof over the crucifix in 1645. The latest renovations were undertaken in 1983-84.

The late-Gothic crucifix is flanked by baroque statues representing Mary (left) and St. John the Baptist (right). At the base of the crucifix is a baroque statue representing St. Mary Magdalene, with her hand on a small reliquary box. Special are the 13 angels that surround the crucifix, of which 11 carry torture tools and instruments that caused Jesus to suffer. This is unique along the Swiss Way of St. James.

St. Martin Church, Schwyz (St. Martin Kirche) 50

Herrengasse 1, 6430 Schwyz

St. Martin, St. Polycarp, St. Nazarius

On a tableau fixed to the last right pew. The stamp depicts the same scene as the painting at the high-altar.

The church as you see it nowadays is the sixth church on this site. The earliest church was built around 730 and was already dedicated to St. Martin. The second church was built around the year 1000 and was possibly destroyed by an earthquake in 1117. The third church followed in 1121 and was built in a Romanesque style. The fourth church, built around 1481, was significantly larger than its predecessors, but burned down in 1642. After the fire a new (fifth) church was built in an early-baroque style. Because of structural weaknesses it was demolished and the (sixth) present-day church was built in a late-baroque style in 1769-74. The oldest parts of the church are the lower walls of the bell tower, which date from 1481 (fourth church). St. Martin is not only the patron Saint of this church, but also of Canton Schwyz.

The church has beautiful baroque interior decorations: marble, frescos, paintings, woodwork, and so forth. Study the pulpit for a moment; it has magnificent artwork and is one of the most elaborately decorated along the Swiss Way of St. James. Even the organ on the gallery at the back of the nave has gold-colored decorations. The marble altars, pulpit, and baptismal font were made by Italian craftsmen in 1769-74. The painting of the high-altar depicts the scene of St. Martin cutting his cape in two and sharing one half with a beggar.

All six side-altars have vitrines with relics. The four vitrines at the front (two left and two right of the chancel) have many small bone particles that have been artfully embroidered and decorated with precious stones, prepared by the Sisters of the Dominican Convent of Schwyz.

Two skeletons dressed in embroidered red Roman military dress lie in the relic vitrines at the altars on the sides of the nave. They are catacomb saints that were purchased from the Vatican in 1652 (Polycarp) and 1676 (Nazarius).

The one in the left vitrine is venerated as Saint Polycarp, the other on the right as Saint Nazarius. Have a closer look at the decorations and embroideries, also prepared by the Dominican Sisters.

The town Schwyz is the capital of the same-named Canton and has several interesting sites. Around the town square (*Hauptplatz*) you see the church, hotel Wysses Rössli (White Horse), town hall (*Rathaus*), and fountain; all against the background of the two Mythen peaks. Unfortunately, half of the square is used as a car park, ruining the historical scene.

The hotel Wysses Rössli already existed in the middle ages and was Schwyz's first inn. It housed famous guests such as Goethe and was also rebuilt after the town's fire of 1642.

The **town hall** was originally built in 1593, but had to be reconstructed several times since (e.g. after the town fire of 1642). The dark brown wall frescos, depicting the Battle of Morgarten of 1315 (*Schlacht bei Morgarten*), were painted in 1891. In this battle troops of the Ur-Cantons Schwyz, Uri, and Unterwalden (nowadays split in Nidwalden and Obwalden) conquered troops of the House of Habsburg to free themselves from Habsburg advances and oppression. This was a historical victory for the first Swiss Confederation, which was formed by the three Cantons in 1291.

For the next three sites in the town Schwyz you need to briefly leave the signposted route: a fortified tower, a Dominican convent and church, and a Capuchin monastery and church. When you cross the square and walk eastward into the *Strehlgasse* (right of the fountain) you see a fortified tower on your right (behind another fountain).

The medieval tower is nowadays called the **Archive Tower** (*Archivturm*) and is the oldest building in the town Schwyz. It was built around 1200 and served as the fortified residence of governors, who managed the local lands and income for the House of Kyburg and later for the House of Habsburg. The three-storied tower is square and 8.5-meters in length with 2.1-meter-thick walls at its foundations (0.9 meter at the top). From its design it is very similar to the castle tower of Pfäffikon; its original entrance door was also on the first floor.

After the House of Habsburg lost the Battle of Morgarten (1315), they withdrew from Schwyz and the town took possession of the fortified tower. They restyled the tower and for many centuries it housed a prison on the ground floor and an archive for important documents on the second floor. Over the centuries the interior was regularly renovated, i.e. a ground floor entrance was made, windows were enlarged, an inside staircase was built, and the wooden roof was often replaced (after a fire or storm). In 1936 the archive relocated to another building that was better protected against fire. Since then it stood empty, housed a museum, and nowadays is used for school workshops by the History Museum, dedicated to the Charter of the first Swiss Confederation of 1291. The present-day appearance dates from renovations in 1776 and 1948. The tower is not publicly accessible.

Other than this fortified residential tower there was never a castle in Schwyz, because the town was not strategically important: it was not along any of the major trade routes from southern Germany to northern Italy (neither along the early East-Switzerland route, nor along the Gotthard route when this opened in 1220). Due to the location of the Benedictine Abbey of Einsiedeln the town was part of the major pilgrimage routes, but not part of the major trade routes. The passage over the Haggenegg Pass was too difficult for carriages and carts (and hardly possible in winter), compared to the much easier trade routes via Zug/Luzern (avoiding pre-Alp mountain passes).

From the Archive Tower continue east on the *Strehlgasse*. At the road split keep left and at km 20.7 you arrive at the Dominican Convent St. Peter am Bach (*Frauenkloster St. Peter am Bach*). The convent is in the narrow streets of the old town and can easily be overlooked in the one-way street.

7 **Dominican Convent St. Peter am Bach** (Dominikanerinnen Kloster)

- Strehlgasse 18, 6430 Schwyz
- Dominican Order
- St. Peter of Verona
- The convent was established under guidance of the Dominican Priory of Zurich in 1275. The local Lord Hartmann donated his house, which was turned into a small convent in 1283. Initially the sisters were a group of religious women living in a community, also called beguines. Around 1300 they adopted the Rule of St. Dominic and became a Dominican convent. In 1347 the convent was named St. Peter am Bach (St. Peter along the Stream), under which name it is still known today. The patron St. Peter of Verona was chosen, as he was considered the first martyr of the Dominican Order. In 1415 the sisters reformed their daily practices. The convent became enclosed, they vowed to poverty, introduced the hourly prayers, and had to become self-sufficient by working in their garden within the confines of the convent. The convent flourished, while the sisters maintained a girls' school in their building.

As with most monastic Orders, decline set in from 15th century. Under influence of the social turbulence caused by the Reformation and the Bubonic Plague, only two sisters occupied the convent in 1531-50. By the beginning of the 17th century their buildings were dilapidated and had to be rebuilt in 1625-29. During the time of the French invasion and the Helvetic Republic in 1798-1803, the convent was closed. Renovations were undertaken in the 1930s, -50s, and -70s. The last one for the celebration of their 700-year existence.

In 1975 the convent still housed 32 nuns, nowadays around seven. It is a closed community with focus on prayer and maintenance of their convent. In earlier centuries the sisters generated income from the preparation and maintenance of paraments; nowadays they concentrate on baking of the Host (25'000 a week) for the surrounding parishes.

Dominican Convent Church, Schwyz (Frauenkloster Kirche) 51

Strehlgasse 18, 6430 Schwyz

St. Peter of Verona

The church has the same construction history as the convent: it was rebuilt in 1639-42 (the previous church was demolished) and renovated in 1932 and 1975. The front porch and the interior decorations date from the 18th century.

Crucifixion way stations line the walls, underneath paintings of former Sisters and Saints. The three marble altars have a typical 18th century baroque style with many statues depicting saints and angels. The large painting of the high-altar depicts St. Peter of Verona. Left of the entrance is a small side-chapel with a Pietà statue and a painting of Jesus at the Cross.

From the church walk back via the *Strehlgasse* to the town square (*Hauptplatz*), and continue straight into the *Herrengasse.* About 300 meters into this street you arrive at the Capuchin Monastery (at km 21.2).

Capuchin Monastery, Schwyz (Kapuziner Kloster) 8

Herrengasse 33, 6430 Schwyz

Capuchin Order

Initially the Capuchin Order settled north of town in a monastery called *St. Josef im Loo* in 1585. The Capuchin friars moved into their present building in 1620. During the time of the Helvetic Republic the monastery was closed (1798-1803). From 1855 until 1972 the Capuchins led the former Jesuit Collegium school. The buildings were last renovated and expanded in 1978-79.

Nowadays nine friars live in the monastery and provide pastoral care for the hospital, retirement home, and others. They also care for the high-aged retired friars living in their monastery.

52 Capuchin Monastery Church, Schwyz (Kapuzinerkloster Kirche)

Herrengasse 33, 6430 Schwyz

St. Anthony of Padua

The church was built in 1620 and last renovated in 1953.

In the traditions of the Capuchin's vow to poverty, the church has a simple interior. The three altars form a unity and wood-colors dominate the interior. Set in the right wall at the back of the nave is a small statue representing St. Anthony of Padua with baby Jesus.

Have a closer look at the vitrines of the two side-altars. They have a large collection of small pieces of bone-relics with different nametags, decorated with embroidery and precious stones. These decorations were made by the sisters of the Dominican convent.

From the church walk back to the main square. In case you are planning to spend the night in Schwyz, you can find a large information board in a recess at the foot of the church (behind the bus stop, close to the signpost with the yellow hiking directions).

The route leaves the square towards the south, across the roundabout, on the pavement along the main road. About 250 meters down the road you arrive at a chapel on the left side of the street (at km 21.7). The Sorrowful Mother of God Chapel of Schwyz stands out against the background scenery of the two Mythen peaks.

Sorrowful Mother of God Chapel, Schwyz (Kapelle zur schmerzhaften Muttergottes) 53

- Schmiedgasse, 6430 Schwyz
- Sorrowful Mother of God
- The chapel was built before the three Ur-Cantons formed the first Swiss Confederation, so before 1291, making it one of the oldest chapels in Schwyz. The first chapel was reconstructed and expanded in 1683, when it was dedicated to the Sorrowful Mother of God and several other saints. Because of reported miracles, the chapel became a pilgrimage destination during the middle ages. Many renovations were undertaken over the last centuries, the last one in 1975-76.
- Its interior is simple. The altar has a statue representing Mary with the corpse of Jesus (a Pietà). Under the front portico two paintings with decorated frames represent the Heart of Jesus and the Heart of Mary.

Only 150 meters further, on the right, you arrive at the reformed Church of Schwyz at km 21.9.

Reformed Church, Schwyz (Evangelisch-reformierte Kirche) 54

- Schmiedgasse 34, 6430 Schwyz
- Right of the entrance, before entering the church hall

The church was built in a modern style in 1957-58, the year the protestant parish of Brunnen received Federal recognition. From 1945 protestant services were held in former army barracks, which were rebuilt and expanded to serve as the protestant church in 1957.

The interior is modern and without religious icons.

Continuing along the main street you pass by the **Victorinox** company building on the left. They make the famous Swiss multiuse pocket knives. In case you are interested in buying one of their pocket knives as souvenir, their factory outlet would be a good place to check out the discounted selection (closed on Sundays).

Another 100 meters down the road, on your right, you pass by the **Mythen Center** Schwyz, a shopping mall with over 50 stores, covering food, fashion, sports, restaurants, and so forth. Are you in need of something specific? Are you hungry? Do you want to buy snacks for the next days? Do you need something from a pharmacy? The Mythen Center is a good place to make a stop (closed on Sundays).

After crossing a roundabout, the trail takes you to the left, between some houses, to a field. There you arrive at the Five Francises Chapel of Ibach at km 22.5.

55 **Five Francises Chapel, Ibach** (Fünf-Franzen Kapelle)

Stägliweg 9, 6438 Ibach

St. Francis of Assisi, St. Francis de Sales, St. Francis Xaver, St. Francis of Paola, St. Francis Borgia, St. Mary, St. Joseph, St. John the Baptist, St. John the Evangelist

The chapel was built in 1675-80, as a smaller replica of the St. Anthony Chapel (see below). During the invasion of French troops in 1798, the chapel was plundered and severely damaged; it was rebuilt in 1811.

It is a so-called farm/yard chapel, in German *Hof*, under which name it is better known. The name five-Francises was derived from the patronage of five Saints with the first name Francis.

The altar painting (1679) depicts these five Saints, below the Holy Trinity, Mary, Joseph, John the Baptist, and John the Evangelist. Notice the pilgrim scallop carved into the door (1811). The door is locked; you cannot enter, as the chapel is still privately owned.

Down the grass field you already see the St. Anthony Church of Ibach. After crossing the *Gotthardstrasse* (road nr. 8) you arrive at this church at km 22.6. The route leads you across the street to the side entrance, covered by a glass portal.

St. Anthony Church, Ibach (St. Antonius Kirche) 56

Gotthardstrasse 87, 6438 Ibach

St. Anthony of Padua

At the parish office; a house across the parking, north of the church. A sign left of the church entrance instructs you how to get there.

The catholic church was built in 1938-39, replacing a smaller chapel. A chapel was first mentioned in official documents in 1430, but must have already existed from the 12th/13th century. In 1520 this chapel was replaced by a second larger chapel. The third chapel replaced the previous one in 1663. Further reconstructions took place in 1783 and 1858. By 1920 the chapel was considered too small for the parish. For nearly 20 years funds and donations were collected to finance the construction of a new and larger church. The new church was consecrated in 1939 and dedicated to St. Anthony, just like its predecessor chapels.

Straight lines shape the exterior and interior of the church. The interior is simple and austere (whereas the previous chapel had three altars and many decorations).

The route follows road nr. 8 (yes indeed still nr. 8, which you also crossed in Rapperswil and Pfäffikon). As you can see, road nr. 8 keeps coming back; it was the historical road connection between St. Gallen and Schwyz/Brunnen.

About 200 meters from the church the route crosses the shallow Muota mountain river. The **Muota River** has a length of around 32 km and flows into Lake Lucerne (*Vierwaldstättersee*). The name Muota was derived from 'wild water', because it regularly flooded the valley. One of the worst floods occurred in 1910, when the whole valley was under water, causing significant damage. The first embankments were already built in the 15th century, trying to tame the wild river. After 1910 the river was increasingly dammed and canalized, and water-power plants were built along it. The river still transports loads of moraine into Lake Lucerne; the location where it flows into the lake needs to be dredged regularly.

After the bridge the signposted route nr. 4 directs left and immediately right. At km 23.0 you arrive at the small Holy Cross Chapel of Ibach, standing a bit lost between several houses.

57 Holy Cross Chapel, Ibach (Heiligkreuz Kapelle)

Feldweg 3, 6438 Ibach

The chapel was first built in 1485, but the present construction dates from the 17th century. The porch and small steeple on the roof were added in 1901-11. It was last renovated in 1974. The chapel is better known as the Erlen Chapel, named after the area.

The crucifixion group at the altar dates from the 17th century. The chapel is a farm chapel, built in the courtyard of a medieval farm (before apartment buildings were constructed around it). It is still in private ownership. The door is locked; you cannot go in.

The route is flat. You walk on a tarmac road between grasslands with wide views toward the Alps. The route turns left onto a narrow gravel footpath through meadows and underneath apple trees. At the end of the gravel footpath you arrive at the Toothache Chapel of Unterschönenbuch (at km 24.4).

Toothache Chapel, Unterschönenbuch (Zahnweh Kapelle) 58

- Unterschönenbuch, 6440 Ingenbohl
- St. Mary, St. Agatha, St. Apollonia, St. Odile
- The chapel was built in the 17th century and was last renovated in 1989-90. It is a farm chapel, built in the courtyard of a medieval farm, and is still in private ownership.
- People visited the small chapel to pray for relief of toothache. The three statues date from the 17th century and represent St. Mary, St. Agatha, and St. Apollonia, while the chapel is dedicated to St. Odile. The statue of St. Apollonia used to be St. Agatha, but was transformed by adding tooth pliers.

Keep looking back to the two Mythen peaks towering high above the town Schwyz. The trail goes up a hill and 400 meters later arrives at the St. Wendolyn Chapel of Unterschönenbuch (at km 24.8).

59 St. Wendolyn Chapel, Unterschönenbuch (St. Wendelin Kapelle)

- Schönenbuchstrasse 4, 6440 Ingenbohl
- St. Wendolyn
- The chapel was built in 1625-35 and dedicated to St. Wendolyn. The present chapel is a reconstruction of the first chapel in 1708-17. Extensive renovations were undertaken in 1828, 1886, and 1992-93.
- For the small settlement of Unterschönenbuch, with a population of only 150, the chapel has an unexpected beautiful baroque interior. Marble altars, statues, paintings, frescos, and gold-plated decorations cover almost the entire interior; a showcase of the importance of catholic religion in the Ur-Cantons. Paintings on the walls tell the story of St. Wendolyn.

The route keeps following the road towards the south and passes by a stone quarry and processing plant. The road goes underneath Highway A4, after which the route turns left immediately.

At this location the nr. 4 signpost directs left, whereas two white signs for the pilgrim inn (*Pilgerherberge*) and the Ingenbohl Convent (*Kloster Ingenbohl*) direct straight. In front you see several long buildings and a church tower. That church, and the pilgrim inn next to it, are indeed the ending point of stage 5. You can either take the direct way (go straight along the tarmac road) or follow the signposted route a little further (and end at the same church). In case you continue to follow the signposted route nr. 4, the path goes parallel to the highway on a poorly maintained boardwalk through a patch of marshland. Where the highway disappears in a tunnel, the signs take you up a hill to the long building.

The long building on your right (in yellow/brown colors) is called the **Theresianum**. In 1860 a private catholic girls' boarding school was established by Capuchin friar Florentini (who rebuilt the catholic boys' Collegium in Schwyz in 1855). The school was named after Mother Theresia (Theresia-num), the co-founder of the Ingenbohl Institute (see below), who was tasked with leading the school. At first the school started in a side wing of the Ingenbohl Convent, until their own building was constructed south of the convent in 1888.

Again you see a white road sign directing right towards the pilgrim inn and convent, but keep going up the hill (you will get to the pilgrim inn with a small detour). The signposted route passes by the Theresianum on its southern side. On your left is a small forested hill, where a gravel path disappears in the tree line. Follow this path and after 50 meters you arrive at the Lourdes Cave (at km 26.3).

Lourdes Cave, Ingenbohl (Lourdes Grotte) 60

Niderzstrasse, 6440 Ingenbohl

Mary-Lourdes

The Lourdes cave belongs to the Ingenbohl convent (see below). Mother Maria Theresia Scherer, co-founder of the convent, went on a pilgrimage to Lourdes, France, in 1886. She had the Mary-Lourdes cave, including a small spring, built as a replica of the one in Lourdes in 1888. The cave is situated just below the cemetery of the convent.

The cave is located in a small patch of forest where three yellow benches invite to sit down. The sounds of birds and trickling water from the spring are conducive to reflection. The permanently burning candles indicate the cave is frequently visited. Mother Theresia brought the Mary-Lourdes statue from Lourdes in 1886. Notice a second small statue underneath a rock.

From the cave follow a small forest trail (with steps) back down the hill to the southern side of the Theresianum. After 50 meters you get to a nr. 4 signpost that directs you to the front of the school. Instead of taking the long staircase with the yellow handlebar on the left down the hill of the school, keep going straight and pass by the entire front of the school. Here you need to leave the signposted route nr. 4 to reach the ending point of stage 5. The path turns right and you get to the *Klosterstrasse*. Turn left and after 100 meters down the hill you arrive at the Ingenbohl Convent at km 26.7.

9 Convent of the Merciful Sisters of the Holy Cross, Ingenbohl
(Barmherzige Schwestern vom Heiligen Kreuz)

Klosterstrasse, 6440 Ingenbohl

Merciful Sisters of the Holy Cross, Franciscan Order

The convent was established by Capuchin friar Florentini (who rebuilt the boys' school in Schwyz and established the girls' school in Ingenbohl) and Mother Maria Theresia Scherer in 1856. The convent housed in a former farmhouse on the same site. For about 100 years the farmhouse was continuously rebuilt and expanded, until it required a comprehensive renovation and modernization. The convent was newly built in a modern design in 1965-75. These are the buildings you see today.

The sisters lead the Ingenbohl Institute, an international organization of nuns active socially, religiously, and educationally, with Ingenbohl as its mother house. See Appendix 3 for more information.

Ingenbohl Convent Church, Ingenbohl (Kloster Kirche) 61

- Klosterstrasse 10b, 6440 Ingenbohl
- At the convent's main entrance (follow the signs to *Klosterpforte*, 140 meters from the church, at a left side-street) or at the convent's pilgrim inn.
- The church was built in 1973. It is a grey concrete building, which does not resemble a traditional church; typical of the modern 1970s church designs.
- Its interior is ascetic and modern too. The absence of richly decorated altars reflects the vows of poverty of the Franciscan Order. Notice how the light comes in through the colored skylight. At the back of the church 14 bronze stations of the crucifixion way, in a modern design, are hanging on the walls.

The crypt (1975) below the church functions as a windowless area for prayers and contemplation, and contains the grave of the convent's founding sister, the blessed Mother Maria Theresia Scherer (died 1888 – canonized as Blessed in 1995). A pilgrim guestbook lies in the crypt.

From the convent's church you pass by the convent's small shop and 200 meters further down the hill you arrive at the iron gate that accesses the St. Leonard church grounds (at km 26.6). You first reach the Cemetery Chapel.

62 Sorrowful Mother of God Chapel, Ingenbohl (Friedhofkapelle)

Klosterstrasse 6, 6440 Ingenbohl

Sorrowful Mother of God

The chapel was built at the same time as the present church, in 1659. The chapel was dedicated to the Sorrowful Mother of God and was reconstructed in 1802.

The crucifixion group at the back wall of the chancel dates from the end of the 18th century.

63 St. Leonard Church, Ingenbohl (St. Leonhard Kirche)

Klosterstrasse 6, 6440 Ingenbohl

St. Leonard

The church is on the site of a first wooden chapel that was already mentioned in official documents in 1387. This first chapel was replaced by a second chapel in 1479-81, which was expanded in 1607. The third and present church, dedicated to St. Leonard, was built in 1658-61 after Ingenbohl became an own parish separated from the St. Martin parish of Schwyz (1618). One of the main reasons for Ingenbohl's separation from the Schwyz parish was that the latter's cemeteries were full, because of the many deceased caused by the Bubonic Plague.

The church stands on a hill above the Muota River valley. It was a strategically chosen location that protected against floods; until the beginning of the 20th century the Muota River regularly flooded the whole valley.

The church was renovated in 1788 and 1832, expanded in 1926-27, and fully renovated again in 1976-78. The oldest bell of the church dates from 1403.

Its interior has a late-baroque and rococo style dating from the renovation of 1788: black and red marble frame the paintings of the three altars and ceiling frescos are framed in stucco. In a side-chapel, left of the entrance, is a beautiful statue representing the Virgin Mary with baby Jesus.

The location of the St. Leonard church and pilgrim inn is on the outskirts of the town Brunnen-Ingenbohl (population of around 9'000). The commercial and tourist center is in Brunnen, about 1 km to the south. Brunnen lies along Lake Lucerne (*Vierwaldstättersee*) and is a tourist hotspot, offering many cafés, restaurants, and hotels close to or directly at the lake's promenade. Just follow the signs to the train station and then the lake.

From the ending point

The St. Leonard church is the ending point of stage 5, about 450 meters aside the signposted route nr. 4.

In case you are a day-hiker, you need to walk 400 meters to the Brunnen train station (in the same direction of the lake).

In case you are a thru-hiker and spend the night in Ingenbohl, you can stay at the pilgrim inn (*Pilgerherberge*) of the Ingenbohl Convent. From the iron gate that leads to the church, retrace your steps for 50 meters to the pilgrim house (*Pilgerhaus Maria Theresia*) (Klosterstrasse 10, 6440 Ingenbohl; tel. 041 825 24 50; haus.maria-theresia@kloster-ingenbohl.ch; www. kloster-ingenbohl.ch). Check out www.jakobsweg.ch or www.viajacobi4.ch for the other accommodation possibilities in Ingenbohl and Brunnen. The Tourist Information Office in Brunnen (200 meters from the boat pier; Bahnhofstrasse 15; Brunnen; tel. 041 825 00 40; www.erlebnisregion-mythen.ch) may assist you in finding the right accommodation as well.

The next Stage

There are two possible next stages upon leaving Ingenbohl/Brunnen. One is stage 6 to Stans (following the Alpine Lakes route), the other is stage L1 to Werthenstein (following the Luzern/Bern route). For the choice of the route via Alpine Lakes or Luzern/Bern, see page 14.

Stage L1 guides you across Lake Lucerne, through the medieval city of Luzern, over a northern foothill of the Pilatus mountain, and along the Small Emme River valley to the Werthenstein monastery. Stage L1 and the subsequent stages L2 to L5 are described from page 285 onwards.

Stage 6 guides you across Lake Lucerne, up to the highland plateau of Emmetten and down again, and along the southern side of Lake Lucerne. Stage 6 has the highest number of churches and chapels (25) of all the stages of the Swiss Way of St. James. Read the next chapter to find out what that entails.

Stage 6: Ingenbohl to Stans 26 km

The Way along the most Churches

Route stats

	Distance in km	*Time in hrs:min*
Boat Brunnen to Treib		0:20
Signposted route nr. 4	24.1	5:30
Churches/chapels	1.9	3:00
Points of interest		0:10
Rest/lunch		1:00
Stage 6	26.0	10:00

In case you hike this stage as a daytrip, you need to add 400 meters in Ingenbohl and 150 meters in Stans (from and to the train stations). For the 8-minute boat crossing of Lake Lucerne from Brunnen to Treib you need to consider that the boat goes only once an hour; time your arrival at the pier to avoid a long wait.

Ascent/descent/total	+787 / -777 / 1'564 altitude meters
Lowest/highest altitude	435 / 788 meters
Pathway/condition	easy (difficult at Stützberg) / difficult
Churches/chapels	Brunnen (3), Volligen, Emmetten (3), Beckenried (5), Buochs (3), Ennerberg, Waltersberg, Oberdorf (2), Stans (6)
Monasteries	Former Capuchin Collegium Stans, Capuchin Convent Stans
Points of interest	Rose Castle Stans

Route summary

Stage 6 starts in catholic Canton Schwyz. Halfway the boat's crossing from Brunnen to Treib you change to catholic Canton Uri. About 1.6 km after disembarking in Treib you leave Uri again (you do not pass through this Canton anymore) and enter **Canton Nidwalden**. The route continues in catholic Canton Nidwalden until the end of the stage.

Stage 6 guides you across Lake Lucerne, up to the highland plateau of Emmetten and down again, and along the southern side of Lake Lucerne.

Stage 6 has the highest number of churches and chapels (25) of all the stages of the Swiss Way of St. James. It promises to be a very spiritual day, with many interesting churches and chapels along the route. The highest concentration is within the last 2 km (the town Stans), where you pass by eight churches and chapels.

The stage starts with an easy 1.2 km walk through Brunnen to the boat pier. An 8-minute boat ride will have to be made to get across Lake Lucerne from Brunnen to Treib. From Treib the route ascends to the highest point of the day at 788 meters over 6 km. This is the only strenuous part of the day. The 500 meters before the top resemble alpine hiking: it is a forested mountain trail, along cliffs, hewn into the rocks to pass by a very steep area on the cliff side of the Stützberg. From the highest point the route enters the highland plateau of Emmetten. After about 4 km on these highlands the route descends again (steep but not difficult) to the southern shore of Lake Lucerne. For most of the following 7 km the route closely follows the shoreline, providing panoramic views over Lake Lucerne. From Buochs, at km 20.5, the route turns away (south) from the lake. The route goes over the northwestern foothills of the Buochserhorn mountain, ascending to 564 meters. After a descent over 1 km, the last 2 km are flat while reaching Stans, the capital of Canton Nidwalden.

Getting to the starting point

Today's starting point in Ingenbohl is at the St. Leonard Church, about 450 meters aside the signposted route nr. 4. You are already at the right location in case you spent the night at the Ingenbohl Convent's pilgrim inn.

In case you hike stage 6 as a daytrip, you need to walk 400 meters from the Brunnen train station to the church. However, you could also walk from the train station directly to the first church along the route, which is opposite of the train station (this saves about 800 meters of walking the same way to and from the St. Leonard church).

Route Map and Profile

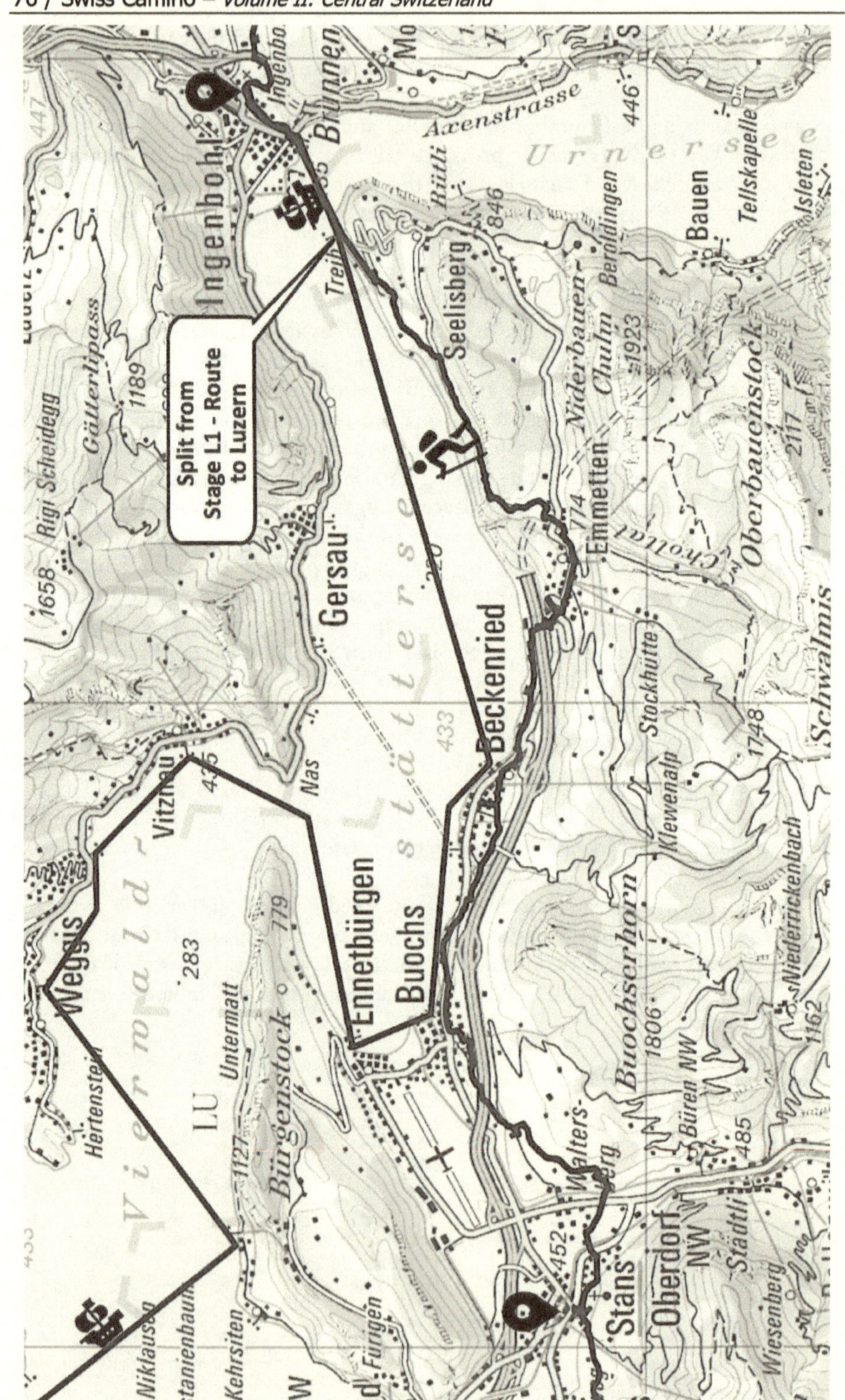
Split from
Stage L1 - Route
to Luzern
Ingenbohl
Brunnen
Axenstrasse
Urnersee
Rütli
Seelisberg
Treib
Gersau
Beckenried
Emmetten
Niderbauen
Chulm
Oberbauenstock
Bauen
Tellskapelle
Beroldingen
Schwalmis
Stockhütte
Klewenalp
Buochserhorn
Buochs
Ennetbürgen
Vitznau
Weggis
Hertenstein
Bürgenstock
Untermatt
Vierwaldstättersee
LU
Rigi Scheidegg
Gätterlipass
Nas
Stans
Oberdorf NW
Büren NW
Wiesenberg
Städtli
Niederrickenbach
Walters-berg
Kehrsiten
Fürigen

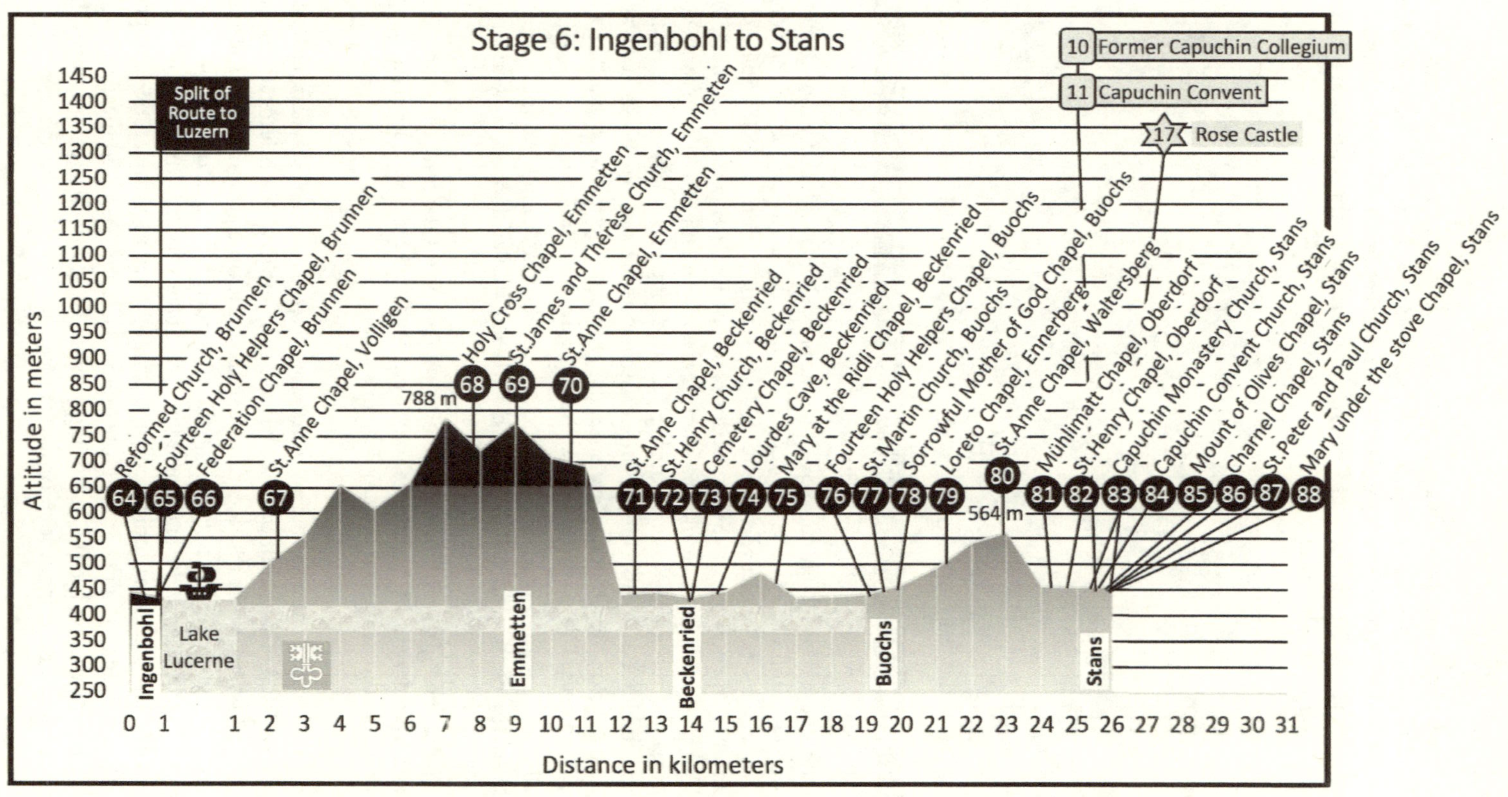
Stage 6: Ingenbohl to Stans
10 Former Capuchin Collegium
11 Capuchin Convent
17 Rose Castle
Split of Route to Luzern
Altitude in meters
1450
1400
1350
1300
1250
1200
1150
1100
1050
1000
950
900
850
800
750
700
650
600
550
500
450
400
350
300
250
Reformed Church, Brunnen
Fourteen Holy Helpers Chapel, Brunnen
Federation Chapel, Brunnen
St.Anne Chapel, Volligen
Holy Cross Chapel, Emmetten
St.James and Thérèse Church, Emmetten
St.Anne Chapel, Emmetten
St.Anne Chapel, Beckenried
St.Henry Church, Beckenried
Cemetery Chapel, Beckenried
Lourdes Cave, Beckenried
Mary at the Ridli Chapel, Beckenried
Fourteen Holy Helpers Chapel, Buochs
St.Martin Church, Buochs
Sorrowful Mother of God Chapel, Buochs
Loreto Chapel, Ennerberg
St.Anne Chapel, Waltersberg
Mühlimatt Chapel, Oberdorf
St.Henry Chapel, Oberdorf
Capuchin Monastery Church, Stans
Capuchin Convent Church, Stans
Mount of Olives Chapel, Stans
Charnel Chapel, Stans
St.Peter and Paul Church, Stans
Mary under the stove Chapel, Stans
788 m
564 m
64 65 66 67 68 69 70 71 72 73 74 75 76 77 78 79 80 81 82 83 84 85 86 87 88
Ingenbohl
Lake Lucerne
Emmetten
Beckenried
Buochs
Stans
0 1 1 2 3 4 5 6 7 8 9 10 11 12 13 14 15 16 17 18 19 20 21 22 23 24 25 26 27 28 29 30 31
Distance in kilometers

Hiking the Route

From the St. Leonard church walk towards the west, passing by two dark-wooden historical houses on white fundaments that look like the typical Swiss chalets. At the second one turn left (south) and walk in the direction of the train station. About 400 meters from the St. Leonard church you arrive at the reformed Church of Brunnen (opposite the train station).

64 Reformed Church, Brunnen (Reformierte Kirche)

Alte Kantonsstrasse 8, 6440 Brunnen

The church was built in 1889-90. Canton Schwyz did not allow protestant worship until the Swiss Confederate Republic declared freedom of religion for the whole of Switzerland in the country's constitution in 1848. Still, it took another 38 years before the protestant parish of Brunnen was established (1886). The first priest came from protestant Canton Bern and had to hold services at a hotel and school in Brunnen during the first four years, until their own church was built. The establishment and organization of the parish, as well as the financing of the church, were strongly supported by the protestant parish of Zurich (as a way to spread Protestantism in the catholic Canton).

The free-standing pointed church tower was not built until 1968; for nearly 80 years the church did not have any bells to call its parishioners to worship. The church was renovated in 1940 and 1990.

The stained-glass windows in the chancel date from the last renovation (1990) and were designed by a sister of the Ingenbohl Convent. The church has a typical protestant interior, without any religious icons.

From the church continue southward on the *Dammstrasse* and stay left (east) of the railway tracks. At the end of the *Dammstrasse* turn left to pass underneath the tracks into the *Olympstrasse*. At this location you are back on the signposted route nr. 4. However, to visit the next chapel, at the fork turn left immediately into the *Alte Gasse* (and briefly leave the signposted route). Have a look at the Way of St. James sign on the lamp post. It indicates 2'450 km/69 days to Santiago de Compostela and 50 m/30 sec to the Fourteen Holy Helpers Chapel. After 50 meters you arrive at the small chapel (at km 0.9), standing a bit squashed between two houses. Duck your head upon entering; the doorpost is low.

Fourteen Holy Helpers Chapel, Brunnen (14 Nothelfern Kapelle) 65

- Alte Gasse 5, 6440 Brunnen
- Fourteen Holy Helpers
- The chapel was built to provide religious support to fight the plague in 1576. The small chapel (only 3 by 2 meters) was renovated in 1844 and 1996.
- The side walls are decorated with two paintings representing the Fourteen Holy Helpers (seven on the left wall and seven on the right wall) dating from 1800. Notice the cord hanging from the ceiling. Just give it a gentle pull to toll the small bell in the steeple on the roof.

From the small chapel continue east and after 80 meters you reach the *Bahnhofstrasse*, where you are back on the signposted route nr. 4. Turn left towards the lake and 50 meters later you arrive at the Federation Chapel of Brunnen, right of the road (at km 1.2).

Federation Chapel, Brunnen (Bundes Kapelle) 66

- Bahnhofstrasse, 6440 Brunnen
- The chapel was built by the chief magistrate of Schwyz in 1632-35 and was dedicated to the Holy Trinity. This first chapel was destroyed when Napoleon's army invaded Switzerland in 1798. After 1803 the chapel was rebuilt in a baroque style. Renovations were undertaken in 1936 and 1990.

The name Federation chapel is linked to the first Swiss Confederation, when the three Ur-Cantons Schwyz, Uri, and Unterwalden (nowadays split in Nidwalden and Obwalden) renewed an initial vow from 1291 to consolidate their efforts to stand up against invaders (in particular the House of Habsburg). This vowing took place in Brunnen, after they had defeated the Habsburg troops in the battle of Morgarten in 1315 (as depicted on the town hall of Schwyz). The Federation chapel stands on the site where these renewed vows were made in 1315.

The chapel has a baroque style with three marble altars. The Holy Trinity is depicted on the painting at the high-altar. Holy Trinity stands for the concept that God is one, yet represented by three Divine Persons, the Father, the Son Jesus Christ, and the Holy Spirit.

After 100 meters you arrive at the Brunnen boat pier at **Lake Lucerne** (*Vierwaldstättersee*). The German name *Vierwaldstättersee* means 'four forest towns at the lake'. In medieval times the lake's shores were densely forested and the four towns (now Cantons) around the lake were Schwyz, Uri, Unterwalden (nowadays split in Nidwalden and Obwalden), and Luzern. Lake Lucerne is Switzerland's fourth-largest lake, with an average depth of 104 meters (maximum depth 214 meters) and a surface elevation of 434 meters. It has an unusual shape that comprises several bays of the lake (each of these bays has an own name). Some parts of the lake are surrounded by steep cliffs. The lake is a popular tourist attraction with boats cruising between idyllic villages (with historical hotels) along the shores.

The turquoise-colored lake against the snow-capped Alps in the background is a postcard scenery, especially with one of the historical steamboats on the lake. The area around the pier and promenade is usually bustling with people, who are enjoying the view from the many cafes' and restaurants' terraces.

At the pier you see a tall hiking signpost with many yellow direction signs. The sign for route nr. 4 directs towards the lake. At this location the Way of St. James

route splits: the Alpine Lakes (via Interlaken) route crosses the lake to Treib (first boat stop; 8 minutes); the alternative route via Luzern/Bern continues on the boat to Luzern (last boat stop; 2hr:30min; see stage L1).

The hiking route continues from Treib in Canton Uri, on the southern shore of Lake Lucerne. From the pier in Brunnen the boat takes only 8 minutes to get you to Treib, which is the first stop. You can buy the ticket (CHF 6) at the counter on the pier. In summer the morning connections to Treib are at 06:33, 08:19, 09:19, 09:49, 10:49, and so forth. So, it is useful to time your arrival at the pier to avoid having to wait an hour. Most pilgrims take the 08:19 or 09:19 boat. You will not be the only one embarking on a nice summer day. Enjoy the short ride and the views back to the two Mythen peaks, towering at the horizon.

The pier at Treib is small and only a few hikers usually disembark. You arrive in catholic **Canton Uri**. Opposite of the pier a cable car takes hikers to the top of the Seelisberg (766 meters). Spend a moment at the hiking signpost. A small board indicates the Way of St. James route to Emmetten (green line) and points out a detour route (red line). The purpose of the detour is to avoid a 500-meter rocky ascent close to some dangerous cliffs (which may be the right decision in bad weather conditions). The detour has a length of 8.9 km with 872 altitude meters; the signposted route nr. 4 has a length of 5.9 km with 619 altitude meters until the routes converge. The detour is, however, not the official Way of St. James, so keep following the signposted route nr. 4 (weather permitting).

For 1 km the route steadily climbs on a narrow tarmac road parallel to Lake Lucerne. The road provides panoramic views of the lake and the surrounding mountains. After a sharp left the sign indicates a sharp right turn, away from the road, steeply up through grasslands. Before making that right turn, though, briefly leave the signposted route and keep walking 100 meters up the road to reach the St. Anne Chapel of Volligen (at km 2.3).

67 **St. Anne Chapel, Volligen** (St. Anna Kapelle)

- Volligen, 6377 Seelisberg
- St. Anne
- The chapel was manually built by local families in 1880-81. It is on the site of an earlier chapel that was first mentioned in 1763. The first chapel had become too small and was replaced by this larger chapel. Renovations were undertaken in 1972 and 2007.
- The altar painting depicts mother Anne teaching Mary to read. This display was to incentivize the local farmer families to also have their daughters educated.

From the chapel return to the signpost that leads onto the grasslands. The trail is a narrow path that goes up steeply through meadows. Some parts of the path have large uneven stones to guide the way through the meadow. After 400 meters you leave Canton Uri and enter catholic **Canton Nidwalden**. You pass by several alpine barns. A green shield warns to be careful around cows with their calves; these may be protective and it is advised to keep your distance. You pass through several metal cattle gates. Be sure to close them after passing. The same for the electrified cattle wires: either step over them or put them back in their position.

The trail changes to a rocky and grass farm road. A narrow steep concrete path leads you to a road. From Treib the route covered 2.7 km with more than 250 altitude meters. The views are great: on the right the blue water of Lake Lucerne and on the left the white cliffs of the Stützberg. At the road the signpost directs to the right. From this altitude of 666 meters the route follows the road downhill for 1.2 km to an elevation of 619 meters.

The road forks: a dirt road goes up steeply (left), while the tarmac road continues to descend (right). There are no signposts, but you need to take the dirt road on the left (the tarmac road is a dead end). You walk a few hundred meters on the rock-covered dirt road with a moss-covered concrete wall on the left, until the path turns right onto a forest trail. The first 800 meters is a forest trail with rocky but good under-footing. In the meantime, you are following the route markings with the three stripes (two white lines with a red one in the middle), signaling that you are on a **mountainous trail** (with rocks, steep climbing along boulders, along cliffs, and beneath overhanging cliffs with the risk of falling rocks).

The following 500 meters are on more dangerous mountain trails that are hewn into the rocks and pass close to cliffs. This is the part where the signpost in Treib warned for. In normal weather conditions this is, however, neither difficult nor dangerous. Just be careful. You do not need heavy mountaineering shoes to get through this part; light sneakers with enough grip (e.g. trail-running shoes) will do too. Under adverse weather conditions (rain or snow on the trail) it will be very slippery. On some parts of the trail wooden or steel-cable handrails enable a safe passage along the abysses. At some areas the trees open up and you have wonderful views over Lake Luzern and the pre-Alps (e.g. the Mythen peaks).

At the altitude of 730 meters you get to a signpost and a split of the trails. Notice the three-striped pointed ends of the yellow signs, signaling the mountainous trails. From here the route nr. 4 turns south, away from Lake

Lucerne, zigzagging further up the mountain until it reaches the highest point of 788 meters, 300 meters later. It is a rocky forest trail, but away from the dangerous cliffs. At the highest point the route comes out of the forest, opening up views over the Emmetten highland plateau with forested hills and barren 2'000-meter-high mountain peaks behind them in the south. This is one of the best 'Swiss' views of the whole Way of St. James; a great reward for the strenuous climb.

For another 150 meters you walk along the edge of the forest, while panoramas open up towards the right, overlooking Lake Lucerne. Through a field you reach a farm, from where the route continues to descend on a tarmac road. About 800 meters later you arrive at the Holy Cross Chapel in Sagendorf (at km 7.9). It is located in a green meadow against the magnificent backdrop of the Alps.

Holy Cross Chapel, Emmetten (Heiligkreuz Kapelle) 68

Brennwaldstrasse, 6376 Emmetten

The chapel was manually built by local families in 1790-91. It replaced a small field chapel (from 1671) that was dilapidated. The latest renovation was completed in 2000.

St. James scallops are hanging from the wall candles left and right of the chancel's iron gate.

Above the entrance door (inside) hangs a half-round painting depicting the Dance of Death (*Totentanz*) in 23 scenes. It has an unusual large width of 4.7 meters and originates from around 1700 (renovated in 1932), making it one of the hidden treasures along the Swiss Way of St. James. The painting depicts that life and death were closely intertwined in society at that time. During medieval times death often came in the form of the Bubonic Plague, which did not exclude kings, bishops, and other noble people from its gruesome fate.

The Dance of Death is a theme that occurs regularly along the Swiss Way of St. James. One of the most famous medieval depictions of the Dance of Death is on the Speuer Bridge in Luzern (see point of interest nr. L-3, stage L1).

The back wall is decorated with many small votive paintings depicting religious scenes and events from the region (the oldest are from the first chapel, dating from 1671). The paintings were donated by parishioners when their prayers were heard. One of the more recent paintings depicts the invasion of Napoleon's troops in 1798.

The chapel is named after the Holy Cross because it (allegedly) has a piece of the original Cross of Jesus, kept at its high-altar. Nowadays it is not known anymore where this alleged piece of the Holy Cross came from or how and when it was obtained.

From the chapel the route continues to descend and crosses road nr. 377 to ascend through the small village Sagendorf. About 400 meters later the route is back on road nr. 377 and follows it for another 400 meters. At this location on your left you have the ground station of the Emmetten cable car (*Seilbahn*) to the Niederbauen peak at 1'570 meters. A sign at the lamp post indicates that this is the location where the Way of St. James from Canton Ticino and Uri connects to the route coming from the north (where you are on). It is still 2'206 km to Santiago de Compostela. During the ascent along the road it was not visible, but when you make a right turn in the street opposite the cable car station you arrive at the St. James and Thérèse Church of Emmetten (at km 9.0).

69 St. James and Thérèse Church, Emmetten (St. Jakob und Theresien Kirche)

- Kirchweg 7, 6376 Emmetten
- St. James the Greater, St. Thérèse of Lisieux
- On a lectern near the right side-altar. Notice the three St. James scallops on the stamp, which are also in the coat-of-arms of the municipality, exhibiting the historical significance of the pilgrimage route dating back to the first chapel in 1307.
- The church was built on the site of three predecessor churches in 1932-33. A first small chapel, dedicated to St. James, was already mentioned in 1307. This chapel was expanded to a church in 1454, which was destroyed by an earthquake in 1601, and rebuilt in 1616. At the beginning of the 20th century this church was in poor condition and had become too small for the growing population. In 1933 the present church was built and dedicated to St. James and Thérèse. Its construction was financed solely by donations. The church was renovated in 1993-96.
- The left side-altar contains a beautifully carved and decorated two-winged retable (folding altar). The right side-altar contains a tall undecorated woodcarving, depicting scenes from the life of St. Thérèse.

  The frescos on the arched wall separating the chancel and nave, and the orange-colored fresco serving as the high-altar at the back of the chancel, date from 1933. This chancel fresco is unique along the Swiss Way of St. James, depicting St. James and St. Thérèse beside Jesus at the Cross. Can you find the St. James statue at the wall?
- The panel below the right side-altar contains relics of St. Thérèse (not visible).

Walk downhill from the church to return to the signposted route nr. 4. Turn right and continue to descend along road nr. 377 through Emmetten for 600 meters. On the left side of the street you pass by three other cable car stations going up the mountains.

Where the road makes an s-curve to the right, the signs direct to continue straight, through the back alleys of a few houses, before returning onto road nr. 377. The trail crosses the road and a signpost directs to a gravel path that curves downhill on the left. At this location you need to briefly leave the signposted route. Instead of turning left, follow the residential road (*Sankt Anna-Weg*) that curves to the right. After 280 meters you arrive at the St. Anne Chapel (at km 10.3).

St. Anne Chapel, Emmetten (St. Anna Kapelle) 70

Sankt Anna-Weg, 6376 Emmetten

St. Anne

The chapel was built by a family who owned a health resort (*Kaltwasserkuranstalt*) in Emmetten at the end of the 19th century. When a family member fell seriously ill, they built a neo-Gothic chapel dedicated to St. Anne in 1902. After 1931 (when the health resort went bankrupt) the plot of land changed owners several times and the chapel was neglected and dilapidated. In 1994 the foundation that owned the chapel was reactivated and initiated a renovation.

The high-altar in the chancel (behind a metal grating) resembles a scale model of a church. Left of the chancel is a stone statue representing St. Anne teaching a young Mary to read. A small rose window above the entrance colors the interior.

From the chapel walk back to the signposted route. The gravel path closely follows a small stream in a zigzagging pattern down the mountain. For the next kilometer the path steeply descends 262 meters to return to the level of Lake Lucerne. The path goes through a patch of forest and grasslands, and underneath Highway A2. While descending you have great views over the lake.

At the lake the signpost directs left (west), where the route follows a quiet road alongside the shore. You walk past luxurious houses with lakefront gardens. In the town Beckenried you arrive at another chapel dedicated to St. Anne at km 13.2.

71 St. Anne Chapel, Beckenried (St. Anna Kapelle)

- Rütenenstrasse 32, 6375 Beckenried
- St. Anne
- On a left pew
- The history of the chapel is depicted on its ceiling. It tells the story of the miller of Beckenried, who survived bad weather while in a boat on the lake, after praying to St. Anne and promising to build her a chapel. He had the chapel built and dedicated to St. Anne around 1600. This first chapel was smaller and did not have the front porch (added in 1753). The reason for expanding the first chapel was a fire at the mill of the owner, which is also depicted on the ceiling. The present chapel was built in 1753. The small chapel was in private ownership until 1855 (since then it has belonged to the parish). The chapel was renovated in 1925 and 1984.
- The painting at the altar depicts St. Anne with a young Mary, as do the many small votives that are hanging on the wall at the entrance. These small paintings were donated by parishioners when their prayers were heard.

The route continues along the southern shore of Lake Lucerne. Next to the shore the water has a transparent light-blue color. You can see small fish and the rocks at the bottom. After 400 meters the Way of St. James re-joins road nr. 377. You can already see the next church and the Beckenried cable car lines going up to Klewenalp (1'593 meters) in the distance. After another 400 meters you arrive at the St. Henry Church in Beckenried (at km 14.0).

St. Henry Church, Beckenried (St. Heinrich Kirche) 72

- Kirchweg 1, 6375 Beckenried
- St. Henry
- On the last pew (together with a basket of fresh apples)
- The church was first built as a small chapel that was mentioned in official documents in 1323. The second church was built in a Gothic style in 1598. The present third church was built over a period of 17 years. The construction started in 1792, but had to be stopped when French troops invaded Switzerland and the Helvetic Republic was declared in 1798. Construction continued again after 1803, and the church was consecrated in 1807. The latest renovations were undertaken in 1975-76 (interior) and 2002-03 (exterior), which restored its original appearance from 1807.
- The church has a baroque style, with three beautiful marble altars, pulpit, chandeliers, and ceiling frescos. The high-altar contains artistic decorations, statues, and several colors of marble. Two gold-winged angels bless you from high above. Even the clock on the arched wall of the chancel is decorated in a rococo style. Church music sounds from the speakers.

South of the church you find the Cemetery Chapel.

73 **Cemetery Chapel, Beckenried** (Friedhof Kapelle)

Kirchweg 1, 6375 Beckenried

The chapel was built in a similar style as the late-baroque church in 1851.

Initially the chapel was used as an ossuary (*beinhaus*), but nowadays it has a multipurpose use for prayers, funerals, exhibitions, and lectures. Notice the rope to toll the bell in the steeple on the roof. The death of Christ is all-around: in the altar painting, in the Pietà, and in the crucifixion way stations.

From the church you pass by the Beckenried boat pier and bus station, and the route zigzags between the houses of Beckenried and leaves road nr. 377 to go inland up a hill. Before the Klewenalp cable car ground-station the route turns right. About 350 meters after the cable car station you reach a road split. The signposted route continues straight, but to go to the next chapel you need to turn right and briefly leave the signposted route. Follow the *Almendstrasse* down the hill for about 260 meters and you arrive at the Lourdes Cave (at km 14.8).

74 **Lourdes Cave, Beckenried** (Lourdes Grotte)

Allmendstrasse 1, 6375 Beckenried

Mary-Lourdes

The cave was built as a replica of the original Lourdes Cave in France in 1898-99. A local widow built it in fulfilment of a promise. During her life she went on many pilgrimages to Lourdes and brought back the Mary statue from one of her trips. The small stone bell tower was added in 1902. Ownership of the cave-chapel was transferred to the Bishopric of Chur in 1904.

The many small candles in the recesses of the left wall demonstrate it is still a frequently visited place of worship. Church music sounds from speakers inside the cave.

From the cave walk back up the hill to the signposted route and turn right. You pass by a school and a dark wooden building on your left, which is the former shooting range that was built in 1902 (nowadays used as a multipurpose building). The Way of St. James is parallel to Highway A2. The constant sounds of speeding traffic accompany you on this section. A tarmac road takes you through the settlement Oberdorf from where you arrive at the Ridli Chapel, built on a small elevation (at km 16.3).

Mary at the Ridli Chapel, Beckenried (Maria zum Ridli Kapelle) 75

Ridlistrasse 32, 6375 Beckenried

St. Mary

In front of the right side-altar, on a shelf at the wall

The present chapel was built in 1700-01. It is the third successor building of a smaller chapel dating from 1605 and another one from 1625. Because it has been a pilgrimage chapel (*Wallfahrtskapelle*) since 1605, attracting many local pilgrims, it was necessary to enlarge/rebuild the chapel twice. The chapel is a pilgrimage destination for the fishers, skippers, and sailors of Lake Lucerne, and especially for Beckenried that historically was a fishermen's village. The chapel stands at an elevated location, making it visible from the lake from afar.

During the renovation of 1957-58 much of the original interior appearance, which had been changed in the renovation of 1863, was restored.

The chapel is richly decorated with marble, statues, and paintings in a baroque style. Noteworthy are the three altars, but also the decorations at the top of the iron chancel gate (rood screen).

Look at the many small plaques and paintings (votives) on the back wall: they all depict the Virgin Mary; some depict how she guides boats to safety in stormy weather. The votives were donated by parishioners when their prayers were heard or as a preventative prayer for safe returns. The Virgin Mary is all-around, even on the chancel grating.

The route continues parallel to Highway A2. Occasionally look back to admire the distant mountains behind you.

Underneath the highway the route turns right (down the stairs), but both hiking signposts guide in the direction from where you just came. Vandals must have turned the signpost guiding to the lake into the opposite direction.

After a short descent you are reunited with road nr. 377. The signs direct to the left and you walk directly along the lake.

For 1.3 km the route follows a smaller road next to the lake, until you return onto road nr. 377. You follow it for 700 meters through the town Buochs.

The signpost for route nr. 4 is fixed to a lamppost behind a hedge on the left side of the street. There the route turns left, ascending in a narrow residential street. About 200 meters later (at km 19.1) you arrive at the Fourteen Holy Helpers Chapel in Buochs. The little chapel is in front of a school complex.

Fourteen Holy Helpers Chapel, Buochs (Nothelfer Kapelle) 76

- Schulstrasse, 6374 Buochs
- St. Sebastian, Fourteen Holy Helpers
- The chapel was built by the local villagers at the time of the Bubonic Plague in 1683-84. The small chapel is dedicated to St. Sebastian, but is better known under the name Holy Helpers.
- Above the arched wall that separates the nave and chancel is a wide painting (dated 1756) depicting the Fourteen Holy Helpers surrounding the Virgin Mary with baby Jesus.

  A fresco (dated 1943) on the outer wall, directly underneath the overhanging roof, depicts the archangel Gabriel announcing to Mary that she will give birth to Jesus.

From the chapel the route zigzags past the school and several modern houses. You can already see the next church tower between the houses. At the bottom of a stairs the nr. 4 sign leads directly to the church. About 400 meters after the chapel you arrive at the St. Martin Church in Buochs (at km 19.5).

St. Martin Church, Buochs (St. Martin Kirche) 77

- Güterstrasse, 6374 Buochs
- St. Martin, St. Mary
- In front of the right side-altar, in a basket on top of a low wooden fence

The present church was built in 1802-05, after the predecessor church (and the whole village) was burned down by invading French troops in 1798. It is the fourth church on this site. Little is known of the three predecessor churches, because the parish's historical archive was also destroyed in the fire of 1798. Archaeological excavations in 1960-61 discovered that a first church was probably built around 1027. The earliest mention of a church on this site dates from 1157, when it was the mother church of a large part of Canton Nidwalden. This first church probably was small, in a Romanesque style, with the chancel inside the base of its tower. This church may have been similar to the St. Martin Church on the Island of Ufenau (see stage 4, Volume I). The second church was probably an expansion, with an enlargement of the nave and a new chancel in Gothic style, built in the period 1445-91. The third church was probably built on parts of the second church in 1718. By 1789 this church was considered to be in poor condition and too small for the growing parish. Nine years later this church was burned down by plundering French troops (1798). The present baroque church from 1805 was renovated in 1884 (exterior), 1893 (interior), and 1960.

The most interesting part of the church is its Virgin Mary chapel, left of the main entrance. The vaulted ceiling and its walls are blackened from the smoke of the burning candles. The side-chapel was originally built at the same time as the church (1100-37). Center stage in the side-chapel is a glass tomb with a lying statue representing the Virgin Mary, originally brought over from Varallo (northern Italy) in 1680. When French troops destroyed the church in 1798, the side-chapel was also destroyed by fire. Though the church was rebuilt relatively quickly, it took nearly 140 years before the side-chapel was restored in its old appearance from before the French invasion.

The interior of the side-chapel as you see it today dates from renovation work in 1937-38. Another replica of the lying statue representing the Virgin Mary was brought from Varallo in 1937. A local painter made all wall frescos in 1940, which depict the main events and dates in the history of the church and its side-chapel. Have a closer look at them and follow the history clockwise, starting on the left wall. The first fresco depicts the construction of the first church by the Abbey of Muri in 1100-37 (though historically it is uncertain whether the Muri monks built this first church; since their monastery's church was dedicated to St. Martin, this could indeed have been the case).

The colorful stained-glass window on the right depicts French troops setting fire to the Virgin Mary chapel in 1798.

Have a closer look at the grid-iron niche with the late-Gothic masonry above it. It is a wall-tabernacle for storage of the Host. It was used in the church from 1718 (or before) and placed in the Virgin Mary chapel in 1937.

West of the church is a modern funeral chapel (built 2016), without interior decorations.

From the church the route continues to the west through a residential area. The Way of St. James route is close to Highway A2 again and its noise is like a constant hum. You have good views to the right over the Buochs valley and the Bürgenberg mountain range behind it. About 400 meters from the church you arrive at the Sorrowful Mother of God Chapel, better known as the Obgass Chapel (at km 19.9).

Sorrowful Mother of God Chapel, Buochs (Obgass Kapelle) 78

- Ennerbergstrasse 35, 6374 Buochs
- Sorrowful Mother of God, St. Nicholas of Flüe, St. Conrad
- The chapel was built by the local villagers in 1661. It is about the same age as the Fourteen Holy Helpers chapel and its interior and exterior have many similarities. The last renovation was undertaken in 1984.
- The frescos (dated 1663) underneath the overhanging roof depict the Holy Trinity, St. Nicholas of Flüe, and St. Conrad. At the small baroque altar, the Pietà depicts Mary with Jesus taken from the Cross, representing one of the Seven Sorrows Mary experienced. These were seven events that caused intense suffering to Mary and were often depicted as seven swords piercing the heart of Mary. Above the Pietà you see a depiction of the heart of Mary, pierced by a sword, radiating golden rays.

  A pilgrim guestbook and fresh apples lie on a crate left of the entrance.

About 300 meters after the chapel the route passes underneath Highway A2. For a short distance the route stays next to the highway, after which the trail turns left. A tarmac country road goes up the hill and passes by some farms. In the distance you see the Stanserhorn mountain peak at 1'897 meters.

About 1.3 km after the Obgass Chapel you arrive at the **Ennerberg** compound. Two tall information boards explain the buildings and grounds. At this location with a great view over the valley, there used to be a stately chateau built by the Canton's chief governor Achermann in 1680. The chateau was destroyed by French troops in 1798 and never rebuilt in its old style.

To go to the compound's chapel do not enter the compound itself. Instead, keep walking straight for 50 meters to a gravel path that accesses the chapel from the southern side. The low stone wall in front of the chapel has a blue/yellow tile with the Way of St. James sign. At km 21.2 you arrive at the Loreto Chapel of Ennerberg.

Loreto Chapel, Ennerberg (Loreto Kapelle) 79

Ennerberg 1, 6374 Buochs

St. Nepomuk, St. Mary, Holy Family

The chapel was built by the Canton's chief governor Achermann in 1713. It is a so-called yard chapel, built by the governor on his estate at Ennerberg. He built it to commemorate his troops' victory over the Bernese in a battle at Sins (a town in Canton Aargau). The painting above the entrance depicts the beginning of the battle, part of the 2nd Villmerger War. This was a religious civil war between the conservative catholic Ur-Cantons and the progressive protestant Cantons (Bern and Zurich), which was ultimately lost by the catholic Cantons in 1712.

Special about this chapel is that it includes a front and a back chapel, the only double-chapel along the Way of St. James through Switzerland.

The front **St. Nepomuk chapel** lets in a lot of light through the windows. The small front chapel has a grey baroque altar, finished with gold decorations. The altar painting tells the story of St. Nepomuk, including the scene where he is thrown off the bridge.

The back **Loreto chapel** can be accessed through the openings left and right of the front altar. This is the actual Loreto chapel, which is dark and windowless. Only the center statue representing the Virgin Mary with baby Jesus is lit by a lamp. Notice how the Holy Family's house is depicted without a roof; stars shine from the ceiling.

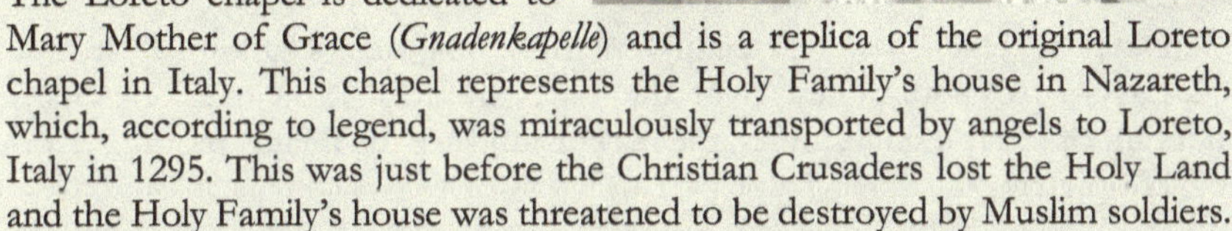

The Loreto chapel is dedicated to Mary Mother of Grace (*Gnadenkapelle*) and is a replica of the original Loreto chapel in Italy. This chapel represents the Holy Family's house in Nazareth, which, according to legend, was miraculously transported by angels to Loreto, Italy in 1295. This was just before the Christian Crusaders lost the Holy Land and the Holy Family's house was threatened to be destroyed by Muslim soldiers.

The Our Lady of Loreto in the Basilica della Santa Casa in Italy is a Black Madonna (like the one in Einsiedeln). In the chapel in Ennerberg the statue representing the Virgin Mary is also darker.

The route continues to climb on a tarmac road through open meadows offering wide views back to Buochs and to the front to the Stanserhorn mountain.

About 1 km after the Loreto chapel you see the next chapel in a field behind a farmhouse. At km 22.3 you arrive at the St. Anne Chapel in Waltersberg.

80 St. Anne Chapel, Waltersberg (St. Anna Kapelle)

- Waltersbergstrasse 10, 6370 Oberdorf
- St. Anne
- The chapel was first built in 1702, but was replaced by the present neo-Gothic chapel in 1889. The chapel is also a farm chapel, belonging to a local farmer's family. Look at its location: behind a farm, in the meadow. It was manually built by the local families. This is the fourth chapel dedicated to St. Anne in stage 6, demonstrating the popularity of this Saint in the region.
- The interior of the chapel is different from the other chapels you have seen today. Instead of whitewashed walls and ceiling, they are completely decorated and colored. It looks very similar to the St. Apollonia church in Alpthal (see church nr. 43), which you visited in stage 5. Stained-glass windows reflect additional color with the incoming sunlight. Small paintings depict the crucifixion way and the altar contains a painting depicting St. Anne with her teenage daughter Mary. The text at the altar says 'pray for us'.

Soon after the chapel you reach a high point of 564 meters (at km 23), from where you have a panoramic view over the valley in front. You overlook Stans, the endpoint of today's stage, and in the background see the Pilatus mountain, peaking at 2'128 meters.

From this viewpoint it is only 3 km until the stage-end at the St. Peter and Paul Church in Stans (you can see its tower in the distance). The first kilometer descends

steeply, after which the route becomes flat. The descent starts at the end of the road, with two narrow concrete tracks (the width of tractor wheels) zigzagging through meadows. You pass by a pig farm and at the foot of the hill need to cross two streams. The first concrete footbridge covers a small irrigation canal, while the second concrete bridge covers the Engelberg Aa River. The route crosses road nr. 374 and continues on a gravel footpath to a small roadside chapel (at km 23.8).

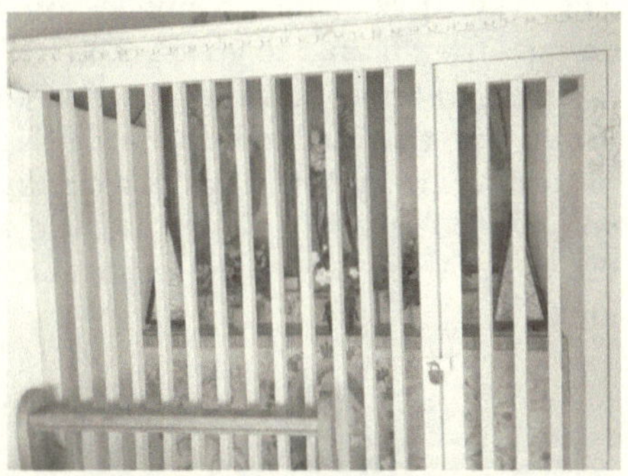

Mühlimatt Chapel, Oberdorf (Mühlimatt Kapelle) 81

- Mühlematt, 6370 Oberdorf
- St. Mary
- The chapel was built in 1743 and was last renovated in 2007. It is another farm chapel, built by the farmer's family living opposite of the chapel (Mühlematt).
- It is one of the smallest chapels along the route, with three small pews and a small statue representing the Virgin Mary at its altar, flanked by two paintings.

The route turns left towards Stans, and after crossing a road and single railway track you arrive at the St. Henry Chapel in Oberdorf (at km 24.7).

82 **St. Henry Chapel, Oberdorf** (St. Heinrich Kapelle)

- Sankt-Heinrich-Strasse 6, 6370 Oberdorf
- St. Mary, St. Henry, St. Beatus
- Left of the entrance
- The chapel was first mentioned in 1541. This first chapel was replaced by a second chapel, which was destroyed by Napoleon's troops in 1798. The present third chapel was built in 1801 and was completely renovated in 2014-15.
- The center piece of the baroque altar is a painting depicting the Virgin Mary with baby Jesus, flanked by a statue representing St. Beatus (slaying a dragon) on the right, and St. Henry on the left.

The Way of St. James continues on the *Sankt-Heinrich-Strasse*, while the path changes from tarmac to gravel. You walk towards and alongside the outer walls of a large red-brown building that is the Collegium St. Fidelis. It is a public gymnasium that used to be part of a Capuchin monastery. The narrow gravel path (watch out for cyclists) ends in a street that leads to the gymnasium. On the right you overlook the school's sports fields. The road continues towards Stans along the walls. At the end of the wall you arrive at the former Capuchin Monastery at km 25.4.

10 **Former Capuchin Monastery and Collegium, Stans** (Kapuziner Kloster)

- Mürgstrasse 18, 6370 Stans
- Capuchin Order
- St. Fidelis
- The monastery was established in 1582 by the Cantonal Governor Melchior Lussi, who donated the land and financed the construction of the buildings (1583-84). He brought the Capuchin Order from northern Italy to Canton Nidwalden to strengthen Catholicism at the time the protestant Cantons (Bern and Zurich) were trying to enforce the Reformation onto the catholic Cantons. During the Reformation in the 1520s-30s Canton Nidwalden had rejected a conversion to Protestantism and in the subsequent decades had to stave off attacks by the protestant Cantons. Very similar to what happened in Rapperswil in 1602, the local ruler established a monastery as a catholic counterforce. Because the Capuchins were a beggar-order, they lived off donations. They were

hardly able to maintain their monastery and a 100 years later their buildings were neglected and dilapidated. The grandson (Ludwig Lussi) of the founder of the monastery, who had also become Cantonal Governor, had the old buildings demolished and financed the construction of a new monastery and church in 1683-84.

During the time of the Helvetic Republic the monastery was closed (1798-1803).

Lack of novices together with an over-ageing of the remaining 12 friars led to the closure of the monastery in 2004. Their buildings have been vacant since. A project called 'the culinary heritage of the Alps' (*'Das kulinarische Erbe der Alpen'*) plans to turn the site into a gastronomy focused regional competence center from autumn 2019.

From 1777 the Capuchins led a Latin boys' school (for the whole of Canton Nidwalden). In 1877 they were asked to take on additional responsibility to lead the collegium, which they led for 111 years. This started as a catholic boys' boarding school in their monastery, until a separate building was constructed in 1895. The dormitory still continued until 1988, when the Canton took over the collegium. At the inauguration the collegium received the name St. Fidelis. From 1972 the school also allowed girls. Until that time, girls attended the girls' school led by the Capuchin Convent (see below).

The ownership of the collegium changed to the Canton in 1988, after which it became a public Cantonal gymnasium.

Capuchin Monastery Church, Stans (Kapuziner Kirche) 83

Mürgstrasse 18, 6370 Stans

St. Mary, St. Fidelis, St. Anthony of Padua, St. Borromeo, St. Nicholas of Flüe, Holy Family

The church shares the same history with the monastery: it was first built in 1583, but demolished and rebuilt in 1683-84. In 1798 Napoleon's troops plundered the monastery and church. The church was used as the student church of the monastery's school and later as the collegium's house church. The church was last renovated in 1980.

Since the Capuchin friars left the monastery in 2004, a society called '*Verein Kapuziner Kirche Stans*' maintains the church. The Capuchin friars of Luzern uphold the tradition with a service once a month.

Eye-catching in the interior of the church is the high extent of woodwork at the ceiling, the side walls, the three altars, the chancel screen, and the pews.

Consistent with the austerity of the Capuchin Order, there are neither stained-glass windows nor decorations on the walls; only three altars, which do have gold decorations and paintings.

The painting at the high-altar depicts the ascension of Mary, with God painted in the medallion above it. The right side-altar depicts St. Anthony of Padua in Capuchin dress; the left side-altar depicts the Holy Family. The top right medallion depicts St. Borromeo, the left top medallion St. Nicholas of Flüe.

The church has a Friar Chancel behind the chancel (not visible). This is another rectangular inside-chancel, which is accessible by the doors left and right of the high-altar. It was used by the friars for their own services (without parishioners). This is similar to the Sister Chancel you saw at the former Capuchin Convent in Wattwil (see stage R2, Volume I). Nowadays the friar chancel is empty.

Right of the chancel is the open-spaced St. Fidelis side-chapel (the chancel and this side-chapel cannot be accessed; a tall wooden rood screen blocks access).

Left of the entrance you find the Cross side-chapel, also gated and not accessible. Below its altar lies a statue representing Jesus in his burial shroud. Above the altar hangs a large wooden crucifix.

Continuing on the same road, you walk past Stans' cemetery and the old armory (*Altes Zeughaus*) built in 1666. At the end of the *Mürgstrasse* you see the St. Peter and Paul church right in front of you (100 meters). Most pilgrims continue walking straight to this church. However, it is worthwhile to turn left and make a 100-meter detour (up the hill) to the Capuchin Convent of St. Clare (at km 25.7).

Capuchin Convent St. Clare (Kapuzinerinnen Kloster St. Klara) 11

Sankt Klararain 2, 6370 Stans

Capuchin Order of Poor Clares

St. Clare

The convent was established when two laywomen (siblings) from Stans were made nuns in an official ceremony with the approval of the local government in 1615. Before them two other laywomen (from Einsiedeln and Schwyz) had already been trying to build a sister community since 1592, but encountered significant resistance for more than 20 years. Women were regarded as second-class citizens and the source of all temptation, so the male government and the friars of the Capuchin monastery were very reluctant to establish a female convent (there was none in Canton Nidwalden yet).

Notwithstanding the local resistance to establish a convent, the first two laywomen started a girls' school upon their arrival in Stans in 1592. This school did receive support from the population and government. After the formal establishment of the convent several more women joined. As the first two nuns, these novices came from wealthy families. Together they had sufficient starting capital (local government refused to support their financing). With additional donations from other monasteries (collected during their beggar-travels) they bought the building that housed their school and built their own monastery with church in 1620-25.

The monastery was built on a plot of land that used to house the gallows, judicial court, and executioner. This was a gruesome place where cruel executions were carried out, and an indication of Stans' skepticism regarding the convent. The convent had to be self-sufficient, which resulted in enduring poverty and hardship. Male supervisors continuously tried to enforce restrictions, seclusion, and isolation.

Their teaching at the school in their convent was often the only allowed contact with society. Because of growing school classes, they expanded their buildings in 1730.

In 1798 Napoleon's troops plundered the convent and church. During the time of the Helvetic Republic (1798-1803) the convent was closed, but the nuns refused to leave. The school building housed an orphanage for children, who had lost their parents during the French invasion. Heinrich Pestalozzi led this orphanage for a period of six months. He became a famous pedagogue and reformer of the Swiss educational system, and established several schools throughout Switzerland (also in Burgdorf; see stage L3). French soldiers reoccupied the school building and turned it into their barracks. The children were relocated to orphanages in Luzern and Bern.

The sisters led the girls' boarding school but closed it in 1988, at the same time as their male counterparts of the Capuchin monastery did. From 1988 the Canton took over the Capuchin collegium, which had already allowed girls since 1972.

Nowadays around 11 sisters live in the convent, still active in the catholic women's community of Stans. They derive most of their income from the rent of their former school building and lease of their farmlands. Despite their high age, they still work in their vegetable garden.

Over the centuries they specialized in embroidering and decorating textiles used in catholic worship, called paraments. They decorated paraments as well as relics of catacomb saints (bones, skulls, skeletons), with gold, silver, and silk embroideries, and precious stones and pearls. For example, the decorated relics in their convent's church were prepared in their workshop. Their work even won an international prize at an exhibition of modern church art in Vienna in 1954. Old age of the nuns forced them to close their workshop in 1973.

84 Capuchin Convent Church, Stans (Kapuzinerinnen Kloster Kirche)

Sankt Klararain 2, 6370 Stans

St. Prosper, St. Anthony of Padua, St. Borromeo, St. Nicholas of Flüe, St. Clare

At the convent's entrance (*Klosterpforte*). Ring the bell (pull down the iron bar) and a nun will open the door.

The church has the same construction history as the convent. It was originally built as part of the convent in 1621-25.

Three altars dominate the interior of the church. Similar to the monastery's church, the right side-altar depicts St. Anthony of Padua in Capuchin dress, below a medallion depicting St. Borromeo.

The treasure of the church is standing in a vitrine on the left side-altar, below the medallion depicting St. Nicholas of Flüe: the relics of St. Prosper, a catacomb saint. Because the convent could not finance the purchase of such relics, a family member of one of the nuns visited Rome and came back with the skeleton in

1675. The skeleton is fully dressed, with a head garment, breastplate, and cape with precious stones sewn in. Rather unusual, the skeleton is standing in its full length (all other catacomb saints along the Swiss Way of St. James are exhibited in a lying position). The skeleton holds a sword and the palm of martyrdom.

The nuns made the embroideries and other decorations in 1740 (restored in 1980). The standing skeleton is, however, not permanently on display. On most days it is hidden behind a screen, with a painting of St. Prosper on clouds above a 17th century map of Stans (1679). In case you want to see the decorated skeleton, you may have to ask the nuns to remove the screen.

The importance of the relics to the convent lies in the miraculous healing powers attributed to St. Prosper. On many occasions prayers to St. Prosper caused miraculous recovery from illnesses. During the large town fire of 1713, prayers to St. Prosper avoided the destruction of the convent, whereas many other buildings burned down.

From the convent descend the hill to return to the signposted route. Turn left and you pass by the war-commemorative **Winkelried Statue** (*Winkelrieddenkmal*). The statue from 1865 represents a violent scene: the Swiss Confederate Winkelried clubbing down soldiers from Habsburg-Austria during the battle of Sempach (1386). Though the Winkelried person never existed, his fictional heroics were important to the self-identification of Canton Nidwalden during the 16th century.

A few meters after the statue you arrive at the grounds of the St. Peter and Paul Church (at km 26.0). You first pass by the Mount of Olives Chapel at the southern side of the church.

85 Mount of Olives Chapel, Stans (Ölberg Kapelle)

Nägeligasse, 6370 Stans

The chapel was built in the 15th century.

Its door is closed, but you can look into the interior from the northern window with the iron meshed bars. Inside you see a relief with a wall fresco depicting the Mount of Olives scene, a cemetery hill outside of Jerusalem where Jesus spent the night before He was betrayed and arrested. The relief depicts a praying Jesus, his sleeping disciples, and approaching Roman soldiers.

A few meters further, west of the church, is the Charnel Chapel that is split in two levels: the lower chapel where the bones and corpses were stored and the upper chapel where the services were held (similar to the two-story ossuary in Schwyz).

86 Charnel Chapel, Stans (Beinhaus Kapelle)

Nägeligasse, 6370 Stans

The Lower Chapel (*Unteres Beinhaus*) has a vaulted ceiling and was used for the storage of bones and corpses of the deceased. It was built in 1482.

The Upper Chapel (*Oberes Beinhaus*) was built in 1560, on top of the already existing Lower Chapel and was used for funeral services.

Have a closer look at the fresco on the outer wall. It depicts a good-death scene. Notice how the last renovation resulted in the lowering of the roof, thereby cutting off the top part of the fresco.

The Upper Chapel contains three altars, with the painting (1761) at the high-altar being most unusual, depicting Jesus chained as a prisoner to a column. This work is a replica of a famous painting in the pilgrimage church of Wies, Bavaria, southern Germany. Most impressive is the wall fresco where Jesus is taken from the Cross and laid in his tomb.

From the entrance under the small protruding red roof, right of the chapel's upper stairs, you can access the Lower Chapel. Next to the entrance a relief depicts purgatory (the fires of hell where the souls of sinners are burning forever). Black marble and gold colored statues and decorations are placed at the northern side of the lower chapel. The southern side is blocked by wooden bars from floor to ceiling. Peek through these bars. You will see a life-size statue representing Christ carrying his Cross, in front of a wall filled with skulls.

From the Charnel chapel walk along the western side of the St. Peter and Paul Church to its main entrance.

St. Peter and Paul Church, Stans (St. Peter und Paul Kirche) 87

- Dorfplatz, 6370 Stans
- St. Peter and Paul, St. Nicholas of Flüe, St. Remy
- Left of the main entrance, in the corner on a desk next to the baptismal font
- The church in its present appearance was built in 1641-47 and is the fifth church on this site. Because this fifth church was larger than the fourth church, its orientation was changed from east to south (which is rather unusual). Settlers from southern Germany (Alemannia) built a first stone church around 750, making it one of the oldest churches in Canton Nidwalden. This made the church the parish church for the whole region, until the St. Martin church in Buochs was built around 1027.

  The Romanesque bell tower dates from around 1200 and is the oldest part of the church. The architectural style of the tower clearly differs from the style of the nave and chancel. You can recognize its typical Romanesque features: narrow windows and Lombard arches around them. Notice the Nidwalden double-key coat-of-arms at the dragon's feet below the clock and how the number of windows increases from two to four. This is the most beautiful maintained Romanesque bell tower along the Swiss Way of St. James. The oldest clock dates from 1533 and is hanging in the tiny steeple above the chancel (not in the bell tower).

The church's three-nave interior has an early-baroque style and is abundantly decorated with black limestone (that looks like marble), statues, paintings, stucco, and so forth. The church has many special features. It has a life-size statue representing St. Nicholas of Flüe, whose birth place and hermitage cell you will visit in stage 7. Notice the artful ironwork of the hinges on the inside of the entrance door. The church has two organs: one above the entrance and one in the chancel. The organ in the chancel dates from 1646 and is the second-oldest still functioning organ in Switzerland. The gold-plated bronze chandelier dates from around 1420; it is of Burgundy origins and was probably brought back as spoils of war. Left of the main entrance is a black limestone baptismal font with a lusciously decorated gold-colored lid (a replica; the original lid was stolen).

At the front-left of the chancel you see a decorated skeleton lying in a vitrine. It is a catacomb saint from Rome (1661) venerated as St. Remy. His dress and decorations were made by the sisters of the Capuchin convent.

When you exit the front door with the artful metal hinges and go down the stairs to the right, you arrive at the Our Lady Chapel. The door behind a bicycle parking (easy to overlook), underneath an elevated walkway, leads to the underground chapel called 'Mary under the Stove' (*Maria unter dem Herd*). Its name is derived from the location being underneath the church.

Mary under the Stove Chapel, Stans (Maria unter dem Herd Kapelle) 88

Dorfplatz, 6370 Stans

Our Lady

The chapel was first mentioned in 1493. Its present appearance dates from 1647, when it was rebuilt together with the church.

The chapel was a place of pilgrimage due to its statue that is a (white-colored) replica of the Black Madonna of Einsiedeln. This statue also wears an embroidered dress with matching cape (made by the Capuchin sisters) that is regularly changed with the festive periods.

The rectangular chapel has a beautiful baroque styled ceiling and chancel.

Stans (population around 8'200) never had a fortified wall protecting it, because the territory was strategically unimportant. The area consisted of moors, swamps, and forests, between the mountain ranges south of Lake Lucerne. Stans was neither at a lake, river, nor trade route. Until the 20th century Nidwalden mostly focused on (valley and alpine) agriculture and cattle farming; the industrial revolution went by without much impact. As a way out of poverty and farming during the middle ages, many men became mercenary soldiers, serving in the armies of France and Spain. For details on the history of late medieval Swiss Mercenaries, see page 27.

In 1713 most of Stans' town was destroyed by a fire, which is why you will not see original buildings from before the 18th century. The buildings around the town square have an early 18th century baroque style. When you walk about 100 meters north of the town square, along the *Alter Postplatz* street, you arrive at the Rose Castle.

The **Rose Castle** (*Rosenburg*), also called *Höfli* (Small Court), derived its name from the small rose garden in its small courtyard. The Rosenburg has three architectural styles: a Romanesque residential tower with 12th century features; Renaissance structures from the 16th century; and baroque features from the end of the 17th century. Together with the Romanesque church tower, the 12th century residential tower is the oldest building in Stans.

The tower has the same features and origins as the castle tower in Pfäffikon: it had meter-thick square walls and an elevated entrance; it was built as an administrative center for a monastery (the Abbey of Murbach, Alsace, France, represented by its subsidiary Abbey in Luzern; see stage L1); and the ground floor was a storage for agricultural produce, collected as taxes from their lands around Stans. After the abbey sold its lands to the House of Habsburg in 1291, the fortified tower was abandoned and citizens used its stones for the construction of other buildings. The tower fell into ruins.

It was not until the beginning of the 16th century that the old tower was reconstructed, with an attached new residential building. Another owner expanded the residential building and built the loggias (arched walkways) in the second half of the 16th century.

Between 1619 and 1692 the castle belonged to the Lussi family (who were Cantonal Governors and brought the Capuchin friars to Stans). From 1692 a new owner (also Governor) expanded the building, gave it a baroque style, and built a small niche-chapel (*Hauskapelle*) that is, however, not publicly accessible.

More changes were made to the building during the 19th century, when it was transformed into a residential and office building. The 12th century tower is now fully integrated in the building and hardly recognizable.

A foundation has owned the building since 1969. In 1977-82 they had it restored to its appearance of around 1750. Nowadays the Rosenburg houses a restaurant, a regional literature organization, and a wedding room. The restaurant occupies the ground floor, first floor, and the old tower with its meter-thick walls. It is closed on Mondays and Tuesdays.

From the ending point

The St. Peter and Paul Church (or the Rose Castle) is the ending point of stage 6, directly on the signposted route nr. 4. Note that the Tourist Office of Stans also provides a pilgrim stamp that can be obtained at the train station, hotel Engel, and several other locations. This stamp displays the Winkelried monument.

In case you are a day-hiker, you need to walk a mere 150 meters to the Stans train station (north of the town's square).

In case you are a thru-hiker and spend the night in Stans, be aware that there is no pilgrim inn, but a few low-priced pilgrim accommodations are available at private residences. Check out www.jakobsweg.ch or www.viajacobi4.ch for the accommodation possibilities. The Tourist Information Office (Bahnhofplatz 2; tel. 041 610 88 33; info@tourismusstans; www.tourismusstans.ch) at the Stans train station can also assist with finding the right accommodation.

Check out *https://www.tourismusstans.ch/geniessen/uebernachtung/pilgerzimmer* for the online booking of pilgrim accommodations.

The next Stage

Stage 7 will guide you out of the Lake Lucerne basin, over the western foothills of both the Stanserhorn and Gräfimattstand mountains, through the Melchaa gorge, and down to the Lake Sarnen basin. Stage 7 is one of the spiritual highlights of the Swiss Way of St. James, because of the visit to the place of Saint Nicholas of Flüe, Switzerland's national patron Saint. Read the next chapter to find out what that entails.

Stage 7: Stans to Sachseln 22 km

The Way to Saint Nicholas

Route stats

	Distance in km	*Time in hrs:min*
Signposted route nr. 4	20.3	4:40
Churches/chapels	1.3	2:30
Points of interest	0.3	0:30
Rest/lunch		0:50
Stage 7	21.9	8:30

In case you hike this stage as a daytrip, you need to add 150 meters in Stans and 500 meters in Sachseln (from and to the train stations).

Ascent/descent/total	+798 / -768 / 1'566 altitude meters
Lowest/highest altitude	454 / 832 meters
Pathway/condition	easy / moderate
Churches/chapels	Kniri, St. Jakob, Wisserlen (2), Halten, St. Niklausen (2), Mösli, Flüeli-Ranft (4), Sachseln (2)
Monasteries	Dominican Convent St. Niklausen, Chemin Neuf Community St. Niklausen
Points of interest	Brother Klaus House, Brother Klaus Museum

Route summary

Stage 7 continues in catholic **Canton Nidwalden** and after 7.6 km enters catholic **Canton Obwalden**.

Stage 7 guides you out of the Lake Lucerne basin, over the western foothills of both the Stanserhorn and Gräfimattstand mountains, through the Melchaa gorge, and down to the Lake Sarnen basin.

Similar to the two previous stages, the route is marked by the high number of churches and chapels (14) along the way. The relatively short distance leaves enough time to immerse in the religious significance of the churches and chapels, particularly those after km 16 in St. Niklausen, Flüeli-Ranft, and Sachseln. The four chapels in Flüeli-Ranft and the church in Sachseln relate to the Swiss Saint Nicholas of Flüe and are one of the spiritual highlights of the Swiss Way of St. James.

Most of the route between Stans and Sachseln follows the so-called **Brother Klaus Way** (*Bruderklausenweg*). Its name is derived from a foot march that priest Heimo am Grund made from Stans to Flüeli-Ranft in 1481, to make an urgent consultation with the counselor Nicholas of Flüe (more commonly called Brother Klaus). His consultation ended a spiraling conflict between the Swiss Confederate Cantons, which could have resulted in a civil war and a split of the Confederation (so-called Treaty of Stans or *Stanser Verkommnis* of 1481). The Brother Klaus Way was established in 1981 and renewed in 2017. Along the route are six stations that invite (in German) to reflect on the life and impact of Brother Klaus, with themes of values, visions, silence, calling, advice, and prayer.

The first 3 km after leaving Stans ascend to 634 meters through open fields offering wide views of the surrounding mountains. The route follows a southwestern direction on easy pathways, around the base of the Stanserhorn mountain (peaking at 1'897 meters). Through a forest the route gradually descends to a highland valley, where it reaches the town of St. Jakob after 6 km. Leaving St. Jakob, the trail goes through some patches of forest (entering Canton Obwalden at km 7.6), after which meadows make up the landscape for most of the ascent. These provide panoramic views of the Pilatus and the Stanserhorn mountains (looking backwards) and of the lower valley with the town Sarnen and Lake Sarnen (on the right). The southward path steadily ascends over the foothills of the Gräfimattstand mountain (peaking at 2'048 meters) to the highest point of the day at 832 meters at the chapel of St. Niklausen (km 16). From this high point the trail descends steeply into the Ranft gorge. The Brother Klaus chapels in the gorge and the historical buildings in Flüeli are the highlight of stage 7. Visit the Saint's cell where he retreated for 20 years, his birth house, and the house where he lived with his family, to gain insight in the rural living conditions of the 15th century. From Flüeli the last 3 km descend through agricultural fields to the level of Lake Sarnen, ending in Sachseln at the church that contains the tomb and several relics of St. Nicholas of Flüe.

Getting to the starting point

Today's starting point in Stans is at the St. Peter and Paul Church, directly on the signposted route nr. 4. In case you hike stage 7 as a daytrip, you need to walk 150 meters from the train station to the church.

Route Map and Profile

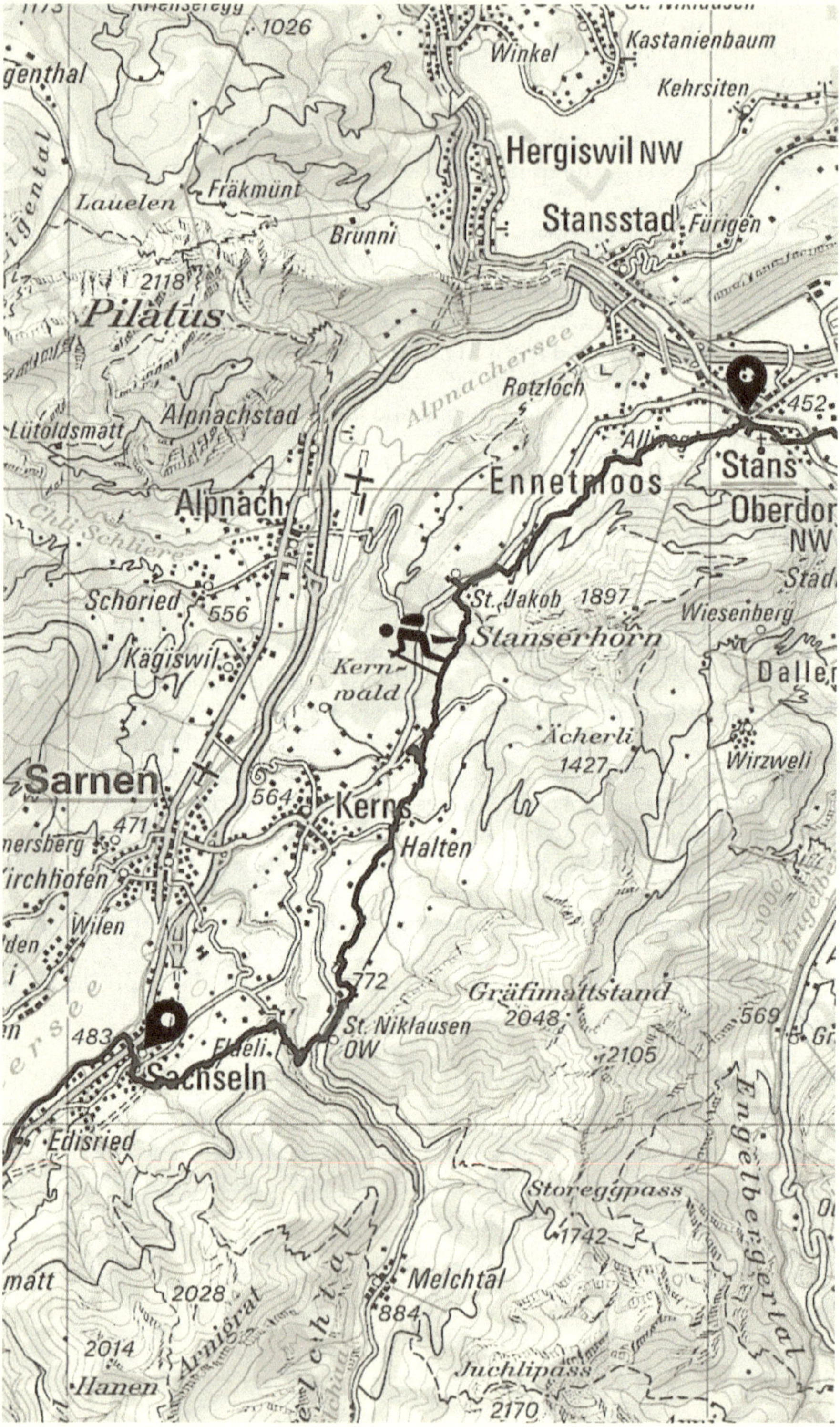

Winkel
Kastanienbaum
Kehrsiten
Hergiswil NW
Stansstad
Fürigen
Fräkmünt
Lauelen
Brunni
2118
Pilatus
Alpnachersee
Rotzloch
Alpnachstad
Lütoldsmatt
452
Stans
Ennetmoos
Alpnach
Oberdorf NW
Schoried
556
St. Jakob
1897
Wiesenberg
Stanserhorn
Kägiswil
Kernwald
Dallen
Ächerli
1427
Wirzweli
Sarnen
564
Kerns
471
Halten
Wilen
772
Gräfimattstand
2048
569
483
St. Niklausen OW
2105
Sachseln
Edisried
Engelbergertal
Storeggpass
1742
Melchtal
2028
884
2014
Arnigrat
Juchlipass
Hanen
2170

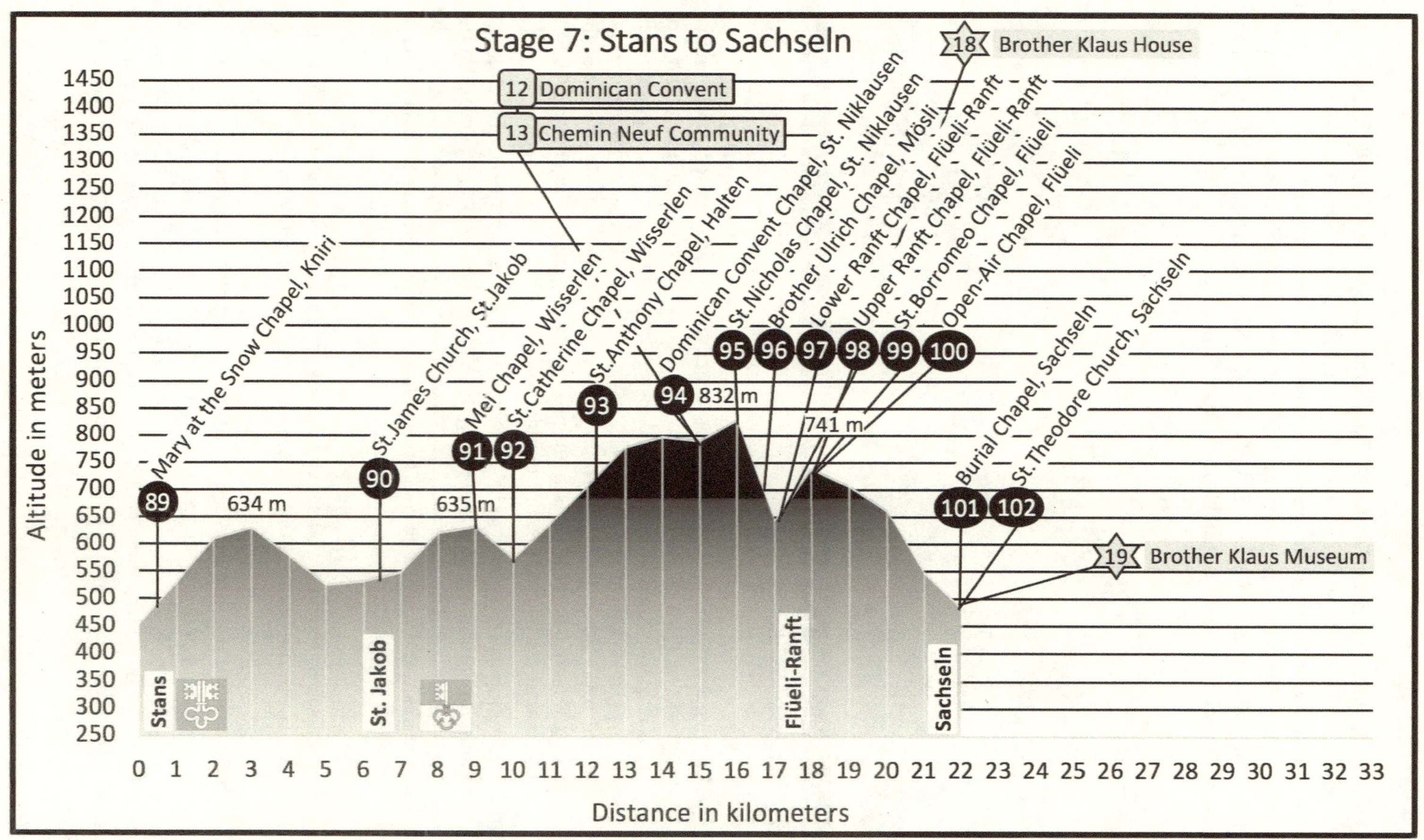
Stage 7: Stans to Sachseln
18 Brother Klaus House
12 Dominican Convent
13 Chemin Neuf Community
Altitude in meters
1450 1400 1350 1300 1250 1200 1150 1100 1050 1000 950 900 850 800 750 700 650 600 550 500 450 400 350 300 250
89 Mary at the Snow Chapel, Kniri
90 St.James Church, St.Jakob
91 Mei Chapel, Wisserlen
92 St.Catherine Chapel, Wisserlen
93 St.Anthony Chapel, Halten
94 Dominican Convent Chapel, St. Niklausen
95 St.Nicholas Chapel, St. Niklausen
96 Brother Ulrich Chapel, Mösli
97 Lower Ranft Chapel, Flüeli-Ranft
98 Upper Ranft Chapel, Flüeli-Ranft
99 St.Borromeo Chapel, Flüeli
100 Open-Air Chapel, Flüeli
101 Burial Chapel, Sachseln
102 St.Theodore Church, Sachseln
19 Brother Klaus Museum
634 m
635 m
832 m
741 m
Stans
St. Jakob
Flüeli-Ranft
Sachseln
0 1 2 3 4 5 6 7 8 9 10 11 12 13 14 15 16 17 18 19 20 21 22 23 24 25 26 27 28 29 30 31 32 33
Distance in kilometers

Hiking the Route

At the Stans village square (*dorfplatz*) the yellow hiking signs already indicate it is 4hr:45min to Flüeli-Ranft. The route is also called the Brother Klaus Way (*Bruder-Klausen-Weg*). The Way of St. James starts with a steep ascent on a tarmac road towards the southwest. The road is called the Kniri alley (*Knirigasse*) and after 400 meters you already arrive at the first chapel, the Mary at the Snow Chapel, which is more popularly known as the Kniri Chapel (km 0.5).

89 Mary at the Snow Chapel, Kniri (Maria zum Schnee Kapelle)

- Knirigasse, 6370 Stans
- St. Mary
- The chapel was built in 1689, but consecrated in 1717. According to legend, the chapel was built on the spot where an avalanche came to a halt, preventing that houses in Stans would be destroyed. As a sign of gratitude, the local people built this chapel and dedicated it to the Virgin Mary. The avalanche had pushed snow, ice, and rocks down the Stanserhorn mountain. A large boulder was left at the spot of the chapel, which was built into the outer wall of the chancel. Have a look around the back to see this boulder.
- The interior was renovated in 1771, from when the late-baroque marble altar, the beautifully dressed statue representing the Virgin Mary, and the painting on the chancel gate date. The eight small votive paintings (19th century) on the side walls of the chancel demonstrate that the locals actively prayed and thanked Mary at this small chapel.

When you look to the west you see the Pilatus mountain (peaking at 2'128 meters) and to the south the Stanserhorn mountain (peaking at 1'897 meters).

The **Stanserhorn** has a revolving restaurant, a main tourist attraction. About 200 meters after the Kniri chapel you cross over the tracks of a historical cable car (originating from 1893). A cable in between the tracks pulls a small train wagon from Stans to the mountain's middle station. From the middle station a unique double-decked areal cable car, with an open upper deck, transports tourists to the peak.

The following 2.6 km the route continues to ascend in a westward direction. After 800 meters on the road the path turns into a grass/gravel trail through meadows. After 1.1 km through meadows you get to a farm road where you reach the altitude of 634 meters in the settlement Obwil. Along the way you have panoramic views of the aforementioned mountains, of Lake Lucerne in the far distance (north), and of the rolling foothills with green meadows, farmlands, and scattered farmhouses.

Along the **Brother Klaus Way** (*Bruder-Klausen-Weg*) from Stans to Flüeli-Ranft you pass by six locations that have information tables (in German) describing the history of Brother Klaus (Saint Nicholas of Flüe). These tables consist of three parts. The first part relates to his life (*Zeittafel*), from his birth in the year 1417 until his death in 1487, and his canonization in 1947. The second part is a message to the pilgrims and hikers, dedicated to a specific theme of the life of Brother Klaus. The third part is several life-related and spiritual thoughts (*Gedanken*), together with an assignment (*Aufgabe*) to personalize the spirit of Brother Klaus for the individual pilgrim. These questions and assignments raise the spiritual side of the Swiss Way of St. James (in case you can read German). With only 22 km, stage 7 is relatively short: this gives enough time to contemplate the thoughts and carry out the assignments.

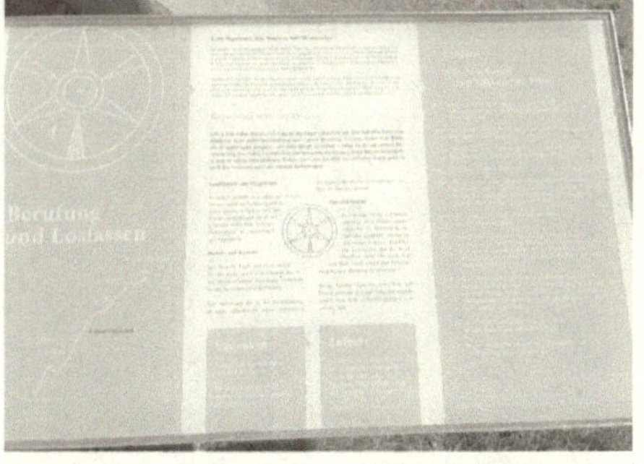

From the high point of 634 meters the path descends over 3 km to the town St. Jakob in a western valley of the Stanserhorn mountain. The descent starts with a 1.8 km trail through, and on the edge of, the Rohrnerberg forest. The beginning of the trail is narrow, after which it widens to a gravel country road as it approaches St. Jakob. You pass by a compound with free roaming deer and a BBQ/shelter place, before arriving in the valley.

On a tarmac road you pass by the Ennetmoos fire brigade (*Feuerwehr*) to arrive at main road nr. 377 (the *Dorfplatz* in Stans was also at road nr. 377). The route turns left and follows the road for 400 meters. On your right a decorative little church and two houses made from stacked fireplace-wood demonstrate the creativity of a local farmer. The route takes a left street into the town St. Jakob, parallel to road nr. 377.

At a crossing in the middle of the village you see a church about 200 meters to the west (right), across road nr. 377. At this location you need to briefly leave the signposted route to arrive at the St. James Church in St. Jakob at km 6.4.

St. James Church, St. Jakob (St. Jakobs Kirche) 90

- Chilenweg, 6372 Ennetmoos
- St. James the Greater, St. Gall, St. Joachim, St. Anne, St. Mary
- On the counter beneath the staircase (left)
- The church was first mentioned as a chapel, dedicated to St. James the Greater, in 1313. It is said to be one of the oldest churches of Canton Nidwalden, though this cannot be validated as archives were burned in a fire in 1707. In 1925 archaeological excavations revealed that the first chapel must have already existed since the early 13th century. Since these early beginnings (until 1972) the chapel was a subsidiary of the mother church St. Peter and Paul in Stans. The chapel became an important station along the Swiss Way of St. James from the 16th century. It was rebuilt and expanded in 1600 to accommodate the increasing number of pilgrims. The chapel was destroyed in a battle between Napoleon's army and troops of Nidwalden in 1798, and reconstructed in 1803-07. The chapel was further expanded several times, until its designation was elevated to church, when the parish separated from Stans in 1972. The building as you see it today (including the tower and the unusual sideway-nave at the entrance) dates from the construction activities in 1925-27.
- The three late-baroque altars and their paintings date from 1807; the remainder of the interior is from 1927 or later. The statues aside the high-altar represent the patron Saints James and Gall (with bear). The painting of the left side-altar depicts St. Joachim and Anne with a young Mary. The painting of the right side-altar depicts the Presentation of Mary. This is based on the story that, in making good on a vow, Joachim and Anne brought three-year-old Mary to the temple, where she would remain until she was 12, as a period of preparation to become the mother of Christ. Left of the main entrance, between two arched windows, is a statue representing St. James. Beneath the staircase a counter contains brochures, St. James candles, apples, a guestbook, scallops, and a pilgrim stamp.

You can get fresh drinking water at the outside fountain. After walking back to the signposted route nr. 4, the route leaves the village and turns left into a forest. The path ascends on a broad gravel road and after 500 meters crosses grasslands. At the beginning of a patch of forest you enter **Canton Obwalden**. For another kilometer the tarmac farm road crosses through meadows and patches of forest.

At km 9.0 you arrive at the Mei Chapel, standing in the shade of some large trees at a road intersection.

91 Mei Chapel, Wisserlen (Maichäppeli)

- Maistrasse, 6064 Kerns
- Holy Family
- The chapel was first mentioned in 1676, because a boy stole three rosaries from the chapel, which his father had to pay for. The date painted above the door is 1699. The chapel was built after a cattle disease, to fulfill a promise and to stave off a repetition of the disease. After an earthquake in 1964 part of the chapel had to be rebuilt. The last renovations were undertaken in 2011.

  The name Mei was derived from its location; it was located on lands that were common property (*Gemei* or *Gemeingut* in German).
- The small chapel has a simple interior. Statues represent the Holy Family; Joseph is displayed with baby Jesus.

  The left statue representing Mary is a Lourdes figure in the typical white cloth. The statue originates from a small plaster Lourdes Grotto that existed in the chapel between 1930 and 1964. After it was damaged in the earthquake of 1964, the grotto was not rebuilt.

  The cord on the right wall tolls the bell in the small steeple on the roof.

In the distance you can see the bell tower of the church in Kerns (which is not along the route). At the intersection of the chapel the route nr. 4 turns right and soon afterwards turns into a small road to the left, and trails up a hill outside the village Wisserlen.

On the hill east of the village the small tarmac footpath forks: route nr. 4 goes left, while a brown sign directs straight to the St. Catherine Chapel. At this location briefly leave the signposted route and follow the brown sign. The tarmac path goes steeply down the hill between several houses. After 400 meters turn left and you arrive at the St. Catherine Chapel of Wisserlen (km 10.2).

St. Catherine Chapel, Wisserlen (St. Katharina Kapelle) 92

- Aecherlistrasse 38, 6064 Kerns
- St. Catherine, St. Wendolyn, Brother Klaus
- On a lectern in front of the chancel: on top lies a guestbook, below the stamp
- The chapel was built on the site of an older gallows chapel (*Galgenchäppäli*) in 1641-42. Until the 14th century the executions of Canton Unterwalden were performed at the gallows in Wisserlen, which stood a little south of the present chapel. As already described for the gallows of Einsiedeln (see point of interest nr. 11, Volume I), gallows have a macabre history demonstrating the cruelty of medieval forms of punishment. As in Einsiedeln, the gallows chapel stood opposite the place of execution. It is logical that this chapel was dedicated to St. Catherine, being the patroness Saint of the condemned. The last major renovation was undertaken in 1952.
- Notice the painting depicting Brother Klaus (1838), the 14 stations of the crucifixion way, and the sculpted angels that hold up the ceiling. The beautifully carved and gold-painted high-altar dates from 1659. Its main painting depicts St. Catherine with baby Jesus. Rather unusual, the chapel has only one side-altar (normally they come in pairs, left and right of the high-altar). The painting of the late-baroque marble right side-altar (1785) depicts St. Wendolyn, the patron Saint of farmers and herdsmen. The oldest decoration is the statue representing St. Catherine on the right wall of the chancel, dating from the middle of the 15th century (it originated from the first gallows chapel).

From the chapel return to the signposted route nr. 4, by walking back the same way through the residential area, steep up the hill. The signposted route nr. 4 continues southward and gradually descends to cross a small stream. The path ascends again, past farmlands, fruit trees (plums, apples), and farmhouses, and provides views of the town Kerns. You pass by a **pilgrim resting place** (*Pilger Stibli*) set-up by a local farmer. A garage has been turned into a place of rest, halfway stage 7. There are toilets, benches and tables, a fridge fully stocked with refreshments, sweet snacks, coffee and tea, and even walking sticks. As in many such places in rural Switzerland, you can serve yourself and just leave the money of your consumptions in the cashbox.

The route continues to ascend on tarmac roads with wide views over grasslands. After passing a horse barn you arrive at the St. Anthony Chapel at km 12.4.

93 St. Anthony Chapel, Halten (St. Anton Kapelle)

- Haltenstrasse 34, 6064 Kerns
- St. Anthony the Hermit, St. Nicholas of Flüe
- The chapel was first built in 1540, consecrated in 1575, and rebuilt in 1639, from when the right side-altar painting depicting St. Nicholas of Flüe dates. The left side-altar painting dates from renovations in 1860. In 1920 the fresco with one Dance of Death scene (dating from around 1640) above the entrance in the front portico was recovered. The last renovations were undertaken in 1974, which uncovered the original frescos in the windowsills.

  The chapel is dedicated to St. Anthony the Hermit, not to be confused with St. Anthony of Padua. The former was an Egyptian hermit who lived in the 4th century; the latter was a Portuguese priest who lived in the 13th century.
- The baroque high-altar is beautifully carved and gold-decorated, and resembles the altar in the St. Catherine Chapel. It was made in a Renaissance retable design with two side panels. At its center is a painting depicting St. Anthony the Hermit.

Over the following kilometer the route ascends steeply, after which you reach a highland plateau and the landscape flattens. Past farmhouses the trail follows a gravel tractor path, after which a narrow gravel, and partially paved, path crosses through grasslands towards the south. Panoramic views open up: in front you can see Lake Sarnen with Sachseln at its shore; to the right you overlook the town Sarnen; to the left you see the green Gräfimattstand mountain range; and looking back you see the Stanserhorn mountain. The hiking trail follows a narrow path on a hill's ridge between cattle fences.

The footpath regularly changes from concrete tractor paths to grass and gravel hiking trails. At km 15.0 you arrive at the Dominican Convent of Bethany.

Dominican Convent of Bethany, St. Niklausen (Dominikanerinnen von Bethanien) 12

- Bethanienstrasse 3, 6066 St. Niklausen
- Dominican Order (of Bethany), Chemin Neuf Community
- St. Mary Magdalene
- The building complex consist of a convent, guesthouse, and chapel. In 1937 several Dominicans nuns of Bethany came from France to Obwalden. They established a convent in an old hotel in the town Kerns (about 4 km north) and divided it in a convent, guest rooms, and chapel. In 1964 an earthquake severely damaged their building. Because of structural damage they built a new convent to house the 54 sisters at the current location in 1969-72. The sisters provided

religious care for the female community of Obwalden and offered a place of retreat in their guesthouse. Fittingly, the convent's patroness Saint is St. Mary Magdalene who witnessed Jesus' resurrection; this reflects the convent's early history of leaving behind a past life (women who were imprisoned) and resurrecting to a new life as nun. Nowadays around 10 nuns live in the convent.

13 Chemin Neuf Community

Chemin Neuf Community

By 2012 the number of nuns was reduced to 17, so they decided on a cooperation with the Chemin Neuf Community (*Gemeinschaft Chemin Neuf*) ('Chemin Neuf' is French for 'new roads'). They reoccupied some of the empty rooms and took over management of the guesthouse.

The Chemin Neuf Community is in charge of the restaurant, accommodations, and meeting rooms for seminars and events. Additionally, they run the guesthouse that offers low-priced pilgrim accommodations (www.haus-bethanien.ch; tel. 041 666 02 00).

94 Dominican Convent Chapel, St. Niklausen (Kloster Kapelle)

Bethanienstrasse 3, 6066 St. Niklausen

St. Mary Magdalene

At the front desk of the guesthouse

The chapel was built in 1969-72. The chapel, the size of a church, has a modern design with a dark wooden exterior. It does not look like a typical chapel, but resembles the modern church designs of the 1960s-70s, with a semicircular footprint.

A descending spiral staircase leads to the crypt below the chapel, a darkened place for silence, prayer, and reflection.

The color brown dominates its interior while sunlight comes in through the narrow floor-to-ceiling windows.

The signposted route nr. 4 follows a road that slightly descends to the village St. Niklausen, after which it ascends steeply to the highest point of stage 7, to reach 832 meters at the St. Nicholas Chapel. Shortly before the chapel you pass by a sawmill and towards the right, in the distance, you see a large building dominating its environment. It is the **hotel Paxmontana** that was built in 1896, and expanded in Jugendstil (German Art Nouveau) in 1906. Its historical interior decorations and design style reflect the period of the Belle Époque. On another hill south of the hotel you see a chapel in Flüeli, which you will visit in about 3 km.

The next chapel stands isolated on the top of a hill, without any other buildings or village around it. An ascending footpath left of the road leads directly to the St. Nicholas Chapel (at km 16.4).

St. Nicholas Chapel, St. Niklausen (St. Niklausen Kapelle) 95

- Schildstrasse 5, 6066 St. Niklausen
- St. Nicholas, St. Lawrence
- The chapel looks more like a church than a chapel due to its free-standing massive and tall bell tower. The tower and chancel were built around 1350 (first mentioned in 1357). The chancel has a Gothic style and initially stood alone, without a nave. The nave was attached to the chancel several decades later.

  The free-standing tower has a Romanesque style with slit-like windows (the steeple was added in 1838) and resembles a medieval watchtower: its walls are 1.5-meter thick at the bottom, narrowing to 90 cm at the fourth level. It was indeed used as a watchtower; it never was a residential tower as its interior space (behind the thick walls) was too narrow.

Major renovations were undertaken in 1703-04 (date on the chancel arch), after the chapel was damaged by a storm. The nave received a baroque interior with a marble pulpit and two marble side-altars. The 100 square medallion paintings on the wooden ceiling of the nave were made during the renovations in 1704. They depict biblical scenes and many popular Saints.

The chancel frescos date from around 1370 and could mostly be recovered during restorations in 1944-46. These frescos are called the Pauper Bible (Biblia Pauperum or *Armenbibel*). They visualized scenes from The Bible and Saints so that the stories were made accessible to those who could not read (they are the medieval version of graphic novels with limited to no text). Since literacy was very low, limited to noblemen and monks, the frescos made the key messages and scenes from The Bible accessible to peasants and illiterates. The frescos depict scenes of the legends of St. Nicholas of Myra (bottom row) as well as biblical scenes of the life of Mary and Jesus. Their age and their depiction of the Pauper Bible are unique along the Swiss Way of St. James; a real treasure.

The text on the chancel arch refers to scenes of the life of St. Nicholas of Flüe. In case you can read German, can you make out the text and the story it tells (it is in rhyme)?

The right side-altar painting depicts the patron Saint Nicholas of Myra in his bishop outfit. The left side-altar painting depicts St. Lawrence who was roasted on a metal grating above hot coal. Rather unusual, the chancel does not have a high-altar; instead a canvas is hanging on the back wall portraying an image of a stained-glass window with a depiction of St. Nicholas.

During the renovations in 1703-04 the chancel also received a baroque high-altar, in a similar style as the two side-altars. When the chancel's frescos were uncovered in 1944-46, this high-altar was in poor condition and removed. The present communion table was placed during the renovations in 1992-94 and is free-standing, so that it does not cover the Pauper Bible at the chancel's back wall.

Another unusual item is the skull in the recess below the pulpit; it still has some teeth. It is of unknown origin, probably from Kerns' cemetery (it is not a relic of a Saint).

From the wooden bench outside the chapel one can enjoy nice views over the forested Ranft valley, Flüeli-Ranft, hotel Paxmontana, Sarnen, and Lake Sarnen against the background of a forested mountain range. From the high point of the chapel an 800-meter trail through grasslands steeply descends to the Brother Ulrich Chapel. The chapel stands isolated (you cannot get there by road) in a meadow at about two-thirds of the descent into the Ranft gorge (at km 17.2).

Brother Ulrich Chapel, Mösli (Mösli Kapelle) 96

Mösli, 6066 St. Niklausen

Brother Ulrich

The chapel was built for Brother Ulrich in 1484. In 1469 Brother Ulrich joined Brother Klaus in hermitage and settled at a large boulder and in a small cave on the eastern side of the Ranft gorge (Brother Klaus was on the western side). The chapel was built next to the cave (access through the narrow door opening on the right) and enclosed the large boulder (front right in the chapel). The original cave served as monk's cell, which Brother Ulrich occupied until he died in 1491.

The 18th century paintings on the left wall of the small chapel tell the story of Brother Ulrich; the last one, nr. 20, describes how his corpse was carried to the parish church in Kerns, where he was buried (his remains still lie there today). The 16th century late-Gothic frescos on the right wall tell the story of Jesus' life (Passion Cycle). The crucifix above the chancel-arch is unusual: it presents Jesus with his right arm released from the Cross. The baroque altar was added during renovations in the 18th century.

From the Brother Ulrich chapel the winding trail descends exceedingly steep into the Ranft gorge. There are 304 steps that help the pilgrim descend the steepest parts, until arriving at the footbridge over the *Grosse Melchaa* stream.

Immediately after crossing the metal footbridge you arrive at the Lower Ranft Chapel (at km 17.6). The word 'ranft' is the old German name for the bottom of a gorge.

97 Lower Ranft Chapel, Flüeli-Ranft (Untere Ranft Kapelle)

Ranftweg, 6073 Flüeli-Ranft

Brother Klaus, St. Mary, St. Mary Magdalene, 10'000 Martyrs, Twelve Apostles

The chapel was built in 1501, as a second chapel to accommodate the increasing number of pilgrims visiting the Upper Ranft Chapel (see below). According to legend, the chapel was built on the location where Brother Klaus had a vision of the Virgin Mary. The Virgin Mary, Mary Magdalene, the Holy Cross, and the 10'000 Martyrs are the patrons Saints of both the lower and the upper ranft chapels.

The mid 16th century frescos in the nave have unfinished scenes from the life of Brother Klaus. In 1650 and 1784 Gothic window-openings were broken through the walls, destroying several of the original scenes. During renovations in 1985-86 these window-openings were bricked up again, but the original frescos in their spots still have to be restored.

Major renovations were undertaken in 1920-21, when the decorated wooden ceiling was reconstructed to its original appearance of 1502.

The vaulted chancel has two special features: a column altar with a canopy and frescos depicting the Twelve Apostles. The unique column altar, from 1741, has a gold-painted statue, representing the Virgin Mary with baby Jesus, in an open half-circle canopy. Both are beautifully decorated.

Large frescos cover the interior walls; have a closer look at the one above the door. It depicts Switzerland untouched by the cruelties of WWI that is raging all around it (notice the national flags of the neighboring countries involved in the war). After a pledge from 1914, it was painted in 1921 to commemorate Switzerland's exclusion from WWI. The painting also depicts Brother Klaus, protected by angels, with raised arms praying for protection of the country towards the Holy Trinity reflected in the stained-glass window.

It is noticeable that the two ranft chapels have to cope with large pilgrim streams: the pathways are tarmacked and have wooden railings. A few paces up the hill lead you to two low dark-wooden chalets on white stone foundations. The second house includes a Brother Klaus giftshop and toilets in its basement. The pilgrim stamp lies in a red basket on the third windowsill of the first house. A St. James scallop and a message to the St. James pilgrims lead you there. Medieval pilgrims on their way to the tomb of St. James in Santiago de Compostela already made a stop at this location (and Brother Klaus' tomb in the church of Sachseln, see below). The Swiss Saint Nicholas of Flüe has become a major pilgrimage destination (together with Einsiedeln) along the Way of St. James through

Switzerland. After a few steps from the souvenir shop up the hill you arrive at the Upper Ranft Chapel (at km 17.7).

98 Upper Ranft Chapel, Flüeli-Ranft (Obere Ranft Kapelle)

- Ranftweg, 6073 Flüeli-Ranft
- Brother Klaus
- The chapel was originally built next to the hermit cell of Brother Klaus in 1468. The present chapel was built in 1693, but resembles the original one.
- The chapel has an austere interior, consistent with the ascetic life of Brother Klaus. Compared to the abundance of interior decorations at the lower ranft chapel, this upper chapel focuses on the pilgrim's spiritual needs and invites to reflect and pray. The paintings depicting scenes of the life of Brother Klaus date from 1821. Look up: the wooden ceiling is decorated in intarsia style panels with recurring patterns (similar to the ceiling decorations in the St. Borromeo Chapel – see below).

Similar to the chapel of Brother Ulrich on the other side of the gorge, the Brother Klaus chapel also has his hermit cell next to it. You can access the cell from the outside, right of the chapel. Up a steep staircase you get to the cell's interior. The wood is worn-out and is very old; much of it is still original from 1468. Notice the two small windows: one looking into the chapel at the altar (where he could see God) and one looking out to the front portal of the chapel (where he could see visitors). From the staircase he had a view of the forested gorge (the lower chapel was built 14 years after his death). Inside his cell hangs a replica of the Meditation Wheel painting, on which he meditated. Brother Klaus died in this cell in 1487, after 20 years of retreat.

From the chapel a 400-meter steep tarmac footpath leads you out of the valley to the level of the village Flüeli. Look back to the two chapels and the forested gorge; it is a unique scenery.

The village Flüeli is fully dedicated to Brother Klaus. You can visit a kiosk (that also serves as tourist information) to buy souvenirs and obtain the pilgrim stamp. Several restaurants and hotels (including Paxmontana) serve individual and group travelers. Many pilgrims arrive by car or coach; you will be one of the few arriving on foot.

Two Brother Klaus sites can be visited in the small village: his **Birth House** (*Geburtshaus*) and his **Residential House** (*Wohnhaus*). Entrance is free (open end of March until end of October). Brother Klaus lived in his birth house until he married Dorothee in 1446. At the time of their marriage he was 30 and she 15. The birth house was restored to its original appearance in 1925. The residential house was built by Brother Klaus only 150 meters from his birth house in 1445-46. He lived there for 20 years with his wife Dorothee and 10 children (until she agreed to his retreat in 1467). The house was restored to its original appearance in 1946. These two houses provide good insight in the primitive living conditions of the 15th century, when these wooden houses stood isolated in a densely forested area.

From the kiosk the route nr. 4 sign leads in the direction of the village's car park. Behind the car park, on a rock, the St. Borromeo Chapel towers above the village. The rock (*fluo* in old German) gave the name to the village Flüeli and Brother Klaus' family name 'von Flüe'. Right of the hill steps lead up to the St. Borromeo Chapel (at km 18.5).

99 St. Borromeo Chapel, Flüeli (St. Borromäus Kapelle)

- Herrenmattli, 6073 Flüeli-Ranft
- St. Borromeo, Brother Klaus
- At the tourist kiosk in the village
- The chapel was built in 1614-18. In 1883 the nave was extended by 4.5 meters, space for several new windows was broken through the walls, and a front portico was attached. The pulpit was taken down from the wall and placed on the floor during the last renovations in 1980-81. For this reason, there is no left side-altar, just a simple statue representing Brother Klaus at the wall where the pulpit used to be. The chapel, which has the size of a church, is dedicated to St. Charles Borromeo. As archbishop of Milan he visited Brother Klaus' grave in 1570. St. Borromeo is called upon for healing, particularly of stomach diseases: many pilgrims visit the chapel to pray for healing of diseases.
- The 17th century paintings on the lower walls of the nave depict scenes from the life of Brother Klaus (right) and St. Borromeo (left). Unfortunately, some of the (German) texts above them have become illegible. The high-altar, in Renaissance retable design, also has a painting depicting St. Borromeo flanked by two angels. The pulpit was made of marble, in the same style as the right side-altar.

  A special feature of the chapel is its woodwork: the wooden gallery inside the chancel; the intarsia wood-inlays in the chancel's walls and door to the sacristy; and the wooden ceiling of the nave and chancel, decorated in intarsia style panels with recurring patterns. These artistic features are not seen in any other chapel along the Swiss Way of St. James.

When you leave the chapel down the stairs on the southern side, you arrive at a square with an open-air chapel (at km 18.6).

Open-Air Chapel, Flüeli (Kapelle im Freien) **100**

- Herrenmattli, 6073 Flüeli-Ranft
- Brother Klaus
- The chapel was built in 1947, to commemorate the canonization of St. Nicholas of Flüe that year.
- A tall bronze statue representing Brother Klaus (1947), standing halfway the hill a bit hidden by the trees, blesses the people. The open-air chapel is used for Brother Klaus festivities and pilgrim services.

From the square it is only a few meters to get back to the signposted route nr. 4. The last 3 km of stage 7 descend into Sachseln. The first 200 meters descend through a patch of forest, where you pass by numbered crucifixion way signs. Grass and gravel trails lead you to a concrete road in the forest. The route nr. 4 sign directs to a leaf-covered forest path on the left, whereas another sign leads to a Lourdes chapel (*Lourdeskapelle*) on the right, following the concrete road.

Neither the St. James Way nor the Brother Klaus Way pass by this Lourdes chapel. The Lourdes chapel lies along an old pilgrimage way and would result in a 700-meter detour as an alternative way to reach Sachseln.

The descending trail crosses through grasslands, and follows a road and tractor paths. The views open up and you overlook Sachseln and Lake Sarnen. You can already see the last church, the end of stage 7, at the foot of the mountain. The final path into Sachseln passes through a residential area, leading straight to the St. Theodore Church. The onion-shaped dome on top of its bell tower serves as a beacon. After a roundabout you reach the church. However, you first pass by a small chapel, standing next to the bell tower. It is the Burial Chapel (at km 21.8).

101 **Buriel Chapel, Sachslen** (Grab Kapelle)

- Dorfstrasse, 6072 Sachseln
- Brother Klaus
- The chapel was built above the original grave of Brother Klaus. At the time of his death (1487) he was buried on the right side of the nave of the old church (see below). Around 1600 a special side-chapel, dedicated to the Virgin Mary, was built around the grave, worthy of the increasing number of pilgrims. After the new church was built in 1679, the tomb was transferred to the new church. The old church was demolished, but the side-chapel was maintained. Around 1703 the Virgin Mary side-chapel was extended to a charnel house and combined into the present burial chapel in 1878. In 1934 the tombstones were transferred from the church to this burial chapel.

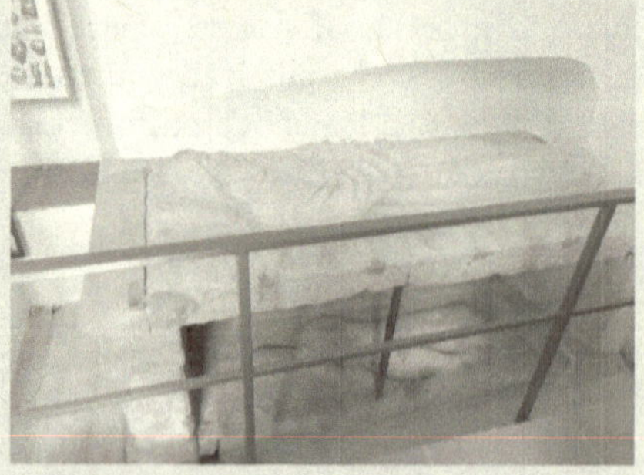

- Two tombstones (effigies) can be seen inside: a lower one dating from 1487 and an upper one dating from 1518. Because of the sandstone, the lower tombstone heavily eroded when it served as the pedestal to the oak coffin from 1518 onwards (the new tombstone lay on top of the coffin). Missing from the arrangement is the coffin, which would have been in between the two slabs of stone. The crucifix at the back wall dates from the mid 14th century and came from the first Romanesque church. The 19th century paintings depict scenes from the life of Brother Klaus.

From the burial chapel continue along the western side of the church to reach its main entrance (at km 21.9).

St. Theodore Church, Sachseln (St. Theodul Kirche) 102

- Dorfstrasse, 6072 Sachseln
- St. Theodore, St. Maurice, Brother Klaus
- On a table left of the main entrance. It is the same one as in Flüeli-Ranft.
- The first church, in a Romanesque design, dated from the 12th/13th century, from which only the lower part of the free-standing bell tower remained. You can still recognize the Romanesque features on the lower part of the tower: narrow windows with decorative Lombard arches. From an architectural style, three construction phases of the bell tower are clearly visible: the first Romanesque tower was relatively low; it was heightened by two levels in 1672, when the new church was built (otherwise the tower would have been lower than the roof of the new nave); and by another two levels (with the baroque onion-dome) after lightning had struck it in 1742.

The first small church, first mentioned in 1234, was oriented to the east, so that the tower stood on its right side. St. Theodore and St. Maurice already were the patron Saints. By the beginning of the 15th century this church was dilapidated and closed for several decades. After reconstruction, services resumed in 1459.

Brother Klaus died in 1487 and was buried on the right side of the nave (nowadays the location of the Burial chapel). During the following centuries the grave of Brother Klaus became a place of pilgrimage; the number of visitors further increased after the Pope allowed the adoration of Brother Klaus in 1649.

The old church was soon too small for the number of pilgrims and a larger church in a baroque style was built in 1672-84. The orientation of the church changed from east to south, which enabled the continuation of services in the old church while the new one was being built; the bell tower now is south of the chancel. The tomb of Brother Klaus was transferred from the old Romanesque church to the new baroque church in 1679, when the new nave was ready. The old church was demolished and in its place the chancel of the new church was built.

The interior has two dominating colors: black and white. The black pillars, floor, and other decorations may look like marble, but they are made of black limestone from quarries near Stans (similar to the St. Peter and Paul church in Stans). The black floor and columns make the interior relatively dark. The church has many interesting interior decorations, altars, statues, paintings, and so forth; too many to describe here – better see them with your own eyes.

Special features are: the woodwork of the entrance door with the inside metal hinges, in the same style decorations you saw at the St. Peter and Paul church in Stans; and the mosaics (under the front portico) that were made in Vatican workshops in 1941, depicting two scenes with Brother Klaus. The left scene depicts his Virgin Mary vision (at the place where the Lower Ranft chapel was built in 1501). The right scene depicts Brother Klaus at the assembly of the Treaty of Stans (*Stanser Verkommnis*) in 1481 (this is fictional: he never was at that assembly – it was priest Heimo am Grund who sped from Stans to Brother Klaus in Flüeli-Ranft to obtain his counsel).

Three main relics of Brother Klaus can be seen: his remains inside the silver effigy integrated in the front side of the communion table; his meditation wheel painting; and his hermit robe.

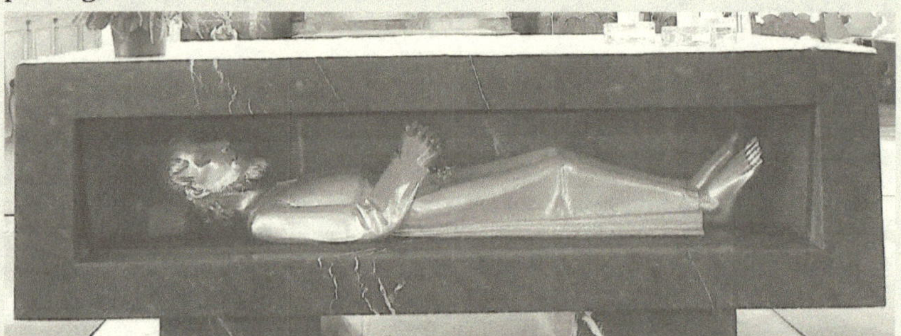

The silver life-size effigy of Brother Klaus, in the front-recess of the communion table, was made in 1934 (inserted in a new altar table in 1976). The bones of St. Nicholas of Flüe were transferred from his coffin to this sculpture in 1934, after which the old tombstones were moved to the Burial chapel. Do you notice the resemblance of the silver effigy with the one at the St. Vincent Church in Eschenbach (see church nr. R-32, stage R3, Volume I)?

A replica of Brother Klaus' Meditation Wheel painting is hanging between the two left side-altars. The original was painted on cloth and dates from 1475-80; it is stored in a secure place at the parish office.

His original dark-brown hermit dress, in which he died, is hanging in an air-controlled vitrine at the front of the right side-nave. It has been on display in the church since 1610. Another original hermit dress of Brother Klaus is displayed in the Jesuit Church in Luzern (see church nr. L5, stage L1).

In 1984 Pope John Paul II visited Switzerland and made a stop in Sachseln. He prayed at the St. Theodore church and celebrated the Eucharist in Flüeli-Ranft.

About 100 meters from the church (in the direction of the train station) across the road you find the **Brother Klaus Museum** (Dorfstrasse 4, 6072 Sachseln) in a white house (ticket CHF 10; open end of March until end of October).

Sachseln has thrived on the many visiting pilgrims since the 15th century. Nowadays many aspects of the town (around 5'000 inhabitants) still revolve around the adoration of Brother Klaus. Pilgrim inns and guesthouses existed for several centuries.

From the ending point

The St. Theodore Church in Sachseln is the ending point of stage 7, directly on the signposted route nr. 4.

In case you are a day-hiker, you need to walk 500 meters to the Sachseln train station (further down the hill towards the lake).

In case you are a thru-hiker and spend the night in Sachseln, be aware that there is no pilgrim inn. The nearest low-priced pilgrim accommodation was offered along the route in the Dominican Convent of Bethany (tel. 041 666 02 00; www.haus-bethanien.ch; from the Sachseln train station about 40 minutes (CHF 6): train to Sarnen, then bus 343 direction Melchtal). Sachseln has several inns and hotels that offer accommodation at fair prices, and pilgrim beds are also available at private residences. The same for Flüeli: from the train station bus 351 direction Flüeli-Ranft; 14 min; CHF 6. Check out www.jakobsweg.ch or www.viajacobi4.ch for the accommodation possibilities in and around Sachseln.

The next Stage

Stage 8 guides you along Lake Sarnen, and after a forested ascent, along Lake Lungern. After another forested ascent to the Brünig Pass, the route passes over the third-highest altitude of the Swiss Way of St. James and descends through the forest to the highland plateau of Brienzwiler. Read the next chapter to find out what that entails.

Stage 8: Sachseln to Brienzwiler 26 km

The Way along Alpine Lakes

Route stats

	Distance in km	*Time in hrs:min*
Signposted route nr. 4	23.9	6:00
Churches/chapels	1.5	1:30
Points of interest	0.4	0:30
Rest/lunch		1:00
Stage 8	25.8	9:00

In case you hike this stage as a daytrip, you need to add 500 meters in Sachseln and 1.4 km in Brienzwiler (from and to the train stations).

Ascent/descent/total	+955 / -773 / 1'728 altitude meters
Lowest/highest altitude	470 / 1'083 meters
Pathway/condition	difficult / difficult
Churches/chapels	Ewil, Giswil (2), Bürglen, Obsee, Lungern, Brienzwiler
Monasteries	none
Points of interest	Former Castle of Hunwil, Ruins Castle of Giswil Dundelbach Waterfalls, Former Castle of Brienzwiler, Open-Air Museum Ballenberg

Route summary

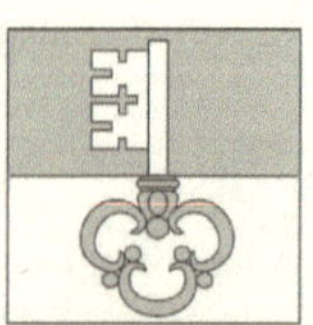

Stage 8 continues in catholic **Canton Obwalden** and at km 21.5 (Brünig Pass) enters protestant **Canton Bern.** The last 4 km of stage 8, as well as the upcoming stages 9, 10, 11, and 12 are all in protestant Canton Bern.

Stage 8 guides you along Lake Sarnen, and after a forested ascent, along Lake Lungern. After another forested ascent to the Brünig Pass, the route passes over the third-highest altitude of the Swiss Way of St. James and descends through the forest to the highland plateau of Brienzwiler.

The Way of St. James follows main road nr. 4 (between Luzern and Brienzwiler) and the railway track (between Luzern and Interlaken) in close vicinity. The first 9 km are an easy hike on gravel footpaths without altitude meters. From Sachseln the route follows the eastern shore of Lake Sarnen, after which the route goes through the Laui River valley to the town Giswil. While hiking km 10 and 11 the trail ascends through a forest from the Lake Sarnen level (at 470 meters) to the Lake Lungern level (at 700 meters). Lake Lungern is the most beautiful turquoise-colored lake against the background of snow-capped mountain peaks glistering in the sun; one of the most beautiful views along the Swiss Way of St. James. The route follows the western shore around the lake (whereas road nr. 4 and the train track stay on the eastern shore). The 6 km along the lake are on easy pathways, though there are some gradual ascents and descents. At km 18 the real ascent starts. Over 4 km the route ascends through the forest to the Brünig Pass at 1'008 meters, where the route changes from Canton Obwalden to Canton Bern. This is followed by an ascent over a kilometer to the highest point of the day (at 1'083 meters), from where the last 2 km descend through the forest to the highland plateau of Brienzwiler.

Getting to the starting point

Today's starting point in Sachseln is at the St. Theodore Church, directly on the signposted route nr. 4.

In case you hike stage 8 as a daytrip, you need to walk 500 meters from the train station to the church. However, since the signposted route nr. 4 passes by the train station, you can also start from the signpost at the train station and skip the 500 meters to the church and the same 500 meters back to the train station (unless you have not yet visited the St. Theodore church).

Route Map and Profile

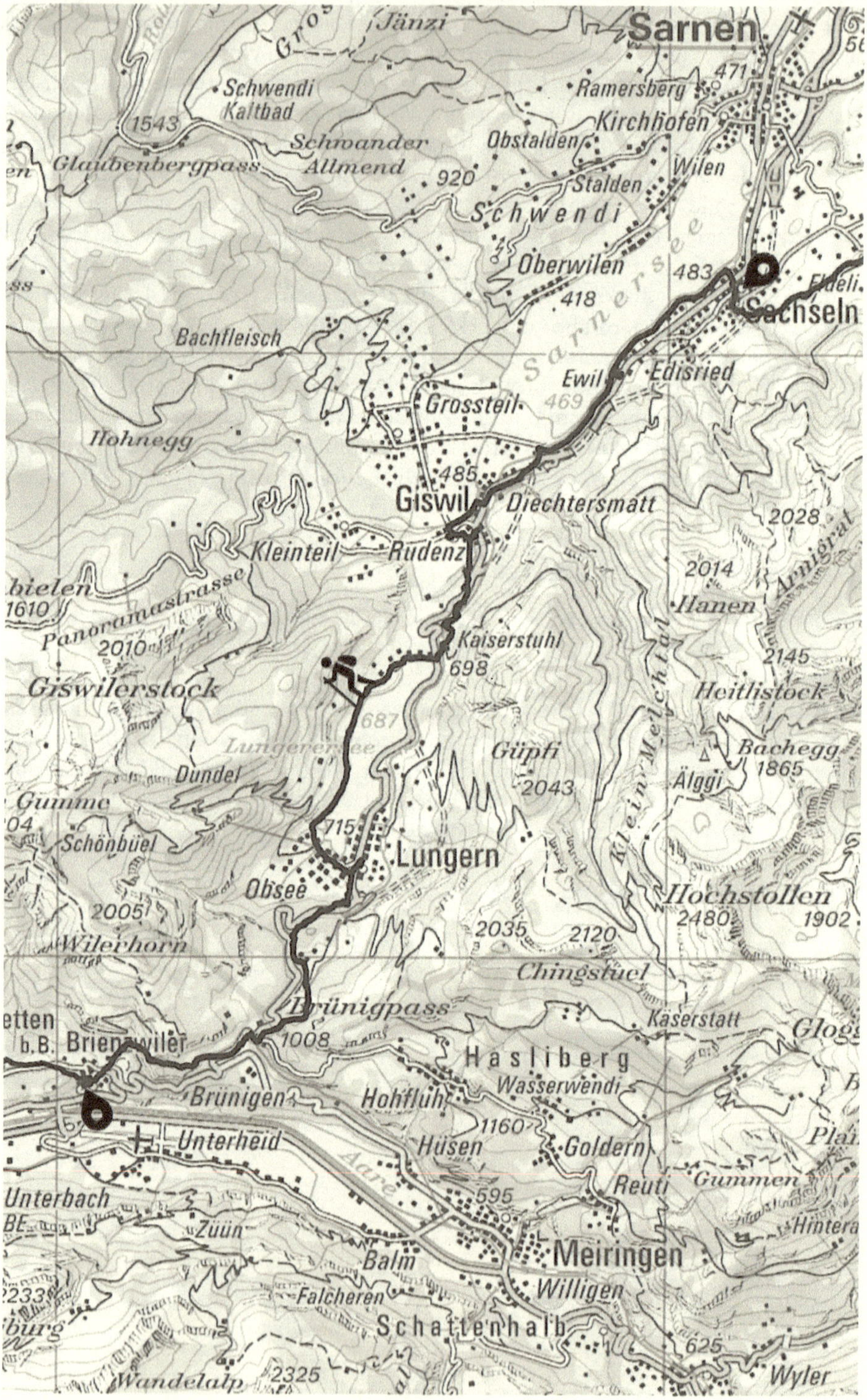
Sarnen
Jänzi
Schwendi
Kaltbad
Ramersberg
471
1543
Kirchhofen
Glaubenbergpass
Schwander
Allmend
Obstalden
920
Stalden
Wilen
Schwendi
Oberwilen
483
418
Sachseln
Sarnersee
Bachfleisch
Ewil
Edisried
Grossteil
469
Hohnegg
485
Giswil
Diechtersmatt
2028
Kleinteil
Rudenz
2014
Panoramastrasse
1610
Hanen
Armigrat
2010
Kaiserstuhl
698
2145
Giswilerstock
Heitlistock
687
Lungerersee
Güpfi
Bachegg
1865
Dundel
2043
Älggi
Gumme
Schönbüel
715
Lungern
Obsee
Hochstollen
2480
1902
2005
Wilerhorn
2035
2120
Chingstuel
Brünigpass
Käserstatt
b.B. Brienzwiler
1008
Hasliberg
Wasserwendi
Brünigen
Hohfluh
1160
Unterheid
Hüsen
Goldern
Aare
Reuti
Gummen
Unterbach
BE
595
Züün
Meiringen
Balm
Willigen
Falcheren
Schattenhalb
625
2325
Wandelalp
Wyler

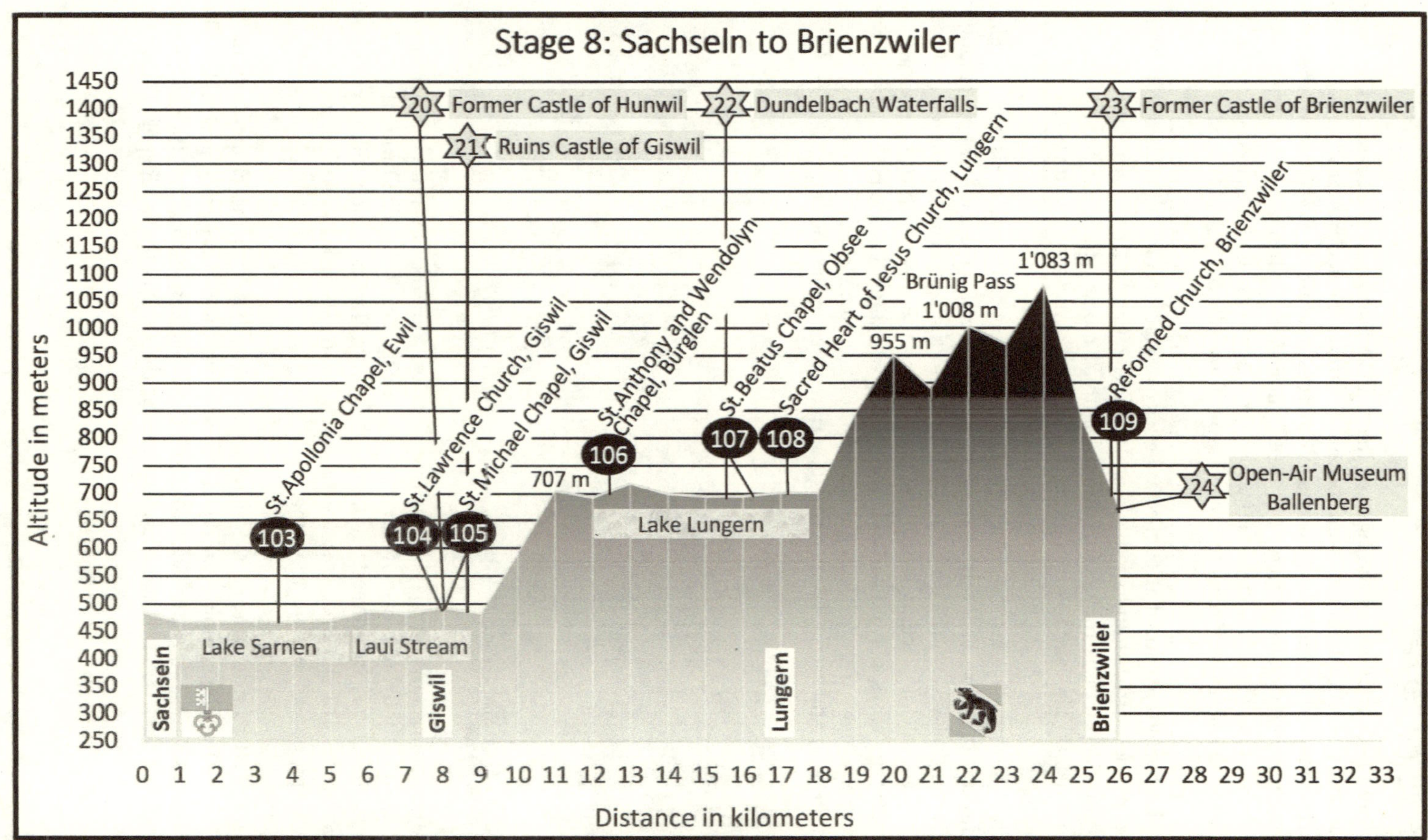
Stage 8: Sachseln to Brienzwiler
Altitude in meters
Distance in kilometers
Sachseln
Lake Sarnen
Laui Stream
Giswil
Lake Lungern
Lungern
Brienzwiler
707 m
955 m
1'008 m
Brünig Pass
1'083 m
103 St.Apollonia Chapel, Ewil
104 St.Lawrence Church, Giswil
105 St.Michael Chapel, Giswil
106 St.Anthony and Wendolyn Chapel, Burglen
107 St.Beatus Chapel, Obsee
108 Sacred Heart of Jesus Church, Lungern
109 Reformed Church, Brienzwiler
20 Former Castle of Hunwil
21 Ruins Castle of Giswil
22 Dundelbach Waterfalls
23 Former Castle of Brienzwiler
24 Open-Air Museum Ballenberg

Hiking the Route

From the church follow the signs to the train station and Lake Sarnen. The route passes by a pedestrian area with a bronze statue representing Brother Klaus in a long-stretched rectangular fountain. You cross road nr. 4 (*Brünigstrasse*) (the main road from Luzern to Brienzwiler), turn right and immediately left, to arrive at the train station. The route turns left and right again to cross the train track. At Lake Sarnen the signpost directs to the left (south) to follow a gravel footpath.

Lake Sarnen is named after the capital city of Canton Obwalden, Sarnen, which lies at the northern end of the lake. It is Switzerland's 21st largest lake, with an average depth of 31 meters (maximum depth 51 meters) and a surface elevation of 469 meters. The lake has a length of 5.7 km and a maximum width of 1.6 km.

The following 4.4 km the signposted route closely follows the eastern shoreline (directly at the water level) of the lake in a southern direction (*Seeweg*). Hiking is easy and relaxed on the gravel footpath next to the lake. The train track and road nr. 4 are in close vicinity left of the path. Along the way you pass by recreational swimming areas, playgrounds, camping sites, and small boat piers. You have early morning views over the tranquil lake to the 1'700-meter-high forested mountains in the west and the 2'010-meter-high barren peaks in the south.

After about 3 km you pass by a camping site on your left. It is not visible from the footpath, but behind (east of) the camping site is a small chapel. During the middle ages this chapel was directly along the Way of St. James, which followed the old road (nr. 4) of the *Brünigstrasse*. The lake's shores, where the path is now, were swamps, not suitable for traveling.

You need to briefly leave the signposted route to get to the chapel. About 50 meters after the camping site, turn left to cross the railway track and follow the *Sagenmattli* for 140 meters east to reach the *Brünigstrasse* (road nr. 4). Turn left at road nr. 4 and after 50 meters you arrive at the St. Apollonia Chapel of Ewil (at km 3.3).

St. Apollonia Chapel, Ewil (St. Apollonia Kapelle) 103

- Brünigstrasse 259, 6072 Sachseln
- St. Apollonia, St. James the Greater
- The chapel was first mentioned in 1593. The present chapel was built in 1746-48 (dates on the inner and outer walls) and last renovated in 1990.
- The altar painting (1844) depicts the patroness Saint Apollonia. To commemorate that the chapel lies along the old Way of St. James, a small statue representing St. James was placed above the door in 2004.

From the chapel walk back the same route to the signposted Way of St. James and continue on the gravel path along the lake for 2 km.

After 5.3 km you leave Lake Sarnen behind and continue in the Giswileraa River valley. The route turns left and goes underneath a concrete railway bridge along a small stream in a rocky riverbed. To your left you see the Highway A8 disappear in the Giswil tunnel (length 2.1 km), a detour for traffic to and from the Brünig Pass. A narrow gravel path follows the stream and leads you to road nr. 4 (*Brünigstrasse*). In the background you see a barren mountain peak pointing to the sky. It is the Giswilerstock at 2'010 meters. Higher mountain peaks are behind it. The route follows road nr. 4 for 600 meters and enters the town Giswil. After crossing the railway track again, you pass by a COOP supermarket (right) and the Giswil train station (left). In the distance the snow-capped peaks of the Rosenhorn, Mittelhorn, and Wetterhorn become visible for the first time.

The route turns right (west), away from road nr. 4. You cross the canalized Giswileraa stream and 200 meters later turn left onto the embankment next to the Laui stream. Until the end of the 19th century these streams used to regularly flood the surrounding lands and cause significant damage. From the beginning of the 20th century the northern sections of these streams were canalized. Around the southern curve of the Laui stream you can already see the next church.

After following the gravel footpath on the embankment along the Laui stream for 600 meters, the route turns left. To the right you see a wooden roofed bridge (built in 1939) over the stream, but the route takes you in the opposite direction (left). About 100 meters later you arrive at the foot of a hill and after following the tarmac road curving up the hill, you arrive at the St. Lawrence Church that stands on the site of the former Castle of Hunwil (at km 7.8).

This hill has a long history as the **site of the former Castle of Hunwil**. After the Abbey of Murbach (Alsace, France) sold its lands in Canton Luzern and Unterwalden to the House of Habsburg-Austria in 1291, the Lords of Hunwil relocated from Luzern to Obwalden. They acted as the regional Governors of the House of Habsburg-Austria. Around 1300 they built a castle on this hill (based on the size of the hilltop it could have been of sizeable proportions). For about 80 years they held dominating political positions, which abruptly ended in 1382, when they were forbidden to claim any public positions in Obwalden. The reason was that their relatives, the Lords of Ringgenberg (Governors of the House of Habsburg south of the Brünig Pass) lost much of their power as a result of the Ringgenberg Dispute in 1381 (see point of interest nr. 30, stage 9). Since the patronage of the Lords of Ringgenberg failed, the Lords of Hunwil were banned from Giswil. By then battles and tensions between the Ur-Cantons and the House of Habsburg were increasing, leading up to the battle of Sempach, where the Habsburg were defeated in 1386; as a prelude the Lords of Hunwil were unable to maintain their representation of the House of Habsburg and were banned from Canton Obwalden.

The family sold their possession in Giswil and returned to Luzern. It is not clear what happened to the castle after they left. Most likely it was not inhabited, its stones might have been used for other buildings, and it fell into ruins over the centuries. Stones of the castle ruins were used in the construction of the St. Lawrence church in 1630, removing the last visible remains. The last remaining fundaments of the old castle are below the northern part of the wall that surrounds the premises.

St. Lawrence Church, Giswil (St. Laurentius Kirche) 104

- Kirchplatz 2, 6074 Giswil
- St. Lawrence
- On a table left of the main entrance. The stamp depicts St. Lawrence above flames.
- The church on the hill in Giswil was built in 1630-35. A predecessor church (first mentioned in 1275) stood about 1 km to the west, on the southern bank of the Laui stream. This church, also dedicated to St. Lawrence, was destroyed by a flood (together with much of the old town) in 1629. The new church was built on the hill that once contained the castle of the Lords of Hunwil; the hill provided protection against floods and stones of the castle ruins could be used to build the church. The destruction of the old church caused an increased witch-hunt for the devilish forces that were considered responsible for the flooding disaster. More than 50 people, most of them branded as witches, were tortured and burned at the ruins of the old church.
- Inside the church the three baroque grey-black marble altars, altar table, and pulpit date from the renovations in 1781, and have all been maintained in the same style. The painting of the high-altar depicts St. Lawrence and dates from 1781. The paintings of both side-altars were purchased during a renovation in 1970.

Next to the church is the St. Michael Chapel.

105 St. Michael Chapel, Giswil (St. Michael Kapelle)

Kirchplatz 2, 6074 Giswil

St. Michael

The chapel was built in 1657-61. It served as ossuary (*Beinhaus*) and nowadays as funeral chapel.

The chapel has a small but beautifully decorated altar piece. Its painting depicts the archangel Michael weighing the souls of deceased people in the Last Judgement, deciding whether they go to heaven or hell. The five statues at the altar are replicas from 2002; the originals from 1661 were stolen in 1992. Notice the rope that tolls the small bell in the steeple.

Small bone relics (1661) of unknown origin are displayed in the vitrines on the left and right side of the arched chancel wall.

From the hill you have wonderful views of the snow-capped peaks of the Rosenhorn (3'689 m), Mittelhorn (3'704 m), and Wetterhorn (3'692 m), towering high above the forested slopes that lead to the next lake. The route ascends on a forest trail left (east) of the large building (*Hotel am Kaiserstuhl*) that you see halfway the hill.

After descending the church's hill, the route follows a tarmac road where you pass by a cemetery and a retirement home. A narrow tarmac footpath through meadows and along apple trees leads to the *Buechholzstrasse.* At this location the signposted route directs south. However, you need to briefly leave the signposted route to reach the ruins of a former castle (200 meters). Keep going straight (past *Hotel Krone*) to the *Brünigstrasse* (road nr. 4), turn left, after 70 meters cross the road, and turn right onto a narrow footpath up the hill to the castle ruins.

21 The **ruins of the Castle of Rudenz, Giswil** stand on a small hill and date from around 1200-50. It was a square fortified residential tower with measurements of 10 by 11 meters. The lower parts of the walls were 1.8-meter thick. Like many other such towers from that period, it must have had a door at an elevated level (first floor), reachable by retractable ladder. Not much more is known about the appearance of the castle. Nowadays, parts of the walls reach about 5 meters

high. The castle consisted of a fortified residential tower built by the Lords of Rudenz, who settled at the beginning of the 13th century to control trade and traffic along the route to/from the Brünig Pass.

They also served the Lords of Ringgenberg, who were regional Governors of the House of Habsburg-Austria. Their arrangement with the Lords of Rudenz served as a northern extension of a line of castles along the trade route between Interlaken and Giswil. In 1366 the last descendants of the House of Rudenz sold the lands in Giswil and relocated to Canton Uri, where they built another castle (they left Canton Obwalden in time before the tensions between the House of Habsburg and the Ur-Cantons reached their peak in the 1380s).

The fortified tower was further used as residence for at least another 200 years (until the mid 16th century), during which time many constructional changes were made (e.g. the ground floor entrance). Sometime after that (it is not known when), the tower was abandoned and fell into ruins. Time and again its stones were used as building materials for other houses. Its present appearance dates from restorations in 2008.

From the ruins walk back the same 200 meters to the signposted route nr. 4 and follow the tarmac road between grasslands to the south. This area is called *Aaried* and used to be a lake and marshlands until 1850. After 400 meters you cross the Giswileraa stream again. The route was flat so far; the first 9.2 km were easy to hike. But that changes now, after crossing the Giswileraa stream.

The following 2 km the trail ascends from 485 to 707 meters. This ascent takes you from the level of Lake Sarnen to the level of Lake Lungern. Most of the ascent over 2 km is through the forest (*Kaiserstuhlwald*) with limited views of the surrounding mountains and lakes. The route follows the ascending and curving road nr. 4 in relatively close vicinity; the sounds of traffic accompany you during the ascent. About 500 meters into the climb the trail passes underneath the elevated road nr. 4. The forest trail is a narrow rocky path; the loose rocks and several landslides add to the difficulty of the steep and zigzagging ascent.

About 1.4 km into the ascent the trail is parallel to the railway track and 200 meters later crosses the track. Views to the north (Giswil and Lake Sarnen) briefly open up.

Still ascending steeply, you leave the forest and enter a path through alpine meadows. Shortly after a sharp right turn at a farmhouse, the route reaches 707 meters. The following 400 meters the trail slightly descends through alpine meadows to reach the Kaiserstuhl train station. After crossing the train station and road nr. 4 the route turns sharp right. In front of you the most beautiful turquoise-colored Lake Lungern appears. High above the lake the eternal snow on the Rosenhorn, Mittelhorn, and Wetterhorn glisters in the morning sun. This is one of the most beautiful views along the Swiss Way of St. James.

Lake Lungern is Switzerland's 37th largest lake, with a length of 3.5 km, a maximum width of 900 meters, and a maximum depth of 68 meters. Its surface elevation varies with the season, between 668 and 692 meters. Because the growing population of Lungern required more agricultural lands, the water level was lowered by about 18 meters (to 657 meters) in 1790-1836. This was done by blasting a 420-meter tunnel as outlet on the northern side of the lake (towards the lower Lake Sarnen). From 1921 the level of the lake was increased again when a water-power plant was built to make use of the water flow through the tunnel. In winter the use of the power plant drops the surface level to 668 meters (because the lake is not refilled with water from the mountains as in summer).

As you walk along Lake Lungern, you are literally in the middle of Switzerland. The geographical center of Switzerland lies about 6 km east of the lake.

Whereas road nr. 4 follows the eastern shore of Lake Lungern, the signposted route nr. 4 follows the western shore of the lake. The western shore continues to offer great views of the snow-capped mountains, providing a much better hike than the eastern shore would have. For 500 meters along the northern shore you can either follow a gravel path (going up and down) or the road (flat). You pass by recreational swimming areas and a pier, after which the route curves around the northwestern corner to the south. Along a tarmac road you arrive at the St. Anthony and Wendolyn Chapel of Bürglen (at km 12.4).

St. Anthony and Wendolyn Chapel, Bürglen (St. Antonius und Wendelin Kapelle) 106

- Bürglenstrasse 39, 6078 Lungern
- St. Anthony of Padua, St. Wendolyn, St. Joseph, Brother Klaus
- The chapel was built around 1680. At that time the municipality of Bürglen was very small (and it still is), but that did not prevent the local authorities, with support from the population, to build their own chapel. The consecration of the chapel took place 43 years later (1723). The chapel was enlarged in 1828-32 (date above the door). The last renovations were undertaken in 1976-77.
- The three baroque marble altars have a similar style. The 17th century painting on the left side-altar depicts St. Wendolyn, the painting on the right side-altar St. Anthony. The treasure of the chapel is the tabernacle, which came from the church in Lungern (see below). It is a beautiful piece of art dating from 1622. Take a closer look; can you recognize the Saints represented by the small statues? The statue representing St. Joseph with baby Jesus (left wall of the chancel) dates from the 17th century. Take a look at the ceiling of the chancel. Do you recognize the portray of the face of Brother Klaus in his Meditation Wheel?

The following 3.2 km the Way of St. James follows the western shore of the lake in a southward direction. The gravel road gently ascends and descends at an elevated level above the lake. The views to the snow-capped southern Alps, and to the 2'000-meter-high mountains on the eastern side of the lake, make the hiking exceptional. Across the lake, at the southeastern corner, you can see the town Lungern and a large church on a hill.

22

At the village Diesselbach, in the southwestern corner of the lake, signs direct to the **Dundelbach Waterfalls** (*Dundelbachfälle*). It indicates 3 minutes to the lower falls and 15 minutes to the higher fall viewpoint. It is worthwhile to walk up the short trail to the lower fall. Water is falling down the rocky cliff in a small basin, after which it continues to flow down to Lake Lungern. Depending on the rainfall, the water flowing from the two falls may be reduced to a small stream.

The route curves around the southern side of the lake, through flat grasslands and some isolated farms and houses. Look back to the waterfalls; you can see both the lower and higher waterfalls against the bare rocks.

You pass by the ground station of the Lungern-Turren cable car, which takes hikers to the Tuggen mountain at 1'531 meters above sea level. Past the parking area of a camping site and recreational areas along the lake, the route follows the *Obseestrasse* towards the St. Beatus Chapel, which you reach at km 16.5.

St. Beatus Chapel, Obsee (St. Beat Kapelle) 107

Obseestrasse, 6078 Lungern

St. Beatus, St. John the Baptist, St. Gall

On the last pew, left of the entrance. The stamp depicts the Sacred Heart of Jesus Church of Lungern (see below).

The chapel was built in 1567, for a specific purpose: to keep the relics of St. Beatus. Until that time these relics were kept in their original place, at the St. Beatus chapel and grave, at the caves on a mountain-side high above Lake Thun (you will visit this place in stage 10). St. Beatus' grave was in Canton Bern and was heavily impacted by the Reformation in the 1520s-30s. The Bernese Church and Authorities forced the conversion to Protestantism during the Reformation and either transformed or closed catholic places of worship in their Canton. The pilgrimage destination of St. Beatus' grave was closed. Since Canton Obwalden was catholic and had rejected the Reformation, the newly built chapel served as a place of refuge for the relics of St. Beatus. This enabled a continuation of the catholic pilgrimage, while the original site of the grave was closed.

The first chapel was small (about 4.5 by 4.25 meters) and stood on the site of the present chancel. About 32 years later (1599) the chapel was extended with a nave. After a village fire destroyed the building, the present chapel was built in 1708. In 1992 renovations of the interior and exterior restored the original appearance from the beginning of the 18th century.

The painting at the high-altar depicts St. Beatus fighting a dragon. This baroque high-altar dates from around 1708, when the present chapel was built. The two side-altars clearly have a different design compared to the high-altar. These two altars were brought over from another church (from Canton Luzern) during renovations in the 1950s. Instead of the usual paintings, they have statues representing St. John the Baptist (left) and St. Gall (right). These were the patron Saints of the old parish church of Lungern (see below).

From the chapel you can already see the main church of Lungern, with its pointed roof on the bell tower. It stands high on a hill, dominating the view towards the east. About 300 meters after the chapel the signpost directs you to the right, south. It is worthwhile to make a 900-meter detour (450 meters to and from) to visit the church. From the signpost keep following the *Obseestrasse* up the hill. Cross road nr. 4 and you arrive at the foot of the hill of the church (at km 17.1).

108 Sacred Heart of Jesus Church, Lungern (Heilig Herz Jesu Kirche)

Brünigstrasse, 6078 Lungern

Holy Family, Brother Klaus, Four Evangelists

In the front portal of the church

The church was built on the hill south of the village in 1891-93. The predecessor church stood at the northern side of the village Lungern, but was destroyed when an overflowing Eibach stream pushed meter-high debris down the mountain in 1887. Only the Romanesque bell tower from 1389 was left standing (nowadays this old tower is about 900 meters north of the present church – going to this tower would mean a 1.8 km detour).

To eliminate the risk of destruction by another flood, the church was rebuilt at a new location on the hill south of the village. This church was constructed as a replica of the Basilica of Lourdes (France); it has a neo-Gothic style and looks like a cathedral. The 'Sacred Heart of Jesus' devotion symbolizes Christ's love and compassion to relieve the suffering of humanity.

Four terraces and 93 steps lead to its main entrance. The higher-level terraces provide wide views over Lungern, Lake Lungern, and the surrounding mountains. A cemetery is spread out over two terraces. Cave-like recesses are left and right of the stairs on the third level. The left-side cavern is a vaulted chapel with a statue representing the Virgin Mary and a small water fountain in a rock recess. The text on the wall translates to: 'Holy Mary Mother of God pray for us'. The right-side cavern is a vaulted chapel with an altar and a carving depicting Jesus and the angel Gabriel. The text on the wall translates to: 'Father not what I want – but what you want'.

When you enter the church you immediately feel like being in a cathedral of a big city (even though Lungern had only around 1'800 inhabitants at the time it was built). The high vaulted ceiling, large sandstone pillars, two wide side-naves, and transept demonstrate large dimensions. The stained-glass windows project a wide array of colors into the interior. The size of the building fully consumed the budget: the interior is relatively austere without opulent decorations.

Originally the interior had several neo-Gothic altars and decorations, but by the 1940s these were considered out of fashion. Except for the pulpit, confessionals, and crucifixion way stations, all neo-Gothic interior decorations (such as the altars) were removed in 1949. Take a closer look at the pulpit: a fine example of neo-Gothic art with its spire and statues representing the Four Evangelists, which were originally at the high-altar.

It is unusual that there is no high-altar; in 1949 it was replaced by the group of statues representing the crucifixion scene. The left side-altar contains a wood-carved statue representing the Holy Family, the right side-altar Brother Klaus. Also notice the hardly visible transparent Plexiglas cross above the communion table.

The church is directly at road nr. 4, and you need to cross it and walk down the hill to get back to the Way of St. James signpost. The sign directs you past the small Obsee industrial area. The ascent to the Brünig Pass starts immediately. This climb is in two stages. The first stage ascends to 955 meters over 2 km. This is followed by a descent to 891 meters over about 1 km. The second stage is the final ascent to the pass level of 1'008 meters over about 1 km. These 4 kilometers (2 steep up, 1 down, 1 steep up) get you to the pass. The descent shortly before the pass level is mentally tough (and nothing on the trail warns you for this). After 2 km you have ascended to 955 meters, almost at the pass level, and any hiker will normally expect the remaining ascent to the pass at 1'008 meters to be short and easy. Nothing of that though. The trail descends in the 3rd km; you need to mentally recharge to conquer the additional altitude meters to the pass level caused by this unexpected descent.

Most of the time the Way of St. James is through the forest, more or less parallel to road nr. 4, which also goes over the Brünig Pass. The traffic may not always be visible through the trees, but you can almost always hear it while hiking the first stage of the ascent. It starts easy, through a patch of forest, across a small road, through patches of meadows, and along the edge of the forest. You follow a crucifixion way, with stations standing on columns or fixed to the rock cliffs.

After 600 meters the route becomes very steep and rocky; the **Holloway** trail was hewn into the rocks, below overhanging cliffs, with steps made of bedrock (at least there are no steep cliffs on the side, like at the Stützberg in stage 5). This is part of the **2'000-year-old Roman road** from southern Germany to northern Italy. Until the Schöllenen gorge was bridged in the 1220s (which opened up the Gotthard route across the Alps), this path over the Brünig Pass was the major military, trade, travel, and pilgrimage route to/from the south. Until the 1220s it was the only passable crossing over the central Alps. You are following in the 2'000-year-old footsteps of Roman Legions. Pilgrims have traversed this route for more than 1'000 years; it was the most frequented Swiss pilgrimage route to Rome, Jerusalem, and Santiago de Compostela. When you stand still and listen, you can hear the heavy breathing of the many pilgrims that went before you (or it may just be your own).

Shortly after conquering the cliff-side, the forest trail is blocked by several fallen trees. You will need to climb over them, go underneath, or walk around them. Because of the remote location it may take a while before foresters cut a path through them. The under-footing through the forest is made up of cobble stones (remains of the 2'000-year-old pathway) and tree trunks, which cause uncomfortable walking.

About 1.1 km into the ascent you need to cross road nr. 4. Be careful as there is no zebra crossing and drivers will not expect people to cross (their speed limit is 80 km/h). For 500 meters the trail continues to ascend parallel to the left side of road nr. 4. Left of the trail, high above, are cliffs from where large boulders regularly loosen and roll down towards the road.

Metal grating, held by steel cables tied to trees and metal posts in the ground, prevents those boulders from rolling onto the road. But the Way of St. James trail passes left of the fence, at the side of the high cliffs; the pilgrims are not protected against falling boulders. Mind the low-hanging steel cables over the trail.

The trail continues to ascend steeply as it approaches the high cliffs. You regularly see large boulders on the trail with a beaten track around it. Shortly before reaching 955 meters altitude (first stage), the trail is next to the high cliffs. Crucifixion way plaques are fixed to the cliff walls. Surprisingly, you come across a small wooden box, fixed in a small recess of the cliff's wall. The box has a St. James scallop imprint and contains a pilgrim guestbook and pen (no stamp). You can leave a message. Left of the box, bright wall drawings catch the attention of the pilgrim.

The trail continues to ascend beneath steep rocky cliffs and reaches road nr. 4 again. [A yellow hiking sign (not Way of St. James) directs to a *Burgkapelle* (castle chapel). A 1.3 km forest trail with quite a few altitude meters leads there. Although it is called castle chapel, there never was a castle there. It is a small chapel that was first built in 1537 (replaced in 1760) as a protest against the Reformation (it is located on the catholic grounds close to the border of protestant Canton Bern). Apart from a small mountain-restaurant (*Bergwirtschaft*), there is nothing else to see. The total detour to visit the small chapel, which is not along the Way of St. James, would be 2.7 km. This book does not cover this chapel].

After a few meters along the side of the road the trail turns into the forest and starts descending. The forest is soon left behind as an alpine meadow opens up the views towards the east. The first part of the descent is on uncomfortable underground of large uneven rocks, remains of the 2'000-year-old Roman road.

The route descends through alpine highland meadows, until you reach a railway track. The train from Luzern to Interlaken uses a cogwheel to pull itself up to the Brünig Pass. From this location the second stage of the ascent to the pass starts. While ascending over 1 km the route closely follows the train track, alternating between its right and left side. At the beginning the gravel path and track are in open landscape, which quickly narrows as the forest and rocky cliffs come closer on both sides. Shortly before the pass level the route joins road nr. 4 again.

In the middle of a low stone wall, a stone pillar with the coat-of-arms of Bern marks the change from Obwalden to **Canton Bern.** From here most churches will be protestant. A narrow walking strip on the left side of the road leads you to the Brünig-Hasliberg train station (1'002 m), where you cross the platform. The route turns back to road nr. 4 and you reach the pass level (in the curve of the road).

The **Brünig Pass** is at 1'008 meters and connects the Ur-Cantons of Central Switzerland to the Bernese Highlands. It is the watershed between the Aare River (flowing south into Lake Brienz and Lake Thun) and the Sarnen Aa River (flowing north into Lake Lucerne). The road over the pass was completed in 1861, the train track in 1888. Nowadays the pass is mostly frequented by tourists visiting the Bernese Highlands, particularly on weekends. The pass level is the 4th highest altitude along the Swiss Way of St. James.

From the pass level road nr. 4 winds down the mountain to the Aare River valley 430 altitude meters lower. For 600 meters the Way of St. James closely follows road nr. 4 in its descent to a level of 973 meters. The trail is on the right side of the road on a separated gravel path (going up and down). The trail turns right, away from road nr. 4, and starts ascending again.

When you believe to have reached the highest point at the Brünig Pass (and the started descent would confirm that belief), you are in for a surprise. Instead of going down, the Way of St. James is going to ascend to a higher elevation of 1'083 meters over the next kilometer. Pay attention to the signposts. At the point of diversion from the road they are not clearly placed; you can easily overlook them and erroneously continue the descent along the road (where there is no walking space aside the heavy traffic).

At first the route ascends through alpine meadows parallel to road nr. 4 to arrive at a tarmac country road. The road turns west and opens up panoramic views of the mountain ranges on the other side of the Aare River valley.

After passing some houses the route turns into the forest and the trail narrows when you reach alpine highland meadows. Rocks protrude the grasslands and low rock walls form natural fences for cattle. About halfway the ascent the trail goes around an alpine barn.

The steep ascent continues into the forest. Steps help to conquer the altitude. The forest is deserted. The sounds of traffic have faded away, replaced by the sounds of the forest. Only few hikers pass through; the Way of St. James seems to be the only trail.

The highest point of 1'083 meters in the middle of the Uoch forest (*Uochwald*) is unspectacular, only marked by a signpost a few meters after the crest. This is the highest point of the day; the remaining 2 km are descending to Brienzwiler. The descent over the first kilometer is through the Uoch forest in a westward direction. Some parts are very steep; the trail zigzags, and steps and wooden hand railings support the hiker. The route passes by rocky cliff walls where a sign warns for falling rocks.

After crossing a wooden bridge over the Dorfbach stream, the route turns left (south), going down the mountain more or less parallel to the riverbed. The trail zigzags down the mountain, with some sections on a rocky underground that makes walking uneven and uncomfortable. After leaving the forest, open fields provide views of the town Brienzwiler and the mountain ranges on the other side of the valley. Brienzwiler lies on a highland plateau at 680 meters.

At the village's main street, the nr. 4 signpost and a white pilgrim inn sign underneath direct west (right). Instead of following these signs, make a 250-meter detour from the signposted route. Continue straight (downhill), take the first street right (*Mattengässli*), cross another road, and in the *Obermoosweg* you arrive at the reformed Church of Brienzwiler (at km 25.8).

109 Reformed Church, Brienzwiler (Reformierte Kirche)

Obermoosweg 11, 3856 Brienzwiler

Left on a bench in the open front portal of the church

The church was built to serve the local parishioners (avoiding the way to Brienz) in 1940-41. A cross on top of the small steeple is unusual for a protestant church, which would normally have a weathercock (reason is that the catholic roofer from Sachseln fit a cross).

The church is a small wooden construction (inside and outside), giving it an ambiance of an alpine chalet. A scene is carved into the chancel's back wall. Its interior is simple and has a strong scent of wood. Typical for protestant churches, there are no lusciously decorated altars, statues, paintings, or frescos. Notice the German texts on the front and back side of the horizontal beams and the stained-glass windows (one of them with the coat-of-arms of Canton Bern). The blue/green cupboard left of the chancel houses the organ (the pipes are behind its doors).

Admire the view from the church towards the mountain ranges in the northeast. Brienzwiler has around 500 inhabitants. It is a charming small village with narrow streets and dark wooden houses in chalet designs, which give the village an alpine atmosphere.

During the middle ages Brienzwiler housed a **fortified tower** belonging to the **Lords of Rudenz** (serving the House of Ringgenberg – see point of interest nr. 30, stage 9). It stood on a small hill on the western side of the village and was part of a line of fortified towers along the trade and travel route over the Brünig Pass. These towers were erected under the patronage of the Lords of Ringgenberg, who served as regional Governors of the House of Habsburg-Austria.

Little is known of the history of this tower and nothing is left of it nowadays. Similar to their tower in Giswil, it was probably built around 1200-50. In 1361 the last descendants of the House of Rudenz sold their lands in Brienzwiler to the Bernese (they retreated from their castle in Giswil only five years later – 1366). Similar to their departure from Giswil, they may have retreated because of the increasing tensions between the House of Habsburg and the Ur-Cantons, culminating in the defeat of Habsburg troops at the battle of Sempach in 1386.

The coat-of-arms of Brienzwiler still depicts this fortified tower.

Brienzwiler is mostly known for its location at the eastern entrance of the **Ballenberg Open-Air Museum** (*Freilichtmuseum*). This museum contains more than 100 original historical Swiss wooden buildings spread over 66 acres (in a forest; nothing is visible from outside their premises). They have imitated the way of life of several centuries ago (including farm animals and crafts). The museum opened in 1978 and nowadays attracts around 200'000 visitors every year. The museum is open from mid of April until end of October. A day-ticket costs CHF 28 (www.ballenberg.ch).

From the ending point

The reformed Church in Brienzwiler is the ending point of stage 8, about 250 meters aside the signposted route nr. 4.

In case you are a day-hiker, you need to walk about 1.4 km to the Brienzwiler train station (continue to follow the road down the hill to descend from the highland plateau to the Aare River level; at the end of the *Museumsstrasse* turn right, at the end of the *Brünigstrasse* right again, and keep following the main road in a westward direction). Alternatively, you can take bus nr. 151 from the bus stop called *Dorf* (beginning of the *Obermoosweg*) or from *Ballenberg-Ost* (museum down the hill to the car park). Beware, this bus goes irregularly. The bus takes 5 minutes and costs CHF 4.40.

In case you are a thru-hiker and spend the night in Brienzwiler, you can stay at the low-priced pilgrim inn that is directly along the signposted route. From the church backtrack the last 250 meters to the signposted route and turn left into the *Dorfstrasse*. The pilgrim inn (*Pilgerherberge Brienzwiler*) is in a charming old wooden building in the village center (open April until October; Dorfstrasse 4, 3856 Brienzwiler; tel. 076 473 90 93; www.herberge-brienzwiler.ch; reservation by phone). Alternatively, a small hotel (Hotel Bären; Brünigstrasse 42, 3856 Brienzwiler; tel. 033 951 13 23; no website) also provides accommodation at fair prices. Check out www.jakobsweg.ch or www.viajacobi4.ch for the accommodation possibilities.

The next Stage

Stage 9 guides you from the highland plateau down to Lake Brienz and, over the lower flanks of both the Tannhorn and Augstmatthorn, along the western side of Lake Brienz to Interlaken. Read the next chapter to find out what that entails.

Stage 9: Brienzwiler to Interlaken 27 km

The Way along Lake Brienz

Route stats

	Distance in km	*Time in hrs:min*
Signposted route nr. 4	24.3	5:30
Churches/chapels	3.0	1:40
Points of interest		0:20
Rest/lunch		1:00
Stage 9	27.3	8:30

In case you hike this stage as a daytrip, you need to add 1.4 km in Brienzwiler and 600 meters in Interlaken (from and to the train stations).

Ascent/descent/total	+875 / -977 / 1'852 altitude meters
Lowest/highest altitude	564 / 759 meters
Pathway/condition	moderate / difficult
Churches/chapels	Brienz (2), Oberried, Ringgenberg, Goldswil, Interlaken (3)
Monasteries	Former Augustinian Monastery Interlaken
Points of interest	Former Castle of Brienz, 80-meter Suspension Footbridge, Ruins Castle of Schaden, Planet Trail, Ruins Castle of Ringgenberg

Route summary

Stage 9 continues in the highlands of protestant **Canton Bern** (*Berner Oberland*).

Stage 9 guides you from the highland plateau down to Lake Brienz and, over the lower flanks of both the Tannhorn and Augstmatthorn, along the western side of Lake Brienz to Interlaken.

In stage 9 you hike the full length of lake Brienz, along its western shore in the southwestern direction. The routes alongside Lake Sarnen and Lake Lungern may have been flat, but this is not the case for the route along Lake Brienz. Stage 9 follows a route with a high number of altitude meters.

From Brienzwiler the first 4 km of the route are on the highland plateau. After a 1 km gradual descent to Brienz, the route stays along the lake for about 3 km. The following 5 km the trail goes up and down the flanks of a mountain. From Brienz the route follows an ascending hiking trail on the southern flanks of the Tannhorn mountain, reaching a first high point of 759 meters. From there the trail descends to Oberried, where the route stays at the lake level for about 2 km. The subsequent 4 km the route ascends and descends along the flanks of a mountain again. From Oberried the trail ascends the flanks of the Augstmatthorn, reaching a second high point of 748 meters, from where the trail descends again to the lake level in Niederried. Following some minor ascents and descents along the shore of Lake Brienz, the village Ringgenberg is reached at km 22. At km 24 you reach the end of Lake Brienz. The lake flows into the Aare River, where the route enters Interlaken and ends at the former Augustinian monastery at km 27.

The hiking trails are easy, the ascents and descents not steep, and the higher altitudes provide panoramic views over Lake Brienz and the surrounding mountains. The 80-meter suspension footbridge over the *Unterweidligraben* at km 11.7 is an adventurous highlight. Several 13th century castle ruins stand along the western shore, signifying the route's importance as the medieval trade and travel route.

Getting to the starting point

Today's starting point in Brienzwiler is at the reformed Church. In case you spent the night in Brienzwiler, just continue from the signposted route in the village.

In case you hike stage 9 as a daytrip, you need to walk 1.4 km from the Brienzwiler train station (in the Aare valley) up the mountain to the Brienzwiler highland plateau. From the Brienzwiler train station walk east and follow road nr. 8 (direction Brünig Pass) up the flanks of the mountain. At the first road turn left (*Brünigstrasse*) and follow the signs to the Ballenberg Parking (eastern gate). After an s-curve take the first left again (to the parking) and keep following the s-curving *Museumstrasse* up the flanks of the mountain. After the parking (left) you reach the church (right). Alternatively, it may be easier to take bus nr. 151 from the Brienzwiler train station to bus stop *Brienzwiler Dorf*. Beware, only the bus at 08:00 has a direct connection, taking only 3 minutes (CHF 4.40). Connections at all other times are indirect and take at least 25 minutes.

Route Map and Profile

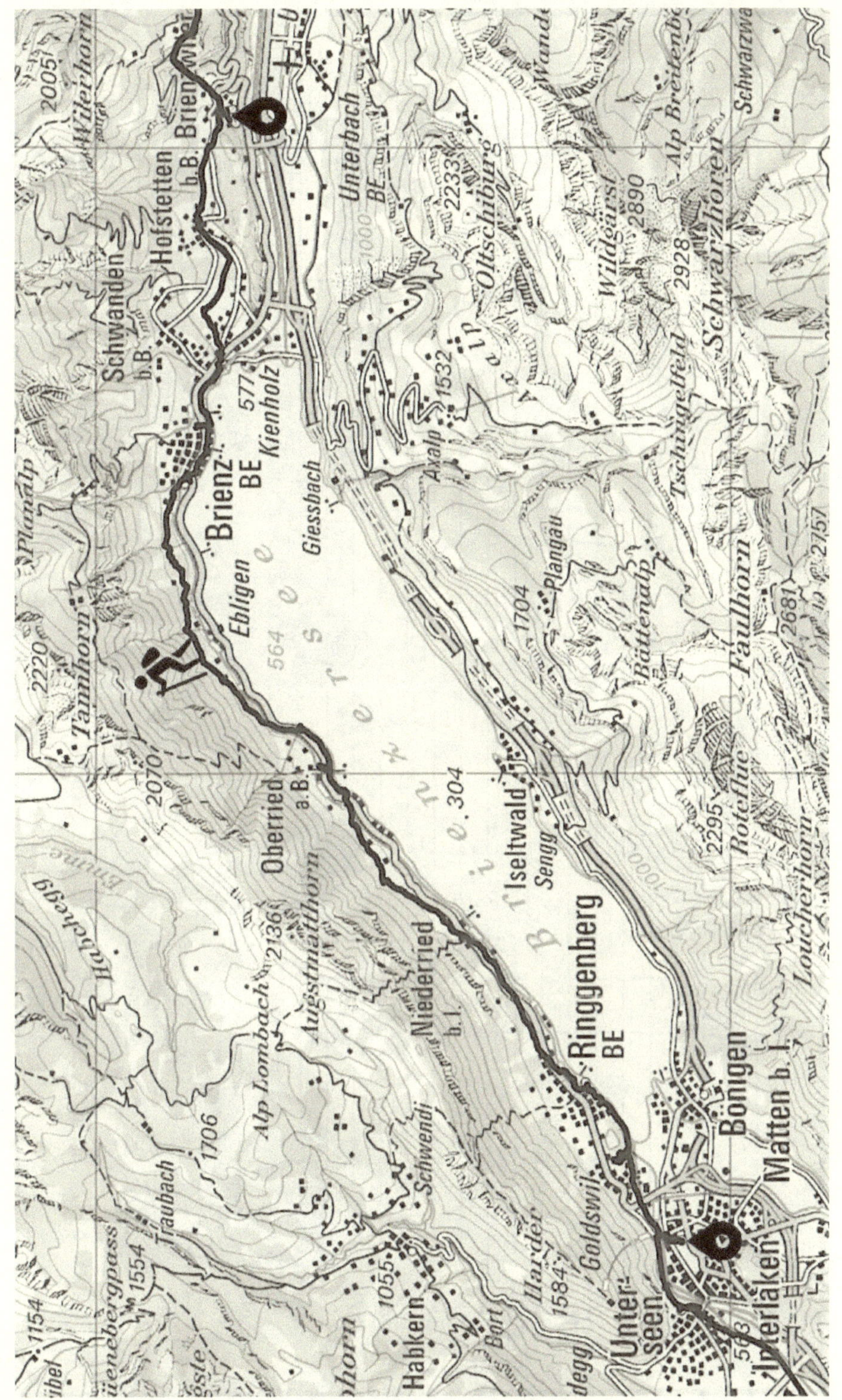
Brienzwiler
Hofstetten b.B.
Schwanden b.B.
Brienz BE
577
Kienholz
Unterbach BE
Giessbach
Ebligen
564
Brienzersee
Axalp
1532
2233
Oltschiburg
Wildgärst
2890
2928
Schwarzhorn
Alp Breitenboden
Tschingelfeld
Faulhorn
2681
2757
Plangäu
1704
Bättenalp
Planalp
Tannhorn
2220
2005
Wilerhorn
2070
Oberried a.B.
304
Iseltwald
Sengg
Ringgenberg BE
Augstmatthorn
2136
Alp Lombach
Niederried b.I.
Hardergrat
2295
Roteflue
Loucherhorn
1706
Traubach
Habkern
1055
Schwendi
Harder
1584
Goldswil
Bönigen
Matten b.I.
Unterseen
Interlaken
Grüenebergpass
1554
1154

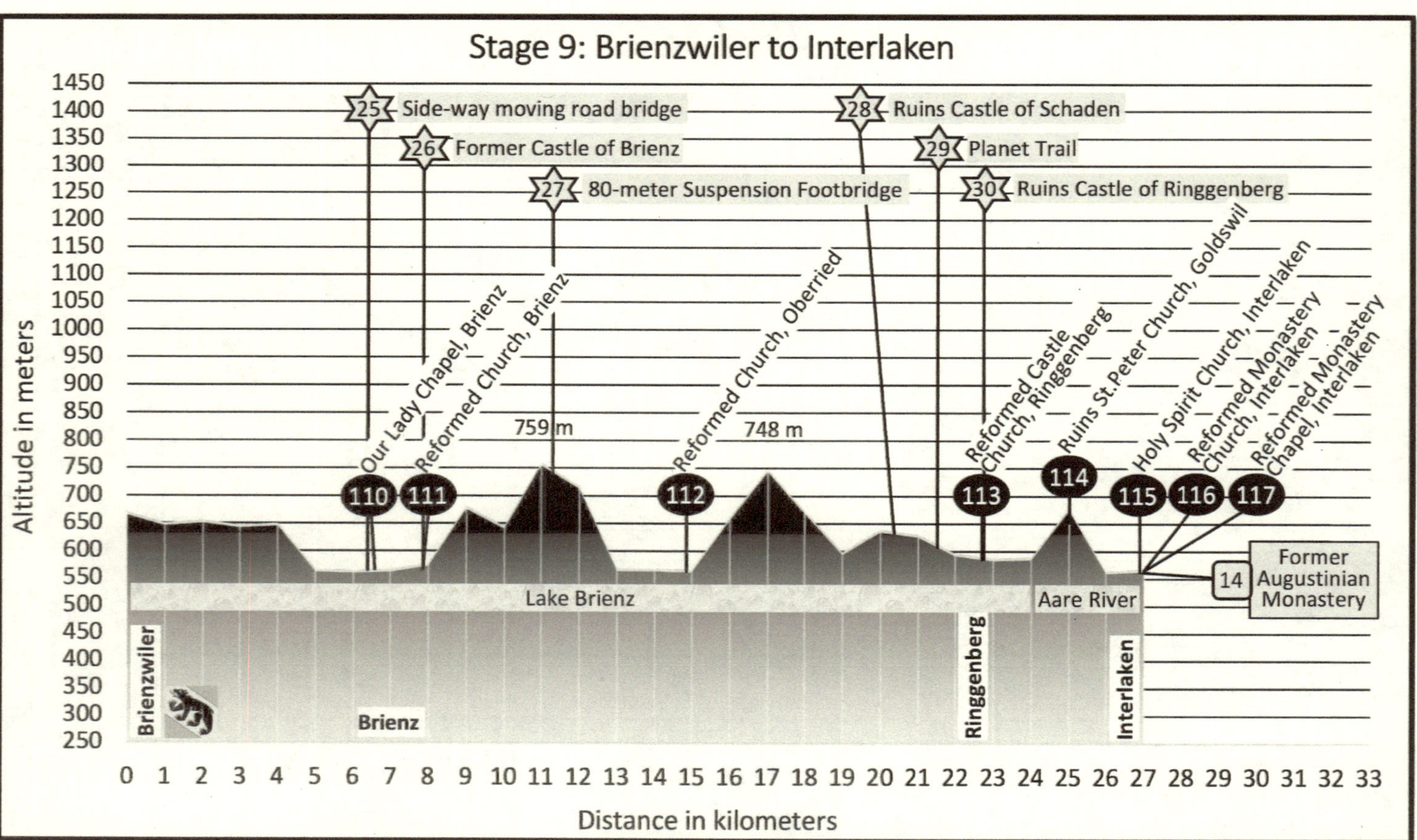
Stage 9: Brienzwiler to Interlaken
25 Side-way moving road bridge
26 Former Castle of Brienz
27 80-meter Suspension Footbridge
28 Ruins Castle of Schaden
29 Planet Trail
30 Ruins Castle of Ringgenberg
110 Our Lady Chapel, Brienz
111 Reformed Church, Brienz
112 Reformed Church, Oberried
113 Reformed Castle Church, Ringgenberg
114 Ruins St.Peter Church, Goldswil
115 Holy Spirit Church, Interlaken
116 Reformed Monastery Church, Interlaken
117 Reformed Monastery Chapel, Interlaken
14 Former Augustinian Monastery
759 m
748 m
Lake Brienz
Aare River
Brienzwiler
Brienz
Ringgenberg
Interlaken
Altitude in meters
1450
1400
1350
1300
1250
1200
1150
1100
1050
1000
950
900
850
800
750
700
650
600
550
500
450
400
350
300
250
Distance in kilometers
0 1 2 3 4 5 6 7 8 9 10 11 12 13 14 15 16 17 18 19 20 21 22 23 24 25 26 27 28 29 30 31 32 33

Hiking the Route

After leaving Brienzwiler the Way of St. James continues on a gradually descending local tarmac road through the forest for 500 meters. The signs direct right and then left again, continuing through patches of forest and meadows, until you reach the village Hofstetten bei Brienz. The path is more or less flat, as you stay on the highland plateau. You pass by farms and to the left you can see a long-stretched carpark along a tree line. It is the western car park of the Ballenberg open-air museum (*Freilichtmuseum*). The museum is behind the tree line. To the right you see mountain ranges with an altitude of 2'200 meters.

For 1 km the route follows the road through the village Hofstetten bei Brienz. You pass by a factory (*Trauffer*) that produces traditional Swiss wood-carved animals (particularly cows). Notice the direction signpost with a wood-carved farmer and cows. The route turns right and follows a gravel road through a patch of forest and meadows for 1 km, until you reach the next village Schwanden bei Brienz. After 4 km on the highland plateau the route starts its decent to the level of Lake Brienz. You have a first view of the lake.

Lake Brienz is 12th in size of the Swiss lakes, with a length of 14 km, a maximum width of 2.8 km, and an average depth of 173 meters (maximum depth 260 meters). Its surface is at 564 meters above sea level. The lake is named after the biggest town on its shore, Brienz. The primary inflow comes from the Aare River at the northern end of the lake. At its southern end lies Interlaken, from where the Aare River flows into Lake Thun.

The route descends from the highland plateau through a patch of forest and on a slightly elevated gravel path. At main road nr. 6 (a continuation of road nr. 4), the route turns right and 100 meters later left. The road descends underneath the railway track to the level of the lake. You arrive at a recreational swimming area (*Strandbad*), where you turn right to follow a gravel path along lake Brienz for the next kilometer. You walk on a narrow path between the lake and the train track. The route passes by recreational and water sports areas. In the distance you can see the town Brienz, boat pier, and train station around the curve of the lake.

Continue to follow route nr. 4 past a small boat port and along the lake. The route passes by the Brienz train station and boat pier. Along the promenade you arrive at a wooden statue representing a laughing pilgrim. At this location you need to briefly leave the signposted route to get to the first chapel. Turn right and follow a narrow gravel path up the hill, across road nr. 6, and on the embankment of a stream.

25

On your right you have a unique **side-way moving road bridge** over the *Trachtbach* stream. In 2005 a fixed bridge caused mud and debris flowing down the stream to accumulate against the bridge, which flooded the area around it. To prevent this from happening again, a side-way moving road bridge was built. In case of significant debris flowing downstream, the bridge can be moved by 25 meters (in the direction of the lake), doubling the space for the debris to flow underneath the bridge.

Up the hill turn left at the road and you arrive at the Our Lady Chapel (at km 6.5).

Our Lady Chapel, Brienz (Mutter Gottes Kapelle) **110**

- Feldstrasse 1, 3855 Brienz
- Our Lady, Four Evangelists
- The chapel was built to serve the Catholics of Brienz in 1939-40. Until that time Catholics had to travel a long way to either Interlaken (west) or Meiringen (east) to attend a service. The chapel is a wooden construction, inside and outside, and its interior footprint is very similar to the wooden reformed church of Brienzwiler (built in the same years).
- Statues representing the Four Evangelists (Matthew, Mark, Luke, and John) decorate the outer wall of the low bell tower. Wood dominates the simple interior, which is logical, because Brienz is well-known for its woodcarving since the beginning of the 19th century.

From the chapel walk back the same way to the lake level with the signposted route nr. 4. Continue to follow the gravel path along the lake promenade. You pass by an oversized statue of a cow, a small boat port, the Brienz Village (*dorf*) boat pier, hotels and restaurants, and a fountain. When you look across the lake towards the southwestern end, you see where you are heading (Interlaken).

In the distance you can also see the reformed Church of Brienz, standing on a small elevation against the background of a 2'000-meter-high mountain range. After 900 meters along the lake's shore the route sign leads away from the water. It will be another 6 km before the route returns to the lake's shore. You cross road nr. 6 and need to briefly (150 meters) leave the signposted route to arrive at the reformed Church of Brienz (at km 7.9).

111 **Reformed Church, Brienz** (Reformierte Kirche)

- Kirchbühl, 3855 Brienz
- St. Peter and Paul, St. Christopher
- On a table behind the door of the right side-room, before entering the church's nave
- The church was built in several phases. A first wooden church, dedicated to St. Peter and Paul, was built by the Lords of Brienz as part of their castle (see below) before 1130. From around 1130-50 this wooden construction was replaced by a church in stone. The chancel was rebuilt and enlarged in 1519. During the Reformation in 1528 Bern enforced the conversion from Catholicism to Protestantism. All catholic decorations (altars, statues, paintings, frescos, organ, and so forth) were removed. Since 1528 the church has an austere interior. In 1679-80 the nave was lengthened by 6 meters, the front portal, gallery, and rooms were added, and the sacristy was built. Its present appearance dates from this expansion in 1680 and renovations in 1939-40. Notice the bricked-up entrance next to the current northern door. The oldest parts of the church are its bell tower and a small bell dating from 1473.
- The bell tower dates from around 1130-50 and has clear Romanesque features: thick walls (1.5 meter at the base) and narrow Lombard arched windows that increase from two to four as the level increases.

  The outer walls have partially recovered frescos dating from the 15th century. The southern wall has a large fresco depicting St. Christopher, which was discovered and renovated in 1976. It served as a beacon protecting the sailors on Lake Brienz. The northern wall had three frescos, of which two were reasonably recovered.

  The interior is modern, in contradiction to the outside appearance. The church has a typical protestant interior, limited to a pulpit, baptismal font, and organ.

The **former Castle of Brienz** was probably built at the beginning of the 12th century (around or after 1100) by the Lords of Brienz, who resided in a residential fortified tower on the hill of the church. They were regional Governors of the House of Habsburg-Austria and from their castle they controlled trade and traffic north of Lake Brienz to the Brünig Pass. Around 1230-40 the House of Habsburg split the Governorship of the region between the Lords of Brienz and the Lords of Raron (the latter were relatives from the southern Canton Valais). As a result, the Lords of Brienz gave up their fortified tower and relocated to Ringgenberg (about 15 km to the south), where they had another castle built (see point of interest nr. 30 below). Little is known of what happened with the castle after they abandoned it. Presumably it fell into ruins and its stones may have been used to expand the church. The last time remains of ruins were mentioned in official documents was at the beginning of the 19th century; nowadays nothing is left of it.

The hill of the church provides superb views over its surroundings, the lake, the dark wooden chalets, and mountain ranges. Back on the route, the path goes through narrow streets between dark wooden chalets, up the hill. After a left and right, the route crosses the railway track, bridges the riverbed of a stream coming down the mountain (*Milibach*), and leaves Brienz behind. The ascent is on a tarmac road, past meadows, that quickly changes to a gravel dirt path.

Wide views over lake Brienz (left) and the mountain ranges (right) make it a wonderful hiking experience. The dirt road changes into a narrow hiking trail through the forest with some gradual descents, as the trail crosses the second riverbed (*Hellgraben*), 400 meters later the third (*Ofenbielengraben*), and 250 meters later the fourth.

The route follows forested hiking trails that are on the lower parts of the Tannhorn mountain range; there are no footpaths along the shore of the lake (only road nr. 6). After a short open field, the trail continues through the forest with a steep ascent and 1 km later crosses the next riverbed (*Mattengraben*). About 500 meters later you reach a first high point of 759 meters (about 11 km into stage 9) in the middle of the forest. The view is blocked by trees. About 200 meters later you arrive at an 80-meter suspension footbridge.

27

The **80-meter suspension footbridge** covers the gorge of the *Unterweidligraben*. The footbridge is north of the village Ebligen, about 2 km east of Oberried and 3.5 km west of Brienz. Many mountain bikers and hikers take this path specifically to experience crossing this wobbly hanging footbridge (bikers need to dismount; horses are not allowed). It is an adventure to walk over it: it swings left and right; it bounces up and down; it makes metal-cracking sounds; while crossing a broad and deep gorge. Not for the fainthearted, but it is Swiss-engineering-safe and the only such spectacular experience on the Swiss Way of St. James.

The bridge is disassembled (floor and side panels are removed) on 1st November and assembled again on 30th March every year. This avoids destruction of the bridge in case of debris avalanches during winter time. In case you should pilgrimage when the bridge has been disassembled, you need to take a different lower route at the trail-split right after the *Mattengraben*. This is then appropriately signposted.

The location provides panoramic views over the eastern part of Lake Brienz, the town Brienz, and the mountain ranges in the east. The following 2 km the forest trail descends to the level of Lake Brienz. The forest blocks the views of the lake and mountains, while only one small stream is crossed. The path descends on a broad gravel path; walking is easy, but watch out for mountain bikers.

At km 12.9 the signposted route suddenly turns left, away from the broad gravel path. The left turn is through a narrow opening in the bushes; you can easily overlook it when not noticing the nr. 4 signpost directing left. A narrow forest trail descends steeply over 300 meters, until you get out of the forest and alongside the railway track. For another 300 meters the route follows the railway track, until reaching the *Hirscherenbach.* The route turns left and passes underneath the track to road nr. 6. You cross the road, after which the path descends to the lake's shore.

At km 13.7 you are back alongside Lake Brienz, after having walked from a 566-meter elevation at the lake level in Brienz to 759 meters alongside the mountain and back again to 566 meters in Oberried, over a distance of about 6 km.

For 900 meters the route follows a path along the shore. The path alternates between gravel and concrete. It becomes concrete when it is a causeway, above the surface of the water. You pass by many boat houses and see the tracks onto which boats are lowered into the water. You pass by a playground and the Oberried boat pier.

To visit the church of Oberried you need to leave route nr. 4 and make a small detour. Turn right, steeply up a small road between houses, cross road nr. 6, continue the ascent, and after 250 meters you arrive at the reformed Church of Oberried (at km 14.8).

112 **Reformed Church, Oberried** (Reformierte Kirche)

- Grauechstrasse 1, 3854 Oberried am Brienzersee
- On a table in the front portal of the church
- The church was built in 1967-68. It is in the typical 1960s-70s modern and concrete style with a free-standing bell tower. Inlaid round rocks in the outer walls give it a special appearance.
- Its interior is as austere as can be expected from a protestant church. Though it has one special feature, not seen at any of the other churches along the Swiss Way of St. James: the large glass window behind the communion table (normally the chancel wall is bricked or has only small windows with stained-glass to ensure focus on the altar).

  In this church the large window behind the communion table provides the parishioners a unique view of the mountains, peaking at 2'040 meters. Though a large wooden cross outside the window is probably meant to attract their focus, not the mountain. In winter the view of the snow-capped mountain behind the chancel must be spectacular.

The front of the church offers a nice view over Lake Brienz, due to its elevated position. Walk back the same route down the hill to the signposted route nr. 4.

For 500 meters the tarmac path continues alongside the lake. Looking back, you have a great view of the lakeside village Oberried. The route crosses the *Louwigraben* riverbed and turns land inward (right). The route zigzags up, crosses road nr. 6, and continues its ascent on a tarmac road through grasslands. With the increasing elevation the views over Lake Brienz and the mountains on the other side increasingly improve. Upon entering a forest, the tarmac turns into gravel. Though relatively steep, the path is broad and easy to walk on. The forest blocks the view, though some openings between the trees provide views of the lake below. Patches of forest alternate with patches of meadow, while you cross the *Grytgraben* riverbed.

The path turns into a narrow forest trail winding up the mountain flank. You cross the *Farlouwigraben* riverbed, after which you reach the second high point of the day at 748 meters at km 17. Look up the mountain along the river bed: the mountain seems to open its mouth – a large cave opening is visible. The rocky forest trail becomes a gravel path. As the descent over 2 km into the village Niederried continues, the path becomes a gravel road and then tarmac. The route passes through the outskirts of Niederried, without going down to the lake level (there is no church in the village). The following 2.5 km the signposted route nr. 4 is more or less parallel to road nr. 6. The route goes through a forest and at km 20.2 you are in close vicinity of the ruins of the Castle of Schaden. These ruins are not on your trail, but about 200 meters higher up a cliff on the mountain (not visible because of the forest). From the signposted route there is no direct path to these ruins (it would require taking a different trail from Niederried, about 1 km back).

The **Ruins of the Castle of Schaden** (*Schadenburg*) have unknown origins. There are no medieval papers that documented this castle. It is likely that the Lords of Brienz had it built to control trade and traffic between Interlaken and Brienz. They were regional Governors of the House of Habsburg-Austria since the beginning of the 12th century (around or after 1100) and already built a castle in Brienz at that time.

They probably had the Castle of Schaden built during the 12th century, long before they relocated their residence from Brienz to Ringgenberg. After they had their own residential castle built in Ringgenberg in 1230-40, they might have given up on this first castle (in an isolated location), which subsequently fell into ruins. The relatively short existence can explain the absence of its medieval documentation.

The strange name Schaden was derived from a legend of Schadenfreude (joy derived from someone else's misfortune). According to legend, the Lord of Brienz wanted relations with a young girl, which her father forbade. As they were fleeing, the Lord killed the girl with an arrow. When the Lord was having his castle constructed many years later, he hired several workmen. One of them was the father of the girl he had killed. Out of revenge the father killed the Lord during the construction of the castle. This legend not only provided the name for the ruins, but according to some people also explained why the castle's construction was never finished.

After the forest the route goes through open fields with a gradual descent into Ringgenberg. Along the way you pass by a fish farm, a boulder deposit area, and a sawmill. The views toward the lake and mountains are rewarding.

The hiking route between Oberried and Ringgenberg follows the **Planet Trail** (*Planetenweg*). The sun is placed in Ringgenberg and all the planets are placed along a distance of 7.7 km of the hiking route, in such a way that they represent a scaled distance to the sun. Information tables and models along the planet trail explain the solar system. This planet trail goes in two directions, mirroring the line-up of the planets from the sun in Ringgenberg. The other direction is from Ringgenberg, past Interlaken, and along the Aare River to Lake Thun, also over a distance of 7.7 km.

In Ringgenberg the route converges with road nr. 6 and crosses the road to reach the Ringgenberg train station, from where it briefly follows the track. The route turns right, back to road nr. 6, takes a left to cross the track, and arrives at the reformed Castle Church of Ringgenberg (at km 22.7). The church is on a hill; 92 steps lead to the entrance.

Reformed Castle Church, Ringgenberg (Burg Kirche) 113

- Kirchgasse 10, 3852 Ringgenberg
- On the black stones at the right wall of the low-ceilinged entrance corridor
- The church was built in 1670. The reason for building this church was the abandonment of the old parish church in Goldswil, a village 1.5 km west of Ringgenberg (see below). The church was built into the existing ruins of the former castle of the Lords of Ringgenberg (see below). This had the advantage that the fortified walls, watchtower, and stones of the ruins could be used for the construction of the church. The church occupies the western half of the rectangular footprint of the former castle. The castle has been in ruins since 1381; three centuries later the church was built inside these ruins. The castle's old watchtower with access gate was restored into the church's bell tower and heightened to hold the bells. The difference in architectural style between the old watchtower and the upper bell part is clearly visible. An extensive renovation of the church was undertaken in 1964.
- When you enter the church, you go through a low cave-like corridor. This used to be the castle's access gate at the base of the tower. The length of this corridor corresponds to the size of the former watchtower. Because of the rectangular

shape of the hill, the church has an orientation to the northeast instead of to the east. The interior of the church has the usual protestant style, with a pulpit, organ (1837), and baptismal font also serving as communion table.

When you walk around the church you reach the castle ruins.

The **Ruins of the Castle of Ringgenberg** have their foundations in 1230-40. At that time the Lords of Brienz relocated from Brienz to Ringgenberg and had a new castle built. From then on they were known as the Lords of Ringgenberg. They served the House of Habsburg-Austria as regional Governor and not only oversaw and controlled the local population, but also trade and traffic that came from/to the Brünig Pass along Lake Brienz. For 140 years (1240-1381) they were the main regional rulers with a distinctive influence on local politics. By the middle of the 14th century they became financially distressed, and had to pledge their castle and lands to the Augustinian Monastery of Interlaken in 1351. After decades of increasing financial difficulties, a new family member became ruler in 1378, and increased taxes. This led to a revolt of peasants from the whole region, including Giswil/Obwalden. The peasants looted and burned down the castle in 1381. Though a court settled the dispute (called the Ringgenberg Dispute – *Ringgenberger Handel*) and the ruler was reinstated, the power had shifted to the disadvantage of the Lord of Ringgenberg. By then the House of Habsburg was already significantly weakened and the Lord of Ringgenberg, as their representative, was not able to maintain a leading role anymore. The ruler did not have the finances to rebuilt the castle and relocated to Bern in 1386, after the House of Habsburg had lost the battle of Sempach. The castle was abandoned, fell into ruins, and was never inhabited again.

The church occupies the western half of the rectangular footprint of the former castle. The middle part contained the courtyard, which included the church's cemetery from 1695 until the middle of the 20th century (for which the level of the courtyard was raised by 2 meters). The whole area was surrounded by a high fortified wall. At the eastern end are the remains of a large residential tower. This tower contained several levels and its entrance was on the first floor, accessible by wooden covered stairs along the inside of the fortified wall (nowadays accessible using the metal staircase, built during the renovations in 2006-08). From around 1300 the upper level functioned as a large ballroom for banquets and parties. Inside the tower you can walk on the metal gallery to the upper level, which used to be the level of the ballroom.

Do you see the rows of small holes at the top of the tower on its southern side? They probably were brooding niches for pigeons, which were used in medieval falconry. The ruins were last renovated to halt further dilapidation in 2006-08.

The tower offers great panoramic views of the surroundings. Information tables (in German and English) explain the history of the castle and church.

From the castle church the route nr. 4 continues westward on a tarmac road parallel to the railway track and shoreline. The route passes by a row of houses and enters a short patch of forest. While the railway track passes through a tunnel, the route follows a narrow gravel path along rocky and overhanging cliffs parallel to the tunnel. The cliffs are very close to the lake and force the pilgrimage route to a narrow trail hewn into the base of these cliffs. A low stone wall separates the path from the train track that comes out of the tunnel. From the elevated position you have a good view over the western end of Lake Brienz.

The railway track turns left to cross to the southern side of the Aare River. The signposted route stays on the northern side of the river. Where the train track bridges the Aare River, leading to the Interlaken-East (*Ost*) train station, you reach the southwestern end of Lake Brienz. Here the lake flows into the Aare River (which flows into Lake Thun 5.5 km later). At this location you need to briefly leave the signposted route to get to the ruins of the church of Goldswil. Turn right on a 90-meter trail that leads to the *Talstrasse.* Follow the *Talstrasse* up the hill for 170 meters. Turn right on a trail that zigzags up the forested hill for 460 meters and you arrive at the ruins of the St. Peter Church in Goldswil (at km 24.7).

114 Ruins of St. Peter Church, Goldswil (Ruinen St. Peter Kirche)

Goldswilhubel, 3805 Goldswil

St. Peter

The ruins have their origins in the 10th-11th centuries, making it one of the first churches in the region (even before the Augustinian monastery of Interlaken was founded in 1130). A first small church with a semicircular chancel was built on top of a cemetery that was on the hill since the 7th-9th centuries. The Romanesque bell tower was built on top of the semicircular chancel around 1050-80. Around 1100 a rectangular church (without a separate chancel) was constructed on the foundations of the first church and an antechamber was added on the western side.

Like all other important medieval constructions along the western side of Lake Brienz, the church, dedicated to St. Peter, was built by the Lords of Brienz. In 1240 the Lords of Brienz/Ringgenberg transferred the patronage to the Augustinian monastery of Interlaken (at the time the Lords relocated from Brienz to Ringgenberg). From 1240 until the Reformation a priest from this monastery held the services at the church.

During the Reformation in 1528 the Augustinian monastery of Interlaken was closed, patronage transferred to Bern, and Bern appointed a protestant pastor to the church. The conversion from catholic worship to Protestantism was enforced, which resulted in the removal and destruction of all catholic icons. After 1528 the church was reconstructed in accordance with protestant worship and a sacristy was attached.

A century and a half later the church was in poor condition; the care that the monastery had provided was replaced by neglect (too far away from the patrons in Bern). It was decided to build a new church inside the ruins of the former castle of Ringgenberg. After the St. Peter church was abandoned in 1671, it fell into ruins. Its stones were probably used as building materials for neighboring houses. Only the tower remained relatively untouched. The cemetery was transferred to Ringgenberg in 1695 and the pastor relocated in 1729.

Renovations of the site and tower were undertaken in 1940-45 and 2015-17.

The restored tower has clear Romanesque features: thick walls; narrow window openings; increasing number of window openings as the levels increase; and decorative Lombard arches. This Romanesque tower is unique in Canton Bern. The appearance of the younger bell tower of the 12th century reformed church in Brienz, which the Lords of Brienz also built, is somewhat similar.

One more feature of the tower is of interest. The highest level of the tower used to contain two statues that served as pillars for the lake-side window openings. Replicas of these statues are now on display inside the base of the tower (the originals are kept at the town hall of Goldswil). The two porous tuff-stone, clearly male figures have their arms stretched out, as they carried part of the roof. These statues represented pagan superstition to provide protection for the church and its parishioners. This demonstrates that Catholicism was not yet fully accepted in the Bernese Highlands during the 10th-11th centuries. It is unique to see such pagan symbols integrated in an 11th century church/tower in Switzerland. This is rare and the only one along the Swiss Way of St. James.

The hilltop provides a great view over the Aare River and Interlaken. From the ruins follow the same way back to the signposted route. The route nr. 4 continues on the northern (right) bank of the Aare River, through the residential area of Goldswil and underneath the elevated road nr. 6 that crosses the river. The final meters of stage 9 along the Aare River are relaxing and easy, offering nice views of the mountains in the south (left). As the lake, the Aare has a beautiful turquoise color.

On the southern bank of the river you see the mooring pier of Lake Brienz's cruise boats. This pier is directly at the Interlaken-East (*Ost*) train station, providing an easy connection between boat and train. The train track crosses back over the river (from southern to northern bank), going from the Interlaken-East train station to the Interlaken-West station. The footpath passes underneath the low iron railway bridge, after which you get to a road (*Brienzstrasse*) that crosses the Aare River.

On the right you see the ground station of the **Harderbahn**; it is a cable track that pulls a wagon to the Harder mountain ridge at 1'305 meters. A panorama restaurant (resembling a small castle) provides unique views over Interlaken, the lakes, and southern Jungfrau mountain ranges.

At the location of the road bridge (*Beaurivage-Brücke*) you need to leave the signposted route nr. 4 (you come back to this location at the start of stage 10). This signposted route continues along the northern bank of the Aare, going around Interlaken. The end of stage 9, however, is at the two large churches and the former monastery in the center of Interlaken, for which you need to cross over the Aare to its southern bank.

Right of the bridge, on the southern river bank, is the Grand Hotel Beau Rivage, dating from the Belle Époque. Turn right at the front side of the hotel (*Höheweg*) and 150 meters later left. You pass by the **Interlaken Japanese Garden** (right side; worthwhile a short visit) and arrive at the catholic Holy Spirit Church in Interlaken at the end of the street (at km 27.2).

115 Holy Spirit Church, Interlaken (Heiliggeist Kirche)

Schlossstrasse 4, 3800 Interlaken

St. Mary, Brother Klaus

On a St. James scallop on a table left of the main entrance

The catholic church was built to serve the Catholics of Interlaken and surrounding municipalities in 1906-08. Since the Reformation in 1528 Canton Bern had prohibited catholic services. After 1842 catholic services were allowed again and held in the small chapel of the former Augustinian monastery in Interlaken (1842-64). When this chapel became too small, as the number of Catholics and tourists attending the catholic services increased, the nave of the former monastery church was used for services (1864-1908).

To fulfil the wish for an own church, a large church was built in 1906-08, after many years of collections and donations. The large size of the church caused a big financial burden on the parish; no money was left for interior decorations, an organ, a clock, or bells. Notice the small protruding roof up the bell tower and the hole in the wall: the planned clock was never installed. Three bells were installed after a Spanish tourist donated money in 1925. The organ was purchased in 1934.

The building looks old from the outside, but its interior is modern and simple with hardly any decorations. The church was in regular need of interior renovations, resulting in major restorations in 1967-68, 1990, and 2013. Notice the wood-carved statue representing Brother Klaus on the wall. Left of the entrance is a small Virgin Mary side-chapel, with blackened walls from the smoke of candles.

From the catholic church continue 50 meters to the south and you arrive at the reformed Church of the former Augustinian monastery of Interlaken (at km 27.3).

Reformed Augustinian Monastery Church, Interlaken (Schloss Kirche) 116

Schloss, 3800 Interlaken

Initially the church was catholic, built as part of the Augustinian monastery (see below) at the beginning of the 12th century. After enforcing the Reformation Canton Bern closed the monastery and its church in 1528. The interior of the church was emptied and all religious icons were removed. Subsequently the chancel was used as a garage for carts, the cellar for storing wine barrels, and the nave for storing wheat and corn. In 1563 the chancel and nave were separated by a wall, dividing the warehouses.

Since the Reformation the town Interlaken did not have a church that was in use anymore. Instead, the Protestants had to go to the reformed church in either Unterseen (1.5 km to the west) or Gsteig (3 km to the south).

In the following centuries there was little care or attention for the former church building. Lack of maintenance dilapidated the building, while its interior became rundown, caused by centuries of storage and neglect.

It was not until more than 300 years later that the space of the former chancel was restored for worship. In 1842 the chancel was restored and back in use for English protestant services, serving the increasing number of English tourists who visited Interlaken (and did not want to go to the church in Unterseen or Gsteig). When the local protestant population wanted to attend a protestant service in Swiss-German, they still had to go to Unterseen or Gsteig until 1911.

From 1864 until 1908 the catholic parish used the run-down nave as a temporary church for their services. Canton Bern allowed them to use the nave under the condition that the Canton did not need to contribute in the costs to repair and restore the nave.

After the catholic parish moved out of the nave into their own church in 1908, the Canton looked for a renewed use of the nave. In 1909 Canton Bern turned the church over to the protestant parish Gsteig-Interlaken. They demolished the old nave and built a new one in 1909-11. Thus, from 1911 the local Protestants could attend the services in the nave of the old monastery church.

It was not until 1950 that the wall separating the chancel from the nave was demolished and the church was 'complete' again. This required new windows in the chancel and in the same year the well-known Swiss stained-glass artist Paul Zehnder created the new windows.

Have a closer look at these stained-glass windows. They are beautiful depictions of biblical scenes. The chancel has unusual dimensions compared to the nave: the vaulted ceiling is much higher and the chancel is unusually long (it must have had a long quire). It is so long that they placed 12 rows of pews that face the back side of the communion table. The nave was renovated in 2000, the chancel in 2018. As you see the church today, its restored Gothic chancel dates from the 14th century, whereas the neo-Gothic nave dates from 1911.

From the reformed monastery church walk a few meters south and you are at the former monastery's inner courtyard. On the eastern side of the courtyard you arrive at the reformed Chapel of the former Augustinian monastery (at km 27.3).

117 Reformed Augustinian Monastery Chapel, Interlaken (Schloss Kapelle)

Schloss, 3800 Interlaken

The chapel was built as part of the Augustinian monastery (see below) around 1450. The small chapel is integrated in the former monastery's compound and lies behind the cloisters, which the monks used to walk from one building to another. The chapel was the house chapel of the monks, until the Reformation in 1528. In 1842-64 the former monastery's small chapel was used for catholic services, after which it was used by the Russian Church. The last renovations were undertaken in 1972-73 and 2003. Nowadays the chapel belongs to the reformed parish of Interlaken.

Notice the beautifully restored (1973) Gothic masonry in the arches of the cloisters. These are the only remaining cloisters in Canton Bern (all others were destroyed during or after the Reformation, when the Bernese secularized, demolished, or reutilized all monasteries). The chapel is small and without decorations.

You are now at the center of the former Augustinian Monastery. Its history is as follows.

Former Augustinian Monastery, Interlaken (Schloss Interlaken) 14

Schloss, 3800 Interlaken

Augustinian Order

The Augustinian monastery was established around 1130 by Lord Seliger of Oberhofen, who resided at a castle at the northern shore of Lake Thun. The monastery was a Collegiate canon-regular led by a provost, under the Rule of St. Augustine (*Augustiner-Chorherren-Propstei*). To establish the small monastery, the Lord of Oberhofen donated lands and built their first housing. Around three years later (1133) patronage of the small monastery changed to Emperor Lothar III of the Roman-German Empire. As an Empire-monastery it started to accumulate lands in the Bernese Highlands. Patronage changed to the City-Republic of Bern in 1224.

By the end of the 13th century the monastery was the biggest landowner in the region. In many parts of the region the monastery replaced the former noblemen as the new owner of the lands and the people who lived on them (serfdom). They received income from fishing rights, forests, vineyards, lease of lands to famers, existing and new churches, donations, and so forth. Through hard work of the monks the monastery became the feudal powerhouse of the Bernese Highlands in little over a century. They became the main financiers and drivers of the regional economy. They were well-known for their management and development of lands (agriculture, cattle) and related rights, but gave little contribution to the scientific and intellectual development of society.

For several centuries the monastery also housed a convent. At its peak it was a double-monastery, housing around 300 Augustinian nuns and 30 monks. Becoming a nun was often the only choice for girls of large peasant families (women had no professions): the convent provided security, care, education, and food. The nuns were generally confined to the convent, where they established a school, cared for the ill, and performed needlework (sewing, weaving). As the Orders were separate institutions, the monks did not share their wealth with the nuns; the convent stayed poor and the nuns lived under much worse conditions compared to the monks. The two separate classes led to intense conflicts triggered by the nuns, who saw how their neighbors lived.

Decline set in from around 1350. The large landownership and extensive rights resulted in debts and continuing clashes and disputes with local Lords, peasants, and the neighboring village Unterseen. The monastery became disorganized and the Rule of St. Augustine (chastity, poverty, and obedience) was often broken, causing escalating conflicts and tensions between the nuns and the monks. The number of nuns and monks steadily decreased. In 1472 the buildings of the nuns burned down, which occurred again in 1479. During the middle ages women were considered the source of all temptation, so the nuns received a large part of the blame for the escalation. At the request of Bern, the convent was closed by order of the Pope in 1484 (when less than 10 nuns were left).

In 1528 Bern accepted the Reformation and decided to close and secularize all monasteries in its Canton. The Interlaken monastery resisted this and sought support from Canton Unterwalden, which sent a small army to fight-off the Bernese. The Bernese came with a much bigger army and seized the monastery, after the troops from Unterwalden fled. The Canton closed the monastery and seized the extensive lands and rights it had accumulated over the centuries. The enforcement of the Reformation enabled Bern to attain significant territory and wealth.

From 1528 the Canton housed its regional sheriff (with administrative and judicial functions) in the former monastery building. Part of the building became a hospital for the poor and ill, and the church was turned into a warehouse. Over the subsequent centuries the buildings were expanded and extended; in 1751 the regional sheriff demolished the old western wing and had the three-winged extension built, which he used as his residence.

After the French invasion of 1798 the buildings became regional administrative offices, housing Bern's regional governor (who relocated from the Castle of Unterseen – see stage 10).

Nowadays the building complex is called the Castle (*Schloss*) of Interlaken, even though it never was as a castle in the traditional sense: it is a former monastery extended with governmental/residential buildings. The buildings still house Cantonal authorities and offices today.

Though stage 9 ends at the former monastery, it is worthwhile to continue to walk westward along the *Höheweg* towards the main tourist area with the historic city center.

Interlaken developed as a main tourist destination for clean air, wellness, and mountains from 1800. The easy access by steamboats on Lake Thun made it a popular destination for English tourists; nowadays they come from all over the world. The town has around 6'000 inhabitants.

You pass by the Casino, luxury-brand watch shops, and the Grand Hotel Victoria-Jungfrau (a famous 5-star hotel dating from the Belle Époque). The hotel has beautiful architecture and interior decorations, and is proud of its unobstructed view of the **Jungfrau mountains** to the south.

Stand in front of the hotel, look over the grass field, and enjoy the view of the permanently snow-capped peaks. Switzerland's most famous mountain peaks (apart from the Matterhorn) appear in a threesome: the *Eiger* (3'970 m), the *Mönch* (4'107 m), and the *Jungfrau* (4'158 m) (translated as Ogre, Monk, and Virgin, respectively).

From the ending point

The former Augustinian Monastery in Interlaken is the ending point of stage 9, about 500 meters aside the signposted route (as the route nr. 4 does not enter the city).

In case you are a day-hiker, you need to walk 600 meters to the Interlaken-East (*Ost*) train station or 1.2 km to the Interlaken-West station.

In case you are a thru-hiker and spend the night in Interlaken, there are many accommodations to choose from (though most are relatively expensive, because Interlaken is a major tourist destination). However, several low-priced alternatives comparable to a pilgrim inn (B&B, Youth Hostel, Backpackers Villa, Happy Inn Lodge) are available. Check out www.jakobsweg.ch or www.viajacobi4.ch for the accommodation possibilities, addresses, and contact details. You can also visit the Tourist Information Office (Marktgasse 1, 3800 Interlaken; tel. 033 826 53 00; www.interlaken.ch) 100 meters from the Interlaken-West train station.

The next Stage

Stage 10 guides you across the bödeli between Lake Brienz and Lake Thun, over the southern flanks of the Beatenberg, along the northern shore of Lake Thun, and by boat across the lake to Spiez. Stage 10 is relatively short with less than 19 km. Read the next chapter to find out what that entails.

Stage 10:
Interlaken to Spiez
19 km

The Way to Saint Beatus

Route stats

	Distance in km	*Time in hrs:min*
Signposted route nr. 4	15.7	3:30
Churches/chapels	3.1	1:10
Points of interest		0:30
Rest/lunch		0:40
Boat Merligen to Spiez		0:40
Stage 10	18.8	6:30

In case you hike this stage as a daytrip, you need to add 600 meters (or 1.2 km) in Interlaken and 700 meters in Spiez (from and to the train stations). Not included in the above time is the wait at the boat pier in Merligen. Given the irregular ferry times, it is advisable to plan your arrival at the pier with the schedule of the boat. The time and distances do not include the sightseeing at the St. Beatus Caves.

Ascent/descent/total	+482 / -448 / 930 altitude meters
Lowest/highest altitude	558 / 724 meters
Pathway/condition	easy / moderate
Churches/chapels	Unterseen, Sundlauenen, Merligen, Spiez (4)
Monasteries	none
Points of interest	Castle of Unterseen, Ruins Castle of Weissenau, St. Beatus Caves, Castle of Spiez

Route summary

Stage 10 continues in the highlands of protestant **Canton Bern** (*Berner Oberland*).

Stage 10 guides you across the bödeli between Lake Brienz and Lake Thun, over the southern flanks of the Beatenberg, along the northern shore of Lake Thun, and by boat across the lake to Spiez.

Similar to the two previous stages, stage 10 offers wonderful views over a turquoise lake along the route and has a relatively low number of churches and chapels. Different from the previous two stages, the distance is relatively short with 19 km. There are two reasons why it is short: you may need time to explore the St. Beatus Caves (60 to 75 minutes); and the boat from Merligen across Lake Thun to Spiez goes infrequently, so that you may incur waiting time of up to two hours (making it important to plan your arrival at the boat pier).

The signposted route nr. 4 follows the northwestern bank of the Aare River for the first 4 km. Hiking across the bödeli is easy; it is flat. Along the way panoramic views of the Eiger, Mönch, and Jungfrau peaks in the south can be enjoyed. At the location where the Aare River flows into Lake Thun, the route follows a boardwalk through the marshlands at the southeastern end of Lake Thun. After 7 km the route leaves the flat area between Lake Brienz and Lake Thun, and follows the northern shore of Lake Thun for the following 8 km. The route along the northern shore is mountainous, trailing on the lower flanks of the Beatenberg. After a minor ascent and descent, the route crosses the Sundlauenen River delta to arrive at the boat pier from where the route ascends over a kilometer on urbanized pathways through the forest to the St. Beatus Caves. These caves (at km 10) are the highlight of the day, providing a unique experience along the Way of St. James through Switzerland. From the caves the route ascends over 1 km through a forest to reach an altitude of 724 meters. The following 3 km the route gradually descends from the flanks of the Beatenberg to the level of Lake Thun. At the town Merligen (northern shore) the route crosses the lake to Spiez (southern shore). The boat takes 27 minutes to get there; its frequency is limited and may require some planning. Since Spiez is built against a hill, the visit of the last churches involves some gradual ascents.

Getting to the starting point

Today's starting point in Interlaken is at the church of the former Augustinian monastery. In case you hike stage 10 as a daytrip, you need to walk 600 meters from the Interlaken-East (*Ost*) train station or 1.2 km from the Interlaken-West station.

In case you have already visited Interlaken and you arrive at the Interlaken East (*Ost*) station, it is quicker to walk directly to the signposted route nr. 4 across the Beau Rivage Bridge. In case you have already visited Interlaken and you arrive at the Interlaken West (*West*) station, it is quicker to walk directly to the signposted route nr. 4 in the town Unterseen. This would avoid the 1.2 km detour into Interlaken and additionally reduce the length of stage 10 by 1.2 km.

Route Map and Profile

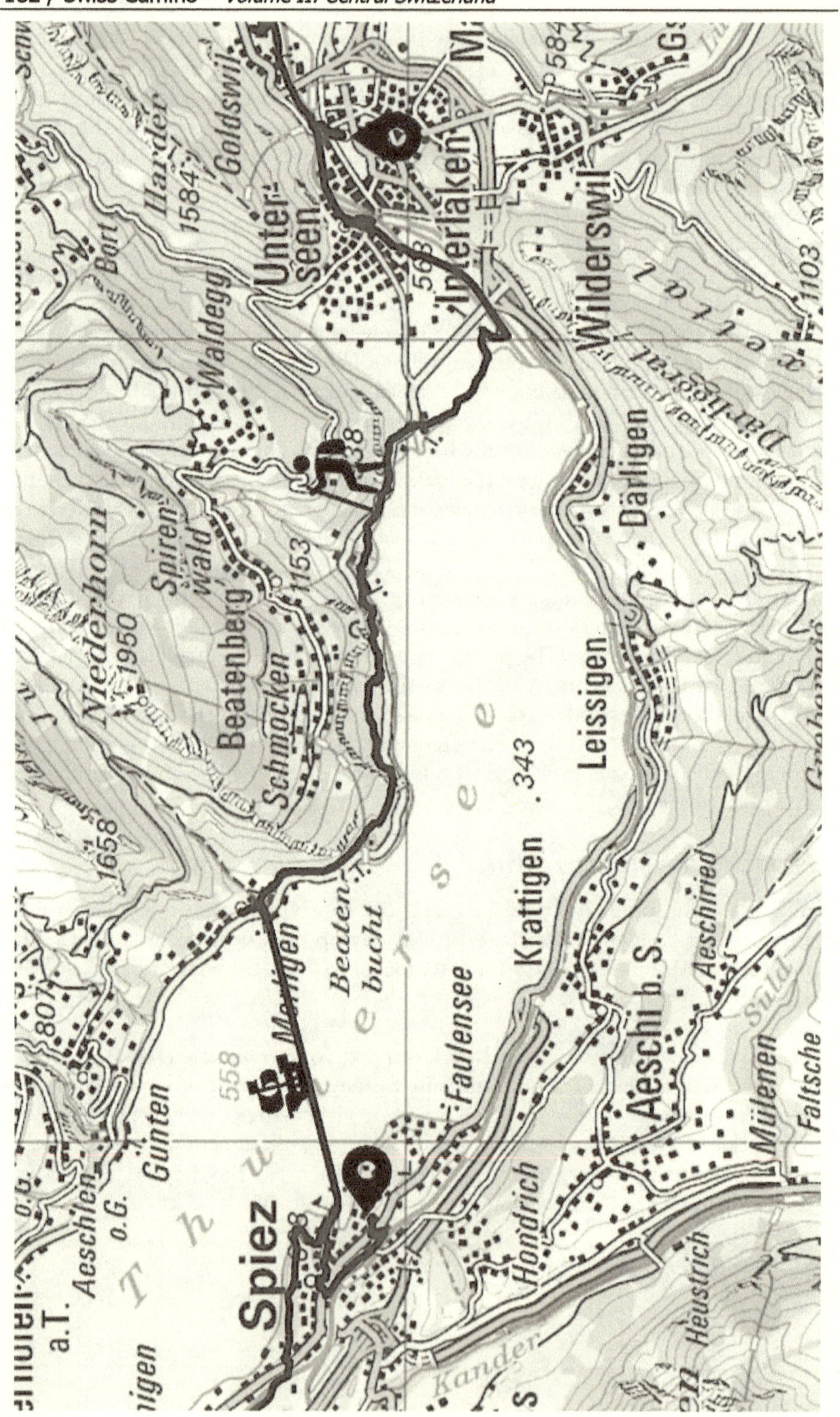
Spiez
Aeschlen o.G.
Gunten
558
Merligen
Beatenbucht
Faulensee
Krattigen
343
Leissigen
Därligen
Wilderswil
Interlaken
568
Unterseen
Goldswil
Harder
1584
Bort
Waldegg
Spirenwald
Niederhorn
1950
1658
Beatenberg
Schmocken
1153
Aeschi b. S.
Aeschiried
Hondrich
Heustrich
Mülenen
Faltsche
Kander
Suld
Därligrat
1103

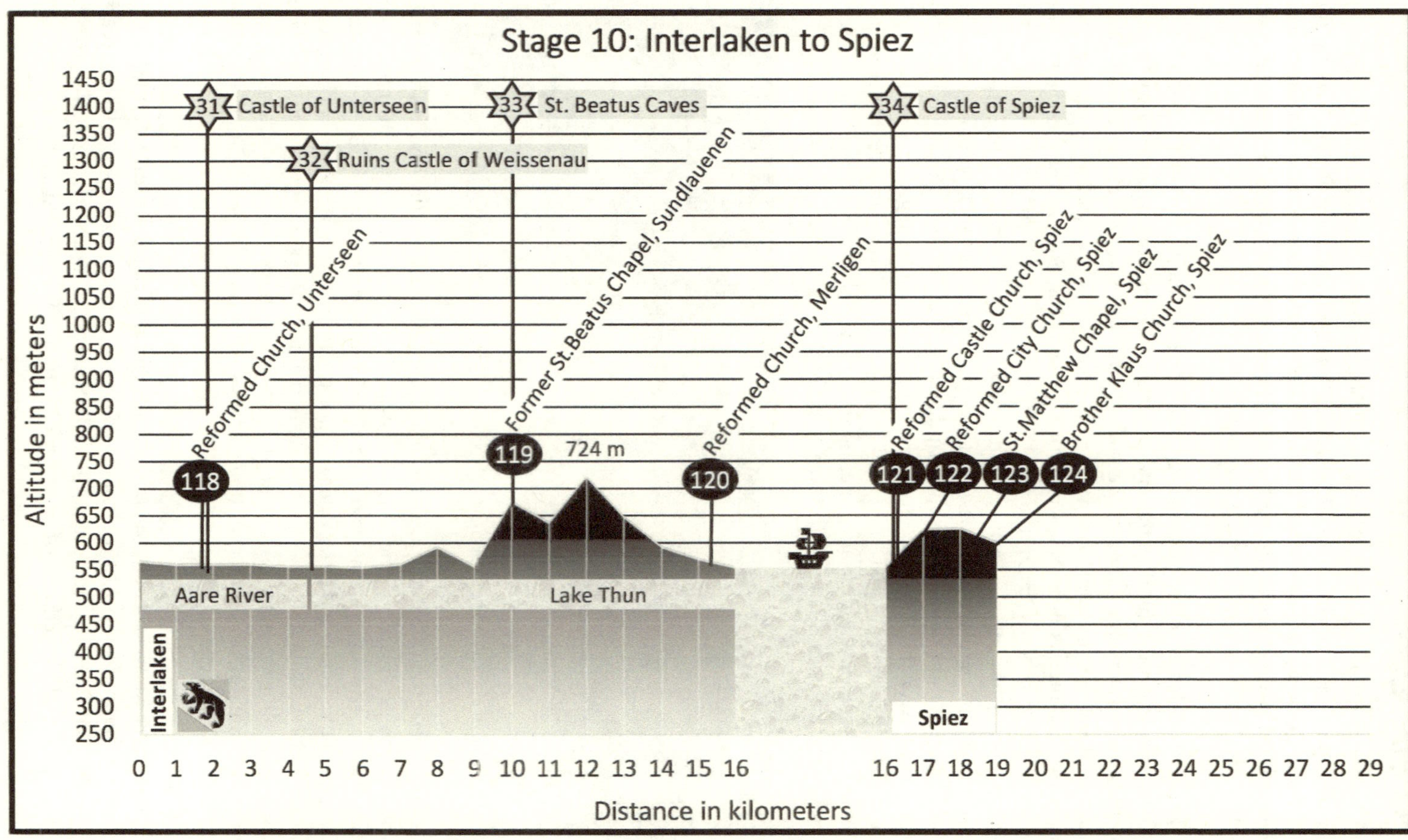
Stage 10: Interlaken to Spiez
31 Castle of Unterseen
33 St. Beatus Caves
34 Castle of Spiez
32 Ruins Castle of Weissenau
118 Reformed Church, Unterseen
119 Former St.Beatus Chapel, Sundlauenen
724 m
120 Reformed Church, Merligen
121 Reformed Castle Church, Spiez
122 Reformed City Church, Spiez
123 St.Matthew Chapel, Spiez
124 Brother Klaus Church, Spiez
Aare River
Lake Thun
Interlaken
Spiez
Altitude in meters
1450
1400
1350
1300
1250
1200
1150
1100
1050
1000
950
900
850
800
750
700
650
600
550
500
450
400
350
300
250
0 1 2 3 4 5 6 7 8 9 10 11 12 13 14 15 16
16 17 18 19 20 21 22 23 24 25 26 27 28 29
Distance in kilometers

Hiking the Route

From the former monastery church walk 500 meters to the north to get back to the signposted route nr. 4 at the northern bank of the Aare River. Pass by the Japanese garden (left), take a right at the *Höheweg*, a left at the corner of the Grand Hotel Beau Rivage, cross the bridge over the Aare River, and take the small path left to the tarmac footpath along the Aare.

The signpost leads you to the west, on the northern bank of the river (continuing where you left route nr. 4 at the end of stage 9). A narrow tarmac footpath goes between the river and a high stone wall. Above the wall the elevated train track follows the same direction. The wall makes room for a lane shaded by trees, as you pass by the Interlaken recreational open-air swimming pool (on the right). The railway track crosses from the northern to the southern bank of the Aare (connecting the Interlaken-East and -West train stations), while the route continues through an underpass. Along the northern bank you can see the Jungfraujoch mountain in the southern distance. On the left you have the Goldey footbridge over the Aare and an information table explaining its more than 100-year history. The Way of St. James continues straight. Together with the river, the route nr. 4 curves to the south, entering the municipality of Unterseen. Trees next to the river provide shade on the tarmac path.

At the end of the tree line you arrive at a riverfront square called the **Haberdarre** (translated as 'grain drying'), a medieval transshipment point at the town Unterseen. The square was used for reloading and storing of goods-in-transit between Lake Thun and Lake Brienz. Since the foundation of the town Unterseen in 1279, it established itself as a transit station along the waterways of the two lakes, for goods shipped between northern Italy to southern Germany. As it lay just outside the gates of Unterseen, no city taxes were levied, making it an attractive location for traders.

The flat area between Lake Brienz and Lake Thun is called the **bödeli** (the Swiss-German diminutive word for ground – *Boden*). After the last ice-age, 10'000 years ago, the two lakes formed one large lake. Sediments left by the *Lütschine* stream (from the south) and the *Lombach* stream (from the north) filled up the narrow and shallow gap between two mountain ranges, until only the Aare River connected the two lakes. As people settled in the region, Interlaken and Unterseen were built on this natural landfill.

Nowadays Lake Brienz is about 6 meters higher than Lake Thun. Already since the 13th century Unterseen and the Monastery of Interlaken tried to tame the **Aare River** that flowed through the bödeli from one lake to the other. They built bridges connecting Interlaken to Unterseen and used the current for powering mills. On the other side of the Aare you see two sluices underneath a wooden bridge over a side arm of the river. A system of sluices was built over a distance of about 5.5 km to regulate the flow of the Aare from Lake Brienz to Lake Thun, covering the 6-meter altitude difference. Weirs were created, used for fishing and water mills since the 13th century.

The fact that Interlaken has two railway stations (West and East) has to do with the Aare River as well. Since there was no waterway connection for boats between Lake Brienz and Lake Thun (because of the sluices, weirs, and bridges), an 8 km train connection between the two lakes was built in 1872-74. The train provided a seamless connection between the steamboats that operated on Lake Thun and Lake Brienz. The **bödeli railway** was one of Switzerland's shortest standalone railway tracks for nearly 30 years (1872-1900), after which it connected to the tracks coming from Thun. The boats from Lake Brienz moored at the East station (built 1874). In 1890-92 a 3-km canal was built that connected the steamboats from Lake Thun to the Interlaken-West station (built 1872). Nowadays both lakes' tourist boats still dock at the two train stations and the historical bödeli railway still covers the 2 km difference (using two railway bridges crossing the river).

At the road bridge over the Aare in Unterseen, leave the signposted route nr. 4 for 100 meters: turn right to enter the village square, where to the right you arrive at the reformed Church of Unterseen (at km 1.7).

118 Reformed Church, Unterseen (Reformierte Kirche)

- Kirchgasse 3, 3800 Unterseen
- On a shelf at the wall of the front portal
- The church was first built as a small chapel at the establishment of the town Unterseen in 1279. This chapel was first mentioned in official documents in 1353. In 1470 a village fire destroyed the town and the first chapel, after which it was rebuilt and expanded as a church in 1470-71. Until 1470 is was a subsidiary of the church in Goldswil, but after the reconstruction it became a separate parish. At the time of the Reformation in 1528 the church and the town Unterseen were eager to convert to Protestantism dictated by Bern, as an offset against their century-long suppressor from the other side of the Aare River. They accepted the Reformation and removed all catholic religious icons from the church.

  The nave of the church was destroyed and rebuilt in 1647 (after a fire) and 1853 (after the roof collapsed from snow). The church as you see it today dates from two construction periods: the bell tower from 1471 and the nave from 1853. Renovations were undertaken in 1932 and 1956.
- The church has a typical protestant interior, without altars, statues, or paintings. The large organ at the back wall of the chancel dates from the last renovation.

The large building in the middle of the village square is the **town hall**. It was built by the City of Bern to support the town Unterseen after the village fire of 1470. Initially it combined a city-inn and a warehouse (in connection with the Haberdarre transshipment location) offering accommodations and storage. As tourism developed at the end of the 18th century, the building accommodated the first international guests, including Goethe and Mendelssohn. Think back to stage 5: at the Haggenegg Pass you already were in the footsteps of these travelers; you journey much of the same route as they did.

After leaving the church walk back 100 meters to the road bridge. From there you have a good view of the second sluice in the river. Turn right along the river and 150 meters later you pass by the Castle of Unterseen (*Schloss Unterseen*).

The **Castle of Unterseen** was first built at the time of the foundation of the town Unterseen by the Lord of Eschenbach-Oberhofen in 1279 (after the King of Habsburg-Austria had given permission). The Lord of Eschenbach-Oberhofen (descendent of Lord Seliger of Oberhofen, who founded the Augustinian monastery in 1133) established the town on the silted-up wetlands between Lake Brienz and Lake Thun. Hence its name Unterseen (between lakes; *unter* means between, *seen* means lakes). The Lord had a fortified castle built (probably a residential tower), together with several houses and a small chapel. The town was surrounded by fortified walls, access gates, drawbridges, and a moat. On the eastern side the Aare River was a natural barrier.

Through the town and its castle, the House of Habsburg (via their allegiant Lords of Eschenbach-Oberhofen and Lords of Brienz/Ringgenberg) controlled trade and traffic from the Brünig Pass to the Alps in the south. In 1317 patronage of the town changed to Bern and in 1386 Bern became owner of the town (after the House of Habsburg lost the battle of Sempach from the Swiss Confederation).

Over the centuries the castle was rebuilt several times, each time changing its appearance: after a fire in 1364; when ownership of the town was transferred to Bern in 1386; after a village fire in 1470; and when the mayor designated by Bern used it as his residence in 1656. In 1746-57 the building was completely renovated.

After the French invasion in 1798 the residence of the Bernese governor transferred to the former monastery in Interlaken and the building lost its Cantonal importance. It was subsequently used by a painter and, after reconstruction in the 19th century, housed a school and the administrative offices of a parquet factory. Finally, the reformed parish acquired the building in 1967 and renovated it for their purposes.

Today's outer appearance mostly dates from 1757 (nothing is left of the earlier fortified residential tower). As you walk through the historical part of Unterseen you will not see any of the fortified walls or watchtowers either: these were demolished in 1855 or destroyed by a fire in 1903.

Since the establishment of the town Unterseen in 1279, the monastery of Interlaken suppressed the town (as the monastery considered itself the ruler of the region). For centuries this led to disputes, conflicts, and disharmony between the two neighbors, during which time Unterseen always sought Bern's support and dispute-settlement. At the time of the Reformation the monastery organized a military uprising (with support from Canton Unterwalden) to resist Bern's interference. Unterseen did not join this uprising and chose to side with Bern. After Bern seized the monastery by military force in 1528, they rewarded Unterseen by transferring some land that belonged to the secularized monastery.

Back on the route, you get to a busy road (*Bahnhofstrasse*) that leads to the Interlaken-West train station. At the *Bahnhofstrasse* turn right and 150 meters later left. After another quick left and right, the route goes through a residential area parallel to the Aare. The Eiger, Mönch, and Jungfrau keep dominating the southern panorama.

After passing by the hospital on your right, the Way of St. James turns left to the western bank of the Aare. The next 1.5 km the route is on a tarmac and gravel path directly alongside the river. You pass by a wooden roof-covered footbridge over the Aare and walk underneath the elevated road nr. 221. You enter a nature protected area (*Naturschutzgebiet*) called Weissenau-Neuhaus, covering marshlands, floodplains, and moors at the eastern end of Lake Thun.

The path along the Aare River ends in a T-crossing: to the left a narrow footbridge crosses the river, to the right a gravel path goes along the edge of the marshlands. Information tables explain the nature protected area. The route turns right and passes by the ruins of the Castle of Weissenau.

The **Ruins of the Castle of Weissenau** originate from the 13th century, when the castle had the purpose to control trade and traffic passing through the northern end of Lake Thun. It was built on a small island in the Aare River delta by the Lords of Wädenswil, under patronage of the House of Habsburg-Austria. The castle itself was protected by high fortified walls and a moat with drawbridge. West of the castle, a protected port provided waterway access to Lake Thun and the Aare River. This port was used to access the castle, store goods in transit, and transfer goods to smaller boats and onto the main road next to the island.

The castle was first mentioned in 1298. Since the foundation of the town Unterseen in 1279, the castle, with its relatively isolated location on an island in the river delta, lost its importance. The haberdarre of Unterseen, with a strategically better location, gradually took over the role as transshipment location. In 1334 the castle was sold to the Augustinian monastery of Interlaken, which tried to use it to suppress the rise of Unterseen as transit station for trade. In 1362 the monastery built a bridge, as an easier transport connection to the bödeli.

After the monastery was secularized in 1528, the castle fell into ownership of the City-Republic of Bern. Bern made the former monastery of Interlaken its governmental office for the region and neglected the castle on the island. It was initially used as a prison, but fell into ruins after it was abandoned.

In 1893 the boat canal to Interlaken was built and the Aare River was canalized; since then the former island has been connected to the land.

The ruins were restored in 1955 and 1989. Nowadays they are the biggest and best maintained castle ruins of the Bernese Highlands. A staircase inside the tower ruins leads up to the top level, where a pine tree is strongly rooted into the walls. You have wide views over Lake Thun and the surrounding mountains.

Along the shores of the marshlands (left) the route curves north, while you pass by the greens and fairways (right) of the Golfclub Interlaken-Unterseen. The lane is lined with tall old trees. About 300 meters after the castle ruins the signpost directs into the marshlands (left). The route follows a boardwalk through marshlands for 1 km, where you are surrounded by nature and can enjoy wonderful views over the lake.

Lake Thun is 9th in size of the Swiss lakes, with a length of 17.5 km, a maximum width of 3.5 km, and an average depth of 136 meters (maximum depth 217 meters).

Its surface is at 558 meters above sea level. The lake is named after the biggest town on its shore, Thun. The primary inflow comes from the Aare River flowing from Lake Brienz.

Back on land, the route continues along the shore of Lake Thun, until you reach a small port and recreational water sports bay at the settlement Neuhaus 600 meters later. The route continues north and follows road nr. 221, across the Lombach stream, and past a large camping site called Manor Farm. In front you see a 900-meter-high forested mountain range.

The route goes into the forest, up the flank of the mountain, parallel to road nr. 221 in a westward direction. This is the first ascent of the day, after 7 km of flat and easy hiking. A narrow gravel trail leads you to an altitude of 594 meters, past rocky walls, with scenic views over the lake. The descent to the lake level (559 meters) is equally short, but partly on uncomfortable rocky under-footing. The route crosses road nr. 211 (*Seestrasse*) and follows it for 400 meters; watch out for traffic.

The route turns left, away from the road, and crosses a partly forested river delta called Sundlauenen for 1 km (the road makes a wide curve around it). The river delta was created by rocks and debris coming down the Sundgraben (gorge) into Lake Thun for centuries (last time in 2012). In the middle of the river delta a debris-avalanche protection-wall was built in 2017. The last 200 meters through the river delta are on a tarmac path next to the lake, until you arrive at the Sundlauenen-Beatus Caves boat pier.

You can see road nr. 221, about 50 meters above the lake level, curving into a tunnel. At the boat pier the route turns right, passing under a blue sign indicating the beginning of the hike up to the St. Beatus caves. This hike from lake level to the St. Beatus caves is 1 km, covering 128 altitude meters, along the rocky and forested flanks of the Beatus mountain (*Beatenberg*). After 300 meters the route crosses road nr. 221; be careful when crossing. Because many tourists undertake this climb, the path has been urbanized: tarmacked, with steps at the steeper parts, and hand railings or walls at the parts near cliffs. The views over Lake Thun are magnificent.

At km 10.0 you reach the St. Beatus caves at 679 meters. The location contains the former grave and hermit's cell of St. Beatus, a former chapel, a restaurant, a museum, and a labyrinth of caves. The area is open from mid of March until mid of November.

Former St. Beatus Chapel, Sundlauenen (St. Beatus Kapelle) 119

- Seestrasse 974, 3800 Sundlauenen
- St. Beatus
- At the ticket counter (you need to ask for it)
- The chapel was first mentioned when it belonged to the Augustinian monastery of Interlaken in 1231. The chapel contained the grave of the hermit St. Beatus, who lived in the cave in the 6th or 9th century (in 1904 excavations at the cave indeed discovered a skeleton).

The chapel was a popular pilgrimage destination from the 12th century, as myths of a cave hermit attracted pilgrims from all around. To improve the attractiveness of the chapel to pilgrims, the Augustinian monastery created a legend around this hermit (see the biography of St. Beatus in Appendix 2) in 1511, which increased the number of pilgrims.

During the Reformation in 1528 the Augustinian monastery of Interlaken heavily resisted the enforcement of Protestantism by the Bernese and clashed over the closure of the chapel. Access to the chapel, grave, and cell were blocked on purpose. Reformed forces demolished the chapel and bricked-up the cave's entrance in 1530. As a continuance for the pilgrimage, the bones and relics of St. Beatus were divided among catholic churches in Cantons Luzern, Unterwalden, and Schwyz, and a chapel dedicated to St. Beatus was built in Obsee, Canton Obwalden (see church nr. 107, stage 8).

Nowadays the former chapel is in use as the seating area of a tourist restaurant. The roof still has a small steeple with bell.

The rock-hewn grave and cave-cell are east (right) of the restaurant. Blue information tables explain the sites in German and English.

33

The **St. Beatus Caves** (*Beatushöhlen*) are the highlight of stage 10, offering cave-exploring unique for the Swiss Way of St. James. The caves are a system of tunnels in the limestone Beatenberg mountain (named after St. Beatus) with a length of more than 14 km. About 1'000 meters of these tunnels have been made safe and accessible for tourists.

You can buy a ticket for CHF 18 at the ticket office (where you also get the pilgrim stamp), which provides access to the cave-exploration museum as well. You can tour the caves individually or in a guided group, taking 60 to 75 minutes. You can leave your backpack at the restaurant (just take your valuables with you). Be aware of the constant temperature of 8 to 10 degrees celsius and 95 percent humidity inside; dress warmly. Along the tour you see underground streams, stalactites, stalagmites, waterfalls, narrow corridors, and large caverns. The well-lit path ascends 87 meters from the cave's opening to its end, 826 meters inside the mountain. When you exit the caves, you pass by a sculpture representing St. Beatus' dragon.

The terrace of the restaurant provides magnificent views over lake Thun. When you arrived at the caves, you came from the eastern side of the mountain. You get the best view of the former chapel and waterfalls below it, when you walk down the zigzagging tarmac path to the lower levels (where you also find the museum).

The signposted route continues along the flanks of the Beatenberg in a western direction. For 600 meters the path (also urbanized) descends through the forest to an altitude of 640 meters, where it crosses a small stream. The route makes a sharp right and zigzagging ascends around a quarry (*Steinbruch*). The quarry left a giant hole in the lower flank of the Beatenberg. The route follows a forest road and reaches the highest point of the day at 724 meters alongside the quarry.

For 400 meters the path gradually descends on a forest gravel path in a nature protected area called Balmholz. The trail ascends again and after 200 meters reaches a wooden roofed footbridge over the Budelbach stream. The path curves around rocky cliffs that are hewn to provide a safe passage. Uneven large stones and small rocks on the path make the walking uncomfortable.

Now and then the tree line opens up and provides great views. When you look back you can see the quarry's hole in the side of the mountain, road nr. 221 far below, the bödeli with Unterseen and Interlaken, and the Jungfrau mountains in the distance.

The following 3 km the trail descends back to the lake level. The path remains in the forest, slowly descending along the flanks of the Beatenberg. The route follows the curves of the northern shore of Lake Thun. At the level of the Beaten bay (*Beatenbucht*) the path passes over the tracks of the Beatenberg cable car (*Beatenbergbahn*). The route approaches road nr. 221 and the lake, as the trail descends. You can see sailing- and motor-boats on the lake. Very appropriately, the route from the St. Beatus caves to Merligen is called the pilgrim path (*Pilgerweg*). At km 14.6 you leave the forest of the Beatenberg behind and arrive in Merligen.

The route follows the streets through residential areas. After crossing the Grönbach stream the nr. 4 sign directs down the hill (left) towards road nr. 221 (*Seestrasse*) and the boat pier. At this location you need to leave the signposted route to reach the church of Merligen. Continue straight in the *Oberdorfstrasse* (curving down the hill to the left for 100 meters), take the first right (*Kirchstrasse*), and after 200 meters uphill you arrive at the reformed Church of Merligen (at km 15.3).

Reformed Church, Merligen (Reformierte Kirche) 120

- Kirchweg, 3658 Merligen
- Holy Family, St. Michael
- On a lectern at the front-left of the nave
- The protestant church was built in 1936-37. Until that time the parishioners had to attend services at the church in Sigriswil, one hour on foot to the west.
- In the center of the chancel the baptismal font also functions as communion table. The wall frescos and the two stained-glass windows in the chancel date from 1937. You will not recognize any Saints or biblical figures in the wall frescos (except for one). The figures left of the windows depict citizens of Sigriswil in a scene comparable to Jesus' parable of the lost son. The figures right of the windows depict citizens of Merligen in front of Jesus in a scene with an adulterer. The stained-glass windows depict the Holy Family below two angels. Compared to the typical austere interior of a protestant church, this one has more colors in the windows and on the walls.

  The protestant parish also allowed the Catholics of Merligen to use the church for their services, for which these donated a stained-glass window of St. Michael.

The elevated position of the church provides beautiful views over Lake Thun and the surrounding mountains. From the church follow the same street back down the hill. At the end turn right to descend to road nr. 221, where you turn left, and pass by the open-air swimming area. Shortly before hotel Beatus turn right into a small road to go down to the lake's boat pier (behind the hotel).

The **BLS ferry connection** between Merligen and Spiez (via Faulensee) takes 27 minutes and costs CHF 13 (to be paid on board). The frequency is limited: 12:05, 13:05, 15:05, 16:05, 17:05 (summer schedule 2019). This frequency is further reduced in autumn, winter, and spring (check out their up-to-date online timetable at *https://fahrplan.bls.ch*). Keep this in mind when planning stage 10 and when you are getting closer to Merligen during the hike. This can avoid you just missing the boat by a few minutes and having to wait one or two hours or not getting across anymore (though the lakeside terrace of hotel Beatus could make the wait very enjoyable). During the boat crossing of Lake Thun you have great views of the

Beatenberg (back) and the triangular Niesen mountain (2'362 meters) towering behind Spiez (front). The boat will be crowded on a sunny summer afternoon.

Spiez is a small picturesque town with less than 8'000 inhabitants, at the foot of the Niesen mountain. Its water sports port and bay at Lake Thun, the 800-year-old castle, and the vineyards against the hills dominate the scenery. Flowerbeds of red geraniums and small palm trees greet you when you leave the boat pier, giving a pure holiday feeling.

From the boat pier follow the route nr. 4 signaling, guiding you up the hill to the right to the castle and its church. Note that the castle and church are only accessible from mid of April until mid of October (the castle's grounds and gardens are accessible year-round). After the steps up to the elevation of the castle's courtyard, you arrive at the reformed Castle Church of Spiez (at km 16.2).

121 **Reformed Castle Church, Spiez** (Schloss Kirche)

Schlossstrasse 16, 3700 Spiez

St. Lawrence, St. Christopher, Twelve Apostles

The church was built around the year 700 (first mentioned in 762), making it one of the oldest churches along the Swiss Way of St. James. This first church was of small size, corresponding to the present space of the nave (without chancel) inside the six thick stone pillars. Around the year 1000 the church was expanded both in width by the six arched pillars and the space of the side-naves, and in length by the 2-meter elevated chancel and an extension of the nave towards the tower. At the same time a crypt was constructed underneath the newly built chancel. At the first church building the bell tower was free-standing; with the expansion and lengthening of the nave it became integrated in the southwestern corner of the church. This Romanesque church was mentioned in official documents from the Bishopric of Lausanne in 1228. St. Lawrence (*St. Laurentius*) was the patron Saint of the church until the Reformation in 1528.

During the Reformation the catholic parish of Spiez converted to Protestantism and cleared out the catholic icons that had been accumulated for more than 800 years. The walls were whitewashed to cover all frescos. In 1670 the church was reconstructed as a baroque church with the nave and chancel at the same level, and three new large windows above the entrance. The gallery with the organ above the entrance was built in 1831.

Excavations and renovations between 1941-50 confirmed the existence of the first church from around 700 and restored the church to its original Romanesque appearance. The nave and chancel were de-leveled, the frescos were recovered from below the whitewash, and the three windows above the entrance were bricked-up (you can still see their contours).

The chancel's ceiling displays the recovered frescos from the 12th century, partially covered by younger frescos. They depict Christ carried by four angels, with the Twelve Apostles on the sides. The recovered fresco above the pulpit depicts St. Christopher and dates from around 1300. St. Christopher is the patron Saint of travelers and frescos depicting him are present in many of the old churches in the Bernese Highlands.

The pulpit, added in the 16th century, does not match the 12th century interior. The wooden chancel chair (front-right) dates from 1516 and has the weapon of the family von Erlach, who owned the castle for more than three centuries.

The church still has clear Romanesque features from its construction around the year 1000: narrow nave with high vaulted ceiling; semicircular chancel, significantly elevated above the level of the nave; narrow, slit-like windows high up the walls; a relatively low bell tower that also served as a watchtower; massive walls; three apses to the east (of which the chancel in the middle is the largest); and decorative Lombard arches on the outer wall of the chancel.

The castle church was the parish church of Spiez for more than 700 years until 1907, when the protestant parish moved its services to a newly built reformed church, about 700 meters west of the castle (see below). The castle church is one of the best maintained Romanesque churches in Switzerland and popular for private events such as weddings. Access to the crypt is via the two side-apses (the gates to the crypt are only opened by appointment).

Notice the bell on the ground next to the entrance of the church. It came from the church of Riggisberg in 1950 (see church nr. 129 in stage 12). On the other side of the courtyard you see the Castle of Spiez.

34

The **Castle of Spiez** (*Schloss Spiez*) was initially a square fortified residential tower, built to control trade and traffic along lake Thun around the year 1200. Clearly visible are the three construction layers: the lower dungeon and storage; the two upper residential areas; and the roof. You can still see the original entrance of the residential area on the first floor, which would have been accessible by retractable ladder. The pointed roof was added around 1600.

At its foundations the tower has massive 3-meter thick walls in a 11.3 by 11.2-meter square shape. The tower was protected by a moat, fortified walls, and two watchtowers (you can still see their square remnants at the corners of the courtyard). The residential building north of the tower was built after 1300; it provided better comfort than the dark and primitive interior of the fortified tower.

Over a period of nearly seven centuries three Bernese families owned the castle. The Lords of Strättligen had the fortified residential tower built around 1200. They were under protection of the Dukes of Zähringen, who founded the City of Bern in 1191. The Lords of Strättligen had their home-castle about 5 km north of Spiez (you pass by their castle ruins in stage 11). From 1260 the fortunes of the family were declining and they were regularly in financial difficulties (like many other noble families around 1250-1350 – compare to the Lords of Ringgenberg in stage 9). The impoverished Lords of Strättligen had to sell their castle and lands to the Bernese Sheriff von Bubenberg in 1338. The Lords of Bubenberg owned the castle until their family lineage died out in 1506. In 1516 the family von Erlach bought the castle and continued to own it until 1877 (when they went bankrupt). They had the buildings south of the tower constructed in a late-baroque style in the 17th-18th centuries.

Between 1877 and 1927 the castle had four owners until the 'Foundation Castle Spiez' (*Stiftung Schloss Spiez*) purchased the castle, church, gardens, and grounds in 1927. The purpose of the foundation was to maintain and restore this cultural heritage and make it accessible to the public. The former residential buildings house a museum that exhibits the 13th century history of the castle and its owners. It is open from mid of April until mid of October (ticket price CHF 10).

The grounds of the castle provide wide views over Lake Thun, the port, the Bernese Alps, the Niesen mountain, and the vineyards.

From the castle's square follow the route underneath its gate towards the west. About 200 meters from the gate the Way of St. James makes a right turn, towards the vineyards. At this location the signposted route nr. 4 already leaves Spiez (it does not pass through town). You need to leave the signposted route to visit three more churches and end stage 10 in Spiez. The four churches you visit indicate the religious history of Spiez along a 1'300-year timeline, which started with the castle church around the year 700. Next is the reformed city church that took over as protestant parish church from the castle's church in 1907. This is followed by a catholic chapel from 1898 and lastly a catholic church from 1974.

Continue walking up the hill along the *Schlossstrasse.* The next church tower is already visible. At the *Seestrasse* turn right and 200 meters later continue on the *Kirchgasse.* Cross the cemetery to arrive at the reformed City Church of Spiez (about 700 meters from the castle) at km 17.2.

Reformed City Church, Spiez (Dorf Kirche) 122

Kirchgasse, 3700 Spiez

On a table right of the front portal. The bunch of grapes on the stamp makes the link to Spiez as a wine region.

The church was built in 1906-07 to take over the role of protestant parish church of Spiez from the castle church, which had become too small. The shape of the roof, inside and outside, and its three small windows (dormers) resemble a traditional Bernese farmhouse more than a church. The bell tower was built to the design of the Romanesque castle church: it looks like a medieval watchtower, with an open gallery just below the roof.

On the inside the ceiling's wooden beams against the white panels resemble a typical half-timbered house. The large organ fills half the space of the chancel. The absence of interior decorations, such as altars and statues, is consistent with the other protestant churches.

From the church walk in the direction of the train station (southeast), cross road nr. 6, and keep following the *Bahnhofstrasse* along the tracks towards the station. Pass by the Spiez train station and keep following the tracks on your right. When the main street turns right over the tracks, continue straight and you are in the *Kapellenstrasse*. Around the corner (left) you arrive at the St. Matthew Chapel (at km 18.3).

123 St. Matthew Chapel, Spiez (St. Matthäus Kapelle)

Kapellenstrasse 4, 3700 Spiez

St. Matthew

The chapel was built by the hoteliers of Spiez in 1898, to offer their catholic holiday guests a place of worship (because the castle's church had converted to Protestantism during the Reformation in 1528). The chapel was enlarged by two windows in 1937, to accommodate the increasing catholic population of Spiez. The catholic parish used this chapel until 1974, when a larger church was built in close vicinity (see below). From 1974 to 2017 the chapel was used by the Evangelic-Methodist parish of Spiez.

Since 2017 the chapel has been closed. The Evangelic-Methodist parish has been trying to sell the chapel since 2017.

From the chapel walk down the hill, cross the *Oberlandstrasse* (road nr. 6), take a right on the *Belvédèrestrasse*, and you arrive at the catholic Brother Klaus Church at km 18.8.

Brother Klaus Church, Spiez (Bruder Klaus Kirche) 124

- Belvédèrestrasse 6, 3700 Spiez
- Brother Klaus
- On a lectern left of the entrance
- The catholic church was built in 1974, to replace the small chapel that was in use since 1898. The church is a bit hidden behind the trees; it is a low building without the usual pointed roof and bell tower. Its exterior and interior have the typical designs of the 1970s, with bare concrete and chairs instead of pews (giving the interior a multipurpose use).
- A bell is hanging at the back wall of the chancel. Notice a large painting of Brother Klaus' Meditation Wheel right of the chancel. The building complex not only houses the church, but also a multipurpose cultural center.

If you want to have a great view of the port of Spiez and the 800-year-old castle and 1'000-year-old church, continue walking down the hill for 200 meters. At the Hotel Belvédère walk around its right side to its back garden and terrace: from there you have a superb view.

From the ending point

The Brother Klaus Church in Spiez is the ending point of stage 10, about 1 km aside the signposted route nr. 4 (which does not enter the town Spiez).

In case you are a day-hiker, you need to walk back 700 meters to the Spiez train station.

In case you are a thru-hiker and spend the night in Spiez, be aware that there is no pilgrim inn, but several regular inns (*Gasthaus*) and hotels offer reasonably priced accommodations. Pilgrim beds are available at B&B at private residences. Check out www.jakobsweg.ch or www.viajacobi4.ch for the accommodation possibilities. Tourist Information Spiez (Bahnhofstrasse 10d, 3700 Spiez; tel. 033 655 90 00; www.spiez.ch) at the train station can also help you find the appropriate accommodation.

The next Stage

Stage 11 guides you along the southern shore of Lake Thun to the eastern highland valleys of the Gantrisch mountain range. Read the next chapter to find out what that entails.

Stage 11:
Spiez to Wattenwil
26 km

The Way along the 1'000-year-old Churches

Route stats

	Distance in km	*Time in hrs:min*
Signposted route nr. 4	22.8	4:50
Churches/chapels	3.3	1:40
Points of interest		0:10
Rest/lunch		0:50
Stage 11	26.1	7:30

In case you hike this stage as a daytrip, you need to add 1 km from the train station in Spiez and 300 meters to the bus stop in Wattenwil.

Ascent/descent/total	+677 / -633 / 1'310 altitude meters
Lowest/highest altitude	564 / 786 meters
Pathway/condition	easy / moderate
Churches/chapels	Einigen, Amsoldingen, Blumenstein, Wattenwil
Monasteries	Former Collegiate Amsoldingen
Points of interest	Former Castle of Strättligen, Former Castle of Blumenstein

Route summary

Stage 11 continues in the highlands of protestant **Canton Bern** (*Berner Oberland*).

Stage 11 guides you along the southern shore of Lake Thun to the eastern highland valleys of the Gantrisch mountain range.

The trails are easy, the distance is moderate, and there are only four churches along the route. The direction is northwest. The stage has many gradual and short ascents and descents, passing through highland valleys and following small streams. Most of the time the route offers panoramic views of the Bernese Alps in the east, behind Lake Thun. These views are behind you and it is worthwhile to regularly turn around, as these views are one of the most beautiful along the Way of St. James through Switzerland.

Stage 11 starts with an ascent of the Spiezberg, through the vineyards on its southeastern slopes. After going up and down the forested Spiezberg, the route passes underneath railway tracks. The trail is parallel to these tracks and after a forest the route goes back to the southern shore of Lake Thun. The church in Einigen is one of the 1'000-year-old-churches around Lake Thun, worthwhile spending a bit more time at. After Einigen the route crosses a footbridge over the Kander River gorge, passes by the former Strättligen Castle, and follows a crest trail called the Burgundy Way. The route turns away from Lake Thun following a highland valley towards Amsoldingen, which has another 1'000-year-old-church and a former collegiate monastery. After passing the Thun military area, the route turns west over a hill and descends to the town Blumenstein. Because the church of Blumenstein is outside the village, a 3.3 km detour from the signposted route is required to visit this church in one of the most beautiful nature settings. After turning back to the signposted route, the trail follows a northern direction, following the Fallbach stream and then the Gürbe stream until reaching Wattenwil with the last church of the day. The last 4 km are easy to hike alongside the streams.

Getting to the starting point

Today's starting point in Spiez is at the reformed Castle Church. In case you hike stage 11 as a daytrip, you need to walk about 1 km from the train station down the hill to the church. Follow the footpath that descends to the recreational swimming area at the small port. The port's promenade offers great early morning views of the castle and Lake Thun, with the Jungfrau mountains at the horizon. A wonderful start of your hiking day. Then circle around the port to the elevated castle grounds.

Route Map and Profile

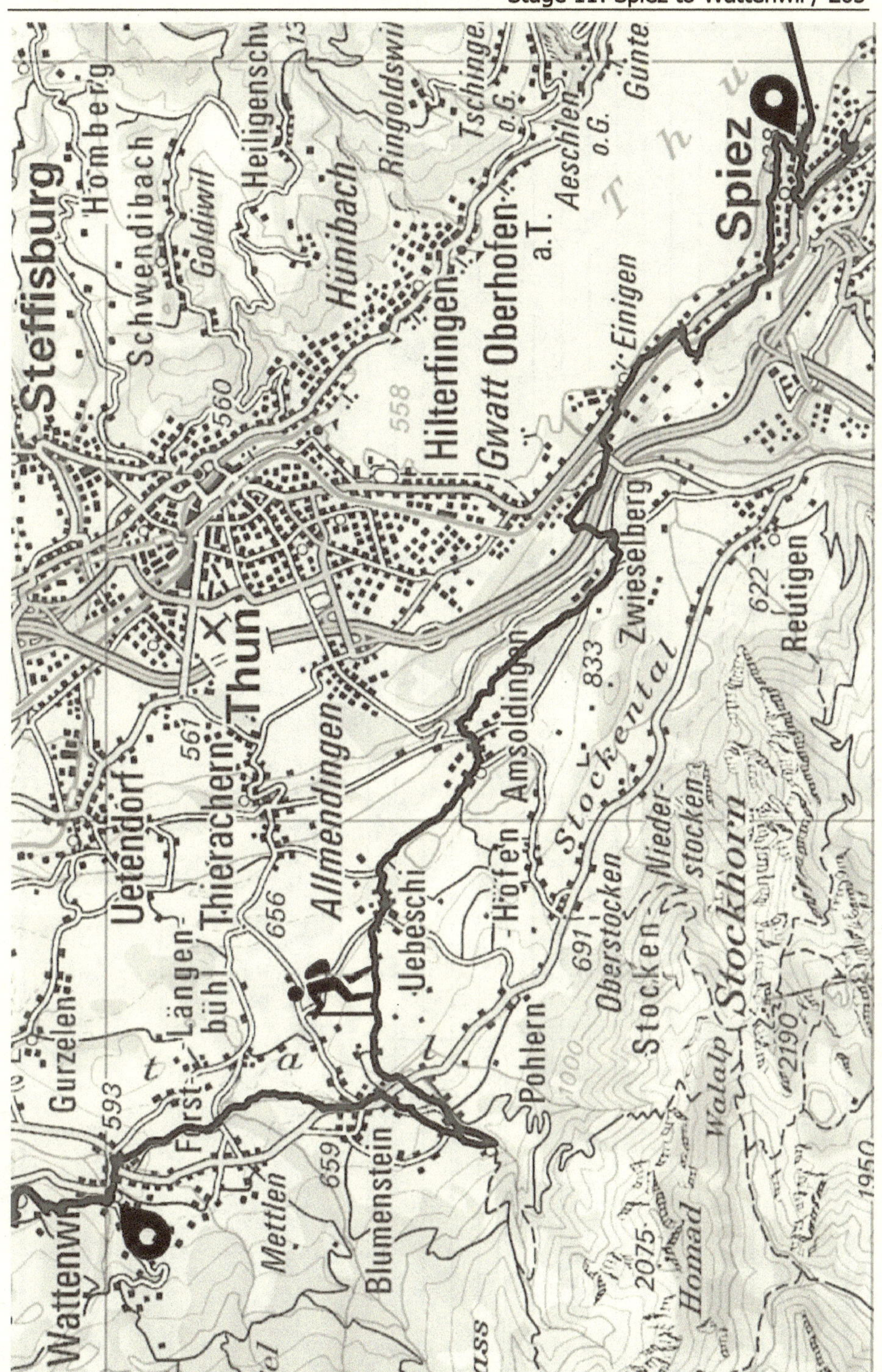
Steffisburg
Homberg
Schwendibach
Goldiwil
Heiligenschw
Hünibach
Ringoldswil
Tschinge
Hilterfingen
Oberhofen
a.T.
Gwatt
Aeschlen
o.G.
Gunte
Spiez
Einigen
558
560
Thun
Uetendorf
Thierachern
561
Allmendingen
Amsoldingen
833
Zwieselberg
622
Reutigen
Stockental
Längen-
bühl
656
Uebeschi
Höfen
691
Oberstocken
Niederstocken
Stocken
Stockhorn
Gurzelen
593
Forst
Pohlern
Blumenstein
659
Mettlen
Wattenwil
2075
Homad
Walalp
2190
1950

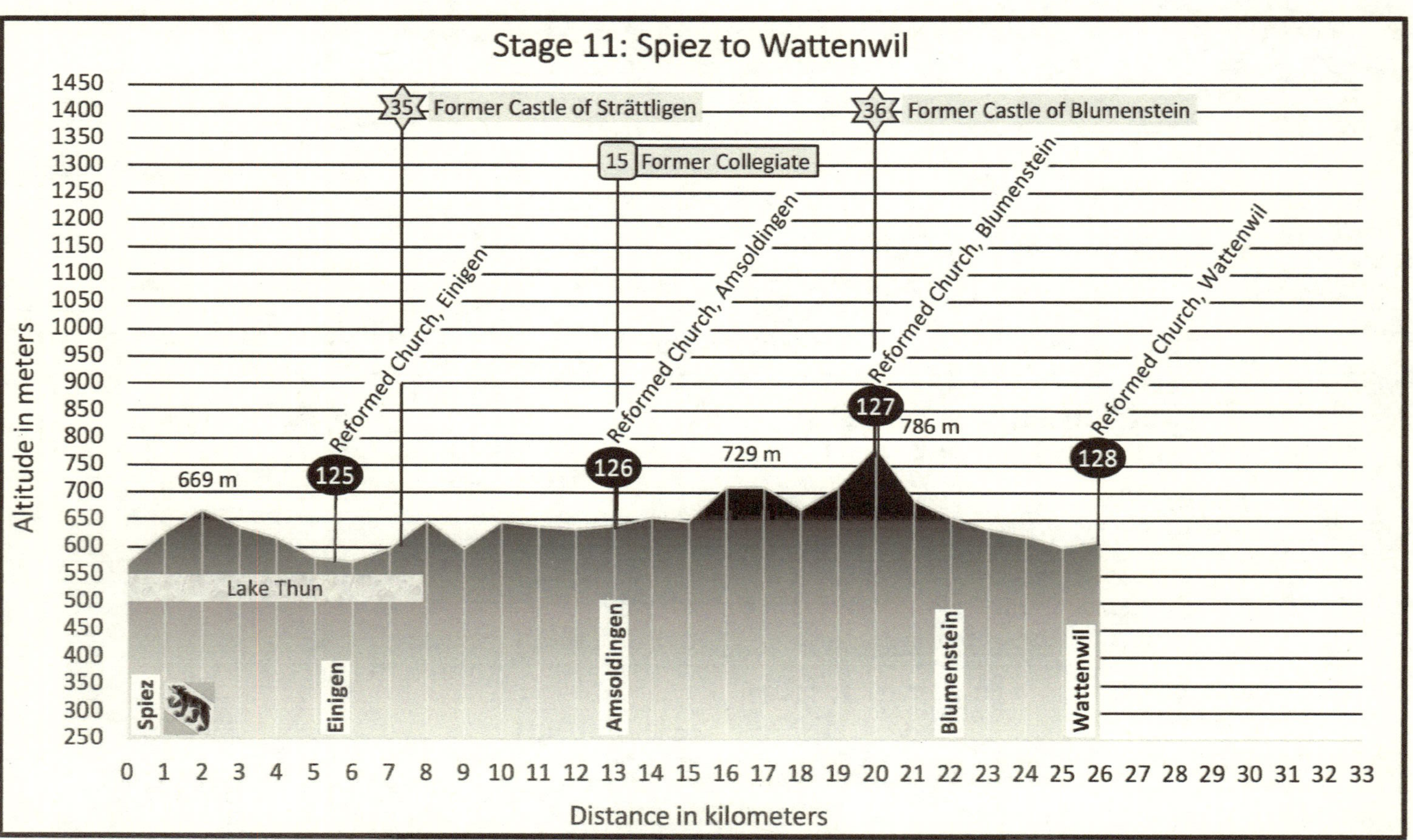

Stage 11: Spiez to Wattenwil
35 Former Castle of Strättligen
36 Former Castle of Blumenstein
15 Former Collegiate
Reformed Church, Einigen
Reformed Church, Amsoldingen
Reformed Church, Blumenstein
Reformed Church, Wattenwil
125
126
127
128
669 m
729 m
786 m
Lake Thun
Spiez
Einigen
Amsoldingen
Blumenstein
Wattenwil
Altitude in meters
1450
1400
1350
1300
1250
1200
1150
1100
1050
1000
950
900
850
800
750
700
650
600
550
500
450
400
350
300
250
0 1 2 3 4 5 6 7 8 9 10 11 12 13 14 15 16 17 18 19 20 21 22 23 24 25 26 27 28 29 30 31 32 33
Distance in kilometers

Hiking the Route

At the end of stage 10 you left the signposted route nr. 4 at the corner of the *Schlossstrasse* and *Reberweg* (the access road to the castle). From the castle grounds follow the signposted route and resume the route at the *Reberweg*. Continue the road up the hill to the vineyards. The road turns into a gravel footpath and steps go up the Spiez mountain (*Spiezberg*) in between vineyards with red and white grapes. Before turning into the forest in a westward direction, the trail on the hill provides a magnificent view over Spiez, its castle and old church, the triangular Niesen mountain, Lake Thun, and the Alps in the background.

The route follows a gravel path on the Spiez mountain for the following 1.1 km. In the middle of the forest on the Spiezberg the route reaches a high point of 669 meters, from where the path descends again. After 400 meters through the residential areas of Spiezmoos the route crosses road nr. 6. (still the same road from Brienz) and soon afterwards passes underneath the railway tracks. The triangular Niesen mountain (2'362 meters) continues to dominate the southern horizon. Immediately after the underpass the route turns right. The trail is parallel to the train tracks for 1.5 km, in a northwestern direction. The route follows the forested edge of the Eggliwald, where the gravel path ascends and descends in short distances. After a last patch of forest, the route joins a country road and turns right. A path through grasslands descends to the railway tracks for 300 meters. A bench invites to sit down and admire the view to the southeast (direction Spiez and Interlaken).

Steps lead down to an underpass of the railway tracks. About 200 meters later, past apple trees and a farmhouse, the route descends to road nr. 6. The yellow hiking sign directs to turn left and you follow the pavement along road nr. 6 to Einigen for 400 meters. Keep looking back to the southeast; the snow-capped mountain peaks remain visible in the distance. The route turns right and follows a small parallel road (*Dorfstrasse*) through the village towards the reformed Church of Einigen, where you arrive at km 5.5. The church is close to Lake Thun, just behind the boat pier.

125 Reformed Church, Einigen (Reformierte Kirche)

- Dorfstrasse 40, 3646 Einigen
- St. Michael
- On a table left of the main entrance, next to the organ and information stand. Two stamps have been pre-printed on stickers: one with a St. James pilgrim and one of the church with the text '*Einigen am Thunersee*' (Einigen at Lake Thun).
- The church was probably first built around 680, making it one of the oldest churches along the Swiss Way of St. James. This first church had a square nave (4 by 4 meters) and a semicircular chancel. This church was rebuilt and enlarged around 933. The church was first mentioned on the list of churches of the Bishopric of Lausanne in 1228. The bell tower was added to the church in 1261 (the steeple is from a later date). The church was destroyed in a battle in 1332, after which it was rebuilt to its present proportions and appearance. From 933 until the Reformation in 1528, the church was dedicated to St. Michael and was an important regional pilgrimage destination (*Wallfahrtskirche*).

  During the Reformation all catholic interior decorations were removed, including a high-altar dedicated to St. Michael, a left side-altar dedicated to the Virgin Mary, a right side-altar dedicated to all Virgins and Martyrs, as well as all relics that were kept at the altars. The last renovation was undertaken in 1954-55, when excavations dated the oldest foundations back to 680.
- The church has typical Romanesque features: narrow windows, thick walls, and decorative Lombard arches on the outer walls of the chancel. Nowadays the oldest decoration is the baptismal font with the coat-of-arms (a star) of the Lords of Bubenberg, dating from 1446. When you look closely, you can identify several special features in the church: a pilgrim with St. James scallops and walking stick on a stained-glass window (1519); stories depicted on the other stained-glass

windows; the different alignment of the chancel and the nave; the parallelogram shape of the nave; and the three devil faces, hidden in the decorative artwork – can you find them?

An important contribution to the late medieval popularity of this church were the so-called **Strättligen Chronicles**, dating from 1464-87. These chronicles were written by Elogius Kiburger, the pastor of the church of Einigen in service of the Lords of Bubenberg (who resided at the castle of Spiez at that time). The name Strättligen refers to the Lords of Strättligen (see below), who had the church built. These chronicles consisted of two main parts: legends about the establishment of 12 churches and legends about the establishment of the mother church in Einigen. Over the centuries there has been much debate about the credibility of these chronicles: many believe them to be a collection of legends (with which the pastor tried to increase the importance of the church and himself), whereas some believe there is a certain degree of historical truth in the stories.

The chronicle's legends about the establishment of 12 churches are as follows. It started with King Rudolf II of Burgundy, husband of the famous Queen Berta (see stage P1, Volume III) and father of the later Queen Adelaide, wife of the German-Roman Emperor Otto I. When King Rudolf II of Burgundy visited the Strättligen Castle in Spiez, he had a dream of a large city with 12 towers, each tower guarded by an angel. He interpreted this as an assignment to build 11 churches around a mother church in Einigen and tasked the land owner, the Lord of Strättligen, with building them. The chronicles list these 12 churches, which have also been listed by the Bishopric of Lausanne in 1228 (of an earlier date than the chronicles). Twelve churches dating from the 10th-11th centuries were indeed located around the shores of Lake Thun (collectively they are called the 1'000-year-old churches around Lake Thun). Since the church in Einigen was considered the mother church, it attracted many pilgrims during the middle ages. Nowadays 11 of these churches still exist (one was destroyed by a fire in 1536), but only four have been restored to their original appearance from a 1'000 years ago. The Way of St. James passes by three of these restored 1'000-year-old churches: the castle church in Spiez (see stage 10); the church in Einigen where you are now; and the church in Amsoldingen (the next church, see below).

The chronicle's legends about the establishment of the mother church in Einigen are as follows. The archangel St. Michael, together with many other angels, appeared in front of the Lord of Strättligen and pointed out the plot of land where a new church in Einigen had to be built. The plot of land (called 'in Paradise') had a spring that flowed into Lake Thun. St. Michael said that this well had healing powers and had to be provided with a particle of the Holy Cross. This was to attract many pilgrims. After the church was built, the archangel Michael and the other angels appeared again and consecrated the church, the relics, and the holy spring, in the presence of the Lords of Strättligen, the Bishop of Lausanne, and the local population. (Notice the similarity with the legend of the consecration by angels of the Our Lady Chapel at the Benedictine Abbey of Einsiedeln – see stage 4, Volume I). During the ceremony of the consecration a peasant became possessed by the devil. The devil spoke to the people and the bishop, and tried to prevent them to honor this new church. The bishop locked the possessed peasant in the high-altar and exorcized the devil (hence the three devil faces hidden in the decorations). After the church was destroyed by Bernese troops (1332), it was rebuilt and St. Michael appeared again at its consecration. Under protection of St. Michael the church was never destroyed again. Over the centuries the church collected many relics brought back from pilgrimages by the Lords of Strättligen, for example: a relic of the cape of St. Michael from Monte Gargano; a piece of the grave of St. Catherine from Sinai; and a particle of the Holy Cross from Jerusalem. The chronicles describe many miraculous healings at the church and its holy spring. If you are looking for the natural healing spring, you will not find it. Neither will you see the relics, as they were all destroyed during the Reformation in 1528.

From the church continue 300 meters along the *Dorfstrasse*, until the route is back on road nr. 6 (*Hauptstrasse*). An underpass leads you to the other side. After 100 meters the route trails left and passes underneath the railway tracks.

The route follows a road left of the tracks for 500 meters, after which it turns left up a forested hill and then down to the Kander River gorge. Some steps down and a sharp right lead you to the metal footbridge over the gorge (the *Strättlisteg* built in 1967, renovated in 2011; length 30 meters, height 20 meters). The bridge's floor is a metal grid; look down to see the foamy river, finding its way between large boulders towards Lake Thun. About 100 meters to the right the railway tracks also bridge the narrow gorge. After the bridge the route turns left and an ascending gravel trail briefly follows the Kander gorge, until a sharp right leads you out of the forest and across a road.

A gravel road goes up the hill with a forest on your left. You arrive at the Strättligen Tower (*Strättligturm*) on the left side. If it was not for the information table you would probably not have realized that there is a castle tower on the hill to the left. It is hidden behind trees (not visible during the approach) and only a narrow gravel path leads up to the fortified walls.

The **former Castle of Strättligen** was originally built by the Lords of Strättligen (their name was derived from *Strasse* – street), most likely as their family residence (though this is not certain as they owned several castles in the region). The family was first mentioned in 1175, as followers of the powerful Dukes of Zähringen (founders of the City of Bern) in the Kingdom of Burgundy. They may have built the castle in the 11th or 12th century.

At the beginning of the 14th century the noble families in the area changed their loyalty to the House of Habsburg-Austria. That triggered the City of Bern to go to war with the nobility in the Bernese Highlands to limit the territorial expansion by the House of Habsburg. In 1332 the Bernese went on a military campaign, conquered the area, and destroyed the Strättligen castle. Because the Lords of Strättligen were bankrupt by then, they did not rebuild the castle.

From 1260 the fortunes of the Strättligen family were declining and they were regularly in financial difficulties. The Lords of Strättligen met the same fate as many of the other nobility in the region (compare to the Lords of Ringgenberg). During the 12th-14th centuries the territorial expansion efforts of the House of Habsburg (from the German-speaking north), the House of Savoy (from the French-speaking south), and the City-Republic of Bern resulted in wars that drained the finances of the local noble houses. By 1290 the Lords of Strättligen started selling and pawning their lands and properties (often to monasteries, such as the Augustinian monastery of Interlaken).

The impoverished Lords of Strättligen had to sell their castle of Spiez, castle of Strättligen, and the church of Einigen (and all surrounding lands) to the Bernese Sheriff von Bubenberg (from the City-Republic of Bern) in 1338.

The Lords von Bubenberg never rebuilt the castle either, as their family resided at the castle of Spiez. The ruins became the property of the City-Republic of Bern and in 1699 they built a fortified tower to be used as a munition depot. This storage depot was in use until 1883. The tower and walls became the property of the City of Thun in 1977, which renovated it in 1978-81 and 2004.

Nowadays the tower can be rented for events. The first two floors have been modernized; the upper three floors are empty. The courtyard offers benches, tables, and a covered fireplace for BBQing.

You can walk around the high walls of the former castle; there is only one steel entrance door, which is locked. There is no chance to peek inside or go up the tower. When you continue to walk 300 meters and look back, you have a much better view of the former castle than when you were near to it.

The route continues to the northwest on the ridge of a hill through grasslands for 600 meters. It is called the **Burgundy Path** (*Burgunderweg*), derived from the fact that this area belonged to the King of Burgundy from 888 to 1033. The hike on the crest offers great views over the city of Thun, the western end of Lake Thun, and behind you to the former Strättligen castle and the distant Alps. Majestic trees are dotted along the hill's crest. A red bench invites to take a break and enjoy one of the most beautiful views along the Way of St. James through Switzerland.

Descending from the crest the route makes a left on a tarmac road and turns south, away from Lake Thun. You pass by cornfields and apple trees, and see the 2'190-meter-high Stockhorn mountain right in front of you. The road curves to the left and makes a short but steep descent through a patch of forest, followed by a passage underneath Highway A6; you could already hear the traffic on the highway from a distance. In the patch of forest the trail crosses the Glütschbach stream and continues through agricultural fields up a hill. At the village Zwieselberg the nr. 4 signpost leads to the right and the route changes from a southern to a northwestern direction. The route goes through the Glütsch stream valley (*Glütschbachtal*) for the following 3.5 km until you reach Amsoldingen, the location of the next church. The route through this highland valley is more or less flat. From Zwieselberg the path is on a tarmac road but quickly forks to the right and changes to a trail through, and on the edge of, the Bodewald forest. Agricultural fields, apple trees, and scattered farmhouses dominate the scenery in the highland valley. You pass by traditional Bernese farmhouses with their overhanging front roof and colorful geraniums at the windowsills. Looking backwards you can still see the white mountain peaks in the southeast. To the left (south) the Stockhorn mountain range dominates the horizon.

The route leaves the agricultural lands and curves to the left to enter the village Amsoldingen. In the distance you can already see the tower of the reformed Church of Amsoldingen. The church in Amsoldingen is mentioned in the Strättligen Chronicles and is one of the 1'000-year-old churches around Lake Thun. At km 13.0 you arrive at the church.

126 Reformed Church, Amsoldingen (Reformierte Kirche)

Chorherrengasse 2, 3633 Amsoldingen

St. Maurice, St. Christopher

On a table, underneath the staircase that leads up to the small museum

The church was built around the year 700, making it one of the oldest churches along the Swiss Way of St. James. This first church was small, corresponding to the present space of the nave (without chancel) inside the thick stone pillars. Around the year 1000 the church was expanded in width with the arched pillars and the space of the side-naves, and in length by the 2-meter elevated chancel with two side-apses. The church was a Collegiate Church, served by the Collegiate that housed south of it (see below). The church was destroyed in a battle by the Dukes of Zähringen in 1191 and rebuilt around 1200, from when the crypt dates. The church was first mentioned in the listing of the Bishopric of Lausanne in 1228. The bell tower was built around 1400, replacing the right side-apse.

During the Reformation the catholic parish converted to Protestantism and cleared the catholic icons from the church's interior. The walls were whitewashed to cover all frescos. The church was dedicated to St. Maurice until the Reformation in 1528. After a fire in 1576 part of the church was rebuilt in a Gothic style and the floor of the nave was elevated to the level of the chancel. In 1978-80 a comprehensive renovation restored the church's original appearance: the floor of the nave was lowered and part of the frescos, which were covered by whitewash for 450 years, were recovered.

Notice the many similarities with the 1'000-year-old Romanesque castle church in Spiez: 2-meter elevated chancel; high and narrow nave with arched pillars; pillared and vaulted crypt below the chancel (the only pillared crypt in Canton Bern; freely accessible); chancel with side-apses; decorative Lombard arches on the outer walls of the two apses; small windows high up the walls; and the fresco depicting St. Christopher from around 1300.

Other interesting features are: the relief-decorated baptismal font from the early 14th century (one of the oldest in Canton Bern); and the small museum (up the wooden stairs).

Have a closer look at the support columns in the crypt. These were originally taken from the old Roman settlement of Aventicum (nowadays called Avenches). During the first centuries the Broye River valley was occupied by the Romans, who had established a large town in Avenches, inhabiting 20'000 people (about 12 km northeast of Payerne). At that time Aventicum was the capital of Roman Switzerland (see stage P1, Volume III, for further references to Aventicum). These Roman columns were removed in 1876, but put back in their place during the renovations in 1979.

At the front of the church you can see that it is part of a building complex. The church is surrounded by the former Collegiate, a pastor house (*Pfarrhaus*), a mill, an ossuary (*Beinhaus*), and a warehouse. The pastor house was built in 1700 and is connected by a wooden bridge to the former ossuary. The wooden shed below it was used to store the natural goods received from the levied church taxes. For a long time, the crypt was used as pastor house basement and for storage of cheese.

West of the church is the former Collegiate St. Maurice.

Former Collegiate St. Maurice, Amsoldingen (Chorherrenstift) **15**

Chorherrengasse 2, 3633 Amsoldingen

Collegiate

St. Maurice

The buildings of the former collegiate were probably constructed around the year 1000. It is believed that the collegiate was established at the same time as the St. Maurice church was built; the collegiate building and the church formed one complex. The first official mention of the collegiate is in the listing of the Bishopric of Lausanne in 1228 (documents before that time were most likely destroyed during battles in the preceding century). It was the only collegiate in the region. The small collegiate and church must have had the same benefactor, who donated a small plot of land and built them their first housing. The collegiate flourished in the first half of the 14th century, when it housed a school, but always stayed small.

In the 14th-15th centuries the collegiate underwent the same downturn as many of the medieval monasteries. By 1484 they were in poor financial condition and their building was neglected. The City of Bern arranged for the collegiate to be closed and their lands transferred into ownership of the St. Vincent Collegiate of the Cathedral of Bern in 1485 (see stage L4). The last remaining five canons changed services as well.

The St. Vincent collegiate sold the old buildings and extensive lands (including the lake) to a rich Bernese merchant in 1496. In the subsequent centuries it changed private ownership many times. Later owners rebuilt the former collegiate into a residential chateau.

📷 Its present appearance mostly dates from 1846, when an owner rebuilt the chateau in the neo-Gothic style. Today the chateau is still in private ownership; it cannot be accessed.

From the church the route turns right (*Seegässli*) and continues through the highland valley in a northwestern direction. The route starts to ascend gradually, as a tarmac country road passes by meadows, apple trees, and a few Bernese farmhouses over the following 2 km. To the left you pass by two small lakes, Lake Amsoldingen (*Amsoldingersee*) and Lake Übeschi (*Übeschisee*). Because of the tree line these are, however, barely visible. You pass by a sign explaining that you are going to walk across a military training area. The Thun military training area, to the right, is extensive: it includes a tank track, airstrip, barracks, infantry areas, storage, and so forth. When the boom gate is up you can enter; in case of military exercises you may have to make a detour around the area.

The route crosses the southern side of the military training area, after which the tarmac road curves up a hill to the village Übeschi. The Way of St. James passes through town and turns west, straight towards the village Blumenstein.

A hill lies between Übeschi and Blumenstein. An ascent over 1 km leads you to an altitude of 729 meters; a gradual descent over 2 km leads to Blumenstein. The route over the hill is mostly on tarmac farm roads, passing by grasslands that provide wide views in all directions.

The Jungfraujoch still towers high above Lake Thun when you look back. In the far distance to the north you can see a white castle standing on top of a hill. That is the Castle of Burgistein, which you will pass in stage 12.

While ascending the hill you pass by a bison farm, where a small herd of bison roams a large meadow. You pass underneath crackling high-voltage power lines twice. The descent is on a rocky dirt road, passing by a small landslide, and continuing on a narrow grassland trail.

In a small patch of forest the route reaches the Fallbach stream, where it makes a sharp right. At this location you need to leave the signposted route to get to the church of Blumenstein. Instead of making a right turn, go straight to cross the Fallbach stream. After 100 meters you get to the *Stockentalstrasse* (road nr. 230). You can see the village Blumenstein to the right, but to get to the church you need to go straight, up the foothills of a mountain range. This is a detour of 3.3 km and 230 altitude meters. Admittedly, this is a big detour; the single biggest along the Way of St. James through Switzerland. But this detour is rewarded with a setting of the church against a unique background, and a church that dates from nearly a 1'000 years ago. Without this detour stage 11 would be less than 23 km (so enough time should be available).

Cross the road and go straight into the *Zelgstrasse*, between meadows up the hill. You are walking towards a mountain range with peaks between 1'800 and 2'100 meters. The road converges with the *Kirchenstrasse*. Keep following this tarmac road, after which you reach the reformed Church of Blumenstein (at km 20.0). At the same time, you reach the highest point of the day at 786 meters.

The church is located far outside the village Blumenstein. In the middle ages the Fallbach and Gürbe rivers frequently flooded the area with sediments and debris; it was not a safe place to build a church. The first church was built in connection with a castle that once stood on a cliff south of the church.

The **former Castle of Blumenstein** stood on a rocky cliff, above the waterfall of the Fallbach stream, on its left bank. There is little documentation of its history: it is not known when it was built or by whom. It is believed that the Lords of Blumenstein established the castle (or expanded an existing one) upon acquiring the village sometime after 1348. The last documentation dates from 1606, when the castle was sold. By the end of the 18th century only some ruins were left. Nowadays nothing remains.

127 Reformed Church, Blumenstein (Reformierte Kirche)

- Kirchenstrasse 26, 3638 Blumenstein
- St. Nicholas, St. Margaret, St. Christopher, St. Mary Magdalene
- On a small table at the front-left of the nave

The church was first built in the 11th century and was dedicated to St. Nicholas. This Romanesque church, with a high vaulted ceiling, was first mentioned in official documents in 1285. This first small church was replaced by a bigger new church at the beginning of the 14th century. It is believed that the smaller old church was demolished only after the bigger one had enclosed it, so that the services could continue during its construction time. The tower was built as an extension to the first church in the 12th or 13th century, and is nowadays its oldest part. In 1522 a storm caused the roof to collapse on the nave. As the church was already the property of Bern, it is likely that the typical Bernese three-paneled ceiling was installed at that time.

During the Reformation in 1528 the parish denounced Catholicism to convert to Protestantism. All catholic icons were removed and the walls were whitewashed, covering all frescos. The church was elaborately restored in 1972-75.

Special features of the church are the stained-glass windows of the chancel and the frescos on the chancel arch. Two stained-glass windows of the chancel, dating from the beginning of the 14th century, are some of the most well-known restored originals from that period. One depicts St. Nicholas/St. Margaret, the other St. Christopher/St. Magdalene. Below the former you see the coat-of-arms of the Lords of Weissenburg (two towers), below the latter the coat-of-arms of the Lords of Strättligen (arrow).

The fresco depicting St. Christopher carrying Jesus and the stars around the chancel arch were partly restored from underneath the whitewash in 1972-75. The stars above St. Christopher extend behind the wooden ceiling, an indication of the higher vaulted ceiling from before 1522.

From the church follow the yellow hiking sign down the hill towards the village Blumenstein. The first 900 meters are on a tarmac road, after which the route follows a grassland trail for 300 meters. On the tarmac *Kirchenstrasse* the route turns left and follows the road for 400 meters to reach the main road *Stockentalstrasse* (road nr. 230). Cross the road to continue straight. After about 50 meters you get to the Fallbach stream, where you turn left. At this location you are back on the signposted route nr. 4.

About 150 meters later the route turns to road nr. 230, continuing on the pavement along the road through the village Blumenstein for 800 meters. You pass by the typical Bernese houses with geraniums; even the municipal office has a curved overhanging roof. That building has a pointed bell tower on its roof, but it is not a church. In absence of a church in the village itself, the municipal office used its bell tower to warn its population.

The signposted route leaves road nr. 230 by turning to the right immediately after a camping site. The route crosses a meadow on a narrow trail, turns left, right, and crosses the Fallbach stream, after which it turns left. A gradually descending broad gravel road is parallel to the Fallbach stream in a northern direction.

About 500 meters after crossing the stream the route suddenly turns left, disappearing into a patch of forest. It is easy to overlook this left fork as, not only is the signpost about 15 meters left of the gravel road and half-hidden in the (shade of the) tree line, but also the path through the grass to the tree line is hardly visible.

The route crosses the Fallbach stream on a small wooden bridge and enters the nature protected area called Längmoos. An information table explains you are in a high-water protection area, a small forest, and the marshlands of the Gürbe stream (on your left).

About 400 meters later the route leaves the area and turns left to cross the Gürbe stream on a wooden roofed road bridge. The nr. 4 route sign indicates to turn right, where the route is next to the Gürbe stream (on its western bank) for the following 1.5 km. The gravel path gradually descends and in the distance you can already see the church tower of Wattenwil against a green hilly background.

The route next to the stream is easy to hike, providing a relaxed ending of stage 11. Because of the tree line and bushes you hardly get to see the stream and its rocky riverbed. Whereas the gravel path and the Gürbe stream continue north, the signpost directs left when reaching a main road (*Bernstrasse*). You have reached Wattenwil.

In medieval times **Wattenwil** was a small settlement in the marshlands of the Gürbe stream, where floods and landslides often occurred. For this reason the area never had a castle. The lands belonged to the Lords of Strättligen and after their lineage died out in 1349, the territory transferred to the Lords of Burgistein (see stage 12). The villagers oriented towards the monastery of Rüeggisberg (see stage 12) and the churches in Riggisberg (see stage 12) and Thurnen. Until 1642 gallows stood in the village, as a place of execution for the courts of the local nobility. Nowadays the town has around 3'000 inhabitants.

On the main road (*Bernstrasse*) turn left and continue walking to the west, straight across the roundabout towards the church tower. About 400 meters from the stream you arrive at the reformed Church of Wattenwil, the end of stage 11 (at km 26.1).

Reformed Church, Wattenwil (Reformierte Kirche) **128**

- Grundbachstrasse 5, 3665 Wattenwil
- On the table in front of the chancel
- The church was first built as a small chapel, probably in the early 15th century. In absence of excavations or earlier documentation of the chapel an exact date or patron Saint could not be determined. The oldest bell of the church dates from 1404 (but it could have come from another church). The chapel was a subsidiary chapel of the church of Thurnen, which was the property of the Augustinian monastery of Interlaken since 1343. During the Reformation in 1528, all catholic icons were removed and the chapel might have been closed or put to a different use. As the properties of the Augustinian monastery of Interlaken fell in the hands of the Bernese, so had this chapel in Wattenwil. In 1659 the designation of the chapel was elevated to parish church. As parish church the building was soon deemed too small and in 1683 the church was significantly expanded to the hall church you see today. The bell tower was heightened in 1692.
- The oldest interior part is the baptismal font, dating from 1659, the year the chapel received the designation of parish church (and thus required a baptismal font). Notice how the number nine was carved wrongly. The church used to have artful stained-glass windows from 1683, but they were sold in 1875, when stained-glass went out of fashion. After receiving a large donation new stained-glass windows were purchased in 1936. The last large renovation was undertaken in 2010, when the new stained-glass window of the chancel was installed. The church has a typical protestant interior.

  The table in front of the chancel offers everything a visiting pilgrim needs: a folder with a list of pilgrim accommodations; a pitcher with fresh drinking water; a pilgrim stamp; a guestbook; candles and matches; and a small bouquet of flowers to brighten up the end of stage 11.

From the ending point

The reformed Church in Wattenwil is the ending point of stage 11, directly on the signposted route nr. 4.

Wattenwil has no train station, but one is nearby. In case you are a day-hiker, you need to take the bus to reach the nearest train station (*Seftigen*). The closest bus stop is 300 meters back (right-side of the road) towards the roundabout and is called *Wattenwil-Bären*. Bus nr. 53 (direction *Seftigen Bahnhof*) departs from there every 7 and 29 minutes past the hour. The bus arrives at the Seftigen train station 8 minutes later.

In case you are a thru-hiker and spend the night in Wattenwil, be aware that there are only a few pilgrim beds in B&B accommodations. Check out the folder in the church, www.jakobsweg.ch, or www.viajacobi4.ch for the accommodation possibilities, addresses, and contact details.

The next Stage

Stage 12 guides you over the eastern and northern foothills that half-circle the Gantrisch mountain range. Read the next chapter to find out what that entails.

Stage 12:
Wattenwil to Schwarzenburg
24 km

The Way along the 950-year-old Cluniac Monastery

Route stats

	Distance in km	*Time in hrs:min*
Signposted route nr. 4	21.0	4:50
Churches/chapels	1.8	1:10
Points of interest	1.2	0:30
Rest/lunch		1:00
Stage 12	24.0	7:30

In case you hike this stage as a daytrip, you need to add 300 meters in Wattenwil from the bus stop and 1.4 km in Schwarzenburg to the train station. Because the ending point in Schwarzenburg is outside of town at a church on a hill in Wahlern, you need to walk back 1.4 km to the Schwarzenburg train station (town center), whether you spend the night there or take the train home.

Ascent/descent/total	+767/ -546 / 1'313 altitude meters
Lowest/highest altitude	614 / 930 meters
Pathway/condition	easy / moderate
Churches/chapels	Riggisberg, Rüeggisberg (2), Schwarzenburg, Wahlern
Monasteries	Former Cluniac Monastery Rüeggisberg
Points of interest	Castle of Burgistein, Castle of Riggisberg, Archive Tower, Castle of Schwarzenburg

Route summary

Stage 12 continues in the highlands of protestant **Canton Bern** (*Berner Oberland*).

Stage 12 guides you over the eastern and northern foothills that half-circle the Gantrisch mountain range.

Stage 12 immediately enters the foothills and starts with a steep climb over 1 km to reach the first highland plateau. The route stays on this highland plateau, with many short ascents and descents, for 6 km. The route passes by traditional Bernese farmhouses with geraniums, as it follows country roads and grass trails through meadows and agricultural fields. The first church is visited in Riggisberg at km 7.5. From Riggisberg the route turns west, crossing the northern Gantrisch foothills. The route gradually ascends over 3 km on farm roads through meadows to Mättiwil, where the Way of St. James route via Luzern/Bern (coming from the north) converges with stage 12. In the village Rüeggisberg the highest point of the day at 930 meters is reached about 1 km later. In Rüeggisberg the second church and the 950-year-old Cluniac monastery ruins are visited. After leaving the monastery ruins the route follows a historical pilgrimage path in a southwestern direction, descending to the Schwarzwasser River over a distance of 3.5 km. The descent is on tarmac country roads and grass trails. The route briefly follows the Schwarzwasser River bank, after which it climbs out of the valley on a steep forest trail to reach the second highland plateau. The route crosses the highland plateau for 3.5 km, on easy and nearly flat tarmac or gravel country roads. The route makes another short but steep ascent through grasslands to reach 855 meters, from where it descends into Schwarzenburg, arriving at the village chapel in the town's center at km 22. The main church is on the hill in Wahlern, outside of Schwarzenburg, which is reached at km 24, the end of stage 12.

Getting to the starting point

Today's starting point in Wattenwil is at the reformed church. Wattenwil has no train station. In case you hike stage 12 as a daytrip, you need to take the bus from the nearest train station (*Seftigen*). In the morning bus nr. 53 (direction *Blumenstein-Post*) departs from *Seftigen* train station at every 41 minutes past the hour, taking only 5 minutes. The nearest bus stop is 300 meters before the church and is called *Wattenwil-Bären*. From the bus stop follow the *Burgisteinstrasse/Grundbachstrasse* heading west, leading straight to the church.

Route Map and Profile

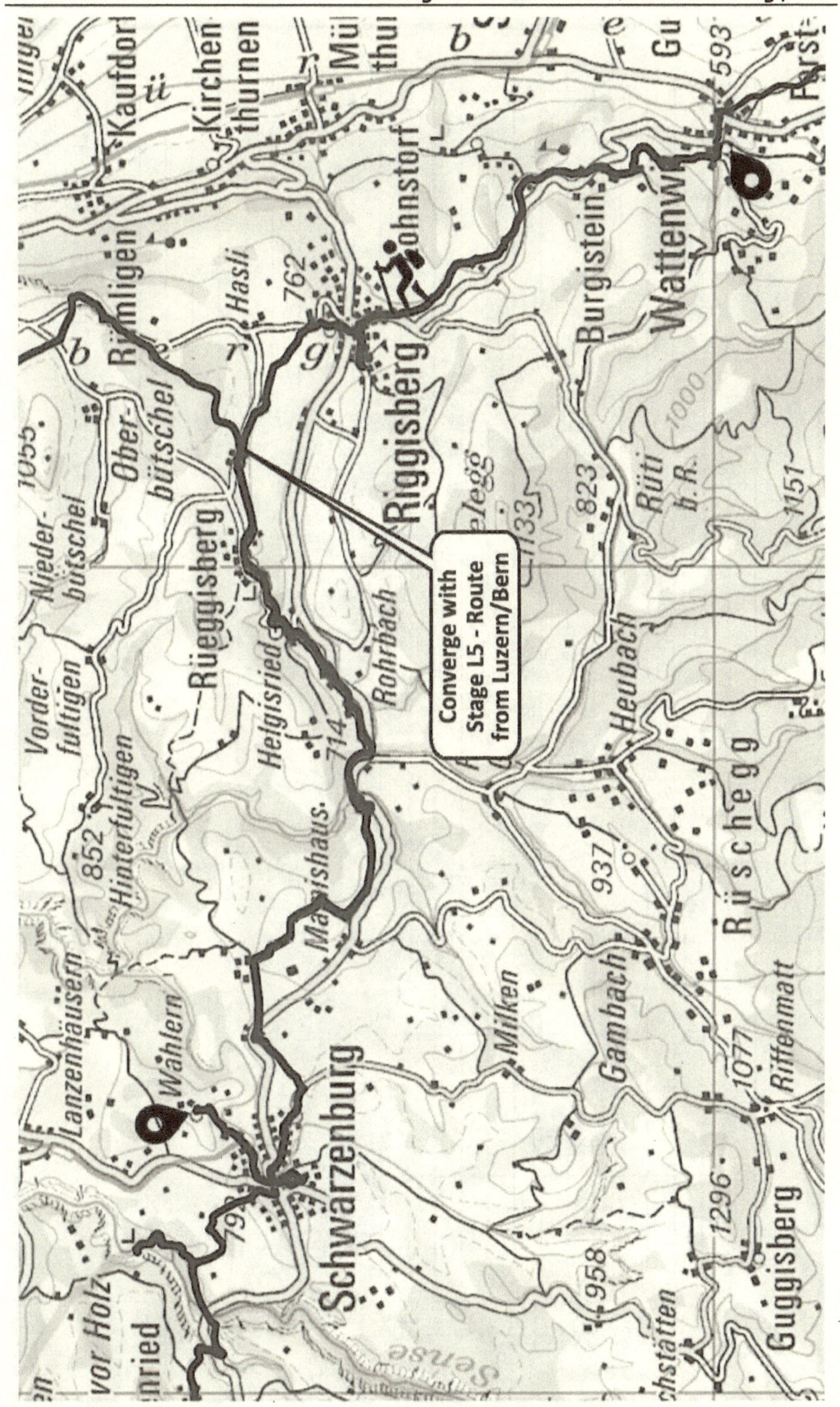
Converge with Stage L5 - Route from Luzern/Bern
Riggisberg
Rüeggisberg
Schwarzenburg
Wattenwil
Burgistein
Rüschegg
Guggisberg
Rümligen
Kirchenthurnen
Kaufdorf
Helgisried
Rohrbach
Heubach
Gambach
Milken
Riffenmatt
Wahlern
Lanzenhäusern
Hinterfultigen
Vorderfultigen
Niederbütschel
Oberbütschel
Hasli
Mamishaus.
Sense
762
714
852
937
958
1055
1077
1151
1296
823
593

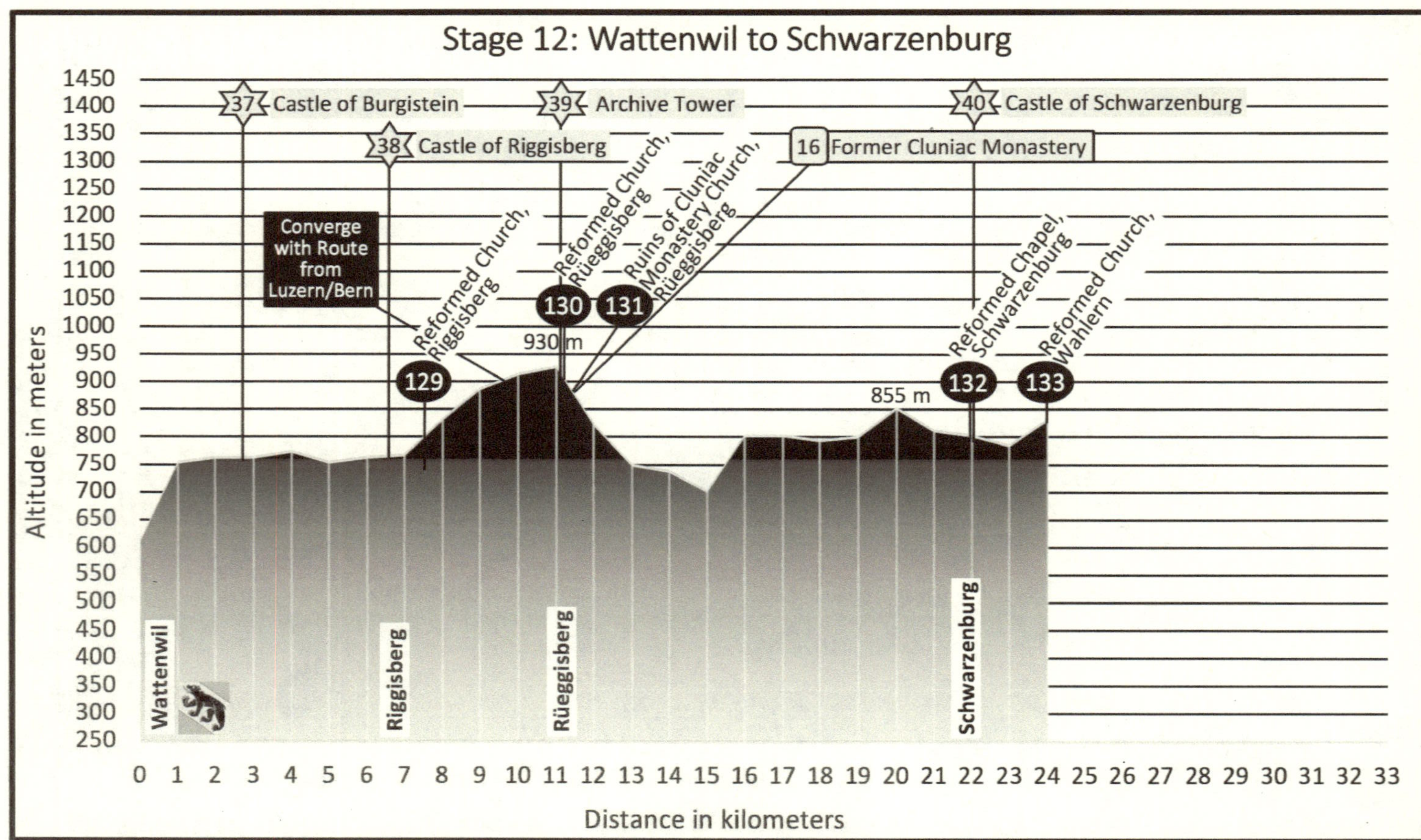
Stage 12: Wattenwil to Schwarzenburg
37 Castle of Burgistein
39 Archive Tower
40 Castle of Schwarzenburg
38 Castle of Riggisberg
16 Former Cluniac Monastery
Converge with Route from Luzern/Bern
129 Reformed Church, Riggisberg
130 Reformed Church, Rüeggisberg
131 Ruins of Cluniac Monastery Church, Rüeggisberg
132 Reformed Chapel, Schwarzenburg
133 Reformed Church, Wahlern
930 m
855 m
Wattenwil
Riggisberg
Rüeggisberg
Schwarzenburg
Altitude in meters
1450 1400 1350 1300 1250 1200 1150 1100 1050 1000 950 900 850 800 750 700 650 600 550 500 450 400 350 300 250
0 1 2 3 4 5 6 7 8 9 10 11 12 13 14 15 16 17 18 19 20 21 22 23 24 25 26 27 28 29 30 31 32 33
Distance in kilometers

Hiking the Route

Wattenwil lies in the Gürbe highland valley, along the Gürbe stream, at the eastern edge of the Gantrisch mountain range. The Gantrisch mountain peak (2'176 m) lies southwest of Wattenwil, but its foothills border the Gürbe highland valley. From the reformed church of Wattenwil the Way of St. James immediately enters these foothills. The route goes steeply up the hill on a tarmac road in a northern direction to Dornere over 1 km. Looking backwards you have a good view of Wattenwil, the Gürbe valley, and even the Jungfraujoch at the horizon. At a traditional half-timbered Bernese farmhouse with geraniums in Dornere, the route makes a sharp right turn, where the steep climb becomes a more gradual ascending trail through the meadows.

You pass by apple trees and a farmhouse, after which the route is back on the country road coming from Wattenwil. To the north you see a white castle on a hill (the same one you saw in the far distance in stage 11); it is the Burgistein Castle. The route follows a concrete road, changes to grasslands, and back to a road, while gradually descending into the village Burgistein.

In Burgistein the route crosses road nr. 230 (the same from Blumenstein and Wattenwil in stage 11). After the restaurant *zur Linde* (in a typical Bernese farmhouse) the route turns right onto a gravel path. The trail goes up the hill to a farmhouse that is at the beginning of a tree-lined lane that leads up to the Castle of Burgistein. The lane is beautiful and to the south you see the wide landscape, through which you passed in the previous stages.

The Castle of Burgistein has been a beacon of the Way of St. James for many kilometers, already in stage 11. The castle can only be viewed from the distance; the closer you get to it, the more it disappears behind a tree line. Unless you want to enjoy the lane and the views, you can save yourself the 220 meters ascent (and return): you will not be able to access the castle grounds. The castle is private property and a viciously growling and barking guard dog will chase you back down the lane (he is not chained) when you approach the front gate.

The **Castle of Burgistein** was built by Lord Jordan I 'of Thun' in 1260, who called himself 'of Burgistein' from 1266. He purchased the lands from the Augustinian monastery of Interlaken to build a new residence.

In 1340 the castle met the same fate as so many other castles in the Bernese Highlands: it was plundered and destroyed by Bernese troops. At the beginning of the 14th century the noble families in the area professed their loyal allegiance to the Kingdom of Habsburg-Austria. At that time the City-Republic of Bern grew increasingly powerful and went to war with the nobility in the Bernese Highlands to limit the territorial expansion by the House of Habsburg. In 1340 the Bernese went on a military campaign and destroyed the Castle of Burgistein. The castle was rebuilt and over the centuries changed ownership several times.

The appearance of the present buildings mostly dates from construction work in the 15th-16th centuries. Since 1717 it has been owned by the family von Graffenried; it is still a private residence today.

From the farmhouse the gravel path goes down the hill to the village Weier. The route makes a broad westward curve around a pond. In the village you see a road-sign directing to a church. Do not bother looking for it as it is in another village, away from the signposted route (this reformed church has a short history, being newly built in 1959).

The route converges with road nr. 230 and forks to the right. The tarmac country road goes through grassland past some farmhouses. You see the rolling foothills of the Gantrisch region all around. After 700 meters the route suddenly turns right, into a meadow, steeply up a hill. The short climb leads you to the edge of a forest. After the small patch of forest the route crosses grasslands to continue on a gravel farm road in a northern direction, more or less parallel to road nr. 230. As a beacon on a hill in the far north you can already see the church of Riggisberg, against the background of higher green hills. The route passes by traditional Bernese farmhouses and cows grazing in the meadows, and follows the Halbbach stream for a while, until the route converges with road nr. 230, shortly before entering the town Riggisberg.

On a hill in the west (left) you see the Castle of Riggisberg. This castle is 400 meters aside the signposted route. At the bus station in the town center turn left (*Vordere Gasse*), instead of going straight. Keep following this road *Gsteigstrasse* up the hill. The castle is up the stairs, on your left behind a rectangular building.

The **Castle of Riggisberg** was first built by the Lords of Riggisberg, probably at the beginning of the 12th century. The family name Riggisberg was first mentioned in official documents in 1140. In 1256 Lord Jakob of Riggisberg founded the Franciscan Monastery in Fribourg (see monastery nr. 19, stage 13). By marriage the castle changed to the Lords of Diesbach around 1337. In 1363 the Lords of Burgistein purchased the castle and surrounding lands. By marriage the castle became the property of the Bernese merchant family von Erlach in 1387. They owned it for more than 400 years until 1799 (they also owned the castle of Spiez from 1516 until 1877). Around 1700 they built the present-day chateau. In the decades leading up to the French invasion in 1798, the last descendants of the family von Erlach became increasingly indebted and continually sold parts of their once extensive estates. They sold the chateau of Riggisberg in 1799. From then the chateau changed hands several times until several municipalities acquired the chateau in 1880. The chateau was remodeled and housed a regional institution for the old and poor. An old rectangular building was demolished and replaced with a new construction in 1938. Nowadays the former chateau from around 1700 is the oldest part of the retirement home complex. The old chateau was extensively renovated and modernized in 1965-70.

From the castle walk back down the hill via the *Gsteigstrasse* and the *Vordere Gasse.* Take the second street on the left (one block before reaching the bus station), cross the *Hintere Gasse* street (on the zebra crossing on the right) after 50 meters, and you are back on the signposted route nr. 4. A footpath leads steeply up the hill to the church. The final steps lead up to the reformed Church of Riggisberg, at km 7.5.

129 Reformed Church, Riggisberg (Reformierte Kirche)

- Kirchweg 12, 3132 Riggisberg
- St. Sebastian
- On a shelf in the anteroom at the entrance
- The church was first built as a small chapel, dedicated to St. Sebastian, in the 12th century. This chapel was first mentioned as a subsidiary chapel of the church of Thurnen in official documents in 1343 (when the church of Thurnen became the property of the Augustinian monastery of Interlaken). Not much is known of its early history.

  During the Reformation in 1528 all catholic icons were removed and the chapel was closed for 11 years (until 1539). As the properties of the Augustinian monastery of Interlaken fell in the hands of the Bernese, so had this chapel in Riggisberg. In 1687-88 the nave was dismantled and rebuilt by the Lords von Erlach. The nave was rebuilt again in 1939, after the designation of the chapel had been elevated to parish church in 1936. In 1950 the church renewed its bells: the small old bell was relocated to the Riggisberg castle tower; the larger old bell was transferred to the castle church of Spiez, where it was placed next to the entrance of the church (do you remember seeing it?). The main western entrance to the church was covered with an externally attached portal.
- During renovations in 1977-79 the church was restored to its original appearance, for which many constructional changes were made to the nave. The interior has a typical protestant appearance, limited to a pulpit, communion table, pews, and

gallery with organ. Nowadays the late-Romanesque chancel tower from the second half of the 12th century is the oldest original part.

The church has several special features. The small stained-glass figures in the windows are originals dating from the 12th to the 17th century. Two of them have the coat-of-arms of the family von Erlach, who owned the neighboring castle between 1387 until 1799.

The bell tower is right above the chancel. The cave-like shape of the chancel seems like it was carved into the base of the tower, which is unique for this region.

Before departing from the church, admire the view to the south over the town Riggisberg and the Gantrisch mountain range. From the church the route briefly continues north, passes by a hospital (on the right), and makes a left turn in a westward direction. The route ascends steadily until reaching the next village Rüeggisberg. Gravel roads through meadows and past Bernese farmhouses change to tarmac country roads that lead up to a main road.

A narrow gravel/tarmac path left of the road passes through the settlement Mättiwil. At km 9.7 (154 km since the splitting of the route in Brunnen at the start of stage 6) the Way of St. James route via Luzern/Bern converges with stage 12 of the Alpine Lakes route. The trail from Bern comes from the right, down the hill from the *Taanwald* forest through a meadow to Mättiwil.

Converge with Route from Luzern/Bern

After Mättiwil the route forks to the left, leaving the road, crossing a meadow for 700 meters. You only see where you have to go by staying in between the agricultural fields left and right, and following a grass trail that is flattened in one direction. The soil is very uneven; it is uncomfortable to walk on. This is compensated by the wide views of the southern Gantrisch mountain and its rolling foothills.

On the outskirts of Rüeggisberg the trail changes from grass to tarmac and you can see the bell tower of the next church. The route joins a main road (*Dorfstrasse*) and reaches its highest point of the day at 930 meters shortly before the church.

39

In front of the church is a low tower that looks like a castle's tower. But it is not. It is a rare **Archive Tower**, built in 1790, which served as the municipal's archive and document storage (you saw a much bigger and older archive tower in the town Schwyz in stage 5). Nowadays it is used for the storage of some materials (not the municipal's archive).

Behind the tower is the reformed Church of Rüeggisberg (at km 11.1).

Reformed Church, Rüeggisberg (Reformierte Kirche) 130

Dorfstrasse 2, 3088 Rüeggisberg

St. Martin

The church was first built in the 11th century and was dedicated to St. Martin. This church pre-dated the Cluniac monastery church (see below) by about 100 years. At the establishment of the monastery in 1072, the Lord of Rümligen donated the church to the monastery. The church was first mentioned in official documents as the property of the Cluniac monastery in 1148. In 1484 the monastery closed and its lands changed ownership to the newly founded St. Vincent Collegium of the Cathedral of Bern, to which also the church changed hands.

During the Reformation in 1528 the parish converted to Protestantism; all catholic religious decorations were removed. A village fire destroyed the old church in 1532. In 1539 the church was rebuilt with bricks plundered from the monastery that had already been abandoned at that time.

In the 18th century the church was significantly expanded: the chancel was enlarged, the nave was extended on the western side, and the gallery was built. The first organ was installed in the chancel in 1789, but was moved to the side-gallery during the renovations in 1956-57.

The church has a typical protestant interior. Apart from one of the church bells dating from before the fire (1516), the baptismal font, serving as communion table, is the oldest part dating from 1688. The three stained-glass windows (1967) in the chancel depict the Holy Trinity: God the Father, Jesus the Son, and the Holy Spirit.

From the church it is only 300 meters to the ruins of the former Cluniac monastery. Follow the gravel path at the back of the church, past the parking lot, down the hill. An information board has a drawing illustrating the monastery in its original state. Across the road you arrive at the ruins of the Cluniac Monastery Church (at km 11.4).

Ruins of Cluniac Monastery Church, Rüeggisberg (Kirche Ruine) 131

Kloster, 3088 Rüeggisberg

St. Peter and Paul

In the windowsill left of the entrance of the small museum

The monastery church was built over a period of 100 years between 1072 and 1175. It was built as a replica of the Basilica of Cluny and was dedicated to St. Peter and Paul. The church had three naves, a large transept, and a chancel with five apses. During the construction the monks used the neighboring St. Martin church for services and prayers. The monastery's church had already fallen in ruins by 1300, after which it was used as a barn. The church and monastery were abandoned by the beginning of the 16th century and fell into disrepair. Its stones were plundered to rebuild the St. Martin church and other village houses after a fire had destroyed them in 1532. The City of Bern decided to demolish the church and monastery in 1541.

The restored ruins of the northern transept of the church is the only part left standing (the main reason why this was not demolished over the centuries was its use as a barn). Renovations were undertaken in 1938-47 and 1988-92. The restored remnant walls of the chancel and side-apses exhibit the typical Cluniac architecture.

Southwest of the ruins a low building houses a small museum dedicated to the former monastery and the Way of St. James pilgrimage in general. A model shows that about nine percent of the former church is still left standing, indicating how sizeable this church must have been.

16 Former Cluniac Monastery, Rüeggisberg (ehemaliges Cluniazenser Priorat)

Kloster, 3088 Rüeggisberg

Cluniac Order

The Cluniac monastery was established by the mother Abbey of Cluny (France), on request of the regional Lord of Rümligen in 1072. His request was accompanied by the donation of extensive lands, including the St. Martin church, to finance the building of the monastery and its church. It was the first Cluniac monastery established in German-speaking Switzerland. The mother Abbey of Cluny sent two monks, who started with a simple cell. Their first small buildings were constructed in 1075. Most of the time the number of monks was below 10, which did not prevent them from building a cathedral-sized church.

During the middle ages their monastery was an important station along the Way of St. James through Switzerland, providing pilgrims with care, food, and shelter. At their peak in the 12th-13th centuries, the monastery owned extensive lands in the region, including the towns Riggisberg and Schwarzenburg.

From the mid 13th century their decline set in, caused by: poor leadership and their distance from the mother Abbey in Cluny; the too costly and oversized church; regional wars; and the looting and ravaging by the poor population of the region. By 1300 most of their buildings were empty or occupied by local farmer families, who used the church as their barn. Part of the buildings were already in ruins and the monks' dormitory had burned down. The once so rich monastery deteriorated and became indebted. At the time the Cathedral of Bern was being built (see stage L4) in 1484, the monastery (with its lands and income) was annexed by the St. Vincent Collegiate of the Cathedral of Bern. They used the income from the extensive lands to help finance the construction of their new cathedral. This is similar to what happened to the St. Maurice Collegium of Amsoldingen in 1485 (see stage 11).

With hardly any income, life at the Cluniac monastery had become very difficult, and successively monks left. It stood empty by the beginning of the 16th century and fell into disrepair. Its bricks were plundered to rebuild the St. Martin church and other village houses after a fire had destroyed them in 1532. The City of Bern decided to demolish the monastery in 1541. Some remaining parts of the former housing were used as a girls' corrective institution in 1834-75, until those buildings burned down in 1875.

The route continues downhill through grasslands in a southwestern direction to reach a road (*Klostergasse*). The Way of St. James follows the old monastery path that used to be the medieval pilgrimage and trade route (first mentioned in documents in 1533) between Schwarzenburg and the Cluniac monastery. The route continues on a road for 100 meters, after which it turns left through a small patch of forest. The forest trail is through a sunken lane and goes over a small stream on a temporary wooden bridge, curving around a small gorge.

The **Sunken Lane** (also called Holloway) indicates the heavy use during the middle ages. The sunken lanes were created by erosion of the soft and humid forest underground, caused by the traffic of carriages, carts, and horses over many centuries. At the time of heavy use, the sunken lanes had more or less straight walls on the left and right side (U-shape). Because these sunken lanes were dirt roads, they made traveling difficult during rainy periods. The development of bigger and heavier carriages made traveling these soft roads increasingly problematic. Wooden boards were used to stabilize the road, when stones or gravel were not available. After the route was abandoned for newer, faster roads that could carry heavy carriages (such as the mail coach), the sidewalls collapsed and the path became a wide V-shape. Erosion and vegetation growing on the sides finally reduced the path to a hollow footpath.

The path leaves the small forest and follows the same road down the hill for another 350 meters, passing through the settlement Helgisried. After turning right, the route crosses the meadows on a tarmac farm road, and after a sharp left and right descends on grass to road nr. 183. The trail stays right of the road and the signs lead to the settlement Rohrbach, going up the hill parallel to road nr. 183. In the village the route forks left and through meadows descends back to road nr. 183. The route enters the lands of Schwarzenburg and crosses the Wislisau bridge (*Wislisaubrücke*). At the narrow valley of the Schwarzwasser ('Black Water') River the route turns right and closely follows the left bank of the river for 650 meters. The area is called the Sense-Schwarzwasser nature protected area.

The hike alongside the river is easy, flat, and relaxing, until the route turns away from the river. In front you see forested steep cliffs on the left river bank. The route goes over those cliffs, for which it first turns left to road nr. 183. The road is enclosed by forested cliffs on the left and right. After 40 meters on the right side of the road the route turns right, away from the road, over a wooden footbridge into a forested climb. The ascent is over 1 km, of which the first part is very steep. Zigzagging steps of the forest path help the ascent. The lower part of the path is overgrown; you need to make your way between overhanging bushes. The next part along the edge of the forest is less steep and easier. The route turns away from the forest and goes steeply up through meadows, where you pass by a Yak and Lama farm. At a cellular tower you reach the end of the ascent.

The route continues west on a tarmac road on the highland plateau. At a settlement called Mami's House (*Mamishaus*) the route turns right and a bit later left. The landscape is flat and the gravel farm road crosses agricultural fields. At the village Elisried the route turns left and follows a tarmac road to the village Schönentannen, where it converges with road nr. 183 again. After 150 meters on this road the route turns left.

The flat part of the highland plateau is over and the route climbs on a grass trail through meadows over 400 meters. At the altitude of 849 meters the trail more or less flattens. You pass by a BBQ area. On a hill on the other side of the valley you can see a steeple above a tree line. That is the destination of this stage: the reformed Church of Wahlern. But before you get there, you need to descend into Schwarzenburg and from there go up the hill to that church.

On a cow trail, along a small patch of forest and a tree line, the under-footing becomes very uncomfortable; hard heaps of earth lie about 50 centimeters apart (like waves), making it difficult to keep a rhythmic walking pace. The waved under-footing changes to a grass trail along a tree line as the route descends to a road (nr. 232). At the road the route turns right in the direction of Schwarzenburg, but forks right after 300 meters, away from the road to follow a grass trail up a hill.

At an altitude of 850 meters a hiking sign indicates that you are at the *Galgenzelg*. This hilltop just outside the town Schwarzenburg was the site of the **Gallows** from the middle ages (until 1798). As in other towns, the gallows stood along the main travel route into town, as a deterrent to thieves, robbers, and other criminals. Nowadays it is a peaceful meadow, but during the middle ages the scenes were gruesome. Death sentences were executed by: hanging (for thieves); decapitation with the sword (for murderers); burning (for witches and arsonists); or with the wheel (for murderers). See point of interest nr. 11 in stage 4, Volume I for a description of the cruel forms of execution in the middle ages.

From the former site of the gallows the route trails through the meadow and down the hill towards town. In the outskirts of Schwarzenburg the route converges with road nr. 232 (*Milkenstrasse*). About 400 meters later you reach the Schwarzenburg train station. Keep the station to your right and follow the *Bahnhofstrasse* until a roundabout, where you need to leave the signposted route (otherwise you will leave Schwarzenburg again). Stage 12 ends in Schwarzenburg and passes by the village chapel, castle, and main church. These final 2.2 km, from the roundabout until the end of stage 12, are aside the signposted route nr. 4.

At the roundabout turn left into the *Bernstrasse,* cross the village square with the fountain, and walk straight into the *Dorfplatz*. The chapel is hidden behind the buildings on the right. Between a wooden garage door and a store (in a typical Bernese house with the overhanging roof) is a small alley (on the right) with steps that lead up to the chapel. About 40 meters from the street you arrive at the reformed Village Chapel of Schwarzenburg (at 21.9 km).

132 Reformed Village Chapel, Schwarzenburg (Dorf Kapelle)

- Käppeligässli, 3150 Schwarzenburg
- St. Mary Magdalene
- At the parish office (about 40 meters from the chapel). From the chapel follow the narrow alley between the old dark-wooden buildings to the east. The alley turns left and right, and the beige-colored building with the green shutters on the

right is the parish house. The stamp is a sticker that lies in a plastic slip, hanging at the front door of the parish house (inside the front portal).

The chapel was built in 1463 (as an early morning chapel, as a subsidiary of the church in Wahlern – see below). Until the Reformation it was dedicated to St. Mary Magdalene. It is assumed that an earlier chapel already stood on this site, which burned down in the village fire of 1448. A private person had the chapel rebuilt in 1463. Nowadays it is the oldest building in Schwarzenburg.

Four years into the Reformation all catholic decorations were removed, the chapel was closed, and put to a different use (1532). In 1535 the unusual pyramidal tiled roof above the chancel was built, serving as a fire watchtower. You can still see the ladder that leads up the tower at the back of the chancel. The interior was rebuilt to house the local school. Because of financial problems the municipality had to sell the building in 1859. A new owner rebuilt the interior and used it as a detention room. Later it was rebuilt as a housing for the poor and homeless. It was restored into a protestant chapel after a complete renovation in 1913. This saved the local population the trouble of having to walk up the hill to the church in Wahlern.

The reformed chapel has been shared between the catholic parish (Saturday nights) and the protestant parish (Sunday nights) since 1963. Its interior is austere, without any altars or religious decorations.

About 200 meters south of the parish office is the Castle of Schwarzenburg. Follow the *Junkerngasse* for 40 meters (south), turn left into the *Herrengässli*, and after 120 meters you see the castle in front of you.

The **Castle of Schwarzenburg** was built in 1573-76, as a replacement for the old 12th century Castle of Grasburg (see point of interest nr. 41, stage 13), which was too isolated and had an outdated residential interior with high maintenance costs. It was considered more useful and cheaper to build a modern new governor's residence adapted to the 16th century style and living conditions. This new castle was built with stones from the castle of Grasburg, which was subsequently abandoned and fell into ruins. The chateau is a typical 16th-17th century residential castle, with crafts space on the ground floor, living quarters on the first floor, and a hall for festivities on the second floor. The chateau's space was divided in the governor's residence, a court, prison, and grain storage. Though the walls and towers may give the castle a fortified appearance, these were only decorative; they never had a military purpose. Bernese/Fribourg regional governors resided at the chateau.

Most of its present-day appearance is from the original construction period, though additional building changes were made in the 18th century. The last large renovation was undertaken in 1980-83. In 2009 the Foundation '*Schloss Schwarzenburg*' purchased the chateau to ensure its maintenance as a cultural object and made it accessible to the public as a museum and historical place for cultural events. Nowadays it hosts exhibitions of regional artists and rooms can be rented for events.

Schwarzenburg has a population of around 4'000 and lies at historical trade and travel roads between Fribourg (west) and Thun/Gürbe valley (east). From 1412 it became an important regional trade market for horses, cattle, and cheese. From 1423 to 1798 the region of Schwarzenburg was under shared governance of the Cities of Fribourg and Bern, who initially housed their representative governors at the Castle of Grasburg (they relocated to the Castle of Schwarzenburg in 1576). Schwarzenburg became the center of a territorial power struggle between Fribourg and Bern that lasted for 375 years. In the 15th century battles between the two forces regularly destroyed properties in the town and region. During the Reformation in 1528 Fribourg (which remained catholic) did not have the power to stop Bern from enforcing Protestantism on Schwarzenburg (they could only delay it by some years). In the 18th century the region of Schwarzenburg endured severe poverty. High population growth, the divided and failing governmental systems, and crop failures caused widespread poverty. Many people moved to other regions to escape a life of poverty. The region was allocated to Fribourg after the invasion of French troops in 1798. At the request of the local population the region switched to Canton Bern in 1802.

Stage 12 does not end at the castle or the village chapel. Schwarzenburg is the only exception on the Swiss Way of St. James, where the stage ends at a main church that is outside of town. From the castle you need to walk about 1.9 km in a northeastern direction to get to this church. Backtrack 450 meters to the roundabout near the train station and continue straight (*Bernstrasse*). About 150 meters later, after the Coop supermarket, turn right and follow the street (*Ringgenmatt*) for 800 meters. Turn right and continue to follow the road.

The last 500 meters the route ascends to 835 meters. The last 100 meters are on a steep tarmac path, separated from the road. The hill of the church offers a great view over the town Schwarzenburg. Across a car park you reach the reformed Church of Wahlern (at km 24.0).

Reformed Church, Wahlern (Reformierte Kirche) 133

- Wahlernstrasse 55, 3150 Schwarzenburg
- St. James the Greater, St. Mary Magdalene
- In a plastic slip that hangs on the information table outside, under the roofed portal at the left side-entrance. The stamp is the same as the one for the village chapel.
- The church was first mentioned in official documents of the Bishopric of Lausanne in 1228, with St. James and Mary Magdalene as patron Saints. It is believed that the hilltop was already used for pagan offerings during the time of the Celts and that a first catholic church might have been built before or around the year 1000. In 1511 the church was completely remodeled: the bell tower was built, the chancel was rebuilt, and the nave was heightened and received new larger windows. Bern forced Protestantism on the church during the Reformation in 1529; all catholic decorations were removed.

  The church history is marked by fires caused by lightning. The hilltop was the highest point in the area and the bell tower was like a magnet for lightning, causing fires in 1603, 1645, 1709, and 1821 (and probably more undocumented fires in the centuries before 1500). In 2010 vandals set fire to the wooden pulpit (which dated from 1649), after which the interior had to be completely renovated.

  Since the Reformation in 1528 organs were forbidden in churches (and removed at the time of the Reformation). As the first church in protestant Canton Bern, this church received permission to install an organ. It was placed at the back of the chancel, irrespective the fact that it blocked two windows, in 1758.

  The front portal was built during the renovations in 1952-53. The last renovations were undertaken in 1994-95.
- Until the renovations in 1953, the organ stood in the chancel and blocked two windows. After its relocation to the gallery, these two windows were also provided with stained-glass in 1954. Have a closer look. The scenes and colors

are beautiful. The artful stained-glass windows of the chancel date from 1936 and 1954. The oldest stained-glass windows are two small round medallions (right window, northern wall) from 1593 and 1596.

The Gothic stone baptismal font, also used as communion table, has the year 1505 engraved (dating from the significant remodeling of the church at the beginning of the 16th century).

Notice how the chancel is not centered with the nave. The remodeling in 1511 intended to expand the nave with a left and right extension. The right side-extension was never built because of insufficient funding.

Nowadays the church is popular for weddings, due to its elevated position and magnificent views of the Jura and Alp mountains.

From the ending point

The reformed Church on the hill in Wahlern is the ending point of stage 12, about 1.4 km aside the signposted route nr. 4.

In case you are a day-hiker, you need to walk back 1.4 km to the Schwarzenburg train station. Note that this is a terminal station, only connecting to Bern.

In case you are a thru-hiker and spend the night in Schwarzenburg, you will also need to walk back the 1.4 km to the town's center. There are several accommodations, two hotels, though no pilgrim inn. Enough comparable low-priced B&B's are available at private residences. Check out www.jakobsweg.ch or www.viajacobi4.ch for the accommodation possibilities or visit the information counter at the Schwarzenburg train station.

The next Stage

Stage 13 guides you over two highland plateaus between the Sense and Sarine rivers to the city of Fribourg. Read the next chapter to find out what that entails.

Stage 13: Schwarzenburg to Fribourg 27 km

The Way to Saint Canisius

Route stats

	Distance in km	*Time in hrs:min*
Signposted route nr. 4	19.6	4:10
Churches/chapels	4.5	3:30
Points of interest	2.5	1:20
Rest/lunch		1:00
Stage 13	26.6	10:00

In case you hike this stage as a daytrip, you need to add 800 meters in Fribourg to go to the train station (in Schwarzenburg the route starts at the train station).

Ascent/descent/total	+692 / -857 / 1'549 altitude meters
Lowest/highest altitude	537 / 817 meters
Pathway/condition	easy / moderate
Churches/chapels	Heitenried (4), Winterlingen, St. Antoni (2), Weissenbach, Rohr, Tafers (2), Menziswil, Uebewil, Schönberg, Fribourg (10)
Monasteries	Former Commandry of the Knights of St. John, Former Augustinian Monastery, Franciscan Monastery, Holy Mary Visitation Convent, Capuchin Monastery, Former Jesuit Collegium
Points of interest	Ruins Castle of Grasburg, Castle of Heitenried, Medieval City Fortifications Fribourg

Route summary

Stage 13 continues in protestant **Canton Bern** and after 5.3 km enters catholic **Canton Fribourg**.

Stage 13 guides you over two highland plateaus between the Sense and Sarine rivers to the city of Fribourg.

In the previous stages through protestant Canton Bern the number of churches and chapels was limited. This number significantly increases in stage 13, when the Way of St. James enters catholic Canton Fribourg. The area between the Sense and Sarine rivers is called the Sense District and together with the city of Fribourg was a historical catholic stronghold. As a result, you will pass by 14 churches and chapels in the Sense District (of which only one is protestant) and 10 within the city of Fribourg (of which seven belong to monasteries/convents).

In the early middle ages the Sense District consisted of dark forests with one main road to travel through the area, which had already been built by the Romans in the 1st century. The present Way of St. James follows this road. Particularly the descent from Schwarzenburg to the Sense River, and the ascent out of the valley, demonstrate the historical prominence of this old road. You will see many small references to the Way of St. James along this route in the Sense District.

Stage 13 starts with a decent towards the Sense River valley. Shortly before reaching the river it is worthwhile to make a 2.5 km side-tour to visit the ruins of the 12th century Castle of Grasburg. After the side-tour the route descends to the Sense River and climbs out of the valley on old trade and pilgrimage roads. At km 8 the route reaches the highest point of the day of 817 meters at the town Heitenried. From km 10 to 14 the Way of St. James crosses the first highland plateau (average altitude 740 meters) of the Sense District. After St. Antoni the route descends to the second highland plateau (average altitude 650 meters) that is crossed from km 15 to 22. The two highland plateaus have only gradual ascents and descents, making the hike easy and relaxed. From the second plateau the route descends to the Sarine River and Fribourg over 2 km. At the end of this descent the route passes by Fribourg's 13th century fortifications (city walls, watchtowers, access gate, wooden bridge) offering the most beautiful view of a medieval city along the Swiss Way of St. James. The last 3 km climb out of the Sarine River valley to the upper historic part of Fribourg, where the route passes by 10 churches/chapels, which require significant time to view the many religious artefacts and treasures. Be aware of this when planning stage 13.

Getting to the starting point

Today's starting point in Schwarzenburg is at the train station, directly on the signposted route nr. 4.

Route Map and Profile

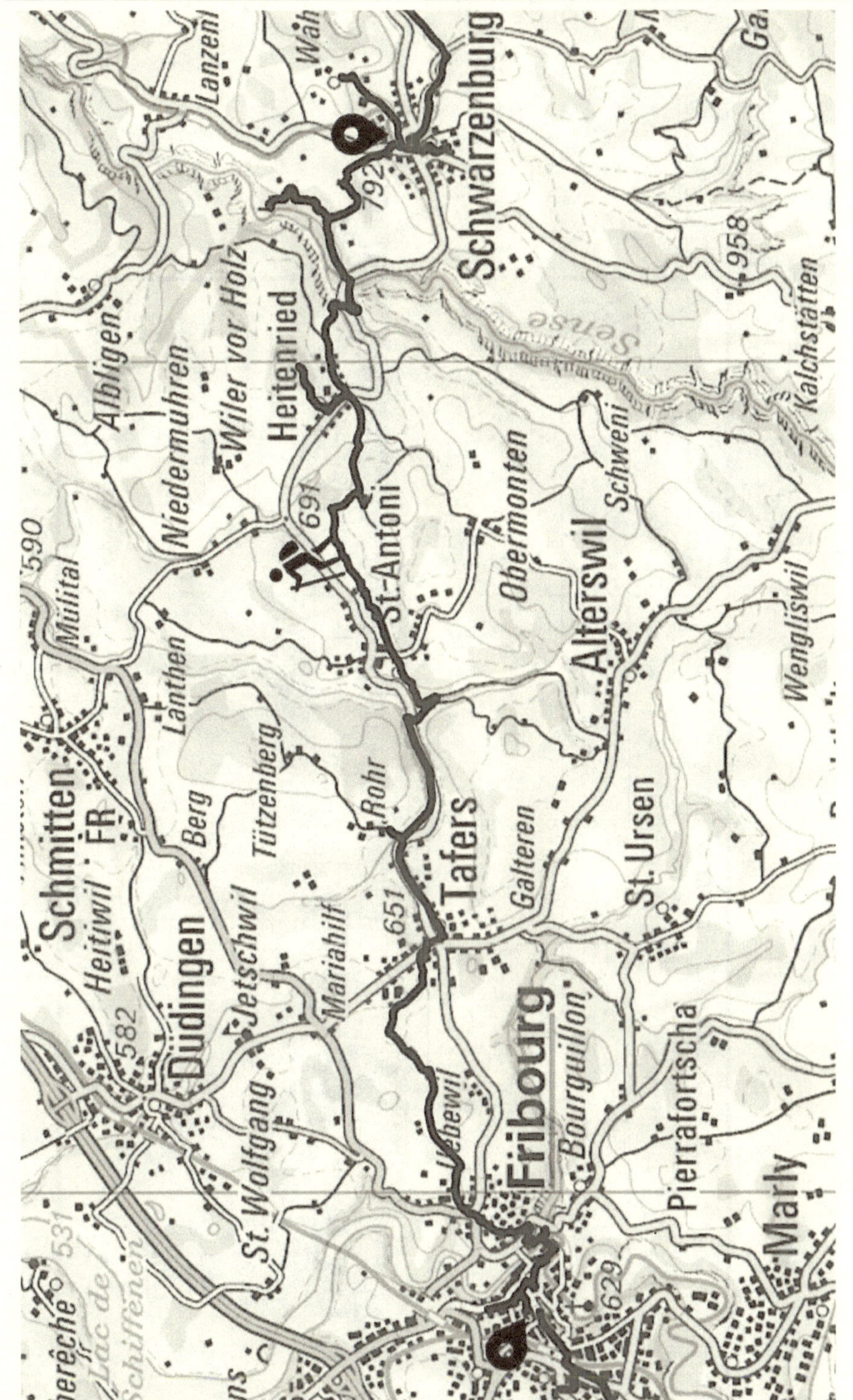
Schwarzenburg
792
Lanzeni
Albligen
Niedermuhren
Wiler vor Holz
Heitenried
Sense
958
Kalchstätten
Schweni
Obermonten
Alterswil
St-Antoni
691
590
Mülital
Lanthen
Tützenberg
Rohr
Tafers
Galteren
St. Ursen
Wengliswil
Schmitten FR
Heitiwil
Berg
Düdingen
582
Jetschwil
Mariahilf
651
Fribourg
Bourguillon
Pierrafortscha
Marly
St. Wolfgang
Lac de Schiffenen
531
629

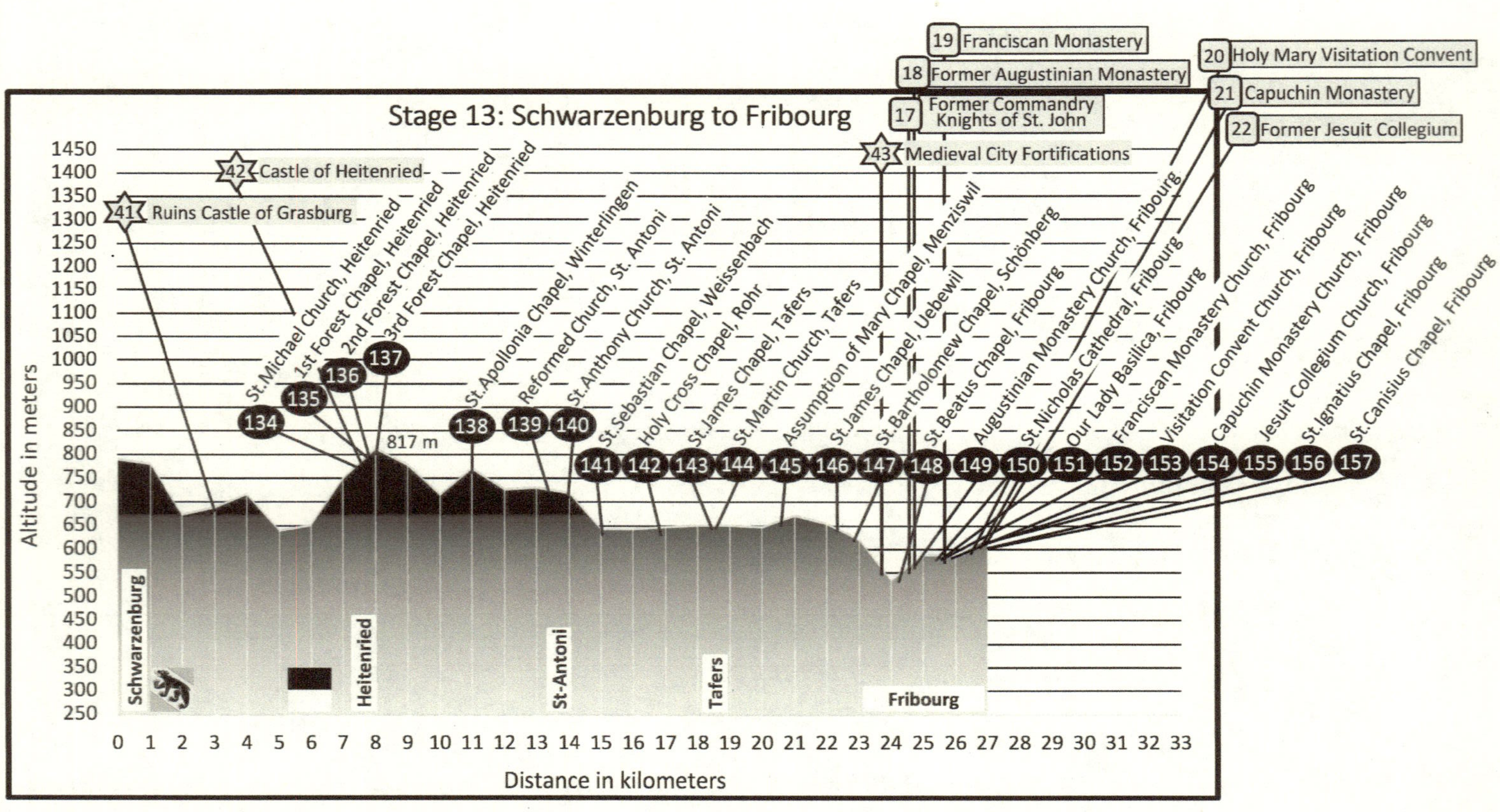
Stage 13: Schwarzenburg to Fribourg
Altitude in meters
Distance in kilometers
Schwarzenburg
Heitenried
St-Antoni
Tafers
Fribourg
817 m
41 Ruins Castle of Grasburg
42 Castle of Heitenried
43 Medieval City Fortifications
17 Former Commandry Knights of St. John
18 Former Augustinian Monastery
19 Franciscan Monastery
20 Holy Mary Visitation Convent
21 Capuchin Monastery
22 Former Jesuit Collegium
134 St.Michael Church, Heitenried
135 1st Forest Chapel, Heitenried
136 2nd Forest Chapel, Heitenried
137 3rd Forest Chapel, Heitenried
138 St.Apollonia Chapel, Winterlingen
139 Reformed Church, St. Antoni
140 St.Anthony Church, St. Antoni
141 St.Sebastian Chapel, Weissenbach
142 Holy Cross Chapel, Rohr
143 St.James Chapel, Tafers
144 St.Martin Church, Tafers
145 Assumption of Mary Chapel, Menziswil
146 St.James Chapel, Uebewil
147 St.Bartholomew Chapel, Schönberg
148 St.Beatus Chapel, Fribourg
149 Augustinian Monastery Church, Fribourg
150 St.Nicholas Cathedral, Fribourg
151 Our Lady Basilica, Fribourg
152 Franciscan Monastery Church, Fribourg
153 Visitation Convent Church, Fribourg
154 Capuchin Monastery Church, Fribourg
155 Jesuit Collegium Church, Fribourg
156 St.Ignatius Chapel, Fribourg
157 St.Canisius Chapel, Fribourg

Hiking the Route

From the front of the Schwarzenburg train station follow route sign nr. 4. It indicates right, and at the roundabout right again, into the *Bernstrasse*, where you pass by a Coop supermarket (a good place to buy any provisions that you might need during the hiking day – closed on Sundays). The route forks to the left into the *Wartgässli*, parallel to the *Bernstrasse*. A narrow gravel path alongside a straight tarmac country road leads you in a northern direction. In the distance to your left you can already see the church in Heitenried, separated from Schwarzenburg by a wide valley. The route turns left and descends steeply into the Sense River valley over a kilometer.

At the beginning of the descent you pass by a wooden Way of St. James sign stating 1'700 km until Santiago de Compostela. Beneath the sign is an information leaflet, stating that you are going to pass through an area which had already been occupied by the Romans in the 1st century. It is believed that they built a watchtower at this site, called ***Wart*** (though nothing is left of it nowadays). In between meadows and cherry trees, the tarmac road curves down towards the Sense River valley. After 500 meters the route forks right, turning onto a gravel path into a patch of forest. The gravel turns into rocks that seem to have been on the path for many centuries. The rocks are unevenly spread making the walking very uncomfortable alongside a 3-meter-high sandstone cliff. On your right you see a small stream, flowing several meters lower. You arrive at a location called ***Torenöli***, where an oil mill (*Oelmühle*) used to be.

A triangular sign warns for flash floods; not at this location, but when you continue to descend and arrive at the river valley. Before continuing on the path, have a closer look at the hiking signpost. A yellow hiking sign directs to the ruins of the Grasburg Castle. This involves a 60-minute detour (20 minutes to get there, 20 minutes viewing, and 20 minutes return) away from the signposted route, but returning to this location. This adds an extra 2.5 km and 330 altitude meters to your day (already included in the 26.6 km distance of stage 13), but is worthwhile doing.

Walk up the rock on the right side of the path. For about 400 meters you follow a forest trail going steep up the hill. After some zigzagging and passing along the edge of a meadow you arrive at a gravel forest road, where you turn left. Walking on this road is easy as it is more or less flat for about 470 meters. At an information sign (also with a flash flood warning) at the curve of the gravel road, the route takes a path to the left. For 350 meters the gravel path steeply descends to the foot of a hill, on which the ruins stand. Several sections of this decent are on **Holloways**, carved through the rocks. This demonstrates that the route was already of importance and heavily used in the middle ages (being the only way to and from the castle). From the last bend on the steeply descending path you have a great view of the ruins. After 157 steps you arrive at the plateau on which the castle was built.

The **Ruins of the Castle of Grasburg** are on a sandstone plateau about 60 meters above the Sense River valley. This valley surrounds the plateau on three sides, which gave the castle a unique natural protection against invading troops. The name 'Gras' originates from the region's name during medieval times. The ruins that you enter at the end of the stairs lie on the eastern side of the 150-meter-long plateau. You are looking at a former fortified residential tower from the 1230s, which was built in a second phase. The ruins of the main building from the first phase construction are at the opposite (western) end of the plateau. It is not certain when the first phase was built. It might have been built by the Dukes of Zähringen (who founded Bern, Fribourg, and Thun) in the 12th century. This first fortified tower had a big hall with two rows of windows and was surrounded by a 15-meter-wide moat with a drawbridge.

During the second construction phase the whole plateau was full of buildings, surrounded by fortified walls on three sides. Storage rooms, prison cells, horse barns, kitchens, a black smith, a chapel, and other crafts houses stood between the two towers, making it a small village. This was the largest fortified castle of the region. Have a closer look at the white information table that describes the castle from around 1500.

The castle stood at a strategic position for the Dukes of Zähringen: at the center of the triangle that their towns Fribourg, Bern, and Thun formed. The castle was used to control trade and traffic in the Schwarzenburg lands at the main medieval crossing of the Sense River. Nowadays it is mostly hidden in the forest, but during medieval times it was visible from afar. The Kingdom of Habsburg probably initiated the second construction phase. From 1250 to 1310 ownership of the castle regularly changed (by battles or pledging) from the House of Kyburg (followers of the Zähringen), to the House of Habsburg, and the House of Savoy. The House of Savoy owned it from 1310 to 1423, after which they sold the castle to Bern and Fribourg, who made it their shared seat of government for the region of the Schwarzenburg lands that was under their shared ownership. Additional fortifications were built around 1485, during a period of battles between the Swiss Confederation and the House of Burgundy.

From 1575 the castle was no longer used as a shared governor's seat. The castle was too isolated, maintenance costs were too high, and it had an outdated residential interior. It was considered more useful and cheaper to build a modern new governor's residence adapted to the 16th century living conditions in the town Schwarzenburg itself (see stage 12). Many of its stones were used to build the new smaller castle and the remainder was abandoned and fell into ruins. The City of Bern became the owner in 1894 and conserved the ruins every few decades (last time in 1984).

From the western side of the plateau you have a great view over the Sense River valley. From the ruins walk back the same 1.25 km to the signpost at the *Torenöli*. Continue on the signposted route. The first 80 meters go steeply down on what is believed to be an old Roman road carved through sandstone rocks; it is paved with round stones from the Sense riverbed. Pilgrims have used this old **Holloway** for more than 1'000 years; you are following in their historical footsteps.

In the valley the path turns from stones to gravel. For 750 meters the route follows the forested southern bank of the Sense River in a western direction. You cross a large gravel parking place with high forested cliffs on your left. The route reaches road nr. 183 and crosses the Sense River on the wooden roofed Sodbach bridge (*Sodbachbrücke*).

On the wooden bridge (from 1867) over the river the route changes from protestant Canton Bern to catholic **Canton Fribourg**. From here on most churches will be catholic. Across the bridge the route keeps left on a gravel path parallel to the road. The route crosses road nr. 183 again, after a short steep climb to the right. A blue sign with a yellow scallop directs to the right, where the path goes steeply up into a forest. This is another 300-meter section of the historical pilgrimage road. You pass by a small round basin, catching water that is trickling down the rocks. The route, carved through sandstone cliffs, climbs out of the valley on a path paved with uneven round riverbed stones.

At the end of the forest a stone pillar displays the scallop sign, a pilgrim, and an arrow with the direction of El Camino. Gradually ascending through grasslands, you pass by a small roadside chapel. It has a typical statue representing St. James with scallop and walking stick. You see Heitenried and its church at the horizon. The route passes by a shooting range and enters the town Heitenried. The Way of St. James passes through the outskirts without going to its church (to the right). However, it is worthwhile to deviate from the signposted route nr. 4 and visit the church and three forest chapels. Shortly before reaching road nr. 183, take the *Dorfstrasse* on the right and follow it up the hill until you arrive at the St. Michael Church (at km 7.6).

St. Michael Church, Heitenried (St. Michael Kirche) 134

- Schlossstrasse, 1714 Heitenried
- St. Michael
- In a small wooden box on the information stand left of the main entrance
- The catholic church was built in a neo-Gothic style in 1904-05, when the predecessor building had become too small for the growing parish. The new building replaced an older and smaller church, also dedicated to St. Michael, that had been in use since the 12th century. The building of this old church still exists; it is the white house south of the cemetery. Nowadays it serves as a party- and concert-hall (*Vereins- und Kulturhaus*).

The church has several artefacts and treasures: the 14 artfully decorated crucifixion way stations; the statue representing St. James (1654); the wood-carved and artfully decorated left and right side-altars; the stained-glass windows (1905); and surely the main treasure, the four-paneled wood-carved retable at the high-altar. This retable with integrated tabernacle is one of the most beautiful along the Swiss Way of St. James. Spend a moment to admire the artwork.

42

Behind the church, at an elevated position, is the **Castle of Heitenried.** The castle was probably first built in the 13th century. Though it is called a castle, it never was a fortified castle in the traditional sense; it was a residential chateau of local Lords. The areas around Heitenried were swamps, which were gradually changed into agricultural fields, without any strategic importance. Over the centuries the chateau changed ownership between noble families many times, until the municipality of Heitenried and the catholic parish of Tafers purchased the buildings in 1878. They reconstructed the buildings to house a school. One building was constructed in the 16th/17th century, the other in the 17th/18th century. Many things had to change to make them suitable for a school; nowadays it still is a school. Its courtyard that once used to have a deep well, a castle chapel, and gardens, now is a playground.

Behind the castle is a forested hill called the castle forest (*Schlosswald*), with a maximum altitude of 825 meters. This forest hides three chapels; the only forest chapels along the Swiss Way of St. James, therefore worthwhile an additional detour of 350 meters (and back). From the church walk up the hill via the *Schlossstrasse*. At the fork take the middle road (*Schlossmatta*) that gets you to the western side of the forest (the forest is on your right). After the last house a sign with *Waldkapellen* directs to a forest trail on the right, with steps up the hill. The steps curve to the left and are followed by a forest trail up the hill. At km 8.0 you arrive at the first Forest Chapel of Heitenried.

135 1st Forest Chapel, Heitenried (I. Kapelle im Schlosswald)

Schlosswald, 1714 Heitenried

The chapel was built in 1707. It is more like a small prayer hut than a chapel: a small wooden construction with a protruding roof and its opening aligned to the southeast. The small chapel does not have a door, so its interior is exposed to the weather, though it does receive protection from the tall trees of the forest.

The only decoration inside is a painting at the back wall. The painting depicts Jesus in the Garden of Gethsemane, at the foot of Mount of Olives near Jerusalem, where Jesus prayed and his disciples slept on the night before his Crucifixion.

From this chapel continue on the forest trail up the hill for another 150 meters and you arrive at the second Forest Chapel (at km 8.2).

2nd Forest Chapel, Heitenried (II. Kapelle im Schlosswald) 136

Schlosswald, 1714 Heitenried

This prayer hut was also built in 1707. Similar to the 1st forest chapel, it is a small wooden construction with a protruding roof and its open entrance aligned to the east.

The only decoration inside is a painting at the back wall. The painting depicts Jesus wearing the Crown of Thornes on the day of his Crucifixion.

Continue through the forest, gradually going up and down, for another 150 meters and you arrive at the third Forest Chapel at km 8.4. This is a unique cave-chapel, the only one along the Swiss Way of St. James.

3rd Forest Chapel, Heitenried (III. Kapelle im Schlosswald) 137

Schlosswald, 1714 Heitenried

St. Mary Magdalene

🏛 On the initiative of the priest of the St. Michael church a small chapel was carved into the rocks in 1700. In 1707 two more small chapels were carved next to the first one. For 160 years the three cave-chapels existed next to each other.

In 1867 the interiors of the three small chapels were heavily eroded because of the humidity, and a complete renovation was undertaken. The inside walls of the three chapels were demolished to create one large cave-chapel, the floors were deepened, and the ceiling leveled. This formed the chapel you are in today. When you look closely, you can still see the three door openings.

The cave-chapel was a regional pilgrimage destination during the 18th and 19th centuries. The chapel was dedicated to St. Mary Magdalene.

📷 A small bell is hanging in a recess in the rocks above; it was placed in 1707 and originates from the former castle chapel. The chain of the bell has carved a long groove in the rocks from its use over the centuries. You can toll the bell.

The chancel has an altar with several statues. A small statue representing the Virgin Mary with baby Jesus stands in a niche in the left wall. The carved windows, with wooden bars, let in warm atmospheric light.

The front of the St. Mary Magdalene cave-chapel offers a wonderful panoramic view of the valley below and the Alps in the distance.

From the cave-chapel walk back to the *Schlossstrasse* and St. Michael church, the same way you came through the forest. From the church walk down the hill to get back to the signposted route nr. 4 at the crossing with road nr. 183.

Cross the road and continue straight. The route follows a gravel road through meadows and passes by a road cross. When you look back you see the church and castle of Heitenried dominate the horizon. Shortly before the settlement Winterlingen the route turns right.

When you briefly leave the signposted route and continue straight up the hill for 150 meters, you arrive at the St. Apollonia Chapel in Winterlingen (at km 10.9). A yellow/blue scallop symbol is in front of the chapel.

St. Apollonia Chapel, Winterlingen (St. Apollonia Kapelle) 138

Winterlingen 119a, 1714 St. Antoni

St. Apollonia

The chapel was built by a private family named Zosso in 1778. The story goes that the sons of the family returned unscathed from the Battle of Murten in 1476. The family built this chapel to commemorate their safe return (a predecessor chapel must have stood on the same site from the end of the 15th century). It is a typical example of a farm chapel; the farmhouse is on the other side of the street.

Today the small chapel is still owned and maintained by the descendants. It is very considerate of the family to keep the small chapel open for pilgrims. Several other privately-owned chapels along the route are either fenced-in (with warning signs of private property) or have their door locked tightly.

Walk back the same 150 meters to route nr. 4 and turn left. The trail switches from grass, to sunken lane in a patch of forest, to an unleveled rocky farm road. You pass by cows in a meadow and a row of wooden beehives. The landscape opens up, providing wide views over the highland plateau.

The route passes through the settlement Niedermonten and in the distance you can already see the tower of the next church. The last 400 meters before arriving at the reformed Church of St. Antoni (at km 13.2) are on a tarmac road.

139 Reformed Church, St. Antoni (Reformierte Kirche)

- Cheerstrasse 22, 1713 St. Antoni
- On a table right of the entrance
- The protestant church was built in 1866. It was the first reformed church in the catholic stronghold of the Sense District, 30 years after the first protestant services were allowed to be held in Canton Fribourg in 1836. It is the only protestant church in stage 13.
- The hall church has a typical protestant interior limited to a pulpit, communion table, organ, and baptismal font.

From the reformed church it is only 600 meters further along the *Cheerstrasse* and *Antoniusweg* to arrive at the catholic St. Anthony Church of St. Antoni (at km 13.7).

140 St. Anthony Church, St. Antoni (St. Antoni Kirche)

- Antoniusweg 32, 1713 St. Antoni
- St. Anthony the Hermit
- On a table right of the entrance
- The church was built in 1894, on the site of a small chapel from 1448. This chapel was erected to commemorate a victory of Fribourg over Bern during the so-called Fribourg War of 1447-48 (in the end Fribourg lost that war, which resulted in Fribourg being annexed by the House of Savoy – and unbound from the House of Habsburg-Austria).

At the time of its construction in 1448, the first St. Antony chapel stood on a rock in the middle of the forest. There was no village yet. Over time people settled east of the chapel and by the middle of the 16th century the village assumed the name of the chapel (*St. Antoni*). The chapel was expanded in 1770 and 1857, and built into the present church in 1894. It is likely that the catholic parish felt compelled to build a church that was at least as large as the protestant church in the village.

Until today the Sense District is characterized by its agricultural farms and for many centuries the district suffered from poverty; St. Anthony the Hermit was a logical name for a chapel isolated in the woods of a poor agricultural district.

Notice that the artfully sculpted side- and main-altars, made of sandstone, are without the usual colorful decorations. This in contradiction to the colorfully designed marble altar of St. Anthony.

The route continues to follow the road to the west. It turns into a gravel road, curving down the hill, descending from the highland plateau to the Taverna stream valley. You can see how the valley curves towards the west with road nr. 183 and the tree lined Taverna stream in the center of it. That is where you are heading. The route makes an s-curve to the left and passes through another **Holloway**, carved through sandstone rocks. Notice a scallop newly carved into the wall (left).

The Holloway ends at a small parking lot, where a signpost next to a stone cross directs to the right. A little later you get to road nr. 183. On the other side you see the St. Sebastian Chapel (at km 14.9).

141 St. Sebastian Chapel, Weissenbach (St. Sebastian Kapelle)

- Thunstrasse, 1713 Weissenbach
- St. Sebastian
- The chapel was built out of gratitude for being saved from the Bubonic Plague in 1750. It is another example of a farm chapel.
- The door is locked; you can only peek through the door's window. The statue at the altar represents St. Sebastian, pierced by arrows.

From the chapel a gravel road leads to the tree lined Taverna stream. The route crosses a small bridge and immediately turns left. For the next 1.6 km a narrow gravel footpath closely follows the stream in the valley of the highland plateau. About halfway you pass by a pilgrim resting area.

The route converges with road nr. 183. Instead of continuing to the left, make a short detour to the right. About 200 meters from the stream you arrive at the Holy Cross Chapel in Rohr (at km 16.9).

142 Holy Cross Chapel, Rohr (Heiligkreuz Kapelle)

- Rohr 1, 1712 Tafers
- Mary-Lourdes, St. John the Baptist, St. Peter, St. Anne, St. Joseph

The chapel was built by a private family in 1842. It is also farm chapel, built by a local farmer on his property; it stands in a meadow next to the road. It is quite large for a private chapel. Today the chapel still is in private ownership.

It is very generous of the owners to keep to chapel open to pilgrims. A Mary-Lourdes statue in a small grotto is at the front-left of the nave. The high-altar has a crucifixion painting and four statues (representing St. John the Baptist, St. Peter, St. Anne with child Mary, and St. Joseph with child Jesus).

From the chapel walk back 200 meters to the stream and then to road nr. 183. For the next kilometer follow the road (*Thunstrasse*) towards Tafers. Around the bend you can already see the tower of the next church. At the beginning of town, a big information table indicates the historic significance of some buildings along the Way of St. James in Tafers. The route follows a road on the left and you arrive at the St. James Chapel in Tafers at km 18.4.

St. James Chapel, Tafers (St. Jakob Kapelle) 143

Kirchweg, 1712 Tafers

St. James the Greater

On a small table against the left wall

The chapel was built by the St. James Brotherhood (*Jakobsbruderschaft*) of Tafers in 1769, replacing an earlier chapel from around 1640. This brotherhood is believed to have been existing since the 15th century. In 2005 it was revived under the name "*Gruppe Santiago*". They still support pilgrims passing through Tafers on their way to Santiago de Compostela.

For St. James pilgrims the small chapel has many special features, outside and inside. In front of the chapel inlaid stones form the shape of a St. James scallop. The eight painted panels above the door (dating from 1790) depict the "Hen and Rooster Miracle" (*Hühnerwunder*). Inside the chapel the marble and wood-carved altar, with the center statue representing St. James, dates from 1640. Walking canes with scallops are left and right of the altar.

The **Hen and Rooster Miracle** (*Hühnerwunder*), sometimes also called the Gallows Miracle (*Galgenwunder*), is a medieval legend. According to this legend, in the 14th century a German family (parents and son) halted for rest in Santo Domingo

(Spain) during their pilgrimage to Santiago de Compostela (still 600 km away). The son rejected romantic advances from the innkeeper's daughter, who hid a silver chalice in his knapsack out of revenge. She told the local sheriff about the theft of a chalice and accused the son, who was arrested for having stolen the chalice. He was sentenced by the local sheriff and hanged at the gallows. The parents continued their pilgrimage to Santiago de Compostela. On their way back they wanted to visit their son's grave, but found him still hanging at the gallows. Miraculously he was still alive; he said that St. Domingo (an 11th century saint, who died in Santo Domingo) had saved him. They went to see the sheriff and asked for their son's release from the gallows. The sheriff responded that their son could not be more alive than the roasted hen and rooster he was about to eat. Miraculously the chicken and rooster came to life, got feathers, and starting crowing. Seeing a miracle by St. Domingo, the sheriff had their son released alive from the gallows.

[This legend is told in different versions, with different dates. The above version comes from the Cathedral of Santo Domingo and ascribes the miracle to St. Domingo instead of to St. James.]

A few meters from the St. James chapel is the St. Michael chapel (*Michaelskapelle*) built in 1753 (replacing an earlier ossuary). It serves as a funeral chapel to store the coffin of a deceased. To the right is the St. Martin Church (at km 18.4).

144 St. Martin Church, Tafers (St. Martin Kirche)

- Kirchweg, 1712 Tafers
- St. Martin
- The church was built, rebuilt, and expanded in six main stages over the centuries. A first small church was probably built in the 6th-8th century. The second church was built on the foundations of the first one in a Romanesque style in the 10th-11th century. This second church was first mentioned in official documents in 1148 and became the mother church of the Sense District. In the 13th century this church was demolished and replaced by the third church in a Gothic style. The fourth church was a remodeling in 1450-54, which attached the sacristy, lengthened the nave, and resulted in other alterations. The fifth church was based on a lengthening of the nave and the addition of a second chancel in 1787. Finally, the sixth version of the church dates from 1968-69, when the nave was lengthened by eight meters.

The present church building dates mainly from 1787; its tower from 1554. The bell tower is special in that it is eight-sided and has a 360-degrees viewing platform (for a medieval fire-watchman).

Inside the church, right side, the St. James Brotherhood put several articles of their 500-year history on display in glass vitrines. A statue representing St. James from 1530 and their membership book from 1620 are the most interesting.

Notice the two areas of the chancel: the space between the nave and the bell tower (from 1787) and the space in the base of the bell tower (from the 13th century). The latter was the chancel of the first churches.

There is no high-altar; instead, a window decorates the chancel's back wall in the base of the tower.

West of the church you see an old wooden house. It dates from 1780 and houses the Sense Museum. The museum exhibits the historical life and culture of the Sense District.

From the church the route turns north, crosses road nr. 183, passes by a soccer field, and turns left to cross road nr. 177. The route continues westward on grass and gravel farm roads in between corn fields, and turns left towards the small settlement Menziswil. The panorama to the south is wide, overlooking agricultural fields with the Alps at the horizon.

At Menziswil the route continues on a tarmac country road. You see the Assumption of Mary Chapel 40 meters right of the road (at km 20.5).

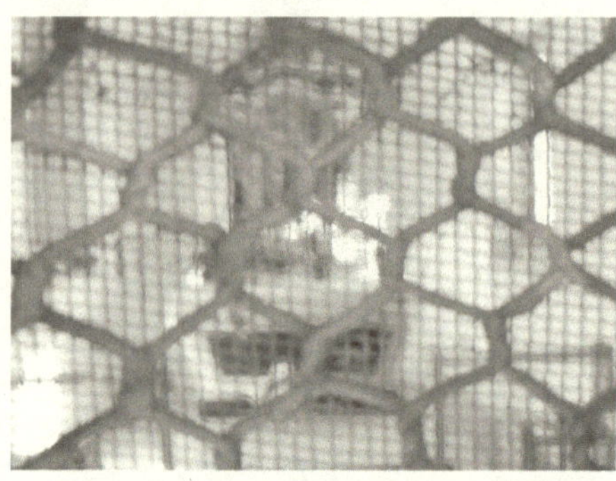

145 **Assumption of Mary Chapel, Menziswil** (Maria-Himmelfahrts-Kapelle)

- Menziswil, 3186 Düdingen
- St. Mary
- The chapel was built around 1780. It is another farm chapel, built by a local farmer; it is in the middle of the meadow and still in private ownership.
- The small chapel cannot be accessed; you can only peek through the metal mesh of the tiny window of the entrance door.

The route turns right and follows a narrow grass path past meadows and corn fields for about 1.3 km. The trail turns to tarmac and after passing by an old estate you arrive at the St. James Chapel of Uebewil (at km 22.2).

146 **St. James Chapel, Uebewil** (St. Jakob Kapelle)

- Uebewil 106, 1700 Fribourg
- St. James the Greater, Sorrowful Mother of God
- The chapel was built in 1788 (inscribed above the altar painting). It was dedicated to St. James, demonstrating the support of the chapel to St. James pilgrims on their way to Fribourg. During the Sonderbund War of 1847 (see page 25 for details) the statue representing St. James was destroyed and replaced by a statue

representing the Sorrowful Mother of God (*Schmerzhaften Mutter Gottes*) – right side of the altar. Becoming the new patroness Saint of the small chapel, the chapel's name changed accordingly.

In 2007 a statue representing St. James was placed back at the altar – left side – after which the chapel's name changed back to St. James.

You have now reached the outskirts of Fribourg. Keep following the street (*Route Villars-les-Joncs*) down the hill for 400 meters to main road nr. 12. Turn left and you arrive at two connected roundabouts. Almost in between the two roundabouts you see the St. Bartholomew Chapel (at km 22.8). As a religious building it seems lost in the urban environment of tarmac roads, busy traffic, and concrete buildings. It stands about 1.5 meters lower than the road and could easily be overlooked. The chapel appears to be in poor condition.

St. Bartholomew Chapel, Schönberg (Schönberg Kapelle) **147**

Route de la Heitera 1, 1700 Fribourg

St. Bartholomew

The chapel was first mentioned in official documents in 1472. The current building probably dates from the 1590s. The altar painting and the extension of the roofed front portal date from 1770-71. For many centuries this chapel was the only place of worship in the area. It was located on an important medieval crossing from Fribourg to Bern and Thun. Even today, the roundabouts split the road towards Bern (road nr. 12 – north) and Thun (road nr. 183 – east).

In 1977 the local parish built a new church about 200 meters east of the chapel. Since then the small chapel has been neglected; its interior was emptied and the walls were plastered, covering all medieval frescos.

The St. Paul parish of Fribourg recently initiated a renovation of the chapel. A partial interior renovation was undertaken in 2018: the interior was cleaned, walls and ceiling painted, old frescos were partially uncovered, and the altar and its painting were restored. The exterior of the chapel still is in poor condition. The door remains locked.

As you are entering the town Fribourg, you will notice that the **Way of St. James signaling** changes. Until you leave the city again, you will not see the yellow sign with the number 4 directing the way. Instead, a small square dark-blue sign with a scallop and a very small arrow and the words *'Chemin de St-Jacques'* direct the way. These signs are fixed to lampposts or on walls of buildings. They integrate well into the historical city of Fribourg. Quite often they integrate too well. Whereas the yellow nr. 4 signs are easy to spot (because of their color and clustering with other yellow hiking signs), the blue signs are easily overlooked (because of their dark color and isolated positions on the walls of buildings). Be aware of this and pay extra attention while following the Way of St. James through Fribourg.

Follow the road (*Route Saint-Barthélemy*) towards the south for 500 meters, until the route turns right into a smaller street (*Route Francois-Arsent*). In the first s-curve of this descending street the hiking signs direct to follow a gravel path towards a square tower.

This tower is part of a chain of **Medieval City Fortifications** around the historical city of Fribourg. It is called the **Red Tower** (because of its red colored bricks). The tower was built around 1387 and is 38 meters high with 3-meter-thick lower walls. The tower also served as a prison and place for executions until 1848. Right of the Red Tower the route descends via steps towards the river valley.

Looking ahead (west) you get the first view over the upper part of town, with the cathedral's 74-meter tower high above the other medieval buildings. Looking left (south) you see: the fortified walls coming down the hill to the Cats Tower and continuing down to the Bern Gate; the Sarine River and the white cliffs; and the lower part of town (the large white building is the former Augustinian monastery with the St. Maurice church behind it). These are the best medieval-city views along the Swiss Way of St. James. Stand still for a moment to absorb this unique scenery.

The **City of Fribourg** is about 900 years old and has one of the largest and best maintained medieval city centers of Switzerland. The city was founded by the Duke of Zähringen in 1157 (he also founded Bern in 1191). Its churches, fountains, and narrow streets transport you back to the middle ages. The city is built on a rocky hill within the s-curving Sarine River and has three historical neighborhoods: Auge, the lower part where the Way of St. James enters the old city; Bourg, the higher part; and Neuveville, the part on the southern side of the Sarine River. The signposted route does not pass through the Neuveville part. Nowadays the city of Fribourg has a population of nearly 40'000.

The route goes around the half-circular building with the red roof (housing the Canton's road- and engineering-offices), crosses the road, and continues on a zigzagging path down the hill to the fortification wall below the Cats Tower.

The **Fortification Wall** was built around 1350, whereas the **Cats Tower** (33 meters high) was built into the wall in 1383. Along the outer wall, underneath a wooden roof, the route descends to the **Bern Gate**. This gate was built around 1350, is 24 meters high, and was the medieval exit towards the Sense District and Bern. Just like today, medieval pilgrims would have passed through this gate, coming down the old Roman road from Schwarzenburg through the Sense District. Around the arched gate you can still see a square outline. This is where the drawbridge used to hang over a moat. Four tall and thick wooden doors, opening on the inside, still operate.

In the footsteps of medieval pilgrims, you pass through the Bern Gate and follow the narrow street to the square of the *Rue de la Palme*.

This square has the **Loyalty Fountain** from the 16th century. The statue in Renaissance style represents a soldier with a loyal dog at his feet. The story goes that this soldier, in full battle dress, is a lookout for Bernese invaders (he is looking towards the Bern Gate, from which direction the Bernese invaders would come). The 12 sides of the basin depict several scenes, amongst others St. Beatus killing a dragon. The fountain has potable water; you can refill your bottle.

At the western side of the square you see the **Auberge de l'Ange** (with a blue Way of St. James sign on its wall). It is one of the oldest inns in Fribourg that already provided pilgrims accommodation in the middle ages (it is just behind the city gate, within the fortifications). It is called the inn of the angel, as it was believed that angels protected the traveling pilgrims.

Towards the east you see the Bourguillon Bridge towering high above the valley. Beneath it is a medieval fortified walkway, bridging the Gottéron stream, leading to the St. Beatus Chapel. It is worthwhile to leave the signposted route nr. 4 for 140 meters to reach this chapel. Take the small road (*Rue de la Palme*) up the hill on the right side (south) of the Gottéron stream. On your right you pass by a heavily eroded limestone rock formation with niches carved into its sides. It forms a natural rock bridge over a large hole at its base and has an interesting story. According to folklore the valley to the east of this small stream was a dangerous and inaccessible place where an ogre terrorized travelers. One day a hermit living in the valley was able to chase the ogre away. The ogre broke through the limestone rocks and fled via the Sarine River.

Through a small alley you arrive at the St. Beatus Chapel (at km 24.1). The chapel is only open on Fridays, from March until October.

St. Beatus Chapel, Fribourg (Chapelle St-Béat Gottéron) 148

Rue de la Palme 10, 1700 Fribourg

St. Beatus, St. Nicholas

The chapel was built, integrated in the medieval fortifications, in 1684. A fortified walkway bridges the Gottéron stream and provided secure access to the chapel in the middle ages. The small chapel was dedicated to St. Beatus, for the symbolism of his tale. The people of Fribourg were afraid of the advancing Reformation that led to civil war and destruction of catholic properties and institutions. As St. Beatus had slayed a dragon, Fribourg wanted to defeat the Reformation to prevent destruction of its churches and chapels. Fribourg obtained relics from St. Beatus from a church in Luzern in 1684, and secured these in the chapel (the St. Beatus caves had been bricked up during the Reformation – see stage 10). Some 30 years later the chapel was in disrepair. It was rebuilt by 1732 and was renovated several times since.

The baroque wooden altar contains three statues, representing St. Beatus (center), St. Nicholas in bishop's outfit (left), and a former abbot (right).

From the chapel walk back to the Loyalty Fountain and turn left to cross the **Bern Bridge** over the Sarine River. A first covered wooden bridge was built around 1250, about 100 years after the foundation of the city; the present bridge dates from 1653. Since medieval times many thousands of pilgrims before you have walked across the bridge.

The bridge offers great views towards the white cliffs (east) and the Auge neighborhood (west); you can see the semicircular chancel of the St. Maurice church, the white former Augustinian monastery, the tip of the St. Nicholas cathedral tower, and the elevated Zähringen bridge.

The Sarine River forms the language border between German- and French-speaking Switzerland. East of the Sarine the Swiss population speaks German, west of it French. As the Sarine cuts right through Fribourg, the city has two official languages, though French is dominating.

From the Bern Bridge follow the small blue signs straight to a square called *Place du Petit-Saint-Jean*, translated as the square of little Saint John. This square used to house the former Commandry of the Knights of St. John and their chapel.

17 Former Commandry of the Knights of St. John, Fribourg (Chevalier de St-Jean de Jérusalem)

- Place du Petit-Saint-Jean, 1700 Fribourg
- Order of the Knights of St. John
- The Commandry of the Knights of St. John of Jerusalem and their chapel stood at this location in 1224-59. They were the first monastic Order that settled in the city of Fribourg and cared for pilgrims and travelers (hence their location close to the Bern Bridge and Gate).

  Because of the increasing influence of the Augustinian monastery (see below), the Fribourg Authorities relocated the commandry to the Neuveville area in 1259. There they built a new commandry, church, and hospital. All they left at this first location was a small chapel, hence the name little John.

  During the French occupation (1798-1803) the Order of the Knights of St. John left Fribourg and only briefly returned to finally leave for good in 1825. The old chapel fell into ruins and was demolished in 1832. The bell of the old chapel was reused in the steeple of the Augustinian monastery church (see below).

  The former commandry and church in Neuveville are still standing, but these are not along the signposted Way of St. James route.

Cross the square diagonally and continue in the *Rue de la Samaritaine.* After 180 meters steep up the cobbled road, make a short detour to a right side-street (*Rue de la Lenda*). It is not visible from the signposted route, but to the right is the St. Maurice Church of the former Augustinian Monastery (at km 24.7).

Augustinian Monastery Church St. Maurice, Fribourg (Eglise St-Maurice) 149

Rue de la Lenda 1, 1700 Fribourg

St. Maurice, St. Victor

At the parish office, across the street from the main entrance of the church

The church was built as part of the Augustinian monastery (see below) over a period of 37 years (1274-1311). The church was dedicated to St. Maurice after receiving relics of St. Maurice from the Abbey of Saint Maurice in Canton Valais (it is believed that St. Maurice and his fellow soldiers were executed on that site). The relics consisted of a jaw bone and a shin bone.

From an architectural point of view, it is unusual for a church of its size to have neither a transept (it is not the shape of a cross) nor a bell tower. The short steeple on the roof above the chancel was added in 1832. It holds the bell from the former chapel of little John. The portal covering the front entrance was added in 1684. Construction in the 17th-18th centuries significantly changed the interior.

The church contains two treasures: the high-altar and relics of a catacomb saint. The high-altar is an enormous three-layered construction, dedicated to the Virgin Mary, reaching to the ceiling of the chancel. The altar dates from 1593 and is one of the largest and most unique in Switzerland. Admire the many artfully sculpted wooden statues, the marble, and the gold-colored decorations.

On the left side of the nave a dressed and decorated skeleton lies in a vitrine. They are the relics of a catacomb saint, dedicated St. Victor. The story goes that the monastery had several relics in storage for a long time. When a plague of beetles destroyed the crops in the year 1747, the Fribourg Authorities asked the Augustinian friars to exorcise this plague. The friars suggested to reinstate the catacomb Saint Victor and to use him as a pilgrimage destination for the farmers to pray to ward off the plague.

Several bones were given to the Capuchin nuns of Montorge (in the Neuveville part of Fribourg, south of the river), who completed the skeleton and made a lusciously decorated Roman dress. In 1748 the restored and decorated skeleton was placed on display near the high-altar of the St. Maurice church and became a pilgrimage destination. According to legends the beetle plague was overcome.

The relics were thought to have the power of healing the ill and even resurrecting dead children. Have a closer look to admire the decorations, precious stones, and attributes of the crown and sword.

18 **Former Augustinian Monastery, Fribourg** (Couvent de Saint-Augustin)

Rue de la Lenda 1, 1700 Fribourg

Augustinian Order

The Augustinian Order was the third monastic Order that settled in Fribourg. Hermit Augustinian friars had already settled at the Sarine River bend underneath the cliffs in 1224. Around 1255 they started to build their monastery next to the river. Little has been documented of the monastery's history.

The present white monastery building (between the church and the river) dates from 1719-47. The Augustinian monastery was forced to close in 1848, under the stipulations of the new Swiss Federal Constitution (after Fribourg had lost the Sonderbund War – see page 25 for a description). Since 1848 the monastery buildings have been used as a prison, cantonal archive, and nowadays as the cantonal court.

When returning to the Way of St. James route, notice a small pilgrim statue in a niche in the wall, right above the blue *Chemin de St-Jacques* sign. Continue the ascent on the cobbled road (*Grand Rue*), climbing out of the Auge area towards the Bourg area. After 400 meters a blue route sign directs right and through the *Rue des Epouses* you arrive at the front entrance of the St. Nicholas Cathedral (at km 25.3).

St. Nicholas Cathedral, Fribourg (Cathédrale Saint Nicolas) **150**

- Rue Cathédrale-St-Nicolas, 1700 Fribourg
- Collegiate
- St. Nicholas
- Left of the front portal, behind the door, in a box below a scallop
- The cathedral was built in a Gothic style between 1283 and 1430. The story goes that the construction of the bell tower stopped because of lack of financing in 1490. This explains the unusual flat top of the tower; does it not look unfinished?

  The cathedral is on the site of an earlier church, dating from around 1157, when the City of Fribourg was founded by Duke Berthold of Zähringen. This first Romanesque church was built on the lands owned by the Cluniac Abbey of Payerne (see stage P1, Volume III). The church was the only parish church in Fribourg until 1511. In 1512 it became an independent Collegiate church (and still is to this day).

  After the Bernese enforced the Reformation in Lausanne in 1536, the Bishop of Lausanne relocated to Fribourg in 1601. The St. Nicholas church continued to be a Collegiate church, despite the presence of the bishop (which would normally have elevated the status to cathedral). It was not until 1924 that the Collegiate church became a cathedral for the newly created diocese of Fribourg, Lausanne, and Geneva. Canton Fribourg has owned the building since 1803 (when the Helvetic Republic was dissolved).
- Similar to the Augustinian monastery church, the cathedral does not have a transept. The cathedral's bell tower is the tallest one in Fribourg: it is 74 meters high, with 365 spiraling steps to the top (providing great views over Fribourg).

  Apart from this tall bell tower, the cathedral has many more interesting features: sandstone sculptures around the entrance doors, dating from the 15th century; balustrades above the arches, on the sides of the nave; twelve side-chapels along the nave with artful statues and paintings; beautiful stained-glass windows in Art-

Nouveau style, a unique collection of church windows from the early 20th century; and a rose skylight in the ceiling of the front portal.

The cathedral is oriented towards (foreign) tourists. Audio guides and information brochures in five languages guide the tourists through the history and sights of the cathedral. You can buy a ticket (CHF 4) to ascend the tower of the cathedral (from April until October) at a counter left of the entrance.

Since 1506 the cathedral has been keeping relics of St. Nicholas. Part of the right arm (from the elbow to the hand) is encased in a standing silver effigy. Depictions of the Saint can be found at several places, but the relic is not on display.

From the main entrance continue straight for 100 meters to a square and roundabout, with a car park on the right. The blue Way of St. James shield directs left, towards the train station. Here you need to deviate from the signposted route for the last 1.3 km to visit five more interesting churches. At the roundabout you see the Our Lady Basilica right in front of you (at km 25.4).

151 Our Lady Basilica, Fribourg (Basilique de Notre-Dame)

Place de Notre-Dame 1, 1700 Fribourg

Our Lady

The church was built on the site of a smaller chapel in 1201. It is the oldest still original church in Fribourg. The first chapel and subsequent church were built and used by the Dukes of Zähringen, after they founded the City of Fribourg in 1157. The church stood at a central location, next to the city's most important social institution, the public hospital that cared for the ill and poor. Between 1250 and 1680 the church also served as the hospital church and provided food and clothing for the poor (the hospital was relocated in 1680).

In the period 1467-1525 the church was significantly remodeled: it was enlarged and changed from a Romanesque to a Gothic architecture. In 1728 it became a Collegiate church (which it is not anymore).

By the mid 18th century the building was dilapidated and in urgent need of renovation. Nowadays you see the results of this renovation (inside and outside) to a Louis XVI style from 1785-87.

The status of the church was elevated to Basilica by Pope Pius XI in 1932, on the occasion of the 350-year celebration of the Congregation of the Holy Virgin. This congregation was established by St. Peter Canisius (see monastery nr. 22 below) in 1582.

The last renovation lasted 25 years and was completed in 2011, revealing old treasures that had been covered over the centuries. Nowadays the interior displays many of these original works. Statues and paintings of the Virgin Mary are all-around.

The oldest furniture are the choir stalls, dating from 1508. The baroque frescos and altar paintings in rococo style date from 1786.

Have a closer look at the front-right side-chapel. Through the metal grating you can see that the walls have been maintained in their original undecorated style. This is what the whole church would have looked like in its original appearance. On the small altar, in front of a narrow stained-glass window, is an artistic statue representing the Virgin Mary.

A unique feature is the manger scene of Jesus' birth, with 75 figures, some dating back to the 18th century. The scene is in a grey booth behind the curtains, left of the entrance. In any other church such a birth scene will only be on display during the Advent and Christmas period; here it is on permanent display. However, outside the Christmas period you need to pay CHF 1 to see it (after inserting a coin a screen lifts and the scene becomes visible).

This particular display is called a Neapolitan Nativity: it places Jesus' birth scene against the background of life in Naples, Italy of around 1700 (instead of Bethlehem at the time of Jesus' birth).

The next church is only a few meters away. Cross the square north of the Our Lady church, past the former tramway depot (turned into the Gutenberg Museum), and you arrive at the Franciscan Monastery and its Church (at km 25.5).

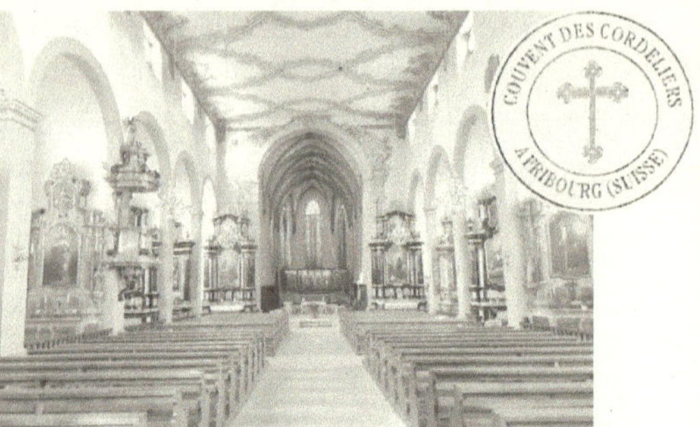

152 Franciscan Monastery Church, Fribourg (Eglise des Cordeliers)

- Rue de Morat 4, 1700 Fribourg
- Our Lady, St. Maximilian Kolbe
- At the pilgrim inn or the reception inside the monastery (follow the signs to the *Accueil du Couvent*, left of the church's main entrance)
- The church was built in 1256-75, together with the monastery that was founded in 1256. Similar to the Augustinian monastery church, the Franciscan monastery church has neither a transept nor a bell tower (only a short steeple on the roof above the chancel). The chancel was newly built around 1300 and the nave was remodeled in 1330-40. In 1745 the nave was newly built in a baroque style, whereas the chancel remained Gothic. The last renovation lasted 17 years (1974-91), resulting in its present-day appearance.
- From the outside the church looks like a dull building not worthwhile visiting (as one might expect from the Franciscans, who vowed to poverty and austerity).

The inside is quite the opposite; it contains many treasures. The retable from 1480 is the largest medieval painted winged high-altar in Switzerland.

When you look around in the nave you see an abundance of marble and many altars in the 11 side-chapels; the 12th side-chapel is the enclosed Our Lady chapel in black marble. In 1694 an exact replica of the black marble Our Lady of Einsiedeln chapel was built inside the nave. It can be accessed from the side of the main entrance of the church. The small chancel of the Our Lady chapel houses an equally lusciously decorated Black Madonna statue.

The oldest of the wooden choir stalls on the sides of the chancel date from 1305, making them the oldest preserved ones in Switzerland.

A unique sculpture of Jesus chained to a column dates from 1438.

The ceiling of the chancel contains four gold-colored keystones dating from 1265.

Another side-chapel inside the church deserves attention: the St. Maximilian Kolbe chapel. You can find the chapel with the vaulted ceiling at the front-right side of the church. During the day this chapel is used for perpetual prayers. The continuous prayers are transferred to the Our Lady of Einsiedeln chapel for the night.

The frescos depicting scenes from the life of Mary, on the cloister wall north of the nave, date from around 1440.

Discover more treasures yourself with the information brochure in several languages available at the church.

Franciscan Monastery, Fribourg (Couvent de Cordeliers) 19

Rue de Morat 4, 1700 Fribourg

Franciscan Order

The Franciscan monastery is dedicated to the Holy Cross. It is the oldest Franciscan Order and the only original one still active in Switzerland today, having settled in Fribourg in 1256. All other medieval Franciscan monasteries in Switzerland were closed either during the Reformation (1520s-30s) or after the Sonderbund War (1848).

The monastery was established after the Lord of Riggisberg (see stage 12) donated his house with gardens in Fribourg to Franciscan friars from Basel. In the 15th century the mendicant Order accumulated significant wealth (as exhibited in its church) – rather in contradiction of the Rule of St. Francis. There must have been a strong competition between the many monastic Orders that settled in Fribourg since the 13th century.

The Franciscan friars became the leading Order, under the protection of wealthy local guardians, from the 15th century. They established strong relationships with the ruling families of Fribourg and received substantial donations and gifts. The Fribourg Authorities held their town meetings at the church between 1404 and 1789, while the monastery accommodated visiting European Royalty, such as the

German-Roman Emperor Sigismund and several Popes. The monastery built an extensive medieval library and was well-known for its bookbinding (1450-1500). Today it still contains more than 100 printed editions from that period.

As the Reformation (1520s-30s) swept through Switzerland, their leading role was taken over by the Jesuit Order, who were the main driver of the Counter-Reformation in Fribourg (see below).

By the beginning of the 18th century the monastery and its church were dilapidated. The old monastery building was demolished and a new one was built in a baroque style in 1712-25, financed by a local guardian. The present-day appearance dates from this time (nothing remained of the medieval buildings).

At the time of Napoleon's occupation and the Helvetic Republic (1798-1803) the monastery was closed. As the Jesuits were banned between 1798 and 1814, and their Collegium was managed by the City of Fribourg, the Franciscan friar Gregor Girard stepped up and took over a leading position in education in Fribourg. He initiated school reforms and together with Pestalozzi (see stages 6 and L4) became a famous pedagogue and reformer of the Swiss educational system.

After Fribourg and other catholic Cantons lost the Sonderbund War in 1847, the monastery was put under state supervision (whereas the monasteries of the Jesuits, Augustinians, and Cistercians in Fribourg were closed and secularized).

In 1857 the state supervision was lifted and the Franciscan friars re-established themselves in the educational system of Fribourg from 1890. They taught at the Collegium St. Michael and built a new dorm in their monastery in 1906-07, to provide boarding for about 100 students. After a fire in the dorm in 1937, the building was partly reconstructed and heightened by two floors. The dorm was closed in 1969. The monastery was renovated in 2013-16.

Nowadays the buildings are too large for the seven remaining friars: space has been reallocated to archives, seminar rooms, and a pilgrim inn.

The monastery still has a large library with 10'000 books that once served the students.

Given all the treasures at the Franciscan monastery church and the pilgrim inn at the monastery, one might think that this would be the end of stage 13. But it is not. There are three more churches to visit. The final church is where a Saint lived and died, and who's relics are still kept there.

The next church is only 200 meters away. From the monastery church follow the main street (*Murtengasse/Rue de Morat*) in a northern direction (slightly up the hill). At a small roundabout continue straight north. From the outside the church building is inconspicuous, fully integrated in the row of buildings along the busy street. You would probably have passed it if you were not looking for it.

On the right side of the street, along the narrow pavement, you arrive at the Church of the Holy Mary Visitation Convent (at km 25.7).

Visitation Convent Church, Fribourg (Eglise Couvent de la Visitation) 153

Rue de Morat 18, 1700 Fribourg

St. Francis de Sales

The church was built as part of the Convent of the Holy Mary Visitation (see below) in 1653-56. The church was dedicated to the Holy Spirit and built with the physical labor of the sisters (the restoration in 1970-71 was done again by the sisters themselves). The church was enclosed, only accessible to the sisters of the convent (which is why its outside is so inconspicuous). It has a round shape and is basically only a chancel in the shape of a Greek cross. No nave was needed as no outside visitors or lay people attended their services (similar to the friar-chancel in Stans and the sister-chancel in Wattwil). It was not until the 1980s that the church was opened to lay people.

The first thing you notice when entering the church is the long iron grating (rood screen) that prevents access from the narrow front corridor to the chancel. Outside the times of services, you can only peek inside through the fence.

You see many statues and paintings representing Saints that are special to the Order: St. Francis de Sales, Visitation, and Scared Heart. Unusual are the two gold-colored triangular reliefs with the all-seeing eye on opposite ends above the northern and southern altars (as if they stare each other in the eye).

Notice the high dome above the center of the church and the tiling of the floor, with four hearts surrounded by another eight hearts.

On the outer wall above the front door you see two statues representing Mary's visit to her cousin Elisabeth (the Visitation).

20 Convent of Holy Mary Visitation, Fribourg (Couvent de la Visitation)

Rue de Morat 18, 1700 Fribourg

Visitation Order

In 1635 several nuns of the French Visitation Order settled in Fribourg to seek refuge from the Thirty Years' War (fought between catholic Habsburg countries and opposing protestant States in Central Europe in 1618-48). The nuns engaged in the embroidery of household and church linen, and had to settle outside the Bern Gate. It was not until 1651 that the City of Fribourg formally allowed them to establish their convent and two years later they settled in their current premises. The nuns provided lower-level education for girls (including a boarding school) and housed a foster home for young girls and older women. In 1696 the sisters added their devotion to the Sacred Heart of Jesus. By 1726 their buildings were dilapidated and the southern wing had to be demolished. It was rebuilt and expanded along the street.

At the time of the French occupation and the Helvetic Republic in 1798-1803, the convent was closed and their property confiscated. From 1803 they resumed their activities and sent out many sisters to France to help rebuilt the French convents. After Fribourg had lost the Sonderbund War in 1847, the convent was closed again and their assets secularized.

Ten years later (1857) the convent was reopened and re-established as a boarding school for the lower-level education of young girls (10-18 years of age). They bought the neighboring building and expanded the school to up to 75 students. In 1922 they closed the school and in 1934 the convent became fully religious and enclosed, with a focus on vows and prayers.

To finance the maintenance of the large convent the nuns entered into several business ventures. In 1950-90 they operated a small industrial laundry, for hotels, restaurants, and private customers. In 1964-87 they housed a home for students and older women. From 1988 a large wing was rented out. Nowadays around 15 sisters still live in the convent.

From the Visitation church continue north along the main street (*Murtengasse/Rue de Morat*), slightly down the hill. After 200 meters, on the right, you arrive at the Capuchin Monastery Church (at km 25.9).

Capuchin Monastery Church, Fribourg (Eglise Couvent des Capucins) 154

Rue de Morat 28, 1700 Fribourg

St. Mary Magdalene

The church was built as part of the Capuchin monastery in 1610-22. The church was dedicated to St. Mary Magdalene.

Consistent with their vows to austerity and poverty, the Capuchin church has a simple interior, without the opulent decorations found in some of the other churches in Fribourg. The three altars are made of wood, in a similar style as seen in the Capuchin churches in Schwyz and Stans. The large wooden high-altar fills the complete back wall of the chancel; other than that, the chancel is not decorated. The most artistic decorations are on the ceiling, with the inlaid wood and medallions.

Capuchin Monastery, Fribourg (Couvent des Capucins) 21

Rue de Morat 28, 1700 Fribourg

Capuchin Order

The monastery was established as part of the Counter-Reformation in 1617, to strengthen Catholicism in the city and Canton Fribourg. The Bishop and the Government of Fribourg had requested the Capuchins to come from northern Italy to Fribourg in 1609. In 1617 a local nobleman donated land and buildings for perpetual use (because of the Order's vow to poverty they could not own it). Whereas the Jesuits (in Fribourg since 1582; see below) focused on the higher-level education of boys, the Capuchins managed the lower-level education of boys. They not only taught the poor, but also took care of them during periods of famine and plague. This made them popular with a large part of the local population and enabled them to strengthen Catholicism in Fribourg.

During the French occupation and the Helvetic Republic in 1798-1803, the monastery was closed, but reopened soon thereafter. It was placed under state supervision after Fribourg had lost the Sonderbund War in 1847. Ten years later the monastery received its independence again and continued to concentrate on the lower-level education of boys and caring for the poor.

The Capuchins helped establish the catholic University of Fribourg in 1889. From then the Capuchins provided professors and housed many international students that came to study Theology at the university. In 1901 the monastery built a new wing to accommodate the increasing number of theology students.

Nowadays the monastery houses only a few young foreign Capuchin friars (from developing countries such as India), who study to become a teacher and preacher at the Theology Faculty of the Fribourg University. The monastery still has an extensive library, though a part of their medieval library was donated to the

University library in 1982. Today around five friars live in the monastery. To support the poor people of society, they accommodate around 20 refugees.

From the Capuchin monastery church walk back 340 meters until you get to a split in the road. The main road (*Murtengasse/Rue de Morat*) continues left, but you need to take the smaller road on the right (*Rue Pierre-Aeby*). About 120 meters into this road you see a small street on the right (*Ruelle des Maçons*). At this corner of the hotel Hine Adon turn right and walk up the short but steep hill. About 100 meters later turn right again and you are in the *Rue Saint-Pierre-Canisius.* At km 26.6 you arrive at the former Jesuit Collegium and its St. Michael Church (accessible during school hours).

22 **Former Jesuit Collegium St. Michael, Fribourg** (Jésuites Collège St-Michel)

Rue Saint-Pierre-Canisius 8, 1700 Fribourg

Jesuit Order

The former Jesuit Collegium St. Michael was established as a higher-level education boys' school by order of Pope Gregor XIII, as an important measure of the Counter-Reformation. From 1536 Fribourg was surrounded by protestant Cantons and the Jesuit school intended to anchor Catholicism in the education of boys and in the city and Canton. Pope Gregor XIII ordered the Jesuit monk Peter Canisius to negotiate the establishment of a school with the Fribourg Authorities in 1580. To finance the new school, Pope Gregor XIII closed the Norbertine monastery of Marsens (about 30 km south of Fribourg) and transferred its assets (lands, vineyards, and forests, i.e. sources of income) to the Collegium St. Michael (see monastery nr. 24 in stage 14, Volume III). From 1582 the Jesuit Order managed the school under leadership of Peter Canisius.

As is normal for a Jesuit Collegium, it consisted of a monastery, a church, and a school within one large building complex. The present buildings were constructed, and gradually expanded, between 1585 and 1660.

In 1773 Pope Clement XIV formally dissolved the Jesuit Order and the Jesuits had to transfer their Collegium to the City of Fribourg, after which they were forced to leave. When Pope Pius VII re-established the Order 41 years later (1814), the Jesuits returned to the Collegium and resumed their educational tasks by 1818. Their boys' boarding school housed nearly 400 students during the following decades.

After Fribourg lost the Sonderbund War in 1847, the Jesuits were banned from Switzerland and had to leave the Collegium again (never to return). Canton Fribourg seized all their lands and buildings, including the church and library. The school continued as a public gymnasium for boys until 1901, after which girls were also given access (though still in separate classes). Only since 1976 have the classes been mixed.

Nowadays the building still houses the Fribourg public gymnasium school with a large campus and sports grounds at the back of the building.

The former courtyard of the Collegium has large trees with low hanging branches and a bust of St. Canisius on a pedestal between two hedges.

To get to the St. Michael church you need to access the Collegium through the door on the right side of the church (from the courtyard). Since the church belongs to the Collegium, it is not open to the public. But, you can obtain the key to the church from the school's office. From the entrance turn right into the long hallway and on the right you find the office (*Secrétariat*). Just ask for the key at the counter. As you walk through the Collegium, you can sense the century-old atmosphere all-around: long hallways, wooden ceilings, spiral staircases, and old portraits of rectors and Jesuits. These transport you back several centuries in time.

Jesuit St. Michael Collegium Church, Fribourg (Eglise Collège St-Michel) 155

Rue Saint-Pierre-Canisius 8, 1700 Fribourg

St. Michael, St. Canisius

The church was built in a late-Gothic style by the Jesuit Order in 1606-13, after the first buildings of the Collegium were built in 1585. In the 18th century the interior of the church was significantly remodeled to a rococo style, nowadays one of the most important representations of this style in Switzerland.

The interior contains many special features. Eye-catching are the many rococo frescos representing the struggle between good and evil. Have a closer look at the figures and scenes they depict.

The tabernacle at the high-altar is one of the most beautifully decorated along the Swiss Way of St. James. The large painting depicts St. Michael. The additional baroque side-altars depict further Saints.

Nowadays the church is mainly used as a concert hall and for school celebrations.

Underneath the high-altar lies the tomb of St. Canisius. His relics are kept in a silver effigy, similar to the ones you saw in Sachseln (Stage 7) and Eschenbach (stage R3, volume I). The silver is already tarnishing.

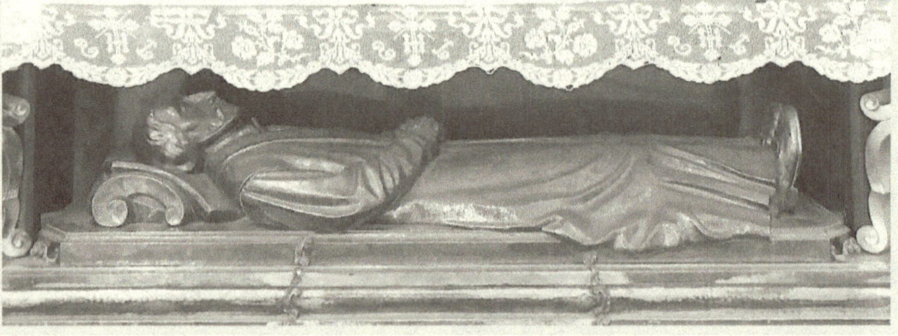

If you go up the stone spiral staircase, right of the door accessing the church from the side of the corridor, you get to the St. Ignatius Chapel.

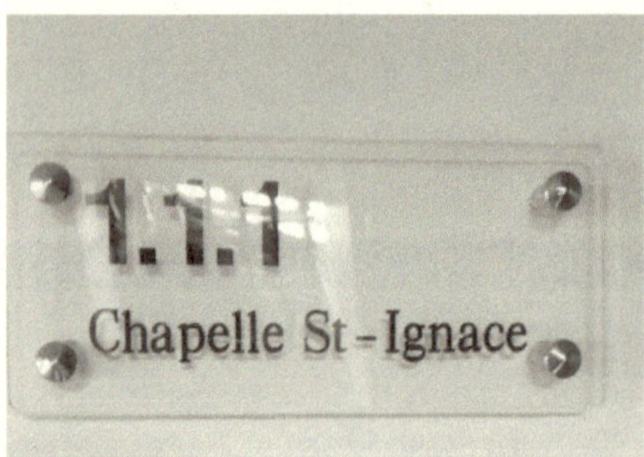

156 St. Ignatius Chapel, Fribourg (Chapelle St-Ignace)

- Rue Saint-Pierre-Canisius 8, 1700 Fribourg
- St. Ignatius
- The chapel was a small prayer room of the Jesuit monks.
- It contains a small altar and portraits of Jesuits on its walls.

The St. Canisius Chapel is on the ground floor in the northern wing. Signs lead you in the right direction; it is in a corridor with red student lockers and classrooms.

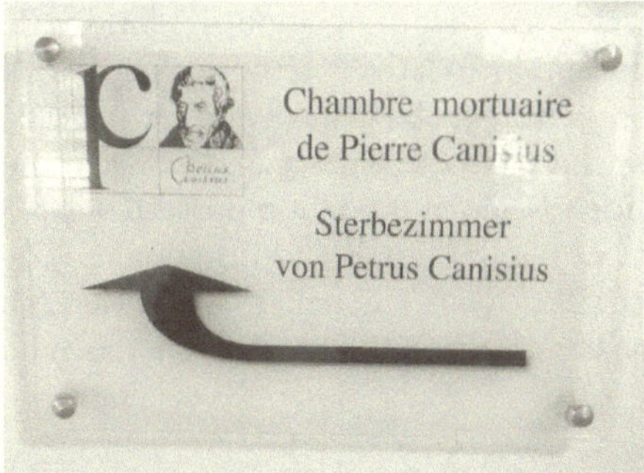

St. Canisius Chapel, Fribourg (Chapelle de Pierre Canisius) **157**

- Rue Saint-Pierre-Canisius 8, 1700 Fribourg
- St. Canisius
- The chapel is the room where St. Canisius died in 1597. It was turned into a chapel dedicated to this Saint in 1636.
- The door has an elaborate wood-carved frame. Inside the room the artful woodwork also dominates the interior. A small altar is dedicated to this Saint.

When you walk around the church to the western entrance, you see a small plaque next to a dent in the wall. According to the information, the dent was caused by a cannon ball, when French troops conquered Fribourg in 1798.

The city of Fribourg has several more churches and monasteries. As a catholic stronghold during the middle ages (first wave in the 13th century: Knights of St. John, Augustinians, Franciscans, and Cistercians) and concentration of the Counter-Reformation (second wave in the 16th-17th centuries: Jesuits, Capuchins, Ursulines, and Visitations) it housed all the major monastic Orders and their churches (except for the Benedictines). In stage 14 you will visit three more churches (and one convent) in Fribourg, after which you will have visited the most interesting ones and those in close vicinity to the signposted route nr. 4. The Way of St. James does not pass through the old Neuveville part of Fribourg, which has several more churches, chapels, and monasteries.

From the ending point

The St. Michael Collegium Church is the ending point of stage 13, about 200 meters aside the signposted route.

In case you are a day-hiker, you need to walk about 800 meters to the Fribourg train station.

In case you are a thru-hiker and spend the night in Fribourg, you are already close to the main pilgrim inn. The pilgrim inn (*Auberge des Pèlerins*) is on the second floor of the Franciscan monastery (Rue de Morat 6; tel. 026 347 11 60; empfang@cordeliers.ch; www.cordeliers.ch). There is a second pilgrim inn at the Maigrauge Abbey (*Abbaye de la Maigrauge*; www.maigrauge.ch), about 1.3 km south, on the other side of the Sarine River (this location is relatively remote). The parish of the St. Nicholas Cathedral has one room with two beds available for pilgrims (tel. 026 321 27 04 or 026 347 10 40; cl.ducarroz@bluewin.ch). Check out www.jakobsweg.ch or www.viajacobi4.ch for the accommodation possibilities. As a tourist city, Fribourg offers a large choice of regular hotels and restaurants. You can also visit the Tourist Information Office (Place Jean Tinguely 1, 1700 Fribourg; tel. 026 350 11 11; www.fribourgtourisme.ch) about 200 meters from the train station.

The next Stage

Fribourg is the end of the routes through Central Switzerland. The Way of St. James continues from Fribourg to Geneva through South-West Switzerland. These stages, together with their churches, chapels, monasteries, castles, chateaus, cities, and other points of interest are described in **Volume III of the Swiss Camino**.

Please continue reading about the next possible stages (number 14 and P1) in Volume III.

ALTERNATIVE ROUTE: INGENBOHL TO SCHWARZENBURG VIA LUZERN/BERN

Stage L1: Ingenbohl to Werthenstein 24 km

The Way with the boat across Lake Lucerne

Route stats

	Distance in km	*Time in hrs:min*
Boat Brunnen to Luzern		2:50
Signposted route nr. 4	19.8	4:10
Churches/chapels	4.0	2:10
Points of interest	0.6	0:20
Rest/lunch		0:30
Stage L1	24.4	10:00

In case you hike this stage as a daytrip, you need to add 400 meters in Ingenbohl and 600 meters in Werthenstein (from and to the train stations).

Ascent/descent/total	+552 / -409 / 961 altitude meters
Lowest/highest altitude	435 / 638 meters
Pathway/condition	easy / moderate
Churches/chapels	Brunnen (3), Luzern (7), Blatten, Malters (3), Schachen, Werthenstein
Monasteries	Former Benedictine Monastery Luzern, Former Jesuit Collegium Luzern, Former Franciscan Monastery Luzern, Former Franciscan Monastery Werthenstein
Points of interest	Lake Lucerne Boat Crossing, Medieval Chapel Bridge, Medieval Speuer Bridge, Mercy Spring

Route summary

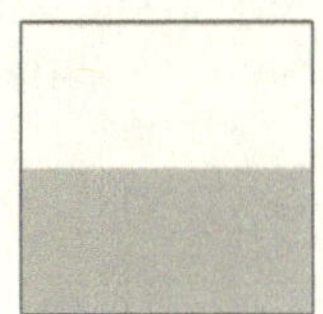

Stage L1 starts in catholic Canton Schwyz and upon arrival with the boat in the city of Luzern continues in catholic **Canton Luzern.**

Stage L1 guides you across Lake Lucerne, through the medieval city of Luzern, over a northern foothill of the Pilatus mountain, and along the Small Emme River valley to the Werthenstein monastery.

Stage L1 consists of three sections: walking from Ingenbohl to the boat pier in Brunnen (1 km); crossing Lake Lucerne by boat (2hr:30min); and hiking the route from the boat pier in Luzern to Werthenstein (23 km). The main challenge of stage L1 is not the hiking distance, but the time needed for the boat crossing from Brunnen to Luzern and the time for sightseeing in Luzern. The hiking distance of 23.4 km from Luzern to Werthenstein should provide some time flexibility.

The hike from Ingenbohl to the Brunnen boat pier is easy and short, only 1 km. Since the ferry times from Brunnen to Luzern are limited, time your arrival at the boat pier. The crossing of Lake Lucerne by tourist boat is the most typical Swiss experience along the Way of St. James. After 2 hours and 30 minutes the boat arrives in Luzern, just before noon (11:47). This leaves the afternoon for the sightseeing in Luzern and the 23 km hike to Werthenstein.

Within the first 3 km in the city of Luzern the route passes by four churches, three chapels, and two points of interest. The route leaves the city and goes up a hill through a forest, slightly descends, and then continues to ascend through the second forest. This is a northern foothill of the Pilatus mountain. In the second forest the highest point of the day at 638 meters is reached. After a steep descent and a crossing of a gorge the route leaves the forest. These two forests make up 6.4 of the 23.4 km from the boat pier. They are the only serious ascents and descents of the day. The remainder of the route closely follows road nr. 2a and the Small Emme River. Along the river the route slopes up very gradually (hardly noticeable). It is an easy path on gravel or soft forest underground, with about half of this distance in the shade of trees.

Several detours from the signposted route nr. 4 are necessary. In Luzern the signposted route skips several interesting churches and one of the points of interest. In Malters the signposted route only follows the Small Emme River, without entering the town, although it includes two churches and a chapel. Similarly, the route passes by the village of Schachen without entering it, despite a chapel that is worthwhile another small detour. Skipping the detours to the churches/chapels in Malters and Schachen would reduce the distance by about 2.6 km, which could make some extra time available for sightseeing in Luzern.

Stage L1 ends at the Monastery of Werthenstein. The monastery's church was the second-most frequented pilgrimage destination in Switzerland during the 17th-18th centuries (up to 80'000 pilgrims per year). It is a worthy ending of the day.

Getting to the starting point

Today's starting point in Ingenbohl is at the St. Leonard church, about 450 meters aside the signposted route nr. 4. You are already at the right location in case you spent the night at the Ingenbohl Convent's pilgrim inn. In case you hike stage 6 as a daytrip, you need to walk 400 meters from the Brunnen train station to the church. However, you could also walk from the train station directly to the first church along the route, which is opposite of the train station (this saves about 800 meters of walking the same way to and from the St. Leonard church).

Alternative: taking the morning train to Luzern (instead of the boat)

From Ingenbohl you have two possibilities to go to Luzern by public transportation. You can either go by train or by boat. This choice may be influenced by the following factors:

- Weather: in case of low clouds, rain, and strong wind, the train might be better. If it is sunny, the boat will offer a wonderful experience.
- Day-schedule: in case you want an early start in Luzern, an early train is best. In case you take the first boat you may have to streamline the schedule for the day, plan for a later arrival in Werthenstein, or speed up the walking.

The direct train from Brunnen to Luzern takes 50 minutes (S3 direction *Luzern*) or 51 minutes (IR26 direction *Basel*). A ticket costs CHF 17.40. For your morning departure, the direct train times from the Brunnen train station are: 07:04, 07:31, 07:41, 08:04, 09:04. Check out the up to date schedules on *www.SBB.ch.*

Alternative: traveling to Luzern the prior evening (end of stage 5)

The city of Luzern is a major tourist destination that offers many points of interest for sightseeing. In case you want to ensure you have sufficient time in Luzern, you could also make your way there at the end of stage 5, after your hike from Einsiedeln to Ingenbohl. This would mean spending the night in Luzern instead of in Ingenbohl. Luzern is a lively town and a major tourist hub in Central Switzerland, offering many possibilities for accommodations and restaurants. The town has several low-cost accommodations (Youth Hostel, Hostel Lion Lodge, Backpackers, Ibis Budget Hotel) that are comparable to a pilgrim inn.

If you are set on taking the boat across the lake to Luzern, you can consider to take the boat late afternoon at the end of stage 5. The afternoon times are 15:49 (arriving 17:47), 16:49 (arriving 18:47), and the last one of the day 17:49 (arriving 19:47). A ticket costs CHF 39.00. Check out the up to date schedules on *www.lakelucerne.ch.*

Another option is to take the late afternoon or early evening train from Brunnen to Luzern. The direct train (S3 direction *Luzern*) takes 50 minutes and departs 4 minutes past the hour: 16:04, 17:04, 18:04 (additional connections are available, but they take longer and require transfer). A ticket costs CHF 17.40. Check out the up to date schedules on *www.SBB.ch.*

Alternative: making Luzern the starting point of a day-hike

In case you are a day-hiker and hike stage L1 as a daytrip, you can also consider to start in Luzern. In this case you skip the lake's crossing and start at the boat arrival pier in Luzern. This is only 200 meters from the Luzern train station. It is straight across the bus terminal towards the lake. A morning start in Luzern would give you sufficient time for sightseeing and exploring the city.

Route Map and Profile

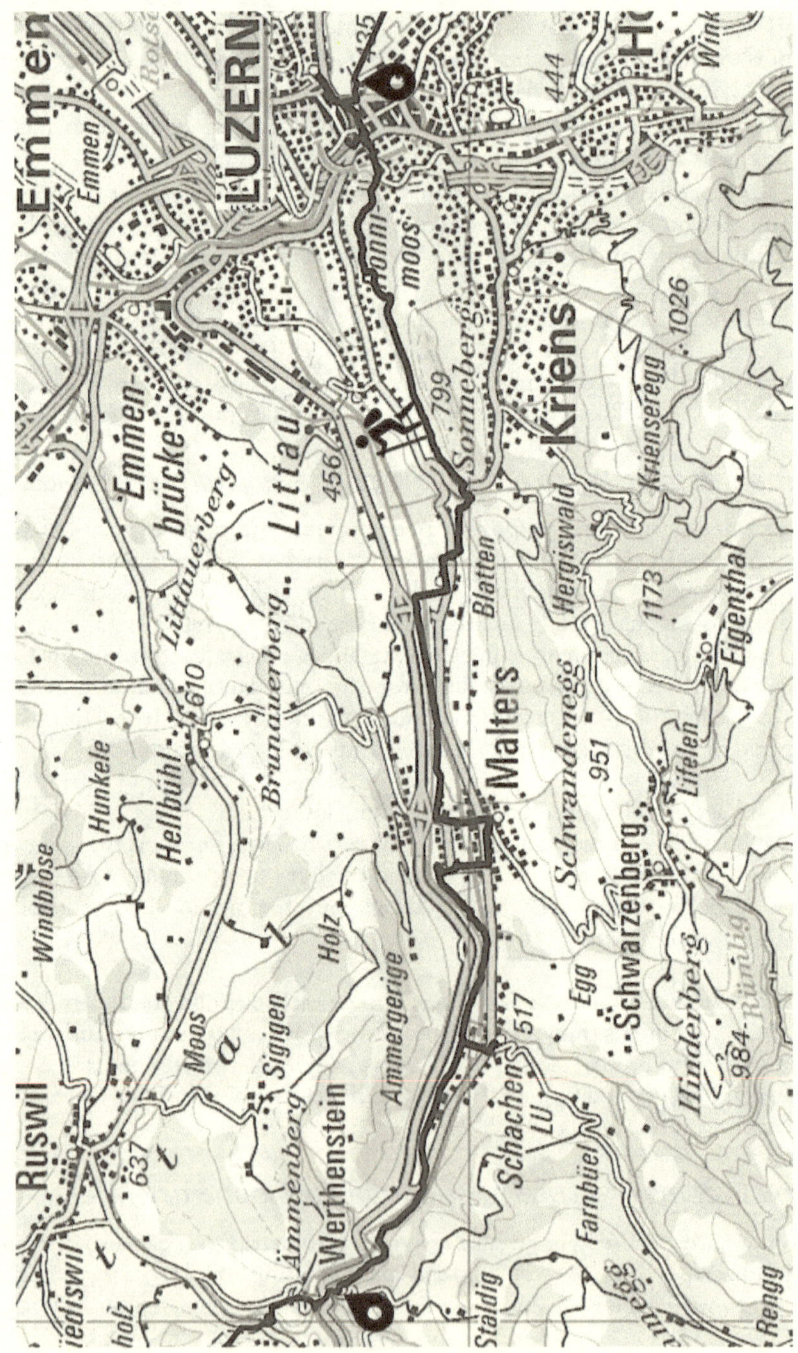

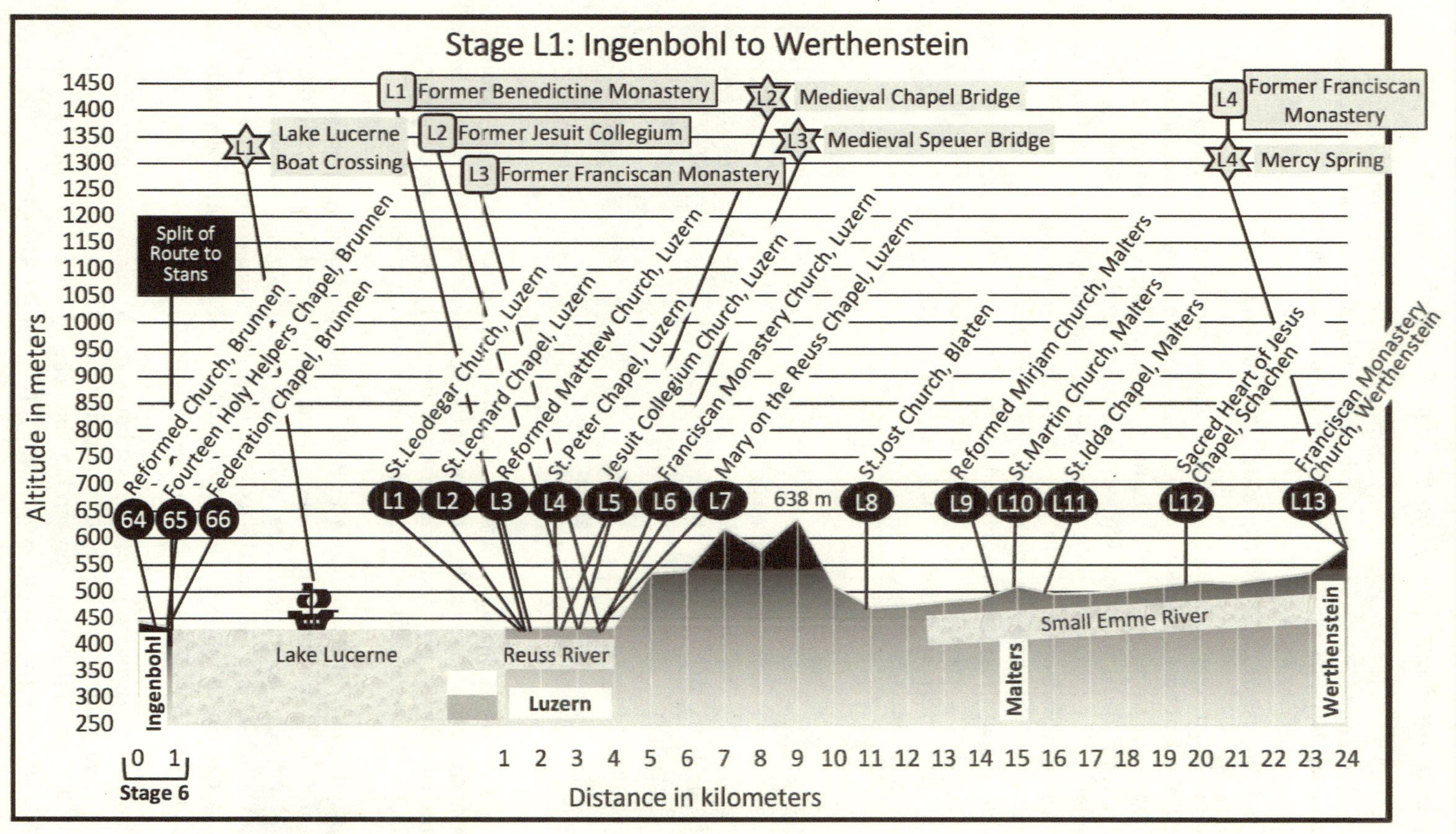
Stage L1: Ingenbohl to Werthenstein
L1 Former Benedictine Monastery
L2 Former Jesuit Collegium
L3 Former Franciscan Monastery
L4 Former Franciscan Monastery
L1 Lake Lucerne Boat Crossing
L2 Medieval Chapel Bridge
L3 Medieval Speuer Bridge
L4 Mercy Spring
Split of Route to Stans
Altitude in meters
1450
1400
1350
1300
1250
1200
1150
1100
1050
1000
950
900
850
800
750
700
650
600
550
500
450
400
350
300
250
Reformed Church, Brunnen
Fourteen Holy Helpers Chapel, Brunnen
Federation Chapel, Brunnen
St.Leodegar Church, Luzern
St.Leonard Chapel, Luzern
Reformed Matthew Church, Luzern
St.Peter Chapel, Luzern
Jesuit Collegium Church, Luzern
Franciscan Monastery Church, Luzern
Mary on the Reuss Chapel, Luzern
St.Jost Church, Blatten
Reformed Mirjam Church, Malters
St.Martin Church, Malters
St.Idda Chapel, Malters
Sacred Heart of Jesus Chapel, Schachen
Franciscan Monastery Church, Werthenstein
64
65
66
L1
L2
L3
L4
L5
L6
L7
638 m
L8
L9
L10
L11
L12
L13
Ingenbohl
Lake Lucerne
Reuss River
Luzern
Malters
Small Emme River
Werthenstein
0 1
Stage 6
1 2 3 4 5 6 7 8 9 10 11 12 13 14 15 16 17 18 19 20 21 22 23 24
Distance in kilometers

Hiking the Route from Ingenbohl to Brunnen (km 0-1)

The 1.3 km route from Ingenbohl to Brunnen overlaps with the beginning of stage 6 (Ingenbohl to Stans). For the detailed description of this route, one church, and two chapels, please refer to the pages 72 to 74 of stage 6.

Crossing Lake Lucerne by boat (2hr:30min)

About 100 meters from the Federation Chapel you arrive at the Brunnen boat pier at **Lake Lucerne** (*Vierwaldstättersee*). The German name *Vierwaldstättersee* means 'four forest towns at the lake'. In medieval times the lake's shores were densely forested and the four towns (now Cantons) around the lake were Schwyz, Uri, Unterwalden (nowadays split in Nidwalden and Obwalden), and Luzern. Lake Lucerne is Switzerland's fourth-largest lake, with an average depth of 104 meters (maximum depth 214 meters) and a surface elevation of 434 meters. It has an unusual shape that comprises several bays of the lake (each of these bays has an own name). Some parts of the lake are surrounded by steep cliffs. The lake is a popular tourist attraction with boats cruising between idyllic villages (with historical hotels) along the shores.

The turquoise-colored lake against the snow-capped Alps in the background is a postcard scenery, especially with one of the historical steamboats on the lake. The area around the pier and promenade is usually bustling with people, who are enjoying the view from the many cafes' and restaurants' terraces.

At the boat pier in Brunnen the tall hiking signpost with the sign for route nr. 4 directs towards the lake. At this location the Way of St. James route splits: the Alpine Lakes (via Interlaken) route crosses the lake to Treib (first boat stop; 8 minutes) and continues on the southern shores of Lake Luzern to Stans (see stage 6); the alternative route via Luzern/Bern continues on the boat to Luzern.

The boat's crossing to Luzern takes 2 hours and 30 minutes; its earliest departure in the morning is at 09:19 from the Brunnen pier, arriving in Luzern at 11:47. A ticket costs CHF 39.00. You can buy the ticket at the counter on the pier. Time your arrival at the pier, to avoid missing the first boat: the next one is at 10:49, arriving in Luzern at 12:47. On a nice summer day you will not be the only one embarking.

L-1 The **Boat Crossing of Lake Lucerne** (*Vierwaldstättersee*) offers one of the most scenic lake tours of Switzerland; very worthwhile to do and a relaxing and enjoyable start of the day. The boat journeys 40 km on the lake and makes seven short stops (Treib, Beckenried, Buochs, Ennetbürgen, Vitznau, Weggis, and Bürgenstock) before arriving in Luzern.

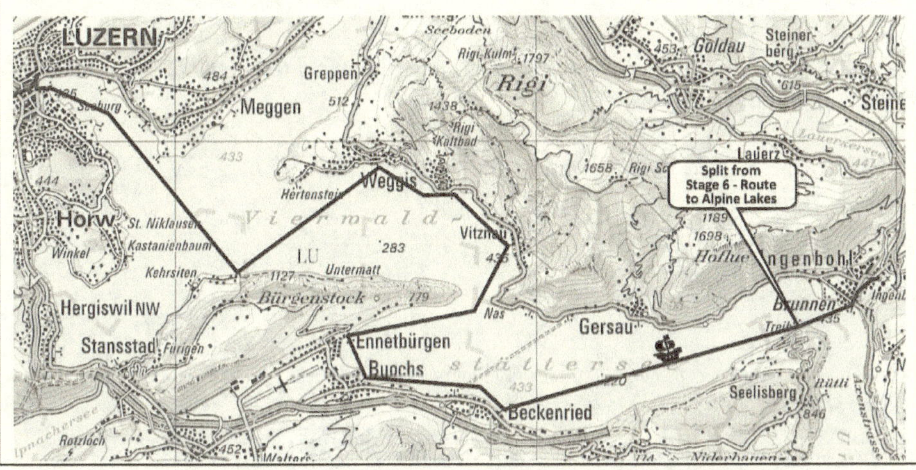

Forested mountain ranges surround the lake: Rigi (1'797 m) in the north; Klewenalp (1'748 m) and Buochserhorn (1'806 m) in the south. The boat circles around the Bürgenstock mountain (1'127 m). Shortly before arriving at the Bürgenstock stop, have a close look at a free-standing elevator at the northern side of the Bürgenstock mountain. This is the Hammetschwand lift: the highest exterior elevator in Europe, with a height of 153 meters. When the boat makes the final crossing from Bürgenstock to Luzern you see the mighty Pilatus mountain (2'118 m) left (south) of Luzern. When you look back you see the jagged peaks of the Alps at the horizon.

Upon approaching Luzern, you can see the fortification towers and church towers rising above the medieval city.

Hiking the Route from Luzern to Werthenstein (km 1-24)

Once you are off the boat, a signpost directs you towards the right (east) to the corner of the road bridge (*Seebrücke*), where a tall hiking signpost marks the first nr. 4 route sign in Luzern. The nr. 4 route directs to go straight and cross the busy road towards the wooden Chapel Bridge. However, at this location you already need to leave the signposted route to visit the main and oldest church of Luzern.

So instead of crossing the road and going straight, turn right and stay along the lake. Walk over the bridge (*Seebrücke*), continue along the promenade next to the lake (*Schweizerhofquai*) passing by the Schweizerhof hotel, and at a big intersection cross the street. Turn right and in front you will already see the two towers of the church. Cross the *Löwenstrasse*, continue in the *Sankt-Leodegar-Strasse*, and go up the steps, where you arrive at the St. Leodegar Church at 0.8 km (all following distances are measured from the signpost at the Luzern boat pier).

St. Leodegar Church, Luzern (Hofkirche St. Leodegar) L-1

Sankt-Leodegar-Strasse, 6006 Luzern

St. Leodegar, St. Maurice

The church is on a site with a long history. A first chapel, dedicated to St. Maurice, was built around 735, and rebuilt around 850. By 1135 the Benedictine Abbey of Murbach (France) came to own the church and dedicated St. Leodegar as patron Saint (who was the patron Saint of the mother Abbey). In 1455 the church became a Collegiate church (see Appendix 3).

During the times of the Reformation, Luzern became a center of the Counter-Reformation, where the Bishop resided for a while, temporarily elevating the status of the church to cathedral.

In 1633 the Gothic church burned down, save for its two towers. A German Jesuit monk was assigned with reconstructing the church in enlarged dimensions (60 meters length and 20 meters height) in 1638-44. The difference in architectural style between the front facade and the two towers is clearly visible. Over the centuries the church was frequently renovated and expanded.

Both patron Saints are present throughout the church; look at the wood-carvings of the entrance doors with St. Leodegar (left) depicted as bishop, and St. Maurice (right) depicted as soldier. Left of the entrance, under the small protruding roof in a niche in the wall, you find colored sandstone statues (dating from 1512) representing the Olive Mountain scene, where Jesus prayed the night before his Crucifixion, while his Apostles slept.

Most impressive are the two side-altars. The left side-altar relief depicts Mary on her deathbed, dating from around 1500. The relief was saved from the fire in 1633. The right side-altar relief depicts Jesus being taken from the Cross (a so-called Pietà). The altar was created in 1640, around the center piece of the Pietà that was also saved from the fire in 1633.

The pipe organ from 1640 (expanded over the centuries) is the third special feature of the church. It has 7'374 pipes, the biggest one measuring 10.7 meters with a weight of 383 kg. It was the largest pipe organ in Europe for a long time. The organ even has a mechanism that imitates the sound of pouring rain.

The iron gate (rood screen), which separates the chancel from the nave, dates from 1643. The tall crucifix dates from the 16th century and was also saved from the fire in 1633. The high-altar dates from 1639 and is one of the tallest classical baroque marble altars in Switzerland.

Nowadays the church is not only used for services, but also for concerts and events. It is, however, mostly a tourist attraction; information brochures are available in several languages.

A few meters north of the church, inside the cemetery cloisters, is the St. Leonard Chapel.

L-2 St. Leonard Chapel, Luzern (Leonhard Kapelle)

Sankt-Leodegar-Strasse, 6006 Luzern

St. Leonard, St. Mary

The chapel was first mentioned in 1461 and renovated in 1608-09. The small chapel escaped the church's fire of 1633, but burned down nine years later (1642). The chapel was immediately rebuilt, but transformed to a cemetery chapel in 1813. The chapel is dedicated to St. Leonard.

The interior contains a beautiful statue representing the Virgin Mary with baby Jesus, several partially-recovered wall frescos, and a colorful stained-glass window at the back of the chancel. Nowadays the chapel is mostly known for the eternal prayer to Jesus, which occurred uninterrupted for the last 11 years.

The church and chapel were part of a Benedictine Monastery that existed for more than 650 years. Its history is as follows.

Former Benedictine Monastery, Luzern (Benediktiner Kloster) L-1

Sankt-Leodegar-Strasse, 6006 Luzern

Benedictine Order, Collegiate

In 735 a small monastery, with a small chapel, was established by south-German noblemen. By the year 800 the monastery was abandoned. The monastery and chapel were rebuilt and reoccupied by monks from the Benedictine Order in 850; they contributed to the establishment of the town Luzern.

Around 1135 these monks gave up their independence and the monastery became a subsidiary of the Benedictine Abbey of Murbach, Alsace (France). By 1291 the mother Abbey of Murbach was in financial difficulties and sold the monastery and all its lands (including Nidwalden and Obwalden) to the House of Habsburg-Austria.

For more than 650 years the Benedictine monks took care of the poor and the religious well-being of the population of Luzern and surroundings. From the beginning of the 13th century the monastery also maintained a school for the higher-level education of boys (this ended in 1574, when the Jesuits were called to Luzern (see below)). As the Swiss Confederation gradually besieged the House of Habsburg, they lost their power over Luzern, and in 1433 the City of Luzern assumed the rights over the monastery. By 1455 the City received approval from the Pope and Bishop of Konstanz to transform the Benedictine monastery to a secular canon (while the church became a Collegiate).

The old monastery buildings have long since disappeared, but the Collegiate still exists today (with nine members). Nowadays the Collegiate of Luzern is one of only three remaining in Switzerland.

From the chapel exit the grounds of the church. Go down the steps and continue straight on the right side of the *Schweizerhofquai.* You pass by expensive watch shops and the majestic five-star hotel Schweizerhof. Turn right immediately after the hotel. In the middle of the square you arrive at the reformed Matthew Church (at km 1.1).

L-3 Reformed Matthew Church, Luzern (Matthäus Kirche)

Seehofstrasse 6, 6004 Luzern

St. Matthew, Four Evangelists

The church was built in a neo-Gothic style in 1860-61, as the first protestant church in the catholic stronghold of Central Switzerland. Until that time the protestant parish had to meet in a small chapel in another part town. This chapel had become too small and the parish wanted to build their own church. The protestant community had to go through a long process to establish this first church. The owner of the nearby hotel Schweizerhof donated the plot of land, and the parish received support from the protestant parishes of Zurich and Bern, and donations from all over Switzerland. This nationwide support was reflected in the stained-glass windows that depict the flags of the Cantons. The church was dedicated to Matthew, without using the word Saint. Given the difficulty of financing the church, Matthew seems to have been an appropriate name indeed.

Queen Victoria of England attended a service at the church when she was on holiday in Luzern in 1868. The four bells in the bell tower were installed based on her donations in 1869. In 1870 the famous German composer Richard Wagner got married in this church.

Renovations in 1951-52 significantly changed its interior appearance, removing many of the original decorations (including the baptismal font). Other than the pulpit, organ, and stained-glass window depicting the Four Evangelists, there is little that makes it a place of worship. Nowadays the church is often used for exhibitions, concerts, and events.

From the church walk back to the *Schweizerhofquai* and turn right towards the bridge. You pass by a tourist coach parking area and expensive watch shops. The mount Pilatus dominates the southern horizon. Shortly before the *Seebrücke* turn right into the *Kapellplatz*. At the small square you arrive at the St. Peter Chapel (at km 1.4).

St. Peter Chapel, Luzern (St. Peter Kapelle) **L-4**

- Kapellplatz 1a, 6004 Luzern
- St. Peter, St. Christopher
- The chapel was first mentioned in official documents in 1178, as one of the oldest churches in the city of Luzern. It was not only used for services, but also for city meetings, making it an important historical building.

  The old chapel was rebuilt in a baroque style in 1746-51, determining its present-day appearance. Further renovations were undertaken in the 19th and 20th centuries. Over time the original rectangular nave was expanded to an almost square footprint. The latest restorations were undertaken in 2017-18.
- Right of the entrance is a small side-chapel, also in a modern style. The tall fresco on the northern outer wall depicts St. Christopher carrying baby Jesus over a river (dated early 20th century). The southern outer wall has an Olive Mountain relief.

In medieval times the quay at the river had a fortified wall, protecting the city against intruders coming from the Reuss River. The wooden Chapel Bridge went through/over these fortifications and led directly into the southern side of the chapel; the northern access to the bridge was from within the chapel. Since the bridge and the chapel were connected, and the chapel was the entry point from the city side, the bridge automatically got its name from the chapel, hence the name Chapel Bridge (*Kapellbrücke*).

Have a look at the northern end of the bridge (the roof is elevated) and in your mind extend the bridge to the chapel: it leads straight to the southern side of the chapel. The entrance existed at an elevated position at the level of the chapel's windows, just underneath the roof, right of the door (there was no tree at that time), above the Olive Mountain relief.

South of the chapel the **Medieval Chapel Bridge** (*Kapellbrücke*) crosses the Reuss River, flowing from Lake Lucerne to the west. Luzern's chapel bridge, with its stone tower (*Wasserturm*), is a big tourist attraction in Switzerland. The wooden covered footbridge has a length of 204 meters, was originally built as part of the town's medieval fortifications in 1333, and crosses the Reuss River diagonally. The eight-sided tower, about 30 years older than the bridge, has been in use as fortification, prison, torture room, treasury, and archive.

To imagine what this looked like in the 14th century, consider that the road bridge (*Seebrücke*) and other footbridges did not exist at that time; the wooden chapel bridge was the only crossing.

Over the centuries the bridge was renovated, renewed, shortened, and rebuilt multiple times (originally it was 285 meters long). In 1993 a devastating fire ruined most of Europe's oldest wooden footbridge and the wooden triangular paintings hanging underneath its roof. Most of the paintings and wooden bridge were restored or renewed in 1994 (though some original paintings are still left). The original paintings in Renaissance style date from 1599 and following years. The 110 triangular paintings tell the history of Luzern and its patron Saints Leodegar and Maurice, as well as the impact of the Counter-Reformation. A gap was left to commemorate the fire of 1993.

About halfway the bridge is a small souvenir shop that has already existed since 1862. Nearly 300 plant pots with colored geraniums decorate the bridge.

The **Reuss River** is the fourth-longest river in Switzerland, with a length of 164 km (the Aare, Rhone, and Rhine are longer). The river springs in the Gotthard mountains and converges into the Aare at Brugg. The Reuss River's water level is shallow and the water is clear. You can see fish swimming between the water plants.

After walking across the Chapel Bridge (north to south), you are back on the signposted route nr. 4. Turn right and walk along the riverside until you arrive at the Jesuit Collegium Church 200 meters later (at km 1.7).

Jesuit Collegium Church, Luzern (Jesuiten Kirche) L-5

Bahnhofstrasse 11, 6003 Luzern

St. Francis Xaver, St. Silvanus, Brother Klaus

The church was initially built in 1574, and served as school church for the Jesuit boys' gymnasium as well as for the Jesuit Order itself. The first church was relatively small and could only accommodate a limited number of students. Because of the large number of students, 300-400 on a population of 4'000 in Luzern, the old church had become too small and a new one was built in a baroque style in 1666-77. The church was reconstructed to connect to the Collegium on its western side in 1756-57.

The church was dedicated to St. Francis Xaver in 1666, who had already been the patron Saint of the City of Luzern since 1654 (a sign of influence of the Jesuits over the City's government).

Since 1773 the church is owned by Canton Luzern and regularly used for services, concerts, and other events. Above all it has become a tourist attraction. The catholic parish of Luzern is allowed to use the church for services based on a contractual agreement with the Canton dating from 1989.

This church is one of the most beautiful examples of baroque style along the Swiss Way of St. James. The interior of the church is artistically decorated with baroque marble, frescos, paintings, woodwork, and so forth. Instead of masonry, the interior appearance is determined by stucco, the fine plaster coating on the walls and ceiling, making the interior very light.

The Brother Klaus side-chapel has a large statue that wears an original robe worn by this Saint (another one is in the church of Sachseln; see church nr. 102, stage 7). Admire the golden altars in the vitrines of several side-chapels.

One side-chapel contains a skull and decorated bones dedicated to St. Silvanus (also called St. Silas). This is a catacomb saint, whose relics were purchased from the Vatican, probably in the first half of the 17th century. They were the center piece in a St. Silas chapel that used to be part of the first Jesuit church.

L-2 Former Jesuit Collegium, Luzern (Jesuiten Kloster)

Bahnhofstrasse 11, 6003 Luzern

Jesuit Order

The Jesuit Order came to Luzern as a City's measure of the Counter-Reformation, for the purpose of strengthening Catholicism in the city and Canton (and stave off Protestantism), in 1574. They set up a school (collegium) for the higher-level education of boys and built a church and monastery.

The Jesuits had significant influence on the development of the educational system in Canton Luzern, and maintained close ties with the patriarchal families and politicians in Luzern (these were often the same people). With political support they could expand their collegium and boarding facilities for students, where they housed up to 400 regional male students at its peak.

The Jesuits were increasingly influencing local educational politics and gathering substantial wealth (as demonstrated in their church). This abruptly ended after 199 years. In 1773 a papal decree formally dissolved the Jesuit Order, after which the Jesuits were expelled from Switzerland. Canton Luzern seized the Jesuit church, the large school and monastery buildings, and all their wealth and assets.

The Canton continued the school in these buildings until 1966, after which the school was relocated to another part of the city. Nowadays the Cantonal government and a college house in the former Jesuit monastery and school buildings.

Continuing westward on the *Bahnhofstrasse*, 120 meters from the Jesuit church you pass by a street on the left, leading to a small square and the Franciscan Church (at km 2.0).

Franciscan Monastery Church, Luzern (Franziskaner Kirche) L-6

- Franziskanerplatz 1, 6003 Luzern
- St. Mary, St. Anthony of Padua, St. John the Evangelist, St. James the Greater, St. Celestine
- At the information table fixed to the wall of the anteroom to the St. Anthony side-chapel
- The church was part of a Franciscan monastery built in 1269-82. The Gothic church, dedicated to St. Mary, was built in several stages from 1270, making it one of the oldest churches in Luzern. Because the church was the largest building in Luzern, it was also used for communal meetings. Above the arches in the nave you see frescos of flags. The City used to hang the coat-of-arms flags (banners) conquered in battles by their mercenaries.

  Because the town's cemetery was full, the gardens of the church were used as a cemetery between 1600 and 1798. Because of the moist soil, caused by the nearby river, the decaying corpses produced unpleasant odors in the church, so that the burial grounds had to be closed and removed in 1798.

  Much of the original Gothic style is still visible, despite the many expansions and the Renaissance, baroque, and rococo renovations that were undertaken in later centuries. Its present interior appearance predominantly dates from renovations and reconstruction in 1622-60. In 1622 an earthquake destroyed most of the nave, which was completely rebuilt and restyled in the subsequent decades.
- The interior of the church is wonderfully decorated with marble, frescos, paintings, statues, woodwork, and so forth. Noteworthy are the wood-carved angels carrying the pulpit (1628), the carvings of the pulpit itself, and the unusual red/white colored marble at the side-altars and the high-altar (1735-37).

  The oldest part of the church is the chancel, which still has the original appearance of the Gothic construction from 1270-82. The chancel used to be the original monastery church (which explains why the chancel is so long); the extensions of the nave and the side-chapels were built in later centuries. The two impressive rows of wood-carved choir stalls in the quire date from 1651. These are the longest double rows, and the best example of a quire section of a chancel, along the Swiss Way of St. James.

The church has two side-chapels: the St. Anthony chapel (1658) and the St. Mary chapel (1626). Although the popular name of the church nowadays is the Franciscan church, its official name is the St. Mary church. Look at the ceiling of the anteroom and the St. Mary chapel: many angels, as frescos complemented with stuccos (1626), look down upon you. This anteroom used to be the St. Anthony chapel (1455), until a new one was built.

The anteroom has an additional exceptional statue: on the wall you see a statue representing St. John the Evangelist and his brother St. James as children. Below these statues is a wooden message board for the Way of St. James pilgrims.

Nowadays the church is frequently used for concerts, particularly during the Lucerne Music Festival over Easter.

Have a closer look at the gold-framed vitrine at the center altar of the St. Anthony chapel. Therein lies an artfully decorated skeleton with crown, sword, and palm branch under the name shield Corpus St. Coelestini Martyris. It is a catacomb saint that was brought from Rome in 1624 (it had to reinstate the good fortunes of the church after it had been devastated by the earthquake in 1622). The skeleton of St. Celestine was decorated by the nuns of the Capuchin Convent St. Clare in Stans (see stage 6).

L-3 Former Franciscan Monastery, Luzern (Franziskaner Kloster)

Franziskanerplatz 1, 6003 Luzern

Franciscan Order

Franciscan friars were sent from southern Germany (area of Lake Constance) to build a monastery in Luzern after 1250. As mendicant Order it took a long time to collect the funds to build the monastery and its church. Donations of lands enabled the Order to maintain a steady income for the maintenance and expansion of their buildings. The Order settled south of the Reuss river and cared for the poor and preached to the local population. They started a boys' school and provided lower-level education for over 260 years. Their school discontinued in 1543, when a public Latin boys' school took over, which in its turn was replaced by the Jesuit boys' Collegium in 1574.

The Benedictines/Collegiate of St. Leodegar (higher-level boys' education) and the Franciscans (lower-level boys' education) were the only two monastic Orders in Luzern until the Counter-Reformation. At that time, Jesuits arrived in 1574 (for higher-level boys' education), Capuchins in 1583 (for lower-level boys' education) und Ursulines in 1659 (for girls' education).

Over the centuries the number of friars residing in the Franciscan monastery varied between a few and 18. During the 15th and 16th centuries the Franciscans went through difficult times, as the Jesuit and Capuchin Orders settled in Luzern and competed in preaching and caring for the poor and needy.

During the first four decades of the 19th century the number of friars steadily declined; only three were left by 1838. The Order was not able to attract novices and the few friars who remained had too many tasks. This led to disorder, mismanagement, and violations of the Rules of the Franciscan Order, as a result of which Canton Luzern increased the supervision over the activities of the remaining few friars.

During the 1820s-30s a wave of liberalization swept through the Swiss Cantons. The liberal forces tried to replace the conservative patriarchal governments of the Cantons and pursued the abolishment of press censorship, separation of Canton and Church, freedom of the individual, and democratically elected Cantonal governments. This wave of liberalization resulted in anti-clerical sentiment and negative press (which contributed to the difficulties of recruiting novices).

By the end of 1838 the Canton decided that the monastery's deficiencies and mismanagement necessitated its closure. The subsidiary Franciscan Order that housed in the Werthenstein monastery (see monastery nr. L-4) met the same fate. The remaining Franciscan friars did not object to the closure and accepted new jobs. After nearly 570 years the presence of the Franciscans ended.

The Canton took possession of the church and monastery buildings, and part of the library. Other assets were liquidated or donated to other monasteries. Nowadays the Cantonal Court houses in the former monastery building.

From the church walk back to the signposted route at the *Bahnhofstrasse* and turn left (west). After a few meters you get to a small square with a fountain. At this location leave the signposted route again to go to the second medieval wooden footbridge over the Reuss River. Turn right into the *Burgerstrasse* and at the river turn left. You can already see the second covered footbridge in front of you. Follow the narrow path between the houses and the river to the bridge.

The **Medieval Speuer Bridge** (*Speuerbrücke)* was built in two phases about 70 years after the Chapel Bridge and was the second medieval crossing of the Reuss. Around 1400 a short bridge was built to connect the northern bank (*Mühlenplatz* – square of the mills) to the small island that occupied several mills, which used the current to turn their wheels. The name *Spreu* means 'chaff'. The downstream position of the bridge was the only place where the mills were allowed to dump their chaff into the river.

About eight years later (1408), the City built an extension of the bridge from the small island to the southern bank of the river. Like the other bridge, it was part of the city's medieval fortifications. It had to be rebuilt in 1568, after the bridge was washed away by the river in 1566.

The bridge is not as famous as the Chapel Bridge, but it is equally impressive. This footbridge has 45 triangular paintings, dating from 1625-35, depicting the Dance of Death (*Totentanz*). The Dance of Death is a medieval theme relating to the Bubonic Plague. The paintings depict skeletons (representing death) that killed people from all walks of life (even religious monks). Many of these paintings are still the originals.

In the middle of the bridge you find a small Virgin Mary Chapel called 'Mary on the Reuss' (at km 2.4).

Mary on the Reuss Chapel, Luzern (Maria auf der Reuss Kapelle) L-7

Speuerbrücke, 6003 Luzern

St. Mary, St. Maurice, St. Catherine

The chapel was first mentioned in a city plan dating from 1597. The small chapel was probably built when the bridge was restored after it had been washed away (1568). The chapel, dedicated to the Virgin Mary, was to protect this second bridge from a reoccurrence of such a disaster. Initially the chapel only contained a painting depicting the Virgin Mary, protected by a bay window. In the following century the chapel was expanded and a small altar was installed. In its present condition the chapel was first mentioned in 1669. The chapel houses in the small red tower with the pointed roof, built on the bridge's middle pillar.

The folktale of the construction of the chapel goes as follows. A wealthy lady was so occupied with her little dog that she neglected her religious routines. To refocus on her religion and receive absolution from God, her confessor asked her to dispose of the dog in the Reuss River. She put the dog in a bag and before throwing the sack from the Speuer Bridge she said to the dog 'how I remorse doing this'. Before the sack disappeared in the water the dog replied 'and I remorse you'. She believed the devil had spoken and expressed regret possessing the little dog (that had made her skip her religious duties). As gratitude for having been shown the path back to religion, she had the small chapel built.

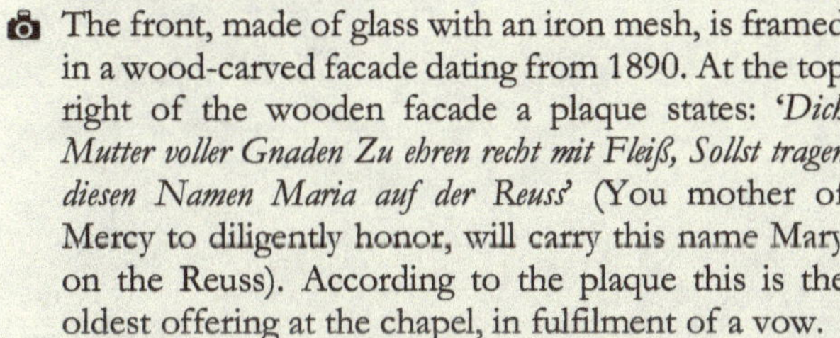

The front, made of glass with an iron mesh, is framed in a wood-carved facade dating from 1890. At the top right of the wooden facade a plaque states: *'Dich Mutter voller Gnaden Zu ehren recht mit Fleiß, Sollst tragen diesen Namen Maria auf der Reuss'* (You mother of Mercy to diligently honor, will carry this name Mary on the Reuss). According to the plaque this is the oldest offering at the chapel, in fulfilment of a vow.

The bridge chapel even has two small stained-glass windows, depicting St. Maurice and St. Catherine, dating from 1905. A statue representing the Virgin Mary stands on the small altar.

This is a unique chapel on a wooden medieval footbridge; one of only two bridge chapels along the Swiss Way of St. James (see stage 4 for the other one).

You can easily spend several more hours sightseeing the medieval city of Luzern. Additional areas for sightseeing are north of the river: the old town (*Altstadt*) with its half-timbered houses; the old town hall (*Altes Rathaus*) from 1606; the narrow streets and small squares with many fountains; and old fortification walls with nine watchtowers (*Museggmauer und Türme*).

Two more churches are spread over the old town: *Mariahilfkirche* (1684; the church of the former Ursuline Convent) and the Christ-Catholic church (1892).

In case you arrived in Luzern the night before or took the early train from Brunnen to Luzern, you may have enough time for this additional sightseeing. In case you took the morning boat from Brunnen, there may not be enough time.

From the Speuer Bridge walk back the same route (about 200 meters) to the small square with the fountain, where you are back on the signposted route. Turn right and continue with the signposted route in a westward direction (*Rütligasse*). Cross main street nr. 2a and continue straight in the *Klosterstrasse.* About 50 meters into the street, the nr. 4 route sign directs to the right (*Hochbühlstrasse*).

At this location you are leaving the town Luzern. In the *Hochbühlstrasse* the route goes steeply up a hill and into a forest. The trail ascends steeply over 700 meters before reaching a high point in the forest (537 meters). The following 1.1 km in the *Gütschwald* are more or less flat, zigzagging through the forest. The trails are mostly wide gravel pathways.

For 600 meters the route passes through a meadow, underneath crackling high-voltage power lines, and past a chalet farmhouse with colorful geraniums at its windowsills.

You enter the next forest, the *Sonnebergwald.* This is also a broad gravel path that slopes up, down, and up again for 2.7 km. The path is more or less straight to the west, and makes a sharp turn to the right only at the end of the *Sonnebergwald.*

You reach the highest altitude of the day at 638 meters. The tree line regularly opens up towards the north, offering wide views over the valley, the towns *Littau* and *Emmen*, and the *Kleine Emme* River. The descent is steep: stairs with 200 steps descend 73 altitude meters. At the bottom of the stairs you cross road nr. 2a and turn into a forest again. Another 100 steep steps down take you to a metal footbridge over a narrow gorge. Some 40 meters below the footbridge the *Ränggbach* flows toward the Small Emme River.

The trail ascends steeply out of the gorge over 150 meters and a little bit later you reach the edge of the forest, where a bench offers a place for rest and panoramic views over the northern valley. The trail changes to grass and you walk through sloping meadows with grazing cows (be cautious), gradually descending towards road nr. 2a.

Upon crossing road nr. 2a, at the foot of the mountain, you have the strenuous part of today's hiking behind you. Over the last 6.4 km you crossed through two forests and ascended from the lake level at 435 meters to 638 meters and down again to 470 meters. The remainder of the route is basically flat; it ascends ever so gradually that you will hardly notice.

After some farmhouses the route turns left on a tarmac road between meadows and corn fields. You can already see the steeples of the St. Jost Church in the distance. You reach the church at km 9.9.

L-8 St. Jost Church, Blatten (St. Jost Kirche)

- Luzernstrasse, 6102 Malters-Blatten
- St. Jost
- In a small basket on a table left of the entrance
- In 1366 a local farmer called Krämer went on a pilgrimage to the grave of St. Jost in northern France, and was captured and robbed along the way. Upon his release he vowed to build a chapel on his lands. He had a small chapel built (financed by donations) in fulfilment of the vow in 1374-75. This farm chapel was consecrated 16 years later (1391) and dedicated to St. Jost.

A hundred years later, in 1483-1511, the chapel already had to be expanded to the size of a church, because it had become too small for all the visiting pilgrims. Around 1500, and in the 17th and 18th centuries, the church was a regional pilgrimage destination.

Further expansion and reconstruction were undertaken in 1629-55, when both side-chapels were built. The right (south) one is called the Marriage chapel (*Vermählungskapelle*); the left (north) one the Holy Grave chapel (*Heiliggrabkapelle*). Have a closer look at the painted figures; they have been artfully created.

The church received its rococo interior in 1767. The latest restauration was completed in 2011.

Attached to the church are two more buildings, which are not accessible without appointment. Left (north) of the entrance is a two-level Confession House (*Beichthaus*), built in 1757-59. The upper level has a small Confession chapel with eight confessionals and small altars with relics. The number of eight confessionals demonstrate the importance of this church as a pilgrimage destination. The lower level was used as a coach house for the visiting aristocrats (a drive-in to the confession). The confession house served as a school room from 1798 to 1838. At the front-right of the nave (south) is the access to the sacristy, which is a two-level building that was attached to the church in 1634. The second level of the sacristy was simply built on top of the first level in 1642. The church owes its unusual footprint to the confession house, sacristy, and the two side-chapels.

The treasures of the church are the Renaissance gold-plated high-altar, created in 1686-89, and the St. Jost paintings at the walls of the nave and above the entrance. See how the story of the farmer Krämer is told in those paintings.

From the church the route goes north, underneath railway tracks, until you reach the river (400 meters). You walk past several tables of the so-called **Blattner Love Trail** (*Blattner Liebesweg*). This trail comprises eight stations that ask couples to reflect on their relationship (through questions that should lead to discussions).

The route follows the Small Emme River (*Kleine Emme*) on its southern bank, while a busy road (nr. 10) is parallel to the river on its northern bank. The continuous traffic noise disrupts any silence you may expect to find alongside the river. The pathway along the river is on gravel or soft forest underground, underneath trees about half of the remaining distance to Werthenstein. This offers a shaded and easy trail, though it has many small curves and minor ascents and descents. The forest around the path, varying between 5 and 30 meters in width, is a narrow strip of trees alongside the river. Most of the time the trees and bushes block the view towards the river (right side, north) and the farmlands (left side, south).

After 3.5 km the trail passes by the outskirts of Malters, but leaves the town on the left. The signposted route nr. 4 continues straight, alongside the Small Emme River. At this location it is worthwhile to leave the signposted route and make a detour into the town Malters. Two churches and one chapel await your visit there. On your left you see a high church steeple. That is where you need to go. Instead of crossing the *Hellbühlstrasse*, turn left and follow it into Malters. After 200 meters and a roundabout, you arrive at the reformed Mirjam Church (at km 13.7).

L-9 Reformed Mirjam Church, Malters (Reformierte Kirche)

Mühlering 2, 6102 Malters

Mirjam

The church was built with significant support of volunteers of the protestant parish of Malters in 1914-15. Because the region was a historical catholic stronghold, the number of protestants only started to grow during the second half of the 19th century.

From 1861 the Protestants could go to the reformed Matthew church in Luzern (see church nr. L-3); from 1880 they could go to a prayer room in the nearby town Ruswil. It was not until 1895 that services were held in Malters itself; initially in the living room of a farmhouse, later in a prayer room of a private house that had been purchased by a group of Protestants.

The sale of the house, donation of a plot of land by a local company, and other donations enabled the construction of the first protestant church in 1914. Because of limited financing, improvements to the church had to be made over a period of 70 years. A community room was built underneath the church in 1965. The church did not have bells until 1986; they could not afford them and initially it was believed that the small steeple was too weak to carry the weight of bells.

The church received its name Mirjam on the occasion of its 75-year celebration in 1990.

The church has a typical austere protestant interior. Its doors are generally locked outside service hours.

From the church continue along the *Hellbühlstrasse* in a southern direction towards the tall bell tower. You pass by the Malters train station and cross the tracks. After crossing road nr. 2a again (here called *Luzernstrasse*), zigzagging through some small streets, and climbing the steps up the hill, you arrive at the St. Martin Church (at km 14.1). A St. James scallop hangs at a pillar of the front porch.

St. Martin Church, Malters (St. Martin Kirche) **L-10**

- Kirchrain 2, 6102 Malters
- St. Martin, St. Jucundus
- On the information stand, left of the entrance
- The church is on the site of several predecessor churches. A first church was mentioned in 1107, back then already dedicated to St. Martin, when the church and lands belonged to the Benedictine monastery of Luzern. The first church was replaced by another one in 1501, which was expanded 100 years later (1602).

  By 1809 the church had become too small, but for financial reasons the construction of the new church had to wait until 1833. Half of the financing for the reconstruction came from a pastor from Willisau. The authorities there had refused his pension entitlement, which motivated the pastor to put all his savings in the construction of a new church in Malters, upon which the municipality of Malters promised him the desired pension entitlements.

  The present church was built in 1833-35. The size of the church, in a small town in the province, is extraordinary. The church could seat 1'200 in 1835, in a village with a population of 3'500 (its original plan was 1'800 seats). Today it still seats 900 people. The church is 53 meters long and 22 meters wide. It has the second-highest bell tower in Switzerland: the top of its needle reaches 97.6 meters (you will visit the church with the highest bell tower of Switzerland in stage L4). The bell tower was newly built in 1935, after the previous one revealed structural weaknesses and had to be demolished.
- Renovations in 1975-77 restored much of the original baroque interior. All windows received plain glass (the stained-glass windows from 1929 were removed) and the ceiling was whitewashed, contributing to the light interior.
- The right side-altar contains a vitrine with the relics of a catacomb saint, lusciously decorated in a Roman dress. The relics were purchased in Rome in 1650 and displayed in the church from that year. The bones were completed with plaster and decorated by the nuns of the Capuchin Convent St. Clare in Stans (see stage 6). The relics were dedicated to Saint Jucundus.

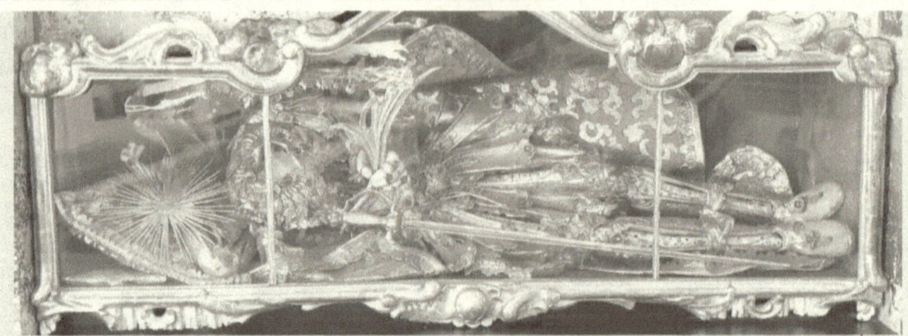

Have a closer look at the relics. Apart from the beautiful decorations, precious stones, palm of martyrdom, and sword, you will see that the skull is missing. The skull and several bones were stolen in 1999. Allegedly a French monk robbed multiple relics in the region and brought them to monasteries in France. Because of border control regulations it is nowadays almost impossible to repatriate relics, such as bones, across the border.

From the church walk back down the hill to road nr. 2a (*Luzernstrasse*) and turn left (west) to follow this road for 300 meters to the St. Idda Chapel (at km 14.6).

L-11 **St. Idda Chapel, Malters** (St. Idda Kapelle)

- Luzernstrasse 52, 6102 Malters
- St. Idda
- The chapel was built in 1642 and dedicated to St. Idda. During the 17th and 18th centuries the small chapel was often visited by people who wanted to pray for recovery from an illness, or before an operation. The chapel was in disrepair by 1849 and could just be saved from demolition, which occurred again by 1875. Since 1899 a local St. Idda foundation has been caring for the regular maintenance of the chapel.
- The Renaissance altar has a beautiful center painting depicting the Rosary Madonna: the Virgin Mary with baby Jesus and four angels surrounded by a rosary. A unique painting, not found elsewhere along the Swiss Way of St. James.

  The chapel's door is locked; it can only be accessed by appointment (an information leaflet hangs next to the door).

From the chapel you need to go back to the signposted route nr. 4 (but not the same way as you came). Continue 100 meters on road nr. 2a to the west, turn right, and follow the *Industriestrasse* in a northern direction. After the railway tracks you see the tree line along the river in front of you. Go straight for the tree line, where you are back on the signposted route.

Continue along the river in a western direction. A little later the forest ends, though the trail keeps following the Small Emme closely. The route passes through an area called *Ettisbühl,* which protects against severe flooding of the Small Emme and includes a water-power plant. A flooding disaster occurred in the downstream towns in 2005 and high-water protection measures have been taken since (e.g. overflowing areas and large posts blocking driftwood from flowing downstream).

After 1.4 km along farmlands, corn fields, and apple orchards, on gravel and tarmac roads, you reach the outskirts of Schachen. When you see the train station on your left (south), after the oil silos, you need to briefly leave the signposted route. Follow the *Schachenweidstrasse* to the small train station of Schachen, pass underneath the tracks, and at road nr. 2a (here called *Kantonstrasse*) turn left (east). Take the first street right and you arrive at the Sacred Heart of Jesus Chapel (at km 18.8).

L-12 Sacred Heart of Jesus Chapel, Schachen (Herz-Jesu-Kapelle)

- Renggstrasse, 6105 Werthenstein
- St. Nicholas of Flüe, St. Mary
- The chapel was built in 1921-22, on the site of a dilapidated predecessor rosary chapel dating from 1623. The construction of the new chapel was financed by a man who had prayed at the old chapel for years. In his testament he donated his wealth to the renewal of the old chapel. During the construction in 1922, elements from other chapels were used in the re-erection. The bell came from Sursee and dates from 1585. The artistic wooden front portal came from Emmenbrücke and dates from 1785. The last exterior and interior renovations were undertaken in 2014.
- The fresco at the top of the chancel-arch depicts the center piece of the Meditation Wheel of St. Nicholas of Flüe (Brother Klaus; see stage 7). The ceilings of the nave and chancel were beautifully restored. The statue representing the Virgin Mary, at the front-left wall, came from the previous rosary chapel and dates from the second half of the 17th century.

From the chapel walk back the same 500 meters to the Small Emme River. You have a great view back towards the east, with the distant Pilatus mountain range towering over the farmlands. The valley keeps getting narrower and the hills on the northern side seem to be closing in. The route past Schachen is along its industrial area, including a large logistical lot that stores hundreds of new cars imported from the USA.

About 2 km before Werthenstein, the railway tracks, road nr. 2a, the Small Emme, and the Way of St. James trail converge in a narrow valley. Road nr. 2a crosses the river to continue westward on its northern bank, while the trail passes underneath the road and closely follows the railway track on its southern bank. The river and trail make an s-curve, passing by high cliffs.

Coming out of the s-curve you can already see the tower of the Werthenstein monastery on the hill in front of you. The last 400 meters to the monastery steeply ascend on a tarmac farm road. At km 23.4 from the Luzern boat pier you arrive at the former Franciscan monastery in Werthenstein.

Former Franciscan Monastery, Werthenstein (Werthenstein Kloster) **L-4**

Oberdorfstrasse 11, 6106 Werthenstein

Capuchin Order, Franciscan Order

The monastery was first built by the Capuchin Order in 1608-12, at the same time as they built the church. Their main purpose was to take care of the visiting pilgrims. The Capuchins were replaced by the friars of the Franciscan Order in 1630, who constructed new monastery buildings in 1631-36. The Franciscan Order had close ties with the Cantonal government and was already home in the city of Luzern. When the Canton was looking to replace the Capuchins, they turned to the Franciscans of Luzern and asked them to open a subsidiary in Werthenstein. They received the assignment to build a monastery to cope with the increasing number of pilgrims.

More than 200 years later, in 1838, Canton Luzern decided to close the Franciscan monastery in Luzern, which automatically affected the monastery in Werthenstein. The Canton closed the Werthenstein monastery, sold its furniture, and used the building as an institution for the deaf and mute for a short time.

However, as its church was a frequented pilgrimage destination (*Wallfahrtskirche*), the Cantonal government was petitioned to reopen the monastery to provide care for the visiting pilgrims. Between 1909 and 1980 the Missionaries of the Holy Family occupied the monastery. Nowadays the parish office resides in the building and offers pilgrim accommodations, just like 380 years ago.

L-13 Franciscan Monastery Church, Werthenstein (Unserer Lieben Frau Kirche)

- Oberdorfstrasse 11, 6106 Werthenstein
- Our Lady
- In the aluminum mailbox of the pilgrim store (right of the store's door) or at the counter of the shop during opening hours.
- During medieval times gold washers frequented the Small Emme River. According to legend, a gold washer from the Netherlands was said to have had a heavenly vision of singing angels and a bright light coming from the top of the cliff when he was saying a Virgin Mary prayer for his safety late at night. He built a small temporary chapel on that site around 1500. A bigger and robust chapel, dedicated to the Our Lady, was built in 1518. The chapel was expanded to a church in 1608-12. The Capuchin Order built the church to cope with the increasing number of pilgrims.

During the middle ages more than 400 miraculous healings took place, which attracted increasing numbers of pilgrims praying and expecting healings of all kinds of diseases. Together with Einsiedeln, the Our Lady church was one of the most frequented pilgrimage destinations in Switzerland during the 17th and 18th centuries (up to 80'000 pilgrims per year; only Einsiedeln received more pilgrims). Nowadays the church is still a pilgrimage destination (*Wallfahrtsort*).

The two small chapels at the front facade were built in 1620, funded by two brothers (named Pfyffer); each received their own chapel, now called the Pfyffer chapels. The Capuchin Order built the cloisters around the courtyard in the same period.

The church received its present-day appearance from renovations in 1953 and 1972-74.

In the church, notice the chandeliers and the beautifully styled and decorated baroque high-altar. The ceiling of the nave used to have the same beautiful frescos as the ones in the chancel. In 1823 the ceiling of the nave caved in, after which new frescos were made on the restored ceiling as you see them today. The interior has a mix of styles: Gothic, Renaissance, and baroque.

A small pilgrim shop (open on Wednesday, Friday, and Sunday; 13:30 until 17:00) is left of the main entrance arch. The shop offers a selection of rosaries, candles, books, incense, and some Way of St. James articles. The small table and chairs in the store invite to rest and have a tea or coffee. In case the store is closed, you can find pilgrimage information on a table at the back of the church.

L-4

Part of the monastery's legend is the **Mercy Spring** (*Gnadenbrünneli*), which you find in a recess on the right side of the road, 150 meters from the monastery's gate (when you walk down the hill towards the village Werthenstein). The water is said to have healing power. The spring was first mentioned in 1638. The current recess and small altar date from 1932 and 1952 respectively. Several candles are always lit in front of the Our Lady statue. Like medieval pilgrims, you can drink the water and fill your water bottle with the clean, fresh, and healing water.

In case you continue to the village Werthenstein (or its train station), you have a wide view over the valley and village (around 2'000 inhabitants), while descending steeply towards the river. After 100 meters you reach a wooden bridge, built in 1775. The wood scent is penetrating the walkway that is separated from the car's crossing.

From the ending point

The Our Lady Church at the Werthenstein Monastery is the ending point of stage L1, directly on the signposted route nr. 4.

In case you are a day-hiker, you need to walk about 600 meters (downhill) from the church to the Werthenstein train station.

In case you are a thru-hiker and spend the night in Werthenstein, you can choose between two accommodations: the pilgrim inn at the monastery or a guesthouse in the village. The monastery has a low-priced pilgrim inn (tel. 079 105 38 62; www.pfarrei-werthenstein.ch; pilgerwohnung.werthenstein@bluewin.ch). The guesthouse is in the valley to the right (north) along road nr. 10, close to the train station. The *Gasthaus zur Emme* offers reasonably priced accommodations, but is closed on Mondays and Tuesdays (tel. 041 490 12 06; mail@gasthauszuremme.ch; www.gasthauszuremme.ch). Check out www.jakobsweg.ch or www.viajacobi4.ch for the details and accommodation possibilities in and around Werthenstein.

The next Stage

Stage L2 guides you over rolling hills to the medieval city of Willisau and across the northern foothills of the Napf mountain to the town Huttwil. Read the next chapter to find out what that entails.

Stage L2: Werthenstein to Huttwil 31 km

The Way over the Napf northern foothills

Route stats

	Distance in km	*Time in hrs:min*
Signposted route nr. 4	30.0	6:30
Churches/chapels	1.2	1:40
Points of interest		0:20
Rest/lunch		1:00
Stage L2	31.2	9:30

In case you hike this stage as a daytrip, you can reduce the distance by 500 meters in Werthenstein and add 500 meters in Huttwil (from and to the train stations).

Ascent/descent/total	+889 / -826 / 1'715 altitude meters
Lowest/highest altitude	549 / 740 meters
Pathway/condition	moderate / difficult
Churches/chapels	Buholz (2), Geiss, Willisau (4), Ufhusen, Huttwil (2)
Monasteries	none
Points of interest	Medieval City of Willisau, Castle of Willisau

Route summary

Stage L2 continues in catholic **Canton Luzern** and at km 28.5, shortly before reaching the town Huttwil at the end of the stage, enters protestant **Canton Bern.**

Stage L2 guides you over rolling hills to the medieval city of Willisau and across the northern foothills of the Napf mountain to the town Huttwil.

The route follows the same direction as roads nr. 2a (east) and nr. 23 (north), half-circling the Napf mountain range over its eastern and northern foothills. These foothills result in a significant number of altitude meters: more than 1'700, though the highest point of the day is a mere 740 meters. The high number of altitude meters is caused by the many ascents and descents – seven 'peaks' between 640 and 740 meters are reached. Combined with the distance of 31 km this is a tough hiking day. Most of the route is on farm roads, grasslands, and forest/dirt trails. The route passes through only three small towns (Geiss, Willisau, and Ufhusen) before reaching Huttwil. Apart from in Buholz, there are no chapels or churches in between the towns, giving the feeling that stage L2 is mostly a hiking day (in contrast to stage L1).

The first 3 km ascend out of the Small Emme River valley. The route is through grasslands, along agricultural fields, and on farm roads. After a short descent to Buholz, the route ascends to the second 'peak'. From there the trail descends along fields and orchards to the town Geiss. From Geiss the route gradually ascends through grassland and between agricultural fields. From the route profile's perspective it looks easy, but there is a lot of ascending and descending over short distances, making the trails tougher than they may look on paper. About 4 km before Willisau the trail descends out of the hills to the valley. Between km 11 and 16 the route is flat, being in the valley of the historic city of Willisau (about halfway stage L2). Willisau is a medieval town where the route passes by two churches and two chapels. From Willisau the route turns west and goes up and down the northern foothills of the Napf mountain over a distance of 10 km, before reaching Ufhusen. Shortly after Ufhusen it reaches the highest point of the day of 740 meters and enters Canton Bern. Through fields and along the edge of forests the route descends into Huttwil, which is reached after 31 km.

Getting to the starting point

Today's starting point is at the Monastery Church of Werthenstein, directly on the signposted route nr. 4. In case you spent the night at the monastery, you are already at the right location.

In case you hike stage L2 as a daytrip, you need to walk only 100 meters from the Werthenstein train station to the signposted route nr. 4. From the *Gasthaus zur Emme* it is less than 100 meters to the trail. This shortens the distance of the day by about 500 meters.

In both these cases there is no need to go back up the hill to the monastery church (since you would be coming back the same way) – unless you want to visit the healing spring and fill your water bottles there, or visit the pilgrimage church for prayers, reflection, or sightseeing (the pilgrim shop is closed in the mornings).

Route Map and Profile

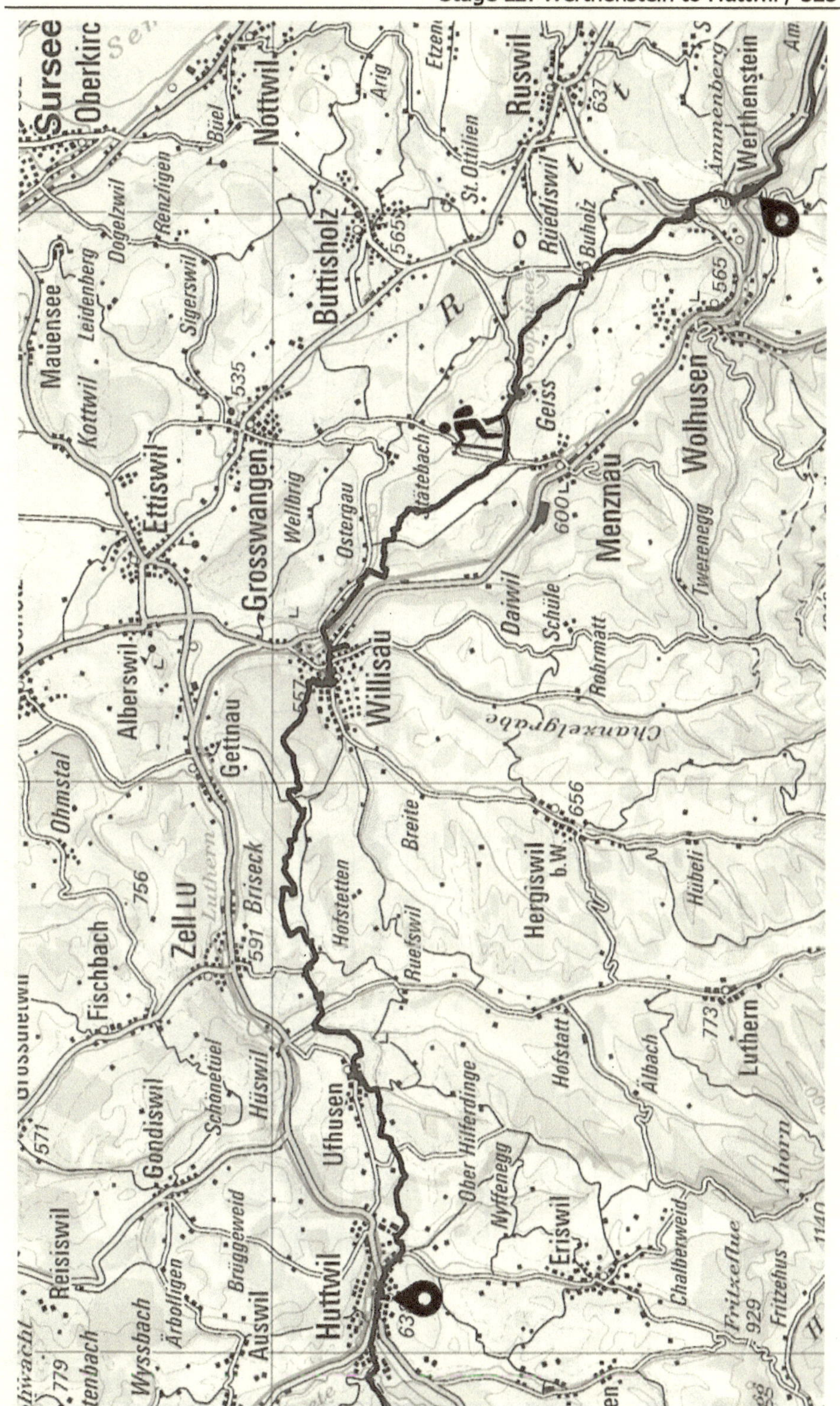
Sursee
Nottwil
Ruswil
Werthenstein
Ämmenberg
Buttisholz
St. Ottilien
Rüediswil
Buholz
Arig
Büel
Renzligen
Dogelzwil
Mauensee
Leidenberg
Sigerswil
Kottwil
Ettiswil
Grosswangen
Wellbrig
Ostergau
Stätebach
Geiss
Wolhusen
Menznau
Twerenegg
Daiwil
Schüle
Rohrmatt
Willisau
Alberswil
Gettnau
Ohmstal
Zell LU
Briseck
Fischbach
Hofstetten
Breite
Ruefswil
Hergiswil b.W.
Hübeli
Hofstatt
Älbach
Luthern
Ahorn
Schönetüel
Hüswil
Gondiswil
Uffhusen
Ober Hilferdinge
Nyffenegg
Eriswil
Chalberweid
Fritzehus
Reisiswil
Wyssbach
Ärbolligen
Brüggeweid
Auswil
Huttwil
565
637
535
600
557
656
756
591
571
773
929
779

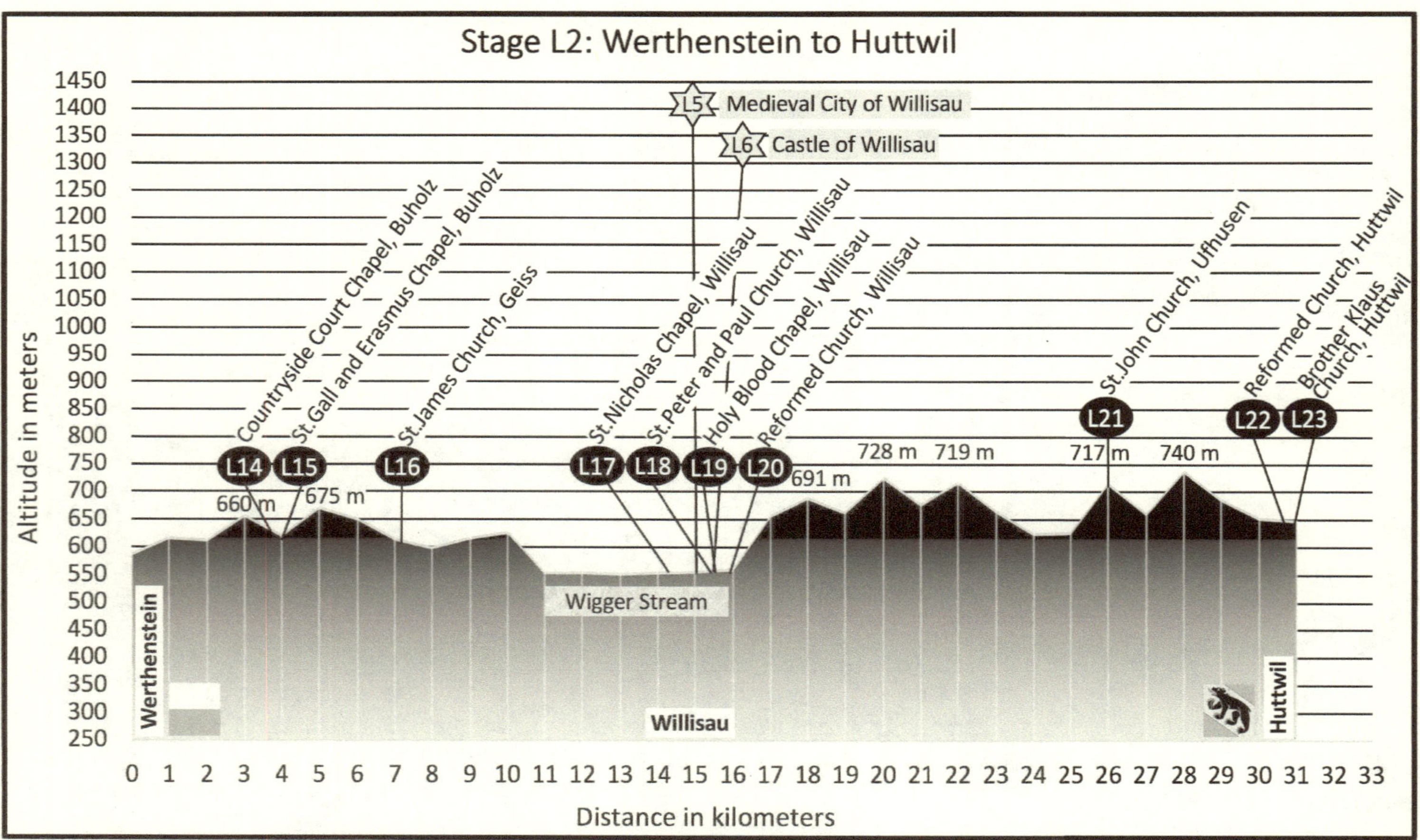
Stage L2: Werthenstein to Huttwil
L5 Medieval City of Willisau
L6 Castle of Willisau
L14 Countryside Court Chapel, Buholz
L15 St.Gall and Erasmus Chapel, Buholz
L16 St.James Church, Geiss
L17 St.Nicholas Chapel, Willisau
L18 St.Peter and Paul Church, Willisau
L19 Holy Blood Chapel, Willisau
L20 Reformed Church, Willisau
L21 St.John Church, Ufhusen
L22 Reformed Church, Huttwil
L23 Brother Klaus Church, Huttwil
660 m
675 m
691 m
728 m
719 m
717 m
740 m
Wigger Stream
Werthenstein
Willisau
Huttwil
Altitude in meters
1450 1400 1350 1300 1250 1200 1150 1100 1050 1000 950 900 850 800 750 700 650 600 550 500 450 400 350 300 250
Distance in kilometers
0 1 2 3 4 5 6 7 8 9 10 11 12 13 14 15 16 17 18 19 20 21 22 23 24 25 26 27 28 29 30 31 32 33

Hiking the Route

From the Werthenstein monastery the route goes down the hill, past the Mercy Spring and wooden bridge (see stage L1), crosses road nr. 2a and the railway tracks, and starts ascending on a tarmac road. While ascending over 300 meters you have panoramic views back to the Werthenstein monastery against the backdrop of the Pilatus mountain range.

The signpost then directs you to a steep narrow trail on the left, going through a patch of forest, after which you walk past a small roadside chapel and an orchard growing blackberries. The following 500 meters are on a local tarmac road, gradually descending. You pass by another small roadside chapel, until a sign suddenly directs you towards the left, to a hardly visible trail through a meadow, which seems to be leading nowhere.

After a short descent through high grass you get to a small patch of forest along the Biel stream (*Bielbach*). The trail crosses the stream on a narrow metal footbridge, after which it turns right. You pass by a local Way of St. James hut (*Jakobs stübli*). It offers a place to rest, but the inside looks unused and is dirty and full of spiderwebs. Ascending out of the stream's valley, the route crosses a road and makes a sharp right on a tarmac farm road. At a pig farm the path changes into a broad gravel farm road. The route leads you to the northwest, through wide agricultural lands, providing good views back to the Pilatus mountain range.

After 500 meters you reach a high point at 660 meters. From there the path gradually descends over the following 1.2 km. The trail changes into a narrow grassland trail that passes by agricultural fields. You hike through a **sunken lane** (for a description of a historical background to sunken lanes, see page 235), covered by trees and overhanging bushes, after which the trail continues along open fields lined with trees and cornfields. The trail passes by a small chapel (at km 3.8), standing in the shade of a tree; notice the height of the entrance door of less than 1.5 meters. A hiking signpost with route nr. 4 is next to it.

L-14 Countryside Court Chapel, Buholz (Landsgericht Kapelle)

Buholz, 6017 Ruswil

It is not known when the small chapel was first built. The area in front of the chapel served as a public place for court proceedings until 1798. Regional governors conducted court proceedings at this location, open and visible to the surrounding local population, for several centuries. In case of a death penalty, the convicted was brought to the gallows that stood on a hill about 1.2 km to the north (see below).

The chapel has a simple interior. A small statue representing Jesus is standing on a small stone altar against the back wall. Behind it is a cross with St. James scallops on each of the four ends. A small table with a candle is fixed to the left wall.

From the chapel it is only 400 meters to the road and the Buholz Chapel at km 4.2.

St. Gall and Erasmus Chapel, Buholz (St. Gallus und Erasmus Kapelle) L-15

Buholz, 6017 Ruswil

St. Gall, St. Erasmus

A chapel on this site was first mentioned in official documents in 1190. This chapel was replaced by another one, which was first mentioned in 1576. The second chapel was a so-called farm chapel, built by a rich farmer who owned the lands in Buholz. It was demolished and the present third chapel was constructed in 1660-62. In 1722 an aristocrat from Luzern bought the lands with the chapel. He enhanced the interior decorations with baroque statues and frescos. The front porch was built during renovations in 1876, while the frescos were whitewashed at that time. These frescos were recovered again during renovations in 1931, while the wall fresco depicting the Virgin Mary with baby Jesus was added.

For a farm chapel the interior is unexpected lusciously decorated. The three baroque marble altars are richly decorated with statues, paintings, other sculptures, and gold paint. The left side-altar has a Pietà statue. The right side-altar has a statue representing St. Gall. The high-altar painting depicts St. Erasmus (dating from 1828). Look up: the ceiling is also richly decorated.

A few meters past the chapel you see an old wooden barn, with 16 cowbells hanging on broad leather straps and old farm tools fixed on its outer walls. At the road crossing in the center of the small village, the signs direct you to the left. Upon leaving the village you pass by another small roadside chapel. A few meters later, the Way of St. James leaves the road and turns right onto a stone/gravel path up the hill to the gallows forest (*Galgebergwald*). At a yellow hiking signpost directing to *Richtstätte,* you can make a 150-meter detour to the site of the former gallows. The path leads deeper into the forest to the highest point of 675 meters.

A large boulder with a plaque and candle marks the spot of the **former gallows**. These gallows were in use until 1798. During the middle ages the gallows stood in an open field on top of this hill (there was no forest then), making the executions visible from afar. The openness was used as a deterrent to thieves, robbers, and other criminals. Nowadays it is a peaceful forest, but during the middle ages the scenes would have been gruesome. See point of interest nr. 11 in stage 4, Volume I for a description of the cruelty of medieval forms of execution.

A hundred meters later the forest trail leads to a viewpoint towards the north, overlooking the Soppi Lake (*Soppisee*) and the low hills behind it. A red bench invites for a short rest. The trail soon leaves the forest and over the following 1.6 km gradually descends into the town Geiss. The route leads you on gravel pathways through farmlands and apple and cherry orchards.

The open terrain offers views back to the Pilatus mountain range and to the front to the town Geiss. You can already see the town's church from afar.

The route descends into town, passing by historical farmhouses. You cannot miss the dark wooden house with the blue-white shutters and the geraniums below its windows. It is an inn (*Landgasthof Ochsen*) with a terrace on its southern side, facing the St. James church. Geiss is a farmer's town that has been living of agriculture since its foundation. During the middle ages the town had an important second source of income: pilgrims. Many pilgrims on the Way of St. James (to Werthenstein and Einsiedeln) passed by this small town, stayed at the pilgrim inn, and left donations at the church. No wonder that the church was named after St. James and that such a sizable church could be built in the middle of agricultural fields. You reach the St. James Church in Geiss at km 7.1.

St. James Church, Geiss (St. Jakobus Kirche) **L-16**

- Kirchenstrasse 1, 6123 Geiss
- St. James the Greater
- On a table right of the entrance
- The church was first mentioned in 1271. A new church was built around 1581 and rebuilt in 1644-47. The nave was enlarged in 1783, 1828, and 1951. The latest renovations were undertaken in the 1993-97.
- Inside the church seven paintings on the southern wall and seven paintings on the northern wall depict the crucifixion way of Christ. The three baroque marble altars have many statues and sculptures. St. James the Greater (*St. Jakobus der ältere*) is well represented. The right side-altar contains a large statue representing St. James, with a pilgrim cane and two scallops at the front of his cloak.

The route leaves Geiss south of the village and goes west on a tarmac road for 1.1 km. You pass by a small roadside chapel and keep going straight. The signpost directs towards the right on a grass trail crossing through farmland.

About 200 meters later you cross a road, pass by another small roadside chapel, and continue for the following 1.8 km through agricultural fields with corn, wheat, or grass. At a group of farmhouses, the trail enters grasslands. On a post a light-green sign warns to be careful when approaching suckling cows and their calves. The cows can be protective, and reports of cows attacking and injuring hikers appear in newspapers several times a year. You pass by a small wooden hut (*Wanderhüsli*) with an outside table and bench set up by a local farmer. The hut has a small refrigerator offering cooled drinks. As so often in the Swiss rural areas, you can take the consumption you want and leave cash on a plate. The route continues along a patch of forest and then onto open meadows. The trail there is not so easy: it is at an inclination along the slope of the hill and on uneven grasslands.

Towards your right you overlook the valley with several ponds, making up the moors of Ostergau (*Ostergauermoos*). The path suddenly turns right and descends steeply through a meadow. At a farm road at the foot of the hill you turn left. It would be easiest to continue straight on that path, but for some unclear reason the signposted route makes a 300-meter detour steep up and down the hill, only to arrive back on the same road again. You can already see the town Willisau in the distance. On a tarmac road the route turns right and 360 meters later left. The route continues along grassland and the edge of a forest, until you reach a tiny stream called *Seewag*. With the stream on your left, you walk through the meadow towards the main road. There the Way of St. James turns left towards Willisau, and 260 meters later makes a left and then a right turn to a small trail next to the *Seewag* stream, parallel to the road.

You follow the small stream for 1 km and pass by the industrial outskirts of Willisau. The signs direct you to an underpass of a roundabout to the other side of road nr. 2a. After a woodwork factory you get to the train tracks with the Willisau train station to your right. The nr. 4 signpost directs to the right, towards the train station. However, at this location you need to leave the signposted route to go to a chapel.

Thus, instead of turning right, cross the railway tracks, and after 200 meters (at restaurant Krone) cross the road (*Menznauerstrasse*). A white sign directs to the next chapel that is at the end of the St. Nicholas path (*St. Niklausweg*). Continue straight onto a small road that curves to the left and turns into a steeply ascending path alongside a patch of forest. After 300 meters you arrive at the St. Nicholas Chapel in Willisau (at km 14.4).

St. Nicholas Chapel, Willisau (St. Niklausen Kapelle) **L-17**

- Bleikimatt, 6130 Willisau
- St. Nicholas, 10'000 Martyrs
- The chapel was part of a Habsburg Castle dating from the end of the 12th century. The castle stood on the hill east of the chapel, but was destroyed in a battle in 1386 (no remains are left nowadays). The Romanesque walls of the small chancel still date from the end of the 12th century. The chapel was partially rebuilt in the 14th century and enlarged around 1497. In 1655 the chapel was remodeled in a baroque style and received a front portal. The latest renovations were undertaken in 1975-76.
- The bell was made around 1200; it is the oldest one in Canton Luzern.

  The wall frescos date from 1497 (the figure at the chancel-arch), the mid 16th century (the decorations and two figures in the chancel and fresco left in the nave), and 1650 (the decorations in the windowsills). The left wall fresco depicts the Martyrs of the 10'000 knights (mid 16th century).

  Notice the beautiful painting depicting Mary with baby Jesus in an array of golden beams (1636) and the details of the statue representing the patron Saint Nicholas (17th century).

The hill of the chapel provides a nice view over the town Willisau.

From the chapel walk back the same 300 meters, down the hill, to the *Menznauerstrasse.* Turn left and follow the street for 350 meters, until you get to a square (*Postplatz*) in front of the access gate to the medieval town Willisau. Here you are back on the signposted route nr. 4.

L-5

The **Medieval City of Willisau** lies in a narrow valley with its main street enclosed by historical town walls, entrance gates, and towers. The historic town is listed under the Swiss Heritage Sites. The original fortifications date from 1302-03 (when the town was founded) and served as protection along the medieval trade and travel route from Luzern to Bern. The fortified walls around the city had a length of 750 meters and a width of 1.2 meters.

Over the centuries the town was raided and destroyed several times. The town suffered four city-wide fires (1375, 1386, 1471, 1704), the first two caused by retreating troops, destroying most buildings. The battle of 1386 that caused the fire in town also destroyed the Habsburg Castle that stood near the St. Nicholas chapel (see above).

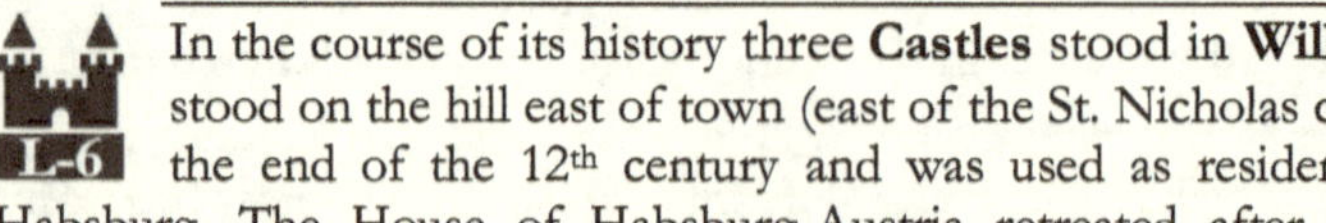

L-6

In the course of its history three **Castles** stood in **Willisau**. The first castle stood on the hill east of town (east of the St. Nicholas chapel). It was built at the end of the 12th century and was used as residence by the Lords of Habsburg. The House of Habsburg-Austria retreated after losing the battle of Sempach against the Bernese in 1386. The Bernese troops plundered the town and destroyed the castle, which was never rebuilt (nothing remains of it today). Excavations discovered a second smaller castle on the eastern side of town, within the fortified walls, which served as an administrative office of the local Lords. This building was also destroyed in 1386, and nothing remains of it today. After the House of Habsburg ceded their control of the region, Willisau was sold to the City-Republic of Luzern in 1407. From 1407 until 1651 the regional governor resided in Luzern and from 1651 until 1695 at a house on the main street of Willisau.

The third castle was built on the hill south of the town (just behind the church) in 1690-95. The chateau was attached to a watchtower (*Kutzenturm*) dating from the end of the 14th century. This baroque chateau was the residence of the governor, until the invasion of the French troops in 1798. Nowadays it houses the municipal offices.

You enter the historical center of Willisau through the eastern gate.

The **Lower Gate** (*Untertor*) was first mentioned in 1347. It was used as a prison and housed torture chambers. The original gate was destroyed by the town fire of 1471 and rebuilt 72 years later (1543). It was severely damaged by the fourth fire in 1704 and subsequently rebuilt by 1768. Because it was dilapidated, the gate had to be demolished in 1854. It was rebuilt, based on old plans, in 1980. As a result of the increased motorized traffic, they made the passageway much wider than the original one. The clock dates from 1543 and the bell in its small steeple from 1706.

Three fountains with potable water are lined along the long street. They were built in 1599, 1601, and 1606, and have a basin with seven sides. The sources of these fountains lie at the top of the hill to the south (inside the walls of the chateau). In 1950-57 these fountains were in poor condition, and were demolished and rebuilt in accordance with their original plans. The figures that decorate the columns date from the 1960s and represent the patron Saints Peter and Paul of the church (see below) and St. Mary with baby Jesus.

Behind the gate you enter into a long street lined with medieval houses, now used as small shops, cafes, restaurants, and hotels. Behind the third fountain you arrive at the St. Peter and Paul Church at km 15.4.

L-18 St. Peter and Paul Church, Willisau (St. Peter und Paul Kirche)

- Müligasse 6, 6130 Willisau
- St. Peter and Paul, Twelve Apostles
- On a shelf right of the main entrance
- The church is on the site of at least four smaller predecessor churches. A church was first mentioned in 1245, making it the oldest building in Willisau; the town was founded around an already existing Romanesque church. The white tower on the western side dates from before 1245 and is one of the best maintained Romanesque towers in Canton Luzern. After lightning struck, the former top of the tower burned down and had to be replaced: the brown onion-dome dates from 1647.

  The first church was expanded several times over the centuries, but still had become too small by the end of the 18th century. Except for the bell tower, the old church was demolished and a new one (the present church) was built in 1804-10, mostly financed by donations. Because of difficulties in financing, the interior decorations were completed with a delay of 12 years (after which the consecration took place in 1822).

  On the roof above the transept was a small steeple until 1928. The parish believed that the small bells in the small Romanesque tower could not be heard far enough and wanted to have a more robust tower that could carry heavier bells. So, the green-colored copper rooftop tower, a unique design from a Rorschach architect, was built in place of the short steeple in 1928-29. It holds six larger bells that can be heard from afar. The copper-based design was so different from the style of the rest of the church that it created a lot of resistance from the local population; they convinced the parish priest to take it down. Canton Luzern prevented this by placing it under architectural protection.
- It is the largest church between Luzern and Bern (56 meters long, 25.5 meters wide – bigger than the church in Malters), seating up to a 1'000 people. The church contains beautiful baroque interior decorations: marble, frescos, paintings, woodwork, and so forth. Statues representing the Twelve Apostles line the pillars and walls, with St. James the Greater as one of them.

Walk down the steps back to the fountain and turn left underneath the western gate.

The medieval western gate is called the **Upper Gate** (*Obertor*). Like the lower gate, this gate was part of the medieval fortifications around the town and was used as a dungeon and housed torture chambers. The fortified tower was also destroyed in the first three town fires but was left undamaged by the fire in 1704. Its present appearance is much like it was when the tower was reconstructed in 1546, 75 years after the third fire of 1471.

Outside the gate you arrive at the Holy Blood Chapel at km 15.5.

Holy Blood Chapel, Willisau (Heilig-Blut Kapelle) L-19

Zehntenplatz 4, 6130 Willisau

The chapel was built in a Renaissance style with a Tuscan front portal in 1674-75. Two earlier chapels (the first one in wood and after 1497 in stone) already stood on this site.

The Holy Blood chapel derived its name from the following legend (events that allegedly happened in 1392). Three men were playing cards. One man lost all his money and while cursing pushed his sword up in the air to stab the body of Christ. Five drops of blood fell on the table. This man was taken away by the devil, while the two others died a gruesome death immediately afterwards. A priest saved the table with the blood drops and built the first wooden chapel to protect it.

This legend made the chapel a regional pilgrimage destination during the middle ages.

The eight oil paintings (1684) on the walls tell this legend. Notice the wooden ceiling (1854) decorated with 70 rectangular paintings depicting New Testament scenes, Apostles, and patron Saints of the chapel. This is one of the biggest chapels along the Swiss Way of St. James, with baroque marble altars bigger than many other altars you find in other chapels (demonstrating its importance as a pilgrimage destination).

From the chapel follow the signpost north, cross the street (*Adlermatte*), pass by the cemetery, and continue straight. You see the reformed Church of Willisau on your right. Cross the parking lot and you arrive at the church at km 15.7.

L-20 **Reformed Church, Willisau** (Reformierte Kirche)

- Adlermatte, 6130 Willisau
- The church is eight-sided and was built in a modern design of the 1950s. The rectangular front portal was added in the 1990s. The square bell tower is separated from the church. Notice the weather cock instead of a cross on top of the tower.
- The church has a typical protestant and modern interior.

From the church cross the parking lot and turn right. The route zigzags up the hill and passes by a playground and a deer park. A steep gravel footpath leads to a large cross at a viewpoint over the town Willisau. Through meadows the route continues to ascend and keeps providing great views. For 500 meters the route crosses through a forest, where the gravel road changes into a forest trail with soft underground. A grass trail continues in a meadow, until you reach a tarmac road.

You pass by several dark wooden farmhouses with colorful geraniums at their windowsills (settlement Olisrüti). You walk across their yards, with two very noisy and smelly pig farms. Horseflies also seem to like pigs, not only horses and cows; be aware of stinging flies in this area. At the last farmhouse the route turns right, crosses its yard, and turns left in a westward direction. From this location the farm's friendly sheepdog may accompany you for several kilometers. On an uneven farm road, the route goes up the hill past meadows and corn fields. The hill offers wide views towards the south. The route passes by several colored beehives and trails along the edge of a forest. Grass and forest trails alternate in short distances.

In the meantime, you have descended somewhat and the view has disappeared; instead, you have a grass hill on your left and the forest on your right. The route follows the edge of the forest while zigzagging at the foot of the hill. On a dirt road the trail climbs out of the small valley. Across even meadows the trail ascends to a high point of 719 meters. The views are wide in several directions.

The route follows a tractor dirt path and changes to a tarmac farm road that gradually descends to the settlement Oberwil. At the entrance of the settlement you pass by a blue Way of St. James sign (put up by the local community) indicating 1'823 km to Santiago de Compostela and a text explaining the Way of St. James. Upon leaving the settlement, do not be alarmed if a large dog barks and growls viciously from a garden on the left, as he jumps up against the fence and follows you as you walk past. Fortunately, the fence is high enough.

On a gravel tractor path, you pass by meadows with apple trees and cows grazing underneath them. Past several farms the route enters a small patch of forest, where a rocky dirt road descends to the Luthern stream. It is a sunken lane, indicating this route was already in use during the middle ages, connecting Luzern to Bern.

On a tarmac road between farmhouses you reach a main road. The route turns right (north), where you pass by a small roadside chapel, and 200 meters later left (south). You enter the industrial area of a sand pit and its processing plant (*Kieswerk Hüswil*). Big sand- and cement-trucks drive here; be careful as the route goes straight over their grounds. After passing through the area you have high pyramidal heaps of deposited sand and stones on your right.

About halfway through the long straight tarmac road leading away from the plant, the route turns right. For about 500 meters the trail crosses meadows with grazing cows. The trail in the grass is barely recognizable. It goes up steeply through rolling hills. Cows are roaming the meadows, so be careful of them and their cow pies; better make a large curve around them. At a tarmac road the route turns right and continues up the hill. You pass by a farm where a big dog roams freely and may chase you while barking viciously. The road curves to the left and the next church appears. At km 26.1 you arrive at the St. John Church of Ufhusen.

St. John Church, Ufhusen (St. Johannes Kirche) L-21

- Obere Seppen 4, 6153 Ufhusen
- St. John the Baptist, St. Helena
- On a shelf right of the entrance
- A first church was already mentioned in 1275. In 1979-80 archaeological excavations during renovations discovered that the church stands on the foundations of a fortified residential tower. The first documentation of a fortified tower on this hill in Ufhusen dates from 1150; this former castle might date from the 11th century or earlier (nowadays nothing is left, other than some foundation remnants underneath the chancel). The lower part of the fortified tower may have contained a chapel or the chancel of the first church.

  This first church was replaced by a second church in 1531-35, which was replaced by a third church (the present one) in a baroque style in 1778-84.

- Special features of the church are a keystone and a 15th crucifixion way station. A Romanesque grey keystone is hanging on the left wall of the chancel (next to the stalls); the only remaining artefact of the 13th century church. The keystone depicts an ox carrying a cross on his back. The story goes that Saint Helena found the Crucifixion Cross in Golgotha (Jerusalem) in the year 310. She gave a small piece to a soldier who transported it back home to Arras in northern France. To check the originality of the piece of wood, it was tied to a wild ox, which suddenly became tame. According to legend, this ox started a journey from Arras and brought the cross-splinter to the town Hasle (about 30 km southeast of Ufhusen), where the ox found its final resting place (a pilgrimage church was built on its location). A small piece of wood, believed to be from the Cross, is still kept at the Holy Cross Church (*Heiligkreuzkirche*) in the town Hasle (the Swiss Way of St. James does not pass by this location). On its way to Hasle, the ox rested in Ufhusen. The replica of the 13th century keystone commemorates this visit.

Most crucifixion ways have 14 stations, but this church has a 15th. The extra station depicts St. Helena, linked to the story of the ox carrying a piece of the Cross.

From the hill of the church the route turns south and descends on a tarmac road to a small stream. You have a wide view over the rolling hills in front of you. At a narrow patch of forest along the small stream the route turns right.

A large information table explains that you will soon cross the border between Canton Luzern and Bern. Until the 17th century this route was the main connection between the two cities. Because the Cantons were independently governed during those times, customs and taxes used to be levied at the Cantonal border crossings. Ufhusen and Huttwil had such customs stations. Canton Bern had more than 30 such stations, each one at a main access road. The constitution of 1848 made Switzerland a Federal State, after which the system of inter-cantonal customs and taxes was abolished.

From the information table the route turns right. For 1 km the trail follows the southern edge of a forest (through meadows) up a hill, where you reach the highest point of the day at 740 meters.

Through meadows along agricultural fields the route reaches a tarmac road, briefly follows the road, and continues on grass while descending towards another patch of forest and a small stream. At this location you change from catholic Canton Luzern to protestant **Canton Bern**. From here you will regularly find its coat-of-arms with the black bear on the yellow hiking signs.

A gravel road follows the northern side of the patch of forest. Over grass fields you can see the industrial outskirts of Huttwil. The route passes by a wood storage area of a local saw mill, with the strong scent of freshly sawed wood. After crossing another small stream, the route crosses a main road, and forks to the right a little later. You enter the town Huttwil and walk past a cemetery (behind a wall on the right). Keep following the *Friedhofweg* until the T-crossing. You can already see the church tower above the houses in front of you. Turn right and immediately left and you arrive at the market square of Huttwil. North of the square, across road nr. 23, is the reformed Church of Huttwil (at km 30.8).

Reformed Church, Huttwil (Reformierte Kirche) **L-22**

- Marktgasse 3, 4950 Huttwil
- In a zip-lock bag on a table with information brochures
- The church was first mentioned in official documents in 1108. During the Reformation in 1528 the catholic church converted to Protestantism and all catholic statues, altars, paintings, and relics were removed, while the walls were

whitewashed to cover the frescos of Saints. The church was newly built in 1705, but had to be rebuilt in 1834, after a town fire destroyed the whole town, including most of the church. The hall church was reconstructed on the foundations of the previous church, while the tower was heightened and topped with an onion dome. Because of lack of financing, stained-glass windows could only replace the normal windows on its 100-year anniversary in 1934. Renovations were undertaken in 1967 and 2003, during which the original appearance (like the green interior color) from 1834 was restored.

The hall church has a typical protestant interior, limited to a pulpit, baptismal font, choir stalls, pews, and organ.

From the church cross road nr. 23 (called *Marktgasse*) and walk back to the square. To go to the final church of stage L2, you need to leave the signposted route nr. 4 (which continues along road nr. 23 towards the train station). From the square turn right and at the crossing turn left onto the *Stadthausstrasse*. At the end turn right (*Hofmattstrasse*) and take the first street on the left (*Südstrasse*). About 400 meters from the protestant church you arrive at the catholic Brother Klaus Church of Huttwil (at km 31.2).

L-23 Brother Klaus Church, Huttwil (Bruder Klaus Kirche)

Südstrasse 5, 4950 Huttwil

Brother Klaus

For nearly 400 years since the Reformation in 1528 (when the catholic church converted to Protestantism) no catholic services were held in Huttwil, until a catholic priest from the church in Ufhusen (Canton Luzern) started with private services in a local restaurant in 1920.

It was not until 1939 that catholic churches/parishes received official state recognition in Canton Bern (which enabled them to change from private to public organizations). In the same year the first new catholic church (dedicated to Brother Klaus) since the Reformation was built in Huttwil.

This first church was in poor condition because of neglected maintenance and was demolished to make room for a new church in 1981. The present church was built in a modern style in 1981-83. From the outside it looks like a villa with a tall chimney.

📷 The church has a modern and austere interior, dominated by the widening wooden roof and the organ at the left wall. The stained-glass colors the interior in shades of red.

Huttwil is a small town with around 5'000 inhabitants. It was built in the narrow valley of the Langete River (flowing from east to west), with hills on its northern and southern sides. Historically the town was dependent on the farms in the surrounding hilly landscape. Many small farm settlements are still dotted in the hills around Huttwil. The area was owned by several regional Lords, but they never built a castle or established a monastery in Huttwil. The area was a hinterland, strategically not important. The town served as an important stop along the medieval road between Bern and Luzern. In 1834 a town fire destroyed most of the medieval buildings. The city center around the village square was rebuilt with stone and half-timbered houses.

From the ending point

The Brother Klaus Church is the ending point of stage L2, about 200 meters aside the signposted route nr. 4 that goes along road nr. 23 (*Bahnhofstrasse*).

In case you are a day-hiker, you need to walk about 500 meters to the Huttwil train station. Walk back to the main road nr. 23 (*Bahnhofstrasse*) and turn left to reach the train station.

In case you are a thru-hiker and spend the night in Huttwil, you can choose between several reasonably priced hotel accommodations, though no pilgrim inn. Check out www.jakobsweg.ch or www.viajacobi4.ch for accommodation possibilities in Huttwil.

The next Stage

Stage L3 guides you over the northwestern foothills of the Napf mountain to the medieval city of Burgdorf in the Emme River valley. Similar to stage L2, L3 is basically a hiking day, though a bit shorter. Read the next chapter to find out what that entails.

Stage L3:
Huttwil to Burgdorf
25 km

The Way over the Napf western foothills

Route stats

	Distance in km	*Time in hrs:min*
Signposted route nr. 4	23.6	5:10
Churches/chapels	1.4	0:50
Points of interest	0.3	1:00
Rest/lunch		1:00
Stage L3	25.3	8:00

In case you hike this stage as a daytrip, you can deduct 600 meters in Huttwil and add 400 meters to the train station in Burgdorf.

Ascent/descent/total	+762/ -853 / 1'615 altitude meters
Lowest/highest altitude	536 / 887 meters
Pathway/condition	moderate / moderate
Churches/chapels	Dürrenroth, Burgdorf (4)
Monasteries	Former Augustinian Monastery Burgdorf
Points of interest	Hotel Kreuz, Lueg Monument, Former Leprosarium, Medieval distance time-marker, Wynigen Bridges, Castle of Burgdorf

Route summary

Stage L3 continues in protestant **Canton Bern.** Stage L3 as well as the upcoming stages L4 and L5 are all in protestant Canton Bern.

Stage L3 guides you over the northwestern foothills of the Napf mountain to the medieval city of Burgdorf in the Emme River valley.

The first 11 km the route follows the direction of main road nr. 23 (and the train tracks and Rotbach stream). This southwestern route curves around the northwestern foothills of the Napf mountain. From km 11 until 25 the route heads west over rolling hills, directly towards Burgdorf. These foothills result in a significant number of altitude meters: more than 1'600. The highest point of the day is at 887 meters; the many altitude meters are caused by two ascents and one long descent from the highest point to the city of Burgdorf. Most of the route is on farm roads, grass fields, and dirt trails. The route passes through only one small town (Dürrenroth) before it reaches Burgdorf. Other than in Dürrenroth, the route does not pass by any chapels or churches, giving the feeling that stage L3 is mostly a hiking day (similar to stage L2 – only a bit shorter).

The route leaves Huttwil and the Rotbach River valley in a western direction, turns southwest through forests and along agricultural fields, and reaches a first high point of 793 meters at km 5. For about 1 km the trail descends to the Rotbach River valley and stays on an altitude between 690 and 710 meters for 5 km (closely following the river and road nr. 23). After Häusernmoos (km 11) the route does not pass through any towns anymore, only some small settlements and isolated farms. For 5 km the route steadily ascends through patches of forest and on grassland trails to the highest point of 887 meters at the Lueg Monument. After a steep descent over 2 km, the route reaches a highland plateau, on which it stays for 3 km. After a 1 km steep and 1 km gradual forested decent the route leads to the Emme River valley and the city of Burgdorf.

Getting to the starting point

Today's starting point is at the reformed Church of Huttwil, directly on the signposted route nr. 4.

In case you hike stage L3 as a daytrip, you are already on the signposted route nr. 4 at the Huttwil train station. Since the route from the reformed church passes by the train station, you can consider to skip 600 meters to the church and the same 600 meters back again.

Route Map and Profile

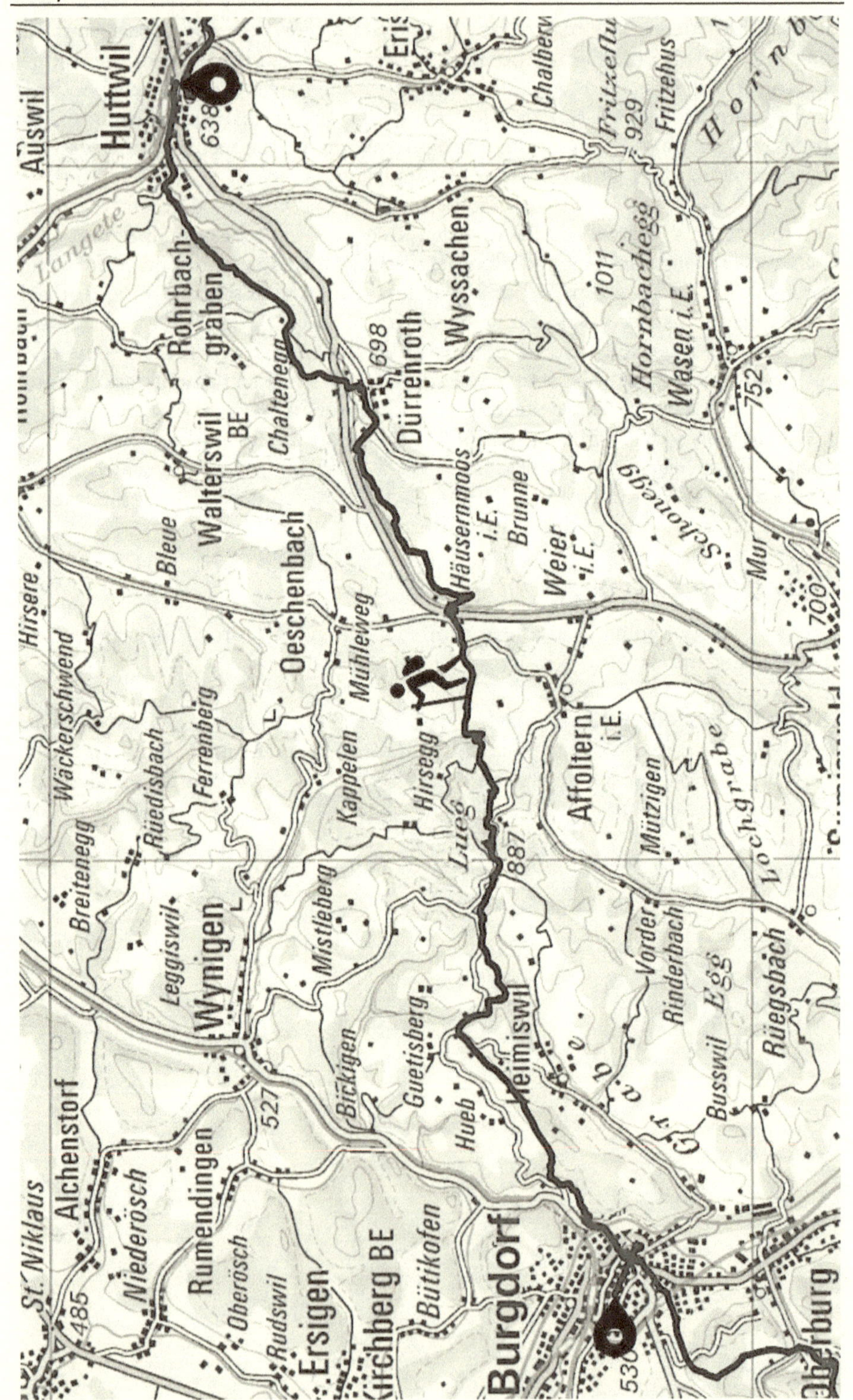
Huttwil
638
Auswil
Langete
Rohrbach-
graben
Walterswil
BE
Chaltenegg
698
Dürrenroth
Wyssachen
Chalberweid
Fritzeflue
929
Fritzehus
Hornbachegg
1011
Wasen i.E.
752
Schonegg
Häusernmoos
i.E.
Brunne
Weier
i.E.
Mur
700
Bleue
Oeschenbach
Mühleweg
Hirsere
Wäckerschwend
Rüedisbach
Ferrenberg
Kappelen
Hirsegg
Lueg
887
Affoltern
i.E.
Mützigen
Lochgrabe
Breitenegg
Leggiswil
Wynigen
Mistleberg
Guetisberg
Bickigen
527
Hueb
Heimiswil
Vorder
Rinderbach
Egg
Busswil
Rüegsbach
Alchenstorf
Niederösch
Rumendingen
St. Niklaus
485
Oberösch
Rudswil
Ersigen
Kirchberg BE
Bütikofen
Burgdorf
530

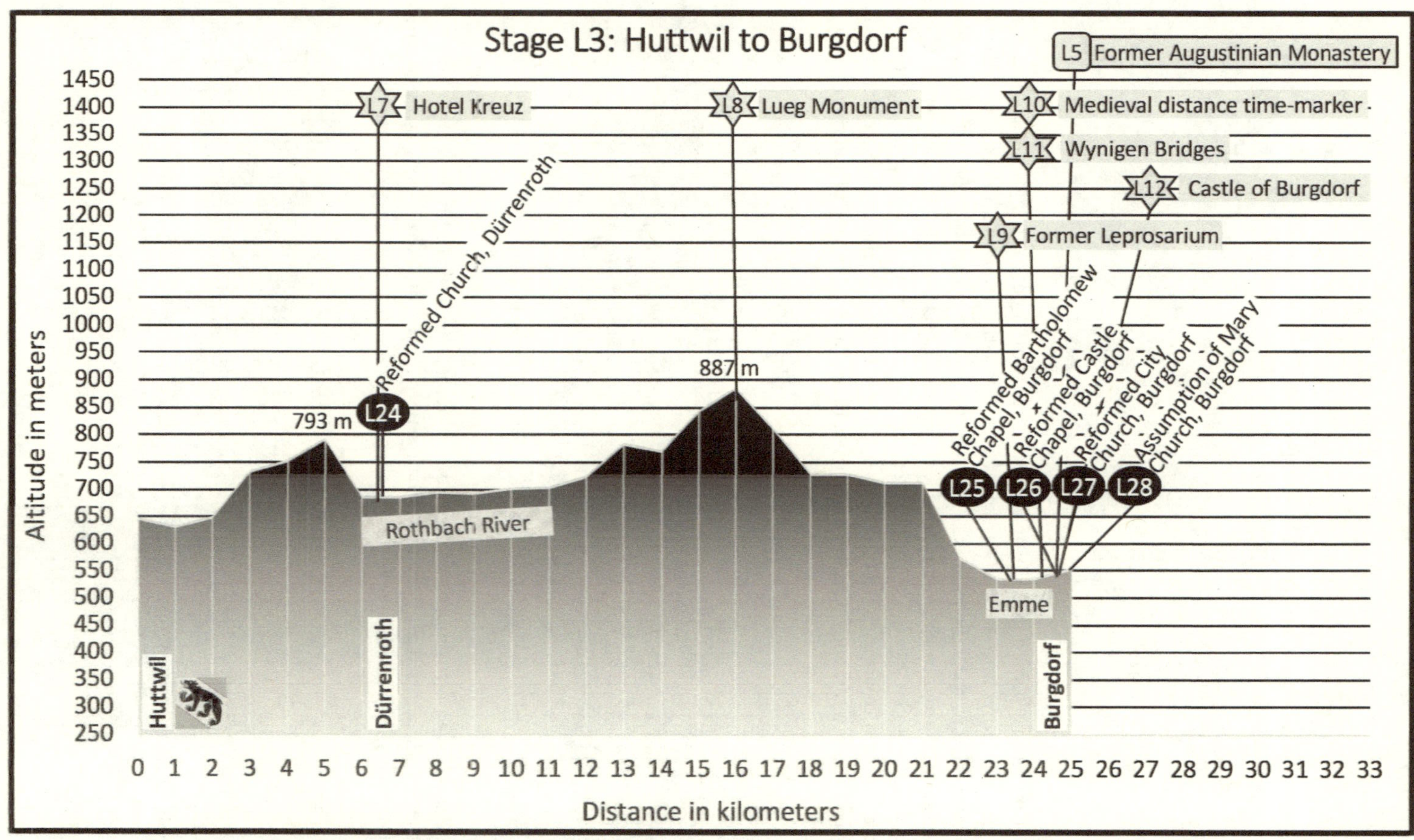
Stage L3: Huttwil to Burgdorf
Altitude in meters
1450
1400
1350
1300
1250
1200
1150
1100
1050
1000
950
900
850
800
750
700
650
600
550
500
450
400
350
300
250
Distance in kilometers
0 1 2 3 4 5 6 7 8 9 10 11 12 13 14 15 16 17 18 19 20 21 22 23 24 25 26 27 28 29 30 31 32 33
L7 Hotel Kreuz
L8 Lueg Monument
L10 Medieval distance time-marker
L11 Wynigen Bridges
L12 Castle of Burgdorf
L9 Former Leprosarium
L5 Former Augustinian Monastery
L24 Reformed Church, Dürrenroth
L25 Reformed Bartholomew Chapel, Burgdorf
L26 Reformed Castle Chapel, Burgdorf
L27 Reformed City Church, Burgdorf
L28 Assumption of Mary Church, Burgdorf
793 m
887 m
Huttwil
Dürrenroth
Rothbach River
Emme
Burgdorf

Hiking the Route

From the reformed church of Huttwil, the route goes west along the main road (*Bahnhofstrasse*) and after 600 meters passes by the train station of Huttwil. The route crosses the railway tracks and 200 meters later forks to the left. Through a residential area the tarmac road (*Fiechtenstrasse*) descends for 500 meters, until you reach the valley of the Rotbach stream. You pass by a saw mill with the scent of freshly sawed wood. The farmhouses have a typical Bernese architecture, with a protruding front roof. On a tarmac road the route climbs out of the river valley.

At a wooden farmhouse the tarmac road ends; the trail continues steeply through the meadow on the edge of a small patch of forest. After passing by another farmhouse the route enters the Chalteneggwald forest and keeps ascending.

After 400 meters on a rocky forest road the tree line opens up along a meadow. On a grass trail you pass by another farmhouse, where you have views over the rolling hills to the south. Dark green patches of forest are surrounded by light green meadows and differently colored agricultural fields. On a farm road the route continues along the southern edge of the forest. The landscape becomes wide and you pass by a small settlement. The route follows the tarmac country road on the highland plateau and reaches a high point of 793 meters. At this location the number 4 signpost directs to the left where you can see the town Dürrenroth, halfway on a hill on the other side of the valley.

For the next 800 meters the route descends steeply on a tractor trail and uneven grasslands. You pass by apple trees and see the white church tower getting closer. The descent ends at road nr. 23, where you turn right (west) and 50 meters later left (south). The route crosses the Rotbach stream (second time) and railway tracks, and passes by the small train station. On a narrow tarmac footpath, the route goes up the hill and reaches the reformed Church of Dürrenroth at km 6.4.

Reformed Church, Dürrenroth (Reformierte Kirche) L-24

- Dorfstrasse 21, 3465 Dürrenroth
- St. Lawrence
- On a table at the back of the church
- The church was built in 1486. Until the Reformation in 1528, the catholic church was dedicated to St. Lawrence (*St. Laurentius*). During the Reformation all

catholic interior decorations were removed. The church was enlarged in 1768-71 and 1833, and renovated in 1942. The front portal was built in 2001, based on historical photos.

The oldest part of the church is its bell, dating from 1392 (originating from another church). Second oldest is the baptismal font from after the Reformation (1562). Despite it being a protestant church, the church tower still bears a cross on its roof, a remnant of once having been a catholic church (protestant churches have a weather cock instead of a cross). The interior decorations are typical of a protestant church, limited to a pulpit, baptismal font, and organ (1833). The stained-glass windows date from 1893, 1910, and 1936.

L-7

In front of the church are the **Hotel Kreuz** (Cross) and *Bären* (Bears), two beautifully restored buildings from 1752 (late-baroque style). Fuchsia-colored geraniums at the windowsills match those of the fountain. The name *Kreuz* is derived from its interior that has the footprint of a Greek cross, with four identical oak doors at the end of the arms. Predecessor inns existed from the 16th century.

During the 16th-19th centuries the town was an important station on the road from Bern to Luzern. Horse-drawn postal coaches halted here until 1908, after which the train took over the main connections. The building left of the hotel (behind the carpark) used to be the stables, where the horses were changed. As 21st century pilgrim you are on the same medieval route between Luzern and Bern.

The Way of St. James leaves the town along the *Dorfstrasse* on a gradually ascending tarmac pavement next to the road, which curves to the right and passes by a settlement with a few stately houses. The pavement ends and you briefly walk on a road lined with apple trees. Shortly before reaching the Rotbach stream valley (with the railway tracks and road nr. 23), the route turns left and after a short grass trail through a meadow, enters the Rotwald forest. The yellow direction arrow is painted on a grey slab of concrete at the entrance to the forest. The slab has some colorful artwork and a grey plaque with a scallop. You might think that the information is about the Way of St. James, but it is not. It states that you are in the northern foothills of the Napf mountain range, and explains the economical and agricultural challenges of the region.

The following 2 km the route trails on the northern edge of the forest in a southwestern direction. Though you cannot see road nr. 23, you can clearly hear the traffic, north of the forest, heading in the same direction. The path in the forest alternates between broad dirt road and narrow footpath. Yellow signs painted on trees confirm the direction. After the route leaves the forest you reach another tarmac country road. You pass by a small settlement with the typical Bernese farmhouses, also with fuchsia-colored geraniums. The tarmac road changes into a grass trail crossing through meadows.

To your right you can see the small Rotbach stream, the railway tracks, road nr. 23, and the small town Häusernmoos. The dirt road enters a small patch of forest, where the route makes a sharp right towards the small town.

You cross the railway tracks, turn left to pass by the small station of Häusernmoos, and turn right on road nr. 23, where you pass by an inn with a Japanese Koi fishpond in its garden (*Restaurant Koi-Gartenteich*). Whereas road nr. 23 and the railway tracks continue to the south, the Way of St. James follows a western direction, straight towards Burgdorf.

The following 12 km the route does not pass through any towns, neither crosses a main road nor railway tracks, until it reaches Burgdorf. The route turns left again and follows an ascending straight road to another village. After the village the route leaves the road and turns right into a patch of forest. The forest trail continues to ascend but is easy to walk on. On a wooden footbridge you cross a small stream and leave the patch of forest. The route continues on a tarmac country road through another patch of forest, where it reaches a high point of 785 meters. You are surrounded by rolling hills that block the views. Up ahead you see the road descend towards another patch of forest, crossing a small stream. Going down the hill the trail is on grass and a tractor dirt path. Ascending out of the small valley the route follows a poorly maintained tarmac road.

You pass by several farmhouses and continue on a straight road through agricultural fields that provide wide views over rolling hills and the Alps in the far distance. The route curves on the side of the hills. On your left (south) you can see a road snaking up the hills too, getting closer to the Way of St. James. After a small patch of forest, the route trails through grass on the slope of a hill. On top of the hill, to your right, you see a five-sided stone pillar. It is the Lueg Monument.

To visit the monument (at km 16.0), you need to briefly leave the signposted route and walk up the steep hill to the monument for 150 meters. The steep climb is rewarded with a great view.

The **Lueg Monument** is at an elevation of 887 meters, the highest point of stage L3. The monument was erected in 1921 for the 54 cavalry soldiers who died of the Spanish Flue during their military service in 1918. Most people, however, visit the monument because of its viewpoint, overlooking the rolling hills of the Emmental valley with the Bernese Alps at the horizon. The word 'lueg' is Swiss-German for 'look'. An information table names all the mountain peaks you can see at the southwestern horizon. Wooden picnic tables, benches, and a BBQ area invite to rest and enjoy the view a bit longer.

The hill top of the Lueg Monument is the highest point of today's hike; from here it is basically a descent to Burgdorf over 7 km. After a steep descent of 150 meters you return to the signposted route. On the road you pass by the Lueg restaurant, after which the route forks to the left. The route goes slightly up again on a tractor trail through fields and a narrow dirt path through a patch of forest. The trail zigzags down the hill through a dense forest. The following 3 km the route is on a highland plateau with just some minor ascents and descents. You pass through patches of forest and walk along a straight highland road, from where you have good views of the Jura mountain range in the northwest.

On a gravel road you pass underneath power lines and enter a forest. The steeply descending trail alternates between narrow dirt paths and grasslands on the edge of the forest. The many loose rocks and stones on the path make the walking uncomfortable; the narrow strip of hardened dirt on the side is easier to walk on.

In the middle of the Leuehölzli forest the steepest part of the decent is through a 50-meter sunken lane called the **Leue Holloway** (*Leuenhohle*). It is a gorge-like medieval path hewn into sandstone walls, several meters high to the left and right. It is one of the best kept Holloways along the Swiss Way of St. James.

At the end of the 50 meters the route turns left and follows the northern edge of the forest for the following 1 km, while gradually descending towards the Emme River. The final part of the descent through the forest is on a path paved with big round stones, making the walking very uncomfortable. It is the medieval road leading up to/down from the Leue Holloway.

As you get out of the forest you need to look back towards the right. Make a small detour on the dirt road that leads to the reformed Bartholomew Chapel of Burgdorf (at km 23.1).

L-25 **Reformed Bartholomew Chapel, Burgdorf** (Bartholomäus Kapelle)

- Kapellenweg, 3400 Burgdorf
- St. Bartholomew
- The chapel, dedicated to St. Bartholomew, was built as a place of prayer for the nearby leper house (*Siechenhaus*) (see below) in 1446. Though most field chapels were destroyed during the Reformation in 1528, this chapel was spared as it prevented lepers from coming into the city of Burgdorf. The word saint was removed from its name, the catholic religious interior decorations were destroyed, and the walls whitewashed.

In 1798 the leprosarium closed, after which the services at the chapel ceased and the chapel was emptied. In 1854 the chapel was sold by the municipality to a private person, who used it for storing equipment. In 1884 the chapel was restored by the Christ-Catholic parish and was in use for services until 1930.

The chapel was renovated by the municipality (who owned it again) and transformed for protestant services in 1955.

Its interior is simple. Nowadays a protestant service is held once a month, while the small chapel is regularly used for weddings. The door is mostly locked.

This is one of two former leper house chapels along the Swiss Way of St. James. The other one is in Lausanne (see stage 17, Volume III).

About 100 meters behind the chapel is the former leprosarium.

The former **Leprosarium** was built outside the city walls in the 13th century (first mentioned in 1316). In the middle ages the lepers had begging rights, so their location near the main travel route (and bridge) Burgdorf-Luzern was meant to stimulate the receiving of alms. The building, as you see it today, dates from 1506-08. It housed a hospital in the 17th and 18th centuries.

Upon the invasion of the French revolutionary troops in 1798 it was closed and the patients were transferred to the local hospital inside the city. The building was used for storage in the 19th century, until the City of Burgdorf purchased it in 1925.

It is one of the few preserved former leper houses in Switzerland (and the only one along the Swiss Way of St. James). Nowadays the building is leased by the protestant parish of Burgdorf; it can be rented for parties and events.

Continuing towards Burgdorf you can see the church tower and the Castle of Burgdorf above the town. Alongside cliffs (watch out for falling rocks) you reach the *Wynigenstrasse* that crosses the Emme River. Left of the road bridge (*Wynigenbrücke*) the Emme River flows past high cliffs.

The **Emme River** and its valley (*Emmental*) have given the name to the famous Swiss Emmental cheese that is produced in this region. The river has a length of 80 km and is known for its sudden spiking of water throughput, which regularly caused severe floods during the middle ages (before containment measures were taken).

Aside the tarmac *Wynigenstrasse*, the route follows a tree lined gravel path that leads to a long wooden covered bridge.

L-10

Notice the slab of stone left of the entrance of the wooden bridge. The engraving is a bit difficult to read, but it says '*V Stunden von Bern*' (5 hours from Bern). This is a **medieval distance time-marker**, indicating that it is 5 hours walking (at 4.8 km per hour) from here to the Clock Tower (*Zeitglockenturm*) in Bern (see point of interest nr. L-18, stage L4).

L-11

The **'outer Wynigen Bridge'** (*äussere Wynigenbrücke*) bridges the Emme River. You just passed over it. A first wooden bridge was built in 1558-59, replaced by a roofed construction in 1858, and demolished and replaced by the current concrete road bridge in 1961. The name Wynigen is derived from the village Wynigen (about 6 km to the north), in which direction the bridges and road lead.

The **'inner Wynigen Bridge'** (*innere Wynigenbrücke*) was built to cross a small river, that was a side-arm and flooding area of the Emme River, in 1776. Predecessor bridges already stood here since 1559. In 1764 a flood destroyed a previous stone bridge, which was replaced by a (not covered) wooden bridge for ten years, until the present one was built. Until 1959 this wooden bridge was used by the road traffic on the *Wynigenstrasse,* located about 10 meters to the right (north). In 1959 the whole bridge was moved to its current position, when a modern concrete road bridge was built to handle the increasing motorized traffic.

It was one of two wooden bridges necessary to go from Burgdorf to the northeastern side of the Emme valley. The city lies in a narrowing of the river valley and during medieval times these bridges were the only connections to the northeast. The bridge was a toll station where tax and duty were levied on traffic crossing the bridge and heading down the river. The Lords and Governors residing in the castle ensured the protection of the bridge and its tax station. This river crossing was an important part of the medieval middle-land route, west of the alpine mountain regions. It connected Geneva via Bern to the south of Germany (Rhone to Rhine), avoiding the alpine mountain passes.

As you approach **Burgdorf** (around 16'000 inhabitants) you will see that the historical town consists of three parts: the castle on the cliff, the upper town, and the lower town. The feudal upper town lies between the castle and the city church, where the town was founded. The lower town housed the traders and craftsmen. As one of the few early cities in the Republic of Bern, the town had a lower court. Executions were carried out at the local gallows. When you tour the city, you will hardly see any of the medieval fortified city walls, towers, or gates (except for the castle). In response to the urbanization most of these fortifications were demolished, starting from 1820. Next to the City Church (see below) you can still see some remnants of the medieval fortified walls.

Former Augustinian Monastery, Burgdorf (Augustiner Kloster) **L-5**

3400 Burgdorf

Augustinian Order

Around 1280 the Counts of Kyburg, who owned the castle, established a small Augustinian monastery with a church. The friars settled to provide spiritual guidance, convert the local population to Catholicism, and care for the poor. They provided pastoral care to the lepers in the St. Bartholomew chapel and to the local population in their monastery's church. As a mendicant Order vowed to poverty, they were dependent on the local Lords and population for donations. In 1475 the Order installed one of the first printing presses of Switzerland in their monastery. The Order was expelled during the Reformation in 1528, their church was demolished in 1541, and the monastery buildings were put to different use, but were finally also demolished in 1821.

From the bridge the route crosses the roundabout (road nr. 23) and goes up the hill through the lower town (*Metzgergasse*). You see the City Church on the hill in front of you. On the left, 81 steps lead you to the level of the upper town. At the top of the stairs the nr. 4 sign directs to the left and through the *Hohengasse* you go further up the hill on a cobbled street in between the medieval houses. At a square called the *Kronenplatz* (with the fountain in front of a house with zebra-striped shutters) you need to leave the signposted route nr. 4. The signposted route leaves Burgdorf again without passing by its churches. At the end of the square take the street left (*Schlossgässli*), which leads up the hill to the Castle of Burgdorf.

L-12

It is not exactly known when the **Castle of Burgdorf** was first built. It was first mentioned in 1090 in ownership of the Dukes of Zähringen (who inherited a small castle from the Kingdom of Burgundy, who were the previous owners of these lands). It was the Dukes of Zähringen who founded Burgdorf around 1200 (they also founded Fribourg (1157) and Bern (1191)). At the same time, they expanded the small castle into a fortified residence with a residential tower, hall, and watchtower (and built the first Romanesque church – see below). Special about these constructions was that they used bricks, a new building technology at that time.

After the Zähringen lineage died out the castle passed to the Counts of Kyburg. Between 1218 and 1382 they added more fortifications, extended the walls, and built new halls. By 1382 the descendants of the Kyburg family had financial troubles and attacked the city of Solothurn, to which they owed a large debt. This raid was unsuccessful and resulted in a war led by the Republic of Bern. Five months later Solothurn troops, with support from troops of other Cantons, launched a counterattack on Burgdorf (*Burgdorferkrieg*). They besieged the city for 45 days but could not take the castle. To settle the debt and end the military dispute the impoverished Counts of Kyburg had to sell their lands and the castles of Burgdorf and Thun to the Republic of Bern in 1384.

From then on Bernese Sheriffs (with administrative and judicial functions) resided at the castle and additionally used it as a prison and granary. They remodeled the castle and gave it the appearance you see today. Most iconic is the large Bernese coat-of-arms painted on the side of the castle.

After the French invasion in 1798 the castle stood empty, briefly housed a military hospital, and a school for 5 years. Heinrich Pestalozzi established a boys' school as an educational institute for the poor, which included an orphanage, dorm, and teacher's seminar. These were new concepts with which he became a famous pedagogue and reformer of the Swiss educational system (he established several schools throughout Switzerland). A year after the dissolution of the Helvetic Republic in 1803, Canton Bern took over the castle and turned it into the residence of a Bernese Governor. Pestalozzi and his new educational institute were forced to leave Burgdorf. In the second half of the 20th century the castle also housed a regional prison. Many renovations were undertaken during the last centuries.

From the castle grounds and its towers, you have a great view over the Emme River valley (*Emmental*) and the city of Burgdorf, all the way to the Jura mountain range. It is one of the biggest and most complete 13th century fortified castles along the Way of St. James through Switzerland. The castle is closed for a two-year renovation and remodeling project, which will last until May 2020. After the renovations the castle will have a museum, a restaurant, a wedding room, event rooms, and a youth hostel (120 beds). The museum has three collections with 60'000 objects, covering the history of the castle and the town Burgdorf, ethnology from around the world, and the history of gold searching and washing (the 'gold room').

For the Castle Chapel you need to go to the second floor, next to the Knights Hall. The small in-house chapel is empty during the renovation, until May 2020.

Reformed Castle Chapel, Burgdorf (Johannes Kapelle) L-26

- Schlossgässli 1, 3400 Burgdorf
- St. John the Baptist
- Prior to the renovation the interior already contained beautiful (though faded) wall frescos dating from 1340. A round window lets in light, but another arched

window was bricked up a long time ago. The walls have several white spots where paintings must have hung or frescos were whitewashed. A sandstone statue is set in the wall, near the corner of the room.

For nearly 700 years this chapel was only accessible to the privileged Dukes and their guests, or administrators working in the office buildings in the later centuries. When the castle opens again in May 2020, this chapel is certainly worth a visit as part of the Way of St. James.

From the castle walk down the hill, back to the *Kronenplatz*. Turn right, backtrack down the hill for about 50 meters, and turn left into the *Kirchbühl* street. At the end of the street is the reformed City Church of Burgdorf (at km 24.6). The church is located at a highest point of the upper town in the medieval city of Burgdorf.

L-27 Reformed City Church, Burgdorf (Reformierte Stadt Kirche)

- Kirchbühl 26, 3400 Burgdorf
- St. Mary, Four Evangelists
- At the parish office, which is the white building opposite the church's entrance. The stamp and ink cushion lie on a small table in the front hall of the office building.
- The church was built in a late-Gothic style under the direction of a master builder of the cathedral of Bern in 1471-90. The church stands on the foundations of a predecessor Romanesque church, which was dedicated to the Virgin Mary, from around 1200. The new church was built around the smaller Romanesque church, so that it could still be used during its 19-year construction period.

The church converted to Protestantism during the Reformation in 1528, after which all its interior decorations were removed.

In 1865 a fire destroyed much of the old town, but the church survived mostly undamaged. Only the top of the church tower had to be rebuilt; its steeple is 71 meters high. Renovations were undertaken in 1968, 1986, and 2004.

The church has a typical austere protestant interior. The dark brown wood-carved choir stalls at the front right and left of the nave date from 1644-47. The stained-glass windows in the chancel date from 1947-54.

The treasure of the church is its rood screen that used to separate the chancel from the nave. It is the most beautiful and prominent work of late-Gothic masonry in Switzerland. Its construction took two years until completion in 1512. It was designed after the rood screen of the cathedral of Bern, which was destroyed during the Reformation. After the town fire in 1865 the sandstone rood screen was moved to the back of the nave, and the statues representing the Four Evangelists were added (1872). When standing in the middle of the nave, look back to the entrance and you will see the magnificent masonry.

Next to the parish office are the last remnants of medieval fortifications.

From the eastern side of the church (behind the chancel) walk down a path and turn left on a footpath down the hill (*Luftgässli*). The path circles halfway around the foot of the hill of the church. At the end turn right, then left, and at the fork right, further down the hill towards the main street (*Technikumstrasse*).

After a road crossing (with the light blue squares painted on the street) you arrive at the catholic Assumption of Mary Church at km 25.3.

Assumption of Mary Church, Burgdorf (Maria Himmelfahrt Kirche) **L-28**

Friedeggstrasse, 3400 Burgdorf

St. Mary, Brother Klaus, Holy Family

On the information shelves in the front portal

🏛 The church was built in a new-Romanesque style in 1902. As one of the few catholic churches in the region, it serves around 3'500 Catholics of 14 surrounding towns and villages.

📷 A wood-carved statue representing Brother Klaus is left of the entrance. The interior is austere, typical for 20th century churches. The two side-altars have a small statue, the high-altar a crucifix. The masonry below the altars depicts the Manger scene (left), the Last Supper (middle), and the Holy Family (right).

From the ending point

The Assumption of Mary Church in Burgdorf is the ending point of stage L3, about 550 meters aside the signposted route nr. 4 that goes through the historical upper City of Burgdorf.

In case you are a day-hiker, you need to walk about 400 meters to the Burgdorf train station (down the hill, to the north).

In case you are a thru-hiker and spend the night in Burgdorf, you can choose between several hotels, which are relatively expensive. Some private persons offer cheaper B&B accommodations. Check out www.jakobsweg.ch or www.viajacobi4.ch for the accommodation possibilities in Burgdorf. You can also visit the Tourist Information Office (Bahnhofstrasse 14; tel. 034 402 42 52; www.emmental.ch) about 50 meters from the train station (350 meters from the catholic church) and have them help you.

From May 2020 onwards the youth hostel (with 120 beds) in the Castle of Burgdorf will serve as a low-priced pilgrim inn (it will have double rooms, not only sleeping halls with bunkbeds – see *www.schloss-burgdorf.ch/Jugendherberge/*; tel. 034 426 10 20; info@schloss-burgdorf.ch). Since it is the biggest and most complete medieval fortified castle along the Way of St. James through Switzerland, and the only one that offers accommodation, it would be great for a pilgrim to spend the night in this 13th century castle.

The next Stage

Stage L4 guides you across the northwestern foothills of the Emmental mountains to the medieval city of Bern in the Aare River valley. Stage 4 is one of the longest and toughest hiking days, with nearly 2'000 altitude meters. It ends at the historical city that is a UNESCO World Cultural Heritage. Read the next chapter to find out what that entails.

Stage L4: Burgdorf to Bern 31 km

The Way to the Center of the Reformation

Route stats

	Distance in km	Time in hrs:min
Signposted route nr. 4	28.6	6:20
Churches/chapels	2.0	2:00
Points of interest		0:40
Rest/lunch		1:00
Stage L4	30.6	10:00

In case you hike this stage as a daytrip, you need to add 750 meters in Burgdorf and 1 km in Bern (from and to the train stations).

Ascent/descent/total	+968/ -1'000 / 1'968 altitude meters
Lowest/highest altitude	520 / 854 meters
Pathway/condition	moderate / difficult
Churches/chapels	Krauchthal, Bern (5)
Monasteries	Former Carthusian Monastery Krauchthal, Former Dominican Monastery Bern
Points of interest	Chateau of Utzigen, Paul Klee Museum, Bear Park, Former Castle of Bern, Medieval Figured Fountains, Medieval Clock Tower, Albert Einstein Museum, Cathedral Terrace

Route summary

Stage L4 continues in protestant **Canton Bern.**

Stage L4 guides you across the northwestern foothills of the Emmental mountains to the medieval city of Bern in the Aare River valley.

Stage L4 does not follow a road or river; rather, it goes over four mountains. The mountains are the northwestern foothills of the Emmental mountain range. Though the altitudes of these four mountains are not very high (623, 729, 854, and 722 meters), they do lead to a substantial number of nearly 2'000 altitude meters.

In combination with a length of 31 km this is a tough hiking day. A significant part of the route is through forests. Country roads through agricultural fields connect the routes between the forests. Between Burgdorf and Bern the route passes through only two towns that are situated in valleys: Krauchthal after the second mountain and Boll after the third mountain (Bern lies after the fourth mountain). A few small settlements are passed while ascending, descending, or on a highland plateau.

The route starts with a 1 km descent from the medieval upper city of Burgdorf to the southern valley. From there a 3 km hike over a first forested hill (623 m) leads you to the Krauchthal stream valley. Between km 4 and 9 the route crosses over the second hill (729 m), until reaching Krauchthal in the same Krauchthal stream valley. Between km 11 and 19 the route crosses over the third hill (854 m), after which it reaches Boll in the Lindental stream valley. Between km 20 and 24 the route goes over the fourth hill (722 m), after which it reaches the eastern agglomerations of Bern. The last 5 km the route goes through an urban environment.

When arriving in Bern, you will notice that the signposted route nr. 4 does not pass through the city. The signposted route circumvents the old town of Bern by staying in the Aare River valley and following the eastern bank to the southern suburbs. Because the historical city of Bern is a UNESCO World Cultural Heritage, the route described in this book does enter the town and deviates from the signposted route for 1.6 km (only). There are many things to see in Bern and the route in this book leads to the four main churches: the Nydegg church, the St. Peter and Paul cathedral, the French church, and the St. Vincent cathedral. For timing your arrival in Bern, consider that these churches have restricted opening times: the St. Peter and Paul cathedral closes its iron gate accessing the nave at 16:30; the French church closes at 17:00; and the St. Vincent cathedral also closes at 17:00. To have sufficient time to explore these churches and other points of interest plan an early start or maintain a good walking pace. A next morning visit could be an alternative, but be aware that the St. Vincent cathedral only opens at 10:00 (for the detailed opening times see the church nrs. L-30 to L-34). Planning a next day for rest and sightseeing in Bern could be an alternative too, given the relatively long distance of 31 km, the nearly 2'000 altitude meters, and the many interesting things to see in Bern.

Getting to the starting point

Today's starting point in Burgdorf is at the reformed City Church. In case you hike stage L4 as a daytrip, you need to walk 750 meters from the train station to the church (which is 150 meters aside the signposted route nr. 4).

Route Map and Profile

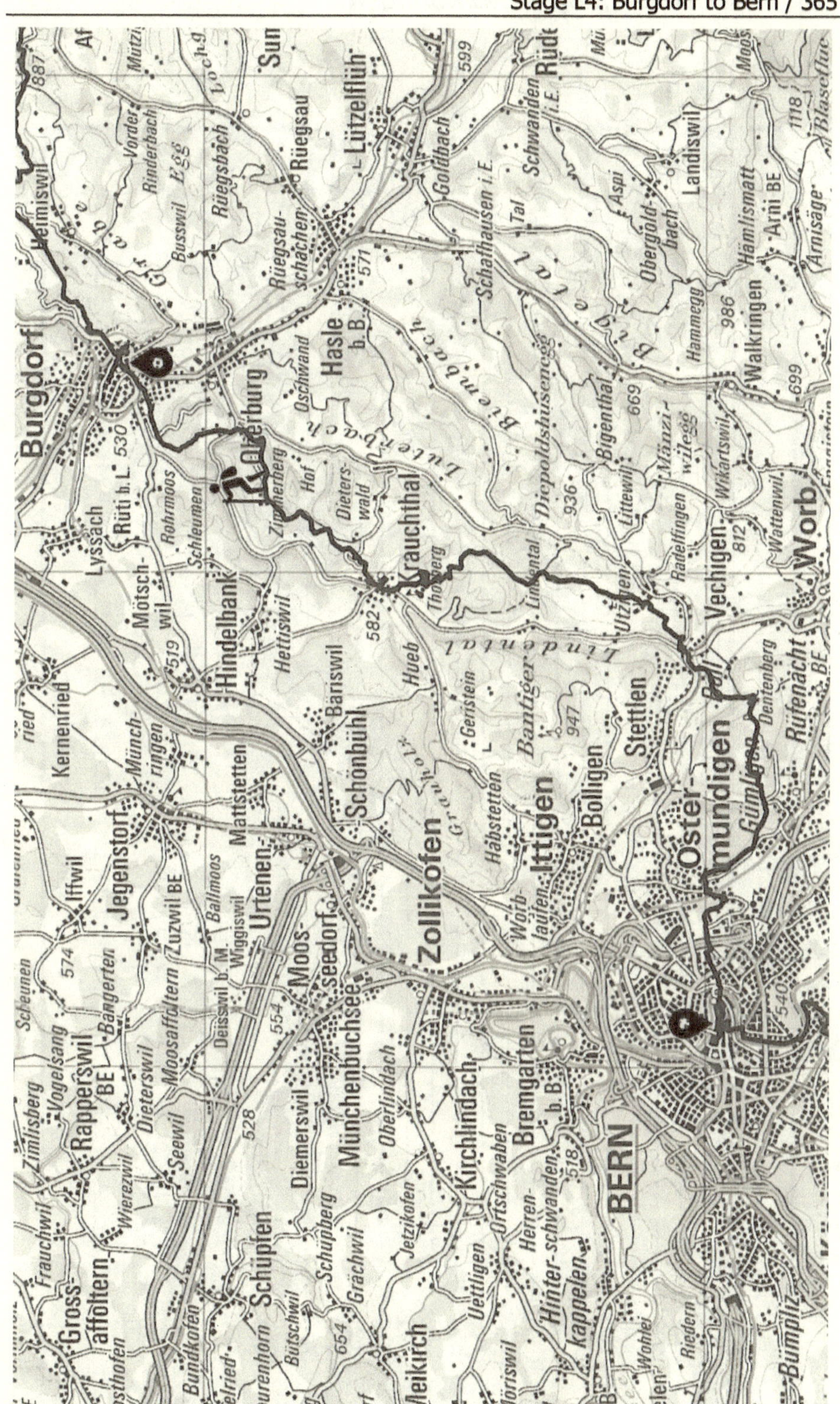
Burgdorf
Oberburg
Hasle b.B.
Rüegsau
Lützelflüh
Krauchthal
Hindelbank
Lyssach
Kernenried
Jegenstorf
Mattstetten
Urtenen
Schönbühl
Bäriswil
Moosseedorf
Zollikofen
Münchenbuchsee
Ittigen
Bolligen
Stettlen
Ostermundigen
Vechigen
Worb
Rüfenacht
Walkringen
Landiswil
Kirchlindach
Bremgarten b.B.
BERN
Schüpfen
Rapperswil BE
Grossaffoltern
Meikirch
Bümpliz

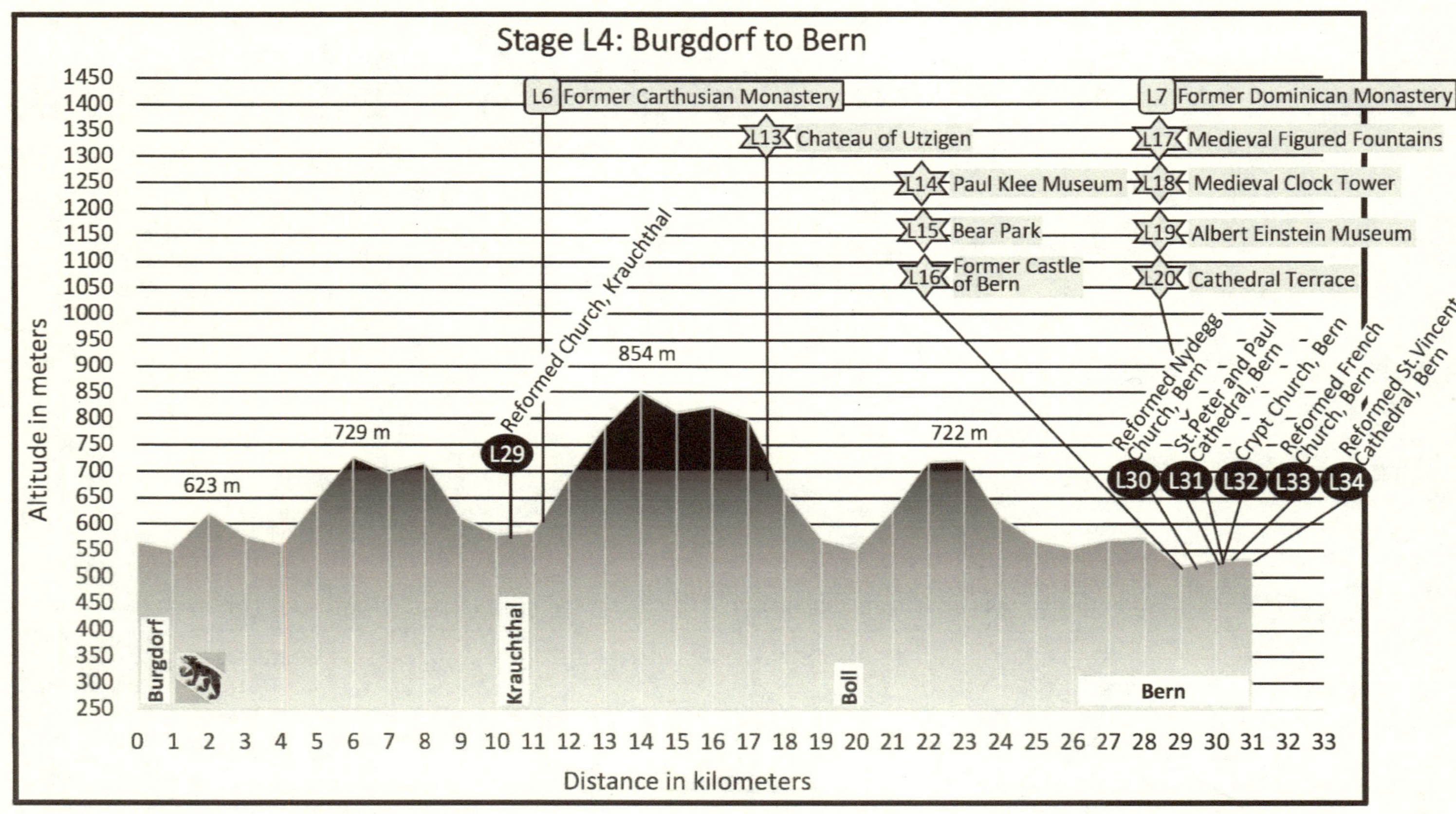
Stage L4: Burgdorf to Bern
L6 Former Carthusian Monastery
L7 Former Dominican Monastery
L13 Chateau of Utzigen
L17 Medieval Figured Fountains
L14 Paul Klee Museum
L18 Medieval Clock Tower
L15 Bear Park
L19 Albert Einstein Museum
L16 Former Castle of Bern
L20 Cathedral Terrace
L29 Reformed Church, Krauchthal
L30 Reformed Nydegg Church, Bern
L31 St.Peter and Paul Cathedral, Bern
L32 Crypt Church, Bern
L33 Reformed French Church, Bern
L34 Reformed St.Vincent Cathedral, Bern
623 m
729 m
854 m
722 m
Burgdorf
Krauchthal
Boll
Bern
Altitude in meters
1450 1400 1350 1300 1250 1200 1150 1100 1050 1000 950 900 850 800 750 700 650 600 550 500 450 400 350 300 250
0 1 2 3 4 5 6 7 8 9 10 11 12 13 14 15 16 17 18 19 20 21 22 23 24 25 26 27 28 29 30 31 32 33
Distance in kilometers

Hiking the Route

From the reformed City Church walk down the hill in a southern direction through the *Neuengasse*. At a crossing turn right, and you are back on the signposted route nr. 4 (*Schmiedengasse*). Follow the street down the hill for 500 meters and turn left to the small train station called Burgdorf-Steinhof.

After crossing the railway tracks turn right and immediately left into the *Schönbühlweg*. The narrow street in the residential area goes up the hill and ends after 250 meters. The trail continues through a meadow. When you look back you can see the Castle of Burgdorf tower above the medieval city. The route goes up the hill on a tractor dirt path and then descends again onto a road. From the elevated position of the hill you have a good view of the distant Jura mountain range in the west. After crossing a road, the route enters the Pleerwald forest and leaves the forest 1.2 km later. The route in the forest ascends on a 300-meter dirt footpath, after which the route descends on a broad gravel road and a dirt path.

On a tarmac road the Way of St. James descends to the Luterbach stream. After crossing a road and the stream the route continues south through agricultural fields. The following 2 km the route ascends again through agricultural fields and past the typical Bernese farmhouses that are surrounded by apple trees. At a settlement called Zimmerberg a high point is reached. After a slight descent the route goes back into a forest (*Eyberg*) and stays at more or less the same altitude (around 710 meters) for 2 km.

Pay attention to the yellow direction signs and marks on the trees, because they are not always clearly visible. The following kilometer the route descends from the Eyberg to the town Krauchthal, going partly through a forest and partly through meadows, with the final section on a tarmac road. Krauchthal lies in a valley, surrounded by rolling hills and some white cliffs in the south. Further south you see a red-white striped antenna that sticks out above the forest. It is the antenna of the **Bantiger TV-tower**, which is 197 meters tall, at the top of a 941-meter high forested mountain. The tower has a viewing platform at 34 meters elevation. The Way of St. James stays about 4 km east of this tower. The antenna is visible most of the time and serves as a distant beacon (on your right/west).

In the Krauchthal valley you get to the *Oberburgstrasse*, where the route turns left. The signposted route nr. 4 passes through town without leading to its church. This requires a 200-meter detour (and return). Turn left at the first road (*Oberdorf*) and you arrive at the reformed Church of Krauchthal at km 9.7.

L-29 Reformed Church, Krauchthal (Reformierte Kirche)

- Oberdorf 3, 3326 Krauchthal
- St. Maurice
- On a table in the front hall
- The church was built on the foundations of a Romanesque church (dedicated to St. Maurice), first mentioned in 1270. At the time of the Reformation in 1528 all the church's catholic icons were destroyed and the walls were whitewashed. This

first church was rebuilt around 1555-60. Several centuries later the church was dilapidated and too small, so that a new, third, church was built in a late-baroque style in 1793-94. The choir stalls, baptismal font, and organ gallery date from this time.

The interior is typical protestant. The stained-glass windows in the chancel date from 1922. Special about this hall church are the two wooden porches (added in 1797), left and right of the bell tower.

From the church walk back the same 200 meters to the signposted route. Turn left and continue on the *Länggasse* for 200 meters. You pass by a typical Bernese house with a protruding roof and south of the town, on top of a forested hill, you see a large building that looks like a monastery. The route turns left into the *Thorbergstrasse* and on your left you pass by an old stone quarry (nowadays overgrown by trees and bushes). Through agricultural fields the road ascends steeply. After 500 meters the tarmac road splits: right goes up to the large building; left continues uphill along a rock wall. The nr. 4 signpost directs to the left, away from the building.

When you have a closer look at the building you see metal fences, barbed wire, floodlights, cameras, and bars in front of the windows. You are looking at the **Thorberg Prison**, which used to be a **Carthusian Monastery**, and before that the fortified **Castle of Thorberg**.

Former Carthusian Monastery, Krauchthal (Kartausen Kloster) **L-6**

Thorberg 48, 3326 Krauchthal

Carthusian Order

The Castle of the Knights of Thorberg was first mentioned in 1175. They ruled the region for more than 220 years and professed allegiance to the Houses of Zähringen, Kyburg, and Habsburg-Austria. In 1397 the last Knight of Thorberg donated his wealth and the castle to the Carthusian Order.

The Carthusian Order occupied the former castle, changed the buildings, and built a church. Through donations and purchases they gathered significant lands and wealth. In the 15th century around 16 monks and 16 support brothers resided at the charterhouse. The Order occupied the buildings for more than 130 years.

The monastery was secularized at the time of the Reformation in 1528. Canton Bern closed the monastery and took possession of the buildings and lands. For more than 260 years the building was the residence of the Bernese regional Governors, and housed a prison and a hospital.

By the middle of the 18th century the former monastery buildings were dilapidated and demolished to make room for a new construction that determined its present-day appearance (1738-63).

After the invasion of the French in 1798, the buildings stood empty. From 1805 they were used as a prison with forced labor (in the stone quarry that you just passed) and a psychiatric ward; since 1848 it has served as a prison.

Only some foundations of the medieval castle's tower are left. From the former monastery nothing remained that is publicly accessible. Nowadays the buildings are still in use as a regional prison.

From the split in the road the signposted route nr. 4 directs to the left. The tarmac road goes steeply up the hill, passes by a smelly and lively pig farm, and circles back to a higher elevation above the prison. The tarmac turns to a white gravel road, which crosses through a patch of forest, still going uphill. After 500 meters in the forest you reach an alpine meadow surrounded by the forest. Opposite a farm is a dark-wooden house (*Spycher-Stüb*) that offers a resting place, drinks, and toilets for pilgrims. The location is called *Schwändi.*

About 30 meters after the resting place the route turns right on another gravel path. Be aware that the signpost may be covered by the overhanging branches and leaves of an apple tree on the side of the large barn. Past cherry trees, the gravel path continues the ascent and, in a curve, there is a great view over the rolling hills to the east. The ascending route turns into the Muelerewald forest, follows the edge of the forest, and goes into the Aebnit forest.

The trail is called the Monastery Path (*Klosterweg*) that was the medieval pathway from Bern to the former Carthusian monastery. In the Aebnit forest you pass by a small forest hut called *Waldhüsli*. The small hut has no lock and is accessible for pilgrims at any time of day (or night). It has a fully equipped interior with pots and pans, an old-fashioned iron stove, grill-charcoal, candles with a lighter, coffee, and so forth (though no water, electricity, or a bed). It invites you to rest and leave a message in the guestbook.

Immediately after the *Waldhüsli* a 50-meter long wall of chopped wood borders the gravel road in the Aebnit forest. The first block resembles a house with two windows with red shutters and geraniums. In the middle of the forest the Way of St. James reaches the highest point of the day at 854 meters (at km 14.0).

From this high point the route starts descending and leaves the forest 400 meters later. You hear dogs howling and barking; on your right you pass by a dog kennel (*Tierheim Tannenboden*). The tarmac road continues along the edge of the forest and provides wide views over the rolling hills, with the red-white antenna of the Bantiger TV-tower as a consistent beacon on your right. You can see the Bernese Alps in the distance for the first time. The gradually descending route passes through another patch of forest (*Brüüschwald*) for 700 meters. The route leaves the forest and continues on a tarmac road through agricultural fields. You are on a highland plateau and have wide views; you can see the Alps at the southern horizon.

The tarmac road ends after a farm; the route continues through grasslands. The descent becomes very steep, where 254 small steps lead down to the village Utzigen. In a small patch of forest, a rope on the side helps to cope with the steepness. As you are descending the steps you see a small chateau in front of you. The route passes left of the chateau, down some more steps, past beehives, the chateau's lower yard with apple trees, and circles to the lower front and its southern driveway. From there you have a good view back to the chateau and its grounds.

L-13

The **Chateau of Utzigen** was first built in the 14th century and served as the (summer) residence of wealthy patrician families from Bern (less than 10 km to the southwest) for many centuries. The residential chateau was reconstructed in 1669 and changed ownership several times, until it was sold to the municipality of Oberland in 1875. The municipality housed an institute for the poor, alcoholics, and unemployed people, and put them to work on the farmlands surrounding the estate. It accommodated more than 500 people at its peak. Since 1964 the chateau houses a retirement home. Modern apartments have been constructed west of the historical building.

The route continues on the former 300-meter driveway of the chateau in a southern direction. Two old pillars that once secured the access gates are still standing on each side of the driveway, under two large trees. A former guard house stands under apple trees. The route turns right and continues its descent on a tarmac road through a patch of forest. You overlook the village Boll.

You would expect to see a church tower, but there is none; the town Boll has a young history, going back to the 18th century, when it housed a customs station. From the patch of forest, the route arrives in the valley and turns left onto the *Lindentalstrasse.* At the roundabout the route turns right, passes by the small train station, turns left to cross the single track a little later, and continues on a road through agricultural fields along the *Lindentalbach* stream.

Beyond the valley you see the hills rise. The route first ascends through a meadow, after which it turns into a forest. A gravel footpath ascends steeply through the forest over 75 meters and at a tarmac road turns right, and crosses through the forest for another 300 meters. The route makes an s-curve and a short but steep ascent leads you to the settlement Dentenberg. You pass by a restaurant and the typical Bernese farmhouses with geraniums. Where the road makes an s-curve, the route crosses steeply through a field to return to the road on a highland plateau. The route stays on the plateau for about 1 km and follows a tarmac road. At the Amselberg settlement the route passes through the yard of a farm and gradually descends on a gravel tractor path. The gravel path splits in two: one going left, the other one right. There is no signpost guiding your way, but you need to turn right. At this location the App of SwitzerlandMobility comes in handy to determine the right direction.

At the entrance of a patch of forest the yellow hiking signs appear again. The forest trail descends steeply over 300 meters, until you arrive at the parking of a shooting range. While descending you cross a small stream called the *Stampflochbächli* in a nature protected area. Opposite the building with the black-red striped shutters and door (*Schützenhaus der Gemeinde Muri*) you find a fountain with potable water.

The route crosses a road and enters another patch of forest. Deforestation has destroyed a large part of this forest (*Harnischberg*). Hardly any tall trees are left along the route; new small trees and bushes provide no protection from the weather, but do allow a view of the city of Bern in the distance. A long staircase leads down the hill until it becomes leveled, and a broad gravel path goes straight between the young trees and bushes. For 1.2 km the route follows the gravel footpath along the southern edge of the forest. Along the way you pass by an open-air recreational area, swimming pool, and tennis courts. To the west you see the residential high-rises in the suburbs of Bern. The route turns left and goes down 106 eroded concrete steps through which you enter the suburbs of Bern. About 500 meters later the route passes underneath the railway tracks and a little later turns right into a small forest (*Schosshaldewald*).

The route curves to the left (west) and behind the tree line on your right is the **Schosshalden Cemetery**. It is Bern's biggest cemetery dating from 1877. It has a park-like structure that offers a sightseeing tour along sculptures, graves of locally well-known people, historical gravestones, and a mammoth tree with a circumference of 8 meters.

You may notice strange street names, such as *Teppich der Erinnerung* (carpet of remembrance) or *Undo-endo.* These are titles of artwork from the Swiss painter Paul Klee (1879-1940), one of the 20th century's most important painters. At the end of the patch of forest you pass by the Paul Klee Center.

L-14 The **Paul Klee Center** is a museum dedicated to the works of Paul Klee, exhibiting the world's largest collection of about 4'000 of his paintings (ticket price CHF 20; closed on Mondays; www.zpk.org). The museum building has a uniquely designed structure of three silver waves that integrate in a hill at their back. Paul Klee is buried at the Schosshalden Cemetery.

Immediately after the Paul Klee Center (on the left) and the cemetery (on the right) you cross over Highway A6. The route zigzags through a residential suburb and descends towards the Aare River valley. At a roundabout you arrive at the eastern bank of the river. You see the Bear Park, the Nydegg Bridge, and the historic city of Bern with the tower of the cathedral rising high above the town.

L-15 The **Bear Park** (*Bärenpark*) houses 3 brown bears, named Finn, Björk, and their daughter cub Ursina. When you walk through the city of Bern you will notice the display of bears everywhere, like on the city's coat-of-arms. According to folklore it was the Duke of Zähringen, founder of the city in 1191, who decided to name the new town after the first animal he would kill during a hunt. This first animal was supposedly a bear; hence, the name Bern derived from bear. It is unlikely that this story is true though. Rather, the name seems to have been derived from the Celtic settlement called Brenodor.

The first bear pit was created when Bernese soldiers captured a bear during one of their battles and placed it in the city's moat in 1513. The Bear Park used to consist of only one pit. In 2009 the bears' living space was extended to a park that goes down the hill and along the Aare River, and includes a pool and cave.

Behind the Bear Park is a statue of Albert Einstein, sitting on a bench. You can take a selfie with this genius. The building to the left (*Altes Tramdepot*) has a restaurant, a kiosk, and a Tourist Information counter (in the black cubic). In case you need Tourist Information to help plan your stay in Bern, this might be a good time to visit the counter (avoiding a detour later).

The signposted route nr. 4 skips the medieval city of Bern, despite it being designated a **UNESCO World Cultural Heritage** in 1983. The signposted route turns left (south) after the Bear Park and circumvents the old town Bern by staying in the Aare River valley, while following the eastern bank until the southern suburbs of Bern are reached. However, it is worthwhile to deviate from this signposted route nr. 4 to visit the medieval center of Bern. Bern has several old and grand churches, of which two cathedrals, and an interesting historical town. It is the capital of Switzerland with the parliament building. In medieval times the pilgrims followed the main travel routes between towns (for safety and accommodations). They would have ended in Bern, visited the churches, and stayed at one of the monasteries or inns. Therefore, this book guides the modern-day pilgrim through the old city of Bern, with the historical churches and cultural buildings, to an interesting ending (only 1.6 km deviation from the signposted route).

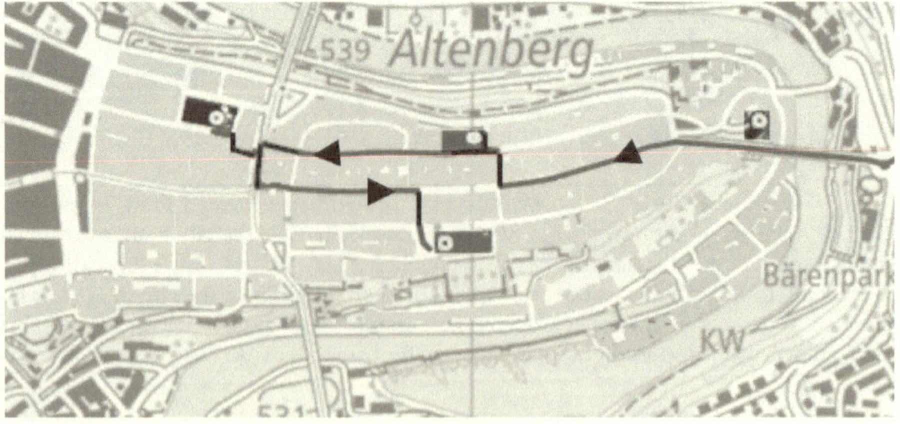

From the Nydegg bridge you have a great view over the turquoise Aare River and the historical buildings on its bank. Right of the bridge you see the tower of the cathedral, left you see the green steeple of the Nydegg church. Cross the bridge, at the end enter the small building on the right, go down the stone steps, and you arrive at the reformed Nydegg Church and site of the former Nydegg Castle (at km 29.2).

The church was built on the **ruins of the Castle of Bern** (called Nydegg) that belonged to the Dukes of Zähringen. The castle was used to control and protect the eastern access (over the s-curve of the Aare River) to the medieval city of Bern. This fortified castle was the first stone building and established Bern as a town in 1191. The Zähringen family lineage died out in 1218, as a result of which the castle fell into the ownership of the House of Habsburg. During a power vacuum in the mid 13th century the Bernese seized the castle, and demolished it in 1268-74 (as a sign to become independent from the European powerhouses, the Habsburg and the Savoy). The only remnants are the 20-meter-deep well and some of the foundations (overgrown by plants) in the courtyard of the church.

L-30 Reformed Nydegg Church, Bern (Reformierte Nydegg Kirche)

Nydegghof 2, 3011 Bern

St. Mary Magdalene, Four Evangelists

The church was built and expanded in different phases over the centuries. At first a small chapel, not much larger than the current chancel, was built around 1344 (making it the second-oldest church in Bern). This chapel was dedicated to St. Mary Magdalene. About 136 years later the expansion of the chapel started with the construction of the bell tower on its western side (1480-83). Eleven years later the nave and chancel arch were constructed (1494-1500). Because the bell tower stood west of the chapel, there was no room to build a large nave there; it had to be built south of the chapel. The small chapel became the chancel and the alignment of the church's chancel changed from east to north. By that time the church was called St. Mary Magdalene at Nydegg.

During the Reformation in 1528 all interior decorations were destroyed and catholic services were forbidden. The building was turned into a warehouse for wood and beer barrels.

From 1566 the building became a church again, where protestant services were held. Because the Protestants did not use the name of Saints, the church's name was reduced to Nydegg.

Until 1841 the bridge over the Aare River was directly above the water, so that the church towered over this part of the city. In 1841-44 the elevated Nydegg bridge was built, connecting the high western bank to the high eastern bank. From then the church stood in the shadow of this elevated bridge. To improve the appearance of the church, its nave was lengthened and heightened, and an entrance from the bridge to the church was built in 1864-65.

The church has a typical austere protestant interior. The interior appearance, and the artistic bronze doors, date from renovation work in 1951-53. The stained-glass windows, depicting the Four Evangelists, were placed in 1958. Notice the harp-playing angel carved on the baptismal font (1953).

In 1995 the church became famous beyond the borders, when Switzerland's first homosexual couple married here. Nowadays the church is mostly used for concerts.

In a recess in the wall below the street level you pass by a small fountain with water flowing from the main basin into two small spillover basins left and right (dating from 1857). A metal statue representing the Duke of Zähringen, together with a small bear, commemorates the founder of the city. Continue to the west towards the medieval city center.

The old city was built along three long axels that go up the hill from east to west. You are standing in front of the middle axle, at the lower eastern end. To your left (south) is the *Junkerngasse* (Young Nobleman alley) that continues in the *Münstergasse* (Cathedral alley) and leads to the reformed St. Vincent cathedral (see church nr. L-34). In the middle, right in front, is the *Gerechtigkeitsgasse* (Justice alley) that continues in the *Kramgasse* (Market alley) and leads to the medieval Clock Tower (*Zytglogge*) and the reformed French church (see church nr. L-33). To your right (north) is the *Postgasse* (Post alley) that continues in the *Rathausgasse* (town hall alley) and leads to the Christ-Catholic cathedral (see church nr. L-31).

L-17

Bern has over 100 fountains, of which 11 are **medieval Figured Fountains** with symbolic statues. These 11 fountains with statues are spread over the historic city and were originally built in the 14th-15th centuries (without statues at that time – these were added in 1535-46). The fountains are in the middle of the streets and served as the main sources of water for households, horses, and travelers. The fountains spring from natural sources and were a public source of water; even today they still spout clean and fresh drinking water, free for everyone. During the middle ages fountain guards would secure the rationed use and prevent poisoning of the springs. The historical water canal runs down the hill in the middle of the street (mostly covered by grating; partly open). In 1520-50 their wooden basins were replaced with stone ones, and they received decorative statues from a Fribourg artist, Hans Gieng. These statues depicted social and moral saga from the 16th century. Along the route you pass by six of these 11 Figured Fountains (in the same order as the photos below): the Justice Fountain (*Gerechtigkeitsbrunnen*); the Banner-Carrier Fountain (*Vennerbrunnen*); the Child-Eater Fountain (*Kindlifresserbrunnen*); the Zähringen Fountain (*Zähringerbrunnen*); the Samson Fountain (*Samsonbrunnen*); and the Moses Fountain (*Mosesbrunnen*).

Continue straight into the *Gerechtigkeitsgasse* (Justice alley). You can either walk in the middle of the street (on the water canal) or through the arched alley-passages right or left of the medieval houses. The passages (along the full length of all three axles) house small restaurants and shops. Slightly up the hill after about 150 meters you arrive at the first figured fountain.

The **Justice Fountain** (1543) depicts the Lady Justice, blindfolded, with balancing scales and a sword. At her feet are four smaller figures with closed eyes, representing the four authorities: Pope, Emperor, Sultan, and Government Official. Their closed eyes represent submission to the authority of Justice. The Pope symbolizes the religious authority, the Emperor the royal authority, the Sultan the dictator authority, and the Government Official the Republic (of Bern) authority. Since the statue was torn down and destroyed in 1986, a replica stands in its place (the renovated original is in the Bern Historical Museum).

From the Justice Fountain continue straight along the *Gerechtigkeitsgasse* for another 150 meters, until you reach the *Kreuzgasse* on your right. Turn right and after 50 meters you reach the *Rathausplatz* (town hall square) with the second figured fountain.

The **Banner-Carrier Fountain** (1542) depicts a Banner Carrier in full armor with the coat-of-arms of Bern on his flag. The fountain is in front of the old town hall, because in Bernese tradition Banner-Carriers held important governmental/military positions, giving them significant power over the city's activities. They held key positions and managed a district of the city.

Diagonally across the *Rathausgasse* (town hall alley) you arrive at the Christ-Catholic St. Peter and Paul Cathedral (at km 29.7).

St. Peter and Paul Cathedral, Bern (Christ-katholische Kathedrale) L-31

Rathausgasse 2, 3011 Bern

St. Peter and Paul

At the parish office (details on an information leaflet left of the entrance)

The catholic church was built in a French late-Gothic style in 1859-64, after the City of Bern had made the plot of land available in 1856. This was the first catholic church that was allowed to be built in the city of Bern in 330 years since the Reformation (1528). Because of limited funding no stone carvings were made. The church was built for the catholic parish of Bern, however, this community split in two over the dogma of Papal Infallibility in 1870-75.

In 1870 the dogma of Papal Infallibility divided Catholics into more liberal Catholics, called Christian-Catholics or Old Catholics, and traditional Catholics, called Roman-Catholics. The Christ-Catholics did not accept the dogma of papal infallibility. The Christ-Catholic Church was mostly limited to Germany, Austria, Switzerland, Czech Republic, and the Netherlands. The Christ-Catholics have no rule of celibacy (priests can be married and have children) and allow female priests (since 1999).

Unsurprisingly, the protestant Bernese Authorities sided with the more liberal Christ-Catholics, who formed the majority over the Catholics in Bern. With support of the Bernese Authorities, the Christ-Catholics assumed control over the St. Peter and Paul church and ousted the Roman-Catholics in 1875. For 23 years these had to hold their services in restaurants and private residences, until their own church was built in 1898 (Trinity Church – *Dreifaltigkeitskirche*).

The church has a female priest since 2012 (she became the second female Christ-Catholic priest in Switzerland in 2005). The St. Peter and Paul church became the seat of the Bishop of the Christ-Catholics in Switzerland and was thus elevated to cathedral. Special features of the cathedral are: the white bishop's seat in the chancel; the ceiling frescos and stained-glass windows in a Jugendstil style; the transparent with the depiction of the Virgin Mary, seemingly floating in the air above the communion table (1998); and the texts in various languages on the rectangular supports at the top of the nave's pillars.

Access to the nave and chancel is limited to the hours 14:00-16:30 from Wednesday to Friday and 13:30-16:30 on Saturday and Sunday. The iron gate of the front portal blocks access outside these days and times.

Below the cathedral is the largest crypt of all the churches along the Swiss Way of St. James, nearly fully extending underneath the cathedral. Historically, crypts were relatively small and only used as burial vaults. Its entrance is a small door on the street north of the cathedral (*Brunngasshalde*).

L-32 Crypt Church, Bern (Krypt Kirche)

Brunngasshalde, 3011 Bern

The crypt church underneath the St. Peter and Paul cathedral was built in 1859-64, at the same time as the cathedral above it. It is one of the few churches built during the last two centuries that has a crypt underneath. The vaulted crypt was renovated in 2014.

The crypt was designed and decorated as a subterranean church, with the same features as a regular church (including floor heating, sound installation, LED lighting, and organ). The crypt is not completely subterranean and has daylight, coming in through the right-side windows.

The Coptic-Orthodox Church of Eritrea uses the crypt for services, as does the Christ-Catholic parish during winter time. Concerts and theater performances also take place in the subterranean church. A curtain in front of the chancel can be closed during performances. The crypt church is only accessible by appointment or during a service.

From the cathedral continue along the *Rathausgasse* (the northern axle of the historical city) to the west. After 400 meters you reach the *Kornhausplatz* (Corn House square) with tram and bus stops. To your left is the third figured fountain.

The **Child-Eater Fountain** (1546) depicts a sitting Ogre putting a little child in his mouth while carrying seven more little kids. The statue depicts a carnival character symbolizing a warning for little children to behave well, because if not, the child-eating Ogre would come and take them away. After the Reformation in 1528 the city's carnival (*Fasnacht*) was forbidden; this statue represented one of the old figures used in the carnival, perhaps as a medieval protest and hint to reinstate this practice.

Enter the street behind (west of) the fountain, the *Schmiedenplatz*, and you see the reformed French Church in front of you. The entrance is on the southern side of the church (at km 30.2).

Reformed French Church, Bern (l'Eglise Française) L-33

Zeughausgasse, 3011 Bern

St. Peter and Paul

The French church is the oldest church in the city of Bern. A Gothic church (dedicated to St. Peter and Paul) was built in 1270-85, as part of a Dominican monastery established in 1269 (see below). From the 15th century the Order's austerity was reduced and the church's interior was enriched with frescos, paintings, and altar pieces.

At the time of the Reformation in 1528 the interior religious statues and altars were demolished, but the frescos on the walls and the stained-glass windows were left intact. The arched wall between the chancel and nave was bricked up (the outline of the former arch is still visible behind the organ) and both were divided into rooms used for storage of grain and corn. For more than 100 years the church was not used for religious purposes.

In 1623 the church was restored for protestant worship. From then the French-speaking protestant community of Bern used the church for services. After the Bernese Authorities offered asylum to French Huguenots, they used the church for both worshipping and lodging.

In 1753-54 the nave was shortened and received a new baroque facade, when the city needed the space to widen the street in front of the church. The separation between the chancel and nave was maintained. The church was renovated several times (last in 1991).

As you can still see today, the organ (1828, replaced in 1991) was placed against the separation wall between the chancel and nave. Thus, instead of the usual round shape, the chancel is rectangular and, apart from the balustrade, merged into the nave. Underneath the balustrade several small chapels with exquisite frescos were created. The (restored) frescos on the arched wall, which used to separate the chancel and nave, date from 1495.

The original, separated, semicircular Gothic chancel still exists. Since 1849 it has been used for exhibitions and events, but also as chapel and cloak room. You can access the old chancel from the rear of the current chancel.

Nowadays the church is still used for French protestant services (hence the name French church) as well as exhibitions and concerts. Its opening times are restricted: Monday closed, Tuesday-Friday 09:00-17:00, weekend 09:00-13:00.

L-7 Former Dominican Monastery, Bern (Dominikaner Kloster)

Zeughausgasse, 3011 Bern

Dominican Order

A Dominican monastery, built around the church, was established in 1269. Both had an austere interior, consistent with the mendicant rules of the Dominican Order. The monastery accommodated the main guesthouse in Bern during the 14th-15th centuries and received distinguished guests such as the German King Sigismund (1414) and Pope Martin V (1418). This Pope visited to approve a request to establish a Bishop's seat in Bern, allowing the City to build an accompanying cathedral (see church nr. L-34).

During the Reformation in 1528 the Dominican Order was expelled from Canton Bern and the monastery's assets and buildings were secularized. Their buildings were turned into a hospital, while the church was turned into a granary. More than 600 years after the monastery was built, it was dilapidated and demolished (1899), to make room for a theater and an administrative building.

From the church walk back to the *Kornhausplatz* and turn right. Cross the square and you reach the backside of the medieval Clock Tower. When you pass underneath its gate, you get to the front side.

L-18

The **medieval Clock Tower** (*Zytglogge*) is probably Bern's most iconic tourist attraction. The tower was built around 1220 and was part of the city's first fortifications, serving as a guard tower and the western access gate to the city. After a second ring of fortifications was built to the west, thereby expanding the city, the tower was heightened by seven meters, so that it could overlook the surrounding houses (1270-75). In 1344-46 a third ring of fortifications was built to the west, further expanding the city. This made the tower less important as a guard tower, after which it was used a women's prison. In 1405 a town fire destroyed much of the city of Bern and caused severe damage to the tower. It was rebuilt, and a mechanical clock and a big bell were installed.

This gave the tower its name of 'time bell' in Swiss-German (*Zytglogge*), back when it was one of the earliest public clocks. This clock was revolutionary in two ways. It was mechanical (with cogs, gears, and a winding mechanism) and it introduced a new standardized measurement of time. It rang every hour (with a fixed length) of the 24 hours, instead of only during the 12 hours of daylight (considering the days' varying duration of daylight depending on the season). The first version of the astronomical clock was installed in 1405 (it was first mentioned in 1443). The moving figures were also installed in the same year, but nothing remained of these originals. The present moving figures date from 1467-83. The mechanism is still driven by stone weights (400 kg in total) that need to be pulled up by hand every day. Over the centuries the tower, clock, and figures were renovated and updated many times.

The present facade dates mostly from the renovation in 1981-83, when it was restored to its appearance from 1770. The top of the tower is 55 meters high and its wall is 2.6-meter thick on the western side (where it was part of the western fortifications). It is possible to visit the interior of the clock tower on a guided tour (bookings at the Tourist Office).

Nowadays the mechanical figures are the main tourist attraction. They start about 3½ minutes before the whole hour and activate a cock (symboling alertness; the hour is going to change), a lion (from the coat-of-arms of the founder of the city, Zähringen), a fool (making the scene humorous), Chronos (the Greek Mythology God of time, directing the change of the hour), a gold man (named Hans von Thann – unknown how he got this name – hitting the bell in the steeple on the roof), and seven parading bears (city guards; symboling alertness). It is wonderful to observe and you will be surrounded by many other tourists shortly before the clock strikes the full hour.

From the medieval Clock Tower continue down the hill (east) in the *Kramgasse* (Market alley) and after 50 meters you arrive at the fourth figured fountain.

The **Zähringen Fountain** (1535) depicts a standing bear, with his head in an iron helmet, with a sword, a banner, a shield, and a cub at its feet. The bear represents the founder of the city, Berthold von Zähringen, in accordance with the legend of him shooting a bear and naming the city after this animal. The Zähringen family coat-of-arms of the lion is depicted on the banner and shield.

About 50 meters further down the hill you pass by the Albert Einstein Museum (*Kramgasse 49*)

The **Albert Einstein Museum** commemorates Albert Einstein's time in Bern, where he worked out his Relativity Theory, while being employed at the local patent office in 1903-05. His apartment (on the third floor) was turned into a small museum and furnished the way it must have looked at the beginning of the 20th century. The museum documents the activities of Einstein during his years in Bern. A ticket costs CHF 6; opening times are 10:00-17:00.

About 50 meters further down the hill in the *Kramgasse* (Market alley) you arrive at the fifth figured fountain.

The **Samson Fountain** (1544) depicts Samson taking on a lion, representing the biblical story of Samson as a symbol of strength. This is symbolic for the protestant City-Republic of Bern taking on Catholicism and the European powerhouses and kingdoms. Samson carries butchers' tools; the fountain was originally called the Butcher Fountain (*Metzgernbrunnen*), probably because the city's Butcher Guild financed the fountain. The original statue is in the Bern Historical Museum; a replica has been in its place since 1973.

From the Samson Fountain turn right (south) into the *Münstergässchen* (Little alley of the cathedral). It is easy to miss this alley, as it is a street-level passage underneath the row of medieval houses on the right. After 50 meters you arrive at the *Münsterplatz* (Cathedral square) with the sixth figured fountain.

The **Moses Fountain** (1544) depicts Moses with the two tablets of the 10 Commandments. His right-hand index finger points to the second Commandment, 'do not worship idols', while facing the main entrance of the reformed St. Vincent cathedral. This is symbolic for the protestant City Authorities commanding the parishioners of the cathedral to renounce the worship of catholic religious icons (statues, relics, paintings, saints, and so forth) – conform the doctrine of the Reformation. The original fountain was dilapidated and replaced in 1791.

Across the square (at km 30.6) you arrive at the reformed Church that used to be the catholic St. Vincent Cathedral until the Reformation in 1528. The church is still known under its name from before its conversion to Protestantism.

Reformed St. Vincent Cathedral, Bern (Berner Münster) L-34

Münsterplatz 1, 3011 Bern

St. Vincent, St. Michael

In the shop left of the entrance (ask at the counter)

The former cathedral is on the site of two predecessor churches. It is believed that a first small Romanesque chapel was built around 1155-60, shortly before the founding of Bern (1191). It was built by the Augustinian Order that resided in Köniz (nowadays a southern suburb of Bern). This chapel, dedicated to St. Vincent, was first mentioned in 1224. In 1226 Emperor Friedrich II transferred the properties of the Augustinian Order to the 'German Order of the Teutonic Knights of the St. Mary Hospital in Jerusalem' (also called the 'German Order' or 'Teutonic Order') that also resided in Köniz. The German Order owned and managed the chapel until 1276, when the City of Bern became an independent parish. Upon becoming a parish, the designation of the small chapel was elevated to church.

After the city of Bern started growing it needed a bigger church. This second church, also dedicated to St. Vincent, was first mentioned in 1289. The Basel earthquake from 1356 (central Europe's biggest earthquake during the middle ages) caused extensive damage to this church, so that most of the church was rebuilt during the subsequent decades. In 1405 a town fire destroyed much of the city of Bern, though the church was mostly undamaged.

The influx of masons and construction workers to restore the city led to a building boom. The City Authorities were so affected by this boom that they also wanted to replace the old church with a bigger and grander one. The authorities increasingly took the religious matters into their own hands and became the builder and major financer of the new cathedral. Wealthy families contributed to the financing and received their private side-chapels as a reward. Construction of the cathedral started in 1421, three years after Pope Martin V approved the bishop's seat and the construction in 1418.

As a common practice, construction of the cathedral started around the existing church, so that it could still be used while the new one was being built. The cathedral's construction started in 1421, but was slow. After 28 years of construction, the nave of the old church could finally be demolished (1449). Five master builders built the chancel and nave over a period of 154 years (1421-1575). The bell tower of the old church still served until 1493, after which it was demolished, being replaced by the cathedral's new tower.

The cathedral's tower was also built in four stages over a long period of time. The lower square part was built in 6 years (1483-89), followed by the upper square part in 29 years (1489-1518), followed by the lower of the eight-sided upper part in 3 years (1518-21); the final upper eight-sided part and top needle were only added 370 years later (1889-93).

Despite the parish's separation from the German Order in Köniz, the Order still interfered with the Bernese parish and its churches for over 200 years, much to the annoyance of the City of Bern. The parish's real independence only came in 1484, when the City of Bern purchased the church rights from the German Order and established a Collegiate for the St. Vincent church. A well-known member of this Collegiate was pastor Elogius Kiburger, who wrote the Strättligen Chronicles (see church nr. 125, stage 11) in 1464. The Collegiate lasted from 1484 until 1528, when the Reformation put an end to it.

During the Reformation in 1528 the church converted to Protestantism, the Collegiate was dissolved, and its interior suffered dearly. All religious figures, paintings, organs, and decorations were removed. All side-altars were removed and their spaces filled with pews, creating the three naves. The 12 side-chapels (family chapels) were emptied. The carpets and textile wall decorations were taken away; some of these are on display at the Bern Historical Museum. Nowadays the interior still looks as austere as it did right after the Reformation.

Regarding the dimensions of the former cathedral: it is 87 meters long, 38 meters wide, the center nave is 21 meters high, and the top of the tower is at 100.6 meters. This is the highest bell tower of Switzerland.

The only sculptures that were spared from destruction were those of the Last Judgement in the front portal, above the main access doors. Carved in 1460-80, the 294 statues represent Heaven and Hell in the Last Judgement, with the archangel St. Michael standing in the center, in front of the others. The small figures are originals; the 47 free-standing larger statues are replicas, the originals being at the Bern Historical Museum. It is a master piece; one of the best maintained and complete late-Gothic sculptures in Europe.

Other special features of the former cathedral are: the highest church tower of Switzerland at 100.6 meters – you can climb the 312 steps leading to the highest viewing platform (64 meters), offering a magnificent view over the city of Bern and the snow-covered peaks of the Bernese Alps, Eiger, Mönch, and Jungfrau; a room in the tower at 46 meters altitude, which was occupied between 1521 and 2007 by a watchman/woman – originally a lookout for fire in the city; the largest and heaviest bell in Switzerland, weighing 9'940 kg (from 1611) – better not stand next to it when it tolls; the first Renaissance-style wood-carved choir stalls in Switzerland (1522-25); the frescos at the vaulted ceiling of the chancel, still the original ones from 1517 (notice the Bernese coat-of-arms in the middle); the stained-glass windows, of which some date from 1441-51; and a unique 20-paneled stained-glass window depicting the Dance of Death (1516-19), as a reminder how the Bubonic Plague (represented by death as a skeleton) killed people from all walks of life during the middle ages.

An outside inscription plaque states 'machs na' (meaning 'copy it') in old German letters, installed by the master builder around 1500 (the original is in the Bern Historical Museum). You find the plaque on the northern outer wall (*Münstergasse*), at the level of the chancel, on the facade about 10 meters high.

Nowadays the church is mostly a tourist attraction. Though open every day, its access times are restricted (summer 10:00-17:00; winter 12:00-16:00). Concerts and cultural events regularly take place in the former cathedral. Left of the entrance you find the information center and shop in a former side-chapel. Here you can buy a ticket to climb the tower (CHF 5). Audio guides and brochures are available in several languages and you can participate in guided tours of the former cathedral.

When you leave the church and turn left, you get to the Cathedral's Terrace.

The **Cathedral's Terrace** was small when they started building it in 1310-34; it was completed by 1531. It was first built by filling up the descending southern slope with many tons of rubble and earth. To avoid the earth from sliding down the slopes, massive meter-high fortified walls were built at the southern base of the terrace. Until 1531 the platform served as the cathedral's cemetery. During the Reformation in 1528 many of the cathedral's interior artworks were dumped in this yard. The platform was changed into a public promenade in the mid 16th century. The baroque corner towers were built in 1778-79, replacing dilapidated bay windows from 1514-19. From the terrace you have great views over the Aare River to the south.

Of the many **monastic Orders** that settled in the 13th century, and maintained monasteries and social activities in the subsequent centuries, none survived the Reformation. The Augustinian Order was the first one to settle in Köniz, south of Bern, and established the first St. Vincent chapel in Bern. More Orders followed during the 13th century: the Franciscan Order in 1255; the Dominican Order in 1269; the Anthony Order in 1283; the Cistercian Order in 1285; as well as Dominican nuns and beguines. Hospital Orders of the Holy Spirit and the German Order also settled. During the subsequent centuries these Orders maintained hospitals, schools, and accumulated wealth and knowledge preserved in their extensive libraries.

The Reformation put an abrupt end to all these Orders in 1528. They were banned and their assets seized. All separate church parishes were combined into one (of the reformed St. Vincent cathedral), under strict control of the City of Bern. Several chapels were demolished and most churches were put to a different use. All monastery buildings were reutilized or demolished. In the historical city, only the church of the former Dominican Order still exists today, nowadays called the French church. All other remnants of the monastic Orders have long since disappeared.

Bern was the biggest **City-Republic** north of the Alps during medieval times. The size of its cathedral (the second-largest Gothic building in Switzerland, after the Cathedral of Lausanne) was a strong expression of the political and economic power of Bern during the middle ages. The rise of Bern as a strong City-Republic and the center of power in Switzerland was based on three main drivers: becoming a self-ruling City from 1218, concentrating aristocratic families within the City, and the Reformation.

At the end of the 12th century the House of Zähringen controlled much of the lands south of the Rhine River, of what is now Switzerland, by decree of the King of Germany. Zähringen established several cities (e.g. Bern, Burgdorf, Fribourg, and Thun). After the last Duke of Zähringen died without descendants, Bern became an independent and self-ruling City (**Free Imperial City**) in 1218. Being able to decide its own fate, the City-Republic began its territorial expansion.

From 1218 the town attracted many of the **high-noble families**. They received income from their lands and had time available to participate in the City's politics. The economic and political interests of these families were intertwined with those of the City. The early rise of politics shared between noble and wealthy families (instead of determined by one lordship) led to smart strategies to expand the influence of the small City to the region and beyond. Apart from military advances, the Bernese purchased and pledged lands, created economic and political alliances, and included other regional nobles into their ruling powers (e.g. by marriage). In 1353 Bern joined the Swiss Confederation together with six other Cantons, which it began to lead. By the end of the 15th century the Swiss Confederation had expanded significantly into Habsburg (German-speaking) and Burgundy (French-speaking) territories and governed most of the lands between the Rhine and Rhone rivers. Bern lay in the middle; the Aare River was the language divide between French in the southwest and German in the northeast.

Ulrich Zwingli started the **Reformation** in Switzerland in the 1520s. He was a priest in Zurich, who was able to convince the City of Zurich to convert to Protestantism in 1523. This spread to other cities, and Bern converted to Protestantism in 1528. The Reformation eliminated the dispersion of hospitals, schools, and knowledge, and concentrated these for the benefit and use of the City (instead of the individual monastic Orders). The hospitals and schools were reorganized and continued by the City of Bern. The reorganized school system led to the development of universities. The libraries were combined and functioned as an important source of knowledge for the government and the universities. The City-Republic of Bern seized the significant wealth accumulated by the monasteries over the centuries. This gave the City the necessary funds and income to continue their expansion and enhance their financial and economic influence. The Reformation had a significant influence on the territorial expansion of Bern. Instead of expanding into the territories of the surrounding Kingdoms, the focus changed to the Cantons that had rejected the Reformation. A strong territorial division between protestant and catholic Cantons incentivized Bern to conduct military quests into the neighboring catholic Cantons.

In 1798 French troops of Napoleon invaded Switzerland and dissolved the independent cantonal structures that made up the loosely organized State of Switzerland. Napoleon created one constitution for the new Helvetic Republic, for the first time centralizing the government of Switzerland. In 1803 Swiss politicians agreed with Napoleon on a restoration of their autonomy and a Confederation of 19 Cantons. The old aristocrats assumed power again and the religious division between protestant and catholic Cantons became deeper.

In 1847 seven catholic Cantons formed their own alliance (*Sonderbund*) to counter the increasing territorial expansion efforts of the protestant Cantons and a centralization of power with the Bernese. The protestant Confederation defeated the Sonderbund without much battle and drew up a new **Federal Constitution**, supported by all Cantons in **1848**. The aristocratic powers were dissolved and the Federal government took seat in Bern (being the most strategic location compared to the alternative cities). Present-day constitutional Switzerland was born, while Bern remained the center of power.

From the ending point

The reformed St. Vincent Cathedral in the middle of the historical city is the ending point of stage L4, about 700 meters aside the signposted route nr. 4.

In case you are a day-hiker, you need to walk about 1 km to the Bern train station.

In case you are a thru-hiker and spend the night in Bern, you can choose from many hotels. Bern is a major destination for tourists, business travelers, and politicians, making the hotels relatively expensive. Even the lower priced Youth Hostel (Weihergasse 4, 3005 Bern; tel. 031 326 11 11; bern@youthhostel.ch; www.youthhostel.ch/bern) and two backpacker hotels (Hotel Landhaus near the

Bear Park and Hotel Glocke) will probably be above the rates of other towns. Check out www.jakobsweg.ch or www.viajacobi4.ch for accommodation possibilities in Bern. You can also visit the Tourist Information Office at the train station (tel. 031 328 12 12; info@bern.com; www.bern.com) and have them help.

The next Stage

Stage L5 guides you out of the Aare River valley, up to the highlands, and over the northern foothills of the Gantrisch mountain range. The stage has the longest distance and the highest number of altitude meters of all stages of the Swiss Way of St. James. Read the next chapter to find out what that entails.

Stage L5: Bern to Schwarzenburg 36 km

The Way over the longest distance

Route stats

	Distance in km	Time in hrs:min
Signposted route nr. 4	32.0	7:00
Churches/chapels	3.7	1:30
Points of interest		0.30
Rest/lunch		1:00
Stage L5	35.7	10:00

In case you hike this stage as a daytrip, you need to add 1 km in Bern and 1.4 km in Schwarzenburg (from and to the train stations).

Ascent/descent/total	+1'177/ -878 / 2'055 altitude meters
Lowest/highest altitude	502 / 980 meters
Pathway/condition	moderate / difficult
Churches/chapels	Wabern (2), Kehrsatz, Rüeggisberg (2), Schwarzenburg, Wahlern
Monasteries	Former Cluniac Monastery Rüeggisberg
Points of interest	Swiss Parliament House, Bern Historical Museum, Archive Tower, Castle of Schwarzenburg

Route summary

Stage L5 continues in protestant **Canton Bern.**

Stage L5 guides you out of the Aare River valley, up to the highlands, and over the northern foothills of the Gantrisch mountain range. The stage has the longest distance and the highest number of altitude meters of all stages of the Swiss Way of St. James.

Stage L5 starts with an ascent in a southern direction to the agricultural and forested highlands above the Aare/Gürbe River valley (east). The route reaches three high points (692 m, 921 m, and 980 m) until reaching the point of convergence with the Way of St. James route coming from Wattenwil (stage 12). Two of the three mountains are high (921 and 980 meters), but the valley between them is not so low, being on a highland plateau. From the highest point the route descends to Mättiwil, where the route converges with stage 12 coming via the Alpine Lakes route (at km 22). For 4 km the route descends from the Gantrisch mountain foothills to the Schwarzwasser River valley. After a steep ascent out of this valley over 1 km, the route stays on another highland plateau for 6 km (with some additional ascents and descents). A gradual descent over 1 km leads to the town Schwarzenburg. The last kilometer ascends a hill (Wahlern) with the last church of stage L5/12.

From the cathedral in Bern the route descends for 1 km to the Aare River valley, which it follows for 2 km. After passing by two churches in the southern suburb Wabern, the route climbs out of the Aare valley over the flanks of the Gurten mountain. The route reaches a first high point of 692 meters at km 7, shortly before a 1 km descent into the town Kehrsatz (in the Aare/Gürbe valley). After passing by the Ecumenical church, the route steeply ascends taking 4 km to reach an altitude of 921 meters on a highland plateau. The subsequent 8 km the route stays on the highland plateau, with some gradual ascents and descents. The route reaches the highest point of the day of 980 meters at km 21, one kilometer before reaching Mättiwil (which lies at 915 meters). In Rüeggisberg the route passes by a church and the 950-year-old Cluniac monastery church ruins. After leaving the monastery ruins, the route follows a historical pilgrimage path in a southwestern direction, descending on tarmac country roads and grass trails to the Schwarzwasser River for 3.5 km. The route briefly follows the Schwarzwasser River bank, after which it climbs out of the valley on a steep forest trail to reach another highland plateau. The route crosses the highland plateau for 3.5 km, on easy and nearly flat tarmac or gravel country roads. The route makes another short but steep ascent through grasslands to reach 855 meters, from where it descends into Schwarzenburg. At around km 34 it reaches the village chapel in the town's center. The main church on a hill in Wahlern, 1.4 km outside Schwarzenburg, marks the ending of stage L5/12 (at km 35.7).

Getting to the starting point

Today's starting point in Bern is at the reformed St. Vincent Cathedral, about 700 meters aside the signposted route nr. 4 (which does not pass through the historic city center). In case you hike stage L5 as a daytrip, you need to walk about 1 km from the train station to the cathedral.

Route Map and Profile

Wohlen b. B
Wohlensee
Wohlei
Frauenkappelen
Riedern
518
BERN
Bümpliz
Matzenried
Köniz
Nieder-
wangen
Heitere
Oberwangen
Herzwil
Liebewil
Mengestorf
Thörishaus
Niederscherli
Oberried
Gasel
Schliern b. K.
Ulmizberg
937
Kühlewil
Englisberg
Wald
BE
Wabern
858
Gurten
Kehrsatz
552
Muri b. B
540
Schlatt
972
Lisiberg
Zimmerwald
Obermuhlern
Oberscherli
782
Oberbalm
Niedermuhlern
Toffen
Gross-
gschneit
Nieder-
mettlen
Mittel-
häusern
Obermettlen
Ueberstorf
Aeckenmatt
Borisried
Converge with
Stage 12 - Route
from Alpine Lakes
1055
Lanzenhäusern
852
Hinterfultigen
Ober-
bütschel
Rümligen
Rüeggisberg
Hasli
Helgisried
762
Wahlern
Schwarzenburg
Mamishaus
714
Rohrbach
Riggisberg
Rüschegg-
Graben
Gibelegg
1133
Milken
958
Gambach
937
Heubach
823
Burgistein
Rüti
b. R.
1000
Rüschegg
1296
1077
Guggisberg
Riffenmatt
1151

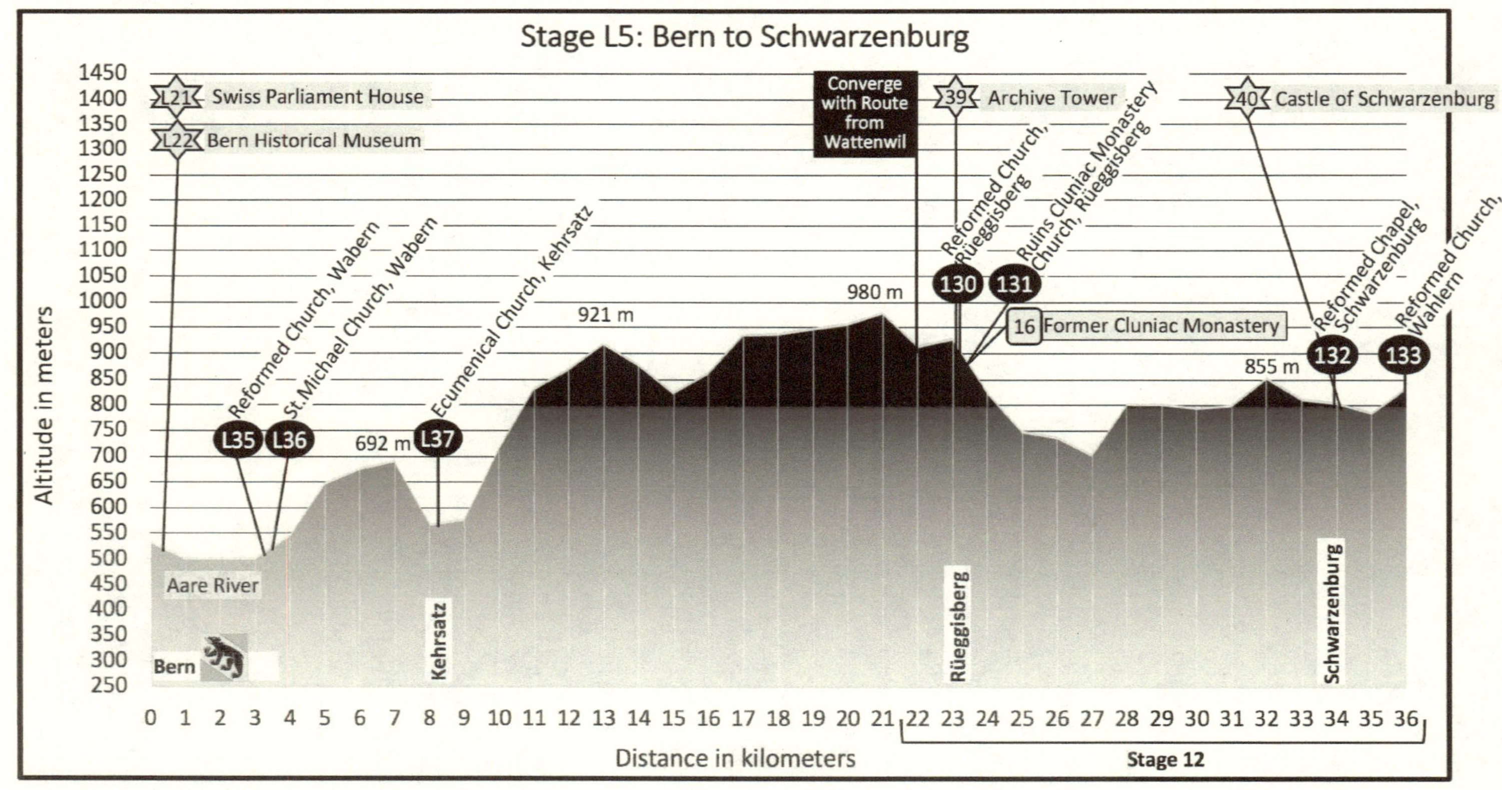
Stage L5: Bern to Schwarzenburg
Altitude in meters
1450
1400
1350
1300
1250
1200
1150
1100
1050
1000
950
900
850
800
750
700
650
600
550
500
450
400
350
300
250
L21 Swiss Parliament House
L22 Bern Historical Museum
L35 Reformed Church, Wabern
L36 St.Michael Church, Wabern
692 m
L37 Ecumenical Church, Kehrsatz
921 m
Converge with Route from Wattenwil
980 m
39 Archive Tower
130 Reformed Church, Rüeggisberg
131 Ruins Cluniac Monastery Church, Rüeggisberg
16 Former Cluniac Monastery
40 Castle of Schwarzenburg
855 m
132 Reformed Chapel, Schwarzenburg
133 Reformed Church, Wahlern
Aare River
Bern
Kehrsatz
Rüeggisberg
Schwarzenburg
0 1 2 3 4 5 6 7 8 9 10 11 12 13 14 15 16 17 18 19 20 21 22 23 24 25 26 27 28 29 30 31 32 33 34 35 36
Distance in kilometers
Stage 12

Hiking the Route

As already explained in stage L4, the signposted route nr. 4 does not pass through the historic city of Bern. Rather, this route follows the Aare River valley from the Bear Park in a southern direction. Therefore, at the start of stage L5 you need to get back to this signposted route. Before you start walking from the *Münsterplatz* in front of the former cathedral, briefly visit the Cathedral's Terrace (see its history described in stage L4) and enjoy the view of the Aare River valley. When you look south you see a bridge high above the valley, connecting the old city to the southern suburbs. Over that bridge and then down to the level of the river is where you are heading (the shortest way back to the signposted route).

From the southern side of the *Münsterplatz* walk westward into the *Herrengasse* and after 200 meters turn left to cross the *Casinoplatz*.

The large building on the corner to your left is called the **Bern Casino**. It was built in 1906-08 and its three halls are used for the city's cultural events and concerts. It is home to the Bern Symphony Orchestra. Though it is called Casino, it never was a gambling hall.

From the *Casinoplatz* continue south to the bridge over the river valley (*Kirchenfeldbrücke*). The **Kirchenfeld Bridge** is a steel construction that was built in 1881-83, with a height of 37 meters and a length of 229 meters. The bridge is infamous for suicides; to prevent people from jumping off the bridge, a 3-meter-wide safety net was attached outside and below the metal railing.

From the bridge look back over your right shoulder and you have a great view of the Swiss House of Parliament.

L-21

The **Swiss House of Parliament** (*Bundeshaus*) is often mistaken for a church because of its dome. The building was constructed in a neo-Renaissance style in three stages in the sequence of west wing, east wing, and central hall, between 1852 and 1902. The central hall has a 64-meter high dome and houses the National Council (*Nationalrat*), the Council of States (*Ständerat*), the Federal Council (*Bundesrat*), and the office of the Federal President (*Bundespresident*). The east- and west-wings are occupied by Federal Departments and a library. Together with the wings the building has a length of more than 300 meters.

The Swiss Confederation has a young history: it was not until 1848 that the current Federal Governmental structures were created (see stage L4 for the history).

Parliament has 246 members, elected every four years. A big difference with other countries is that Swiss Parliament does not have a governing or opposing party (consultation of all political parties is required, after which a vote determines the passing of a law or policy) and that parliament meets only four times a year (for a duration of three weeks). Most representatives have a regular job outside parliament.

Parliament is split in two Councils with 246 members: the *Nationalrat* with 200 members representing the Swiss people, where the size of a Canton's population influences the number of their representatives; and the *Ständerat* with 46 members, where 20 Cantons each have two representatives and six former half-Cantons each one representative.

The *Bundesrat* has seven members who collectively form the highest executive and directional authority of the Swiss Federation (like a Cabinet in other countries). On a rotational basis one of these seven members assumes the role of Federal President for the duration of one year.

The Federal government oversees the 26 Cantons that have a relatively high degree of autonomy (very similar to the Federal and State structures of the USA – in Switzerland the States are called Cantons). Federal legislation is restricted, only concerning topics for Switzerland as a whole (covering all Cantons); a substantial part of legislative power lies with the Cantons.

A special feature of Swiss democracy is its process of referendums, which can be held at Federal, Cantonal, and Communal levels. The optional referendums give the Swiss population a direct influence on legislative decisions. The formal initiation of a Federal referendum requires at least 50'000 signatures supporting a cause.

Free of charge guided tours, with a duration of one hour, lead through the House of Parliament and explain the workings of Parliament (online reservation via *https://www.parlament.ch/en/services/visiting-the-parliament-building/guided-tours-of-the-parliament-building*).

At the end of the *Kirchenfeldbrücke* is the triangular *Helvetiaplatz* with the Bern Historical Museum.

L-22

The **Bern Historical Museum** was built in 1894, designed after medieval castles. The museum's permanent exhibitions (with around 500'000 objects) cover the history of Bern, exhibit artefacts from the tombs of ancient Egypt, and artefacts from cultures in America, Asia, and Oceania. Since 2005 it has been housing an additional museum dedicated to Albert Einstein (separate ticket). He developed his Relativity Theory while living in Bern and working in the patent office in 1903-05 (see stage L4 if you want to visit his former apartment, which was turned into a small museum). A statue of Albert Einstein sitting on a bench is in front of the museum (similar to the one at the Bear Park). You can sit down next to him and take a photo with this genius. A ticket to the museum's permanent exhibition costs CHF 13; the museum is closed on Mondays.

To reach the signposted route you need to take the stairs down the hill on the right, at the end of the bridge (near the yellow zebra-crossing – before the *Helvetiaplatz*). These stairs go to the *Schwellenmattstrasse*, where a left turn leads downhill to the Aare River. Do not cross the Dalmazi bridge, but stay on the eastern side of the river (*Dalmaziquai*) and you are back on the signposted route nr. 4.

The **Aare River** is Switzerland's longest river with a length of around 295 km. It springs at the Aare glaciers in the Bernese Alps, flows through Lake Brienz (see stage 9), Lake Thun (see stage 10), Bern, Lake Biel, Aarau, and finally flows into the Rhine River at the Swiss town Koblenz.

The next 1.1 km the route follows the *Dalmaziquai* on the eastern bank of the river in a southern direction. At the *Schönausteg* footbridge the route crosses to the western bank. Many padlocks are hanging in the metal mesh underneath the railing. Most have the names of couples and a date symbolizing the locked-in love for each other. The following 800 meters the signposted Way of St. James follows the riverbank in its upstream direction.

At the Eichholz camping site the route turns right (south), away from the river, into a residential suburb called Wabern. At the roundabout of road nr. 221 (*Seftigenstrasse*) the route turns right. About 50 meters later you need to briefly deviate from the signposted route (that continues straight on the *Seftigenstrasse*). After the Coop supermarket turn left into the *Waldblickstrasse* and another 50 meters later you arrive at the reformed Church of Wabern (at km 3.6).

L-35 Reformed Church, Wabern (Reformierte Kirche)

- Kirchstrasse 210, 3084 Köniz
- The church was built in 1946-48, to serve the growing protestant population of Wabern, a southern suburb of Bern.
- Because of limited budget the artistic fresco (the resurrection of Jesus in a size of nearly 9 by 9 meters) at the back wall of the chancel could only be realized in 1955-62. During the interior renovation new modern furniture was placed in 2004. The cubic forms of the pews, and the similar cubic style tall wooden construction that houses the organ, give the interior a distinctive modern look.

From the church walk back the same 50 meters to the signposted route on the *Seftigenstrasse* and turn left. After another 50 meters you need to briefly leave the signposted route again to visit the next church. Turn right into the *Gossetstrasse* and after 50 meters you arrive at the catholic St. Michael Church (at km 3.9).

St. Michael Church, Wabern (St. Michael Kirche) L-36

- Gossetstrasse 8, 3084 Köniz
- St. Michael
- At the parish office, right of the church
- The church was built in 1958-59, to serve the growing catholic parish. The growing apparatus of Government in Bern attracted many civil servants from the catholic Cantons, as well as Italian and Spanish immigrants, during the 1950s. The pyramidal bell tower is typical of the modern church designs of the 1950s-60s.
- The interior is as austere as a protestant church. Because of budget constraints it took 11 years before the organ was purchased (1970) and 19 years before the stained-glass windows were placed (1978).

From the church walk back to the *Seftigenstrasse* and turn right. About 100 meters later the route turns left into the *Dorfstrasse* and you pass over train tracks (with the Wabern railway station on your right).

In front you see the ground station of the **Gurtenbahn**. This funicular railway (built in 1899) has a length of about 1'100 meters and takes tourists to the Gurten mountain summit at an altitude of 858 meters in 5 minutes. It is a major recreational area of the city of Bern with a hotel, restaurants, and a park, visited by about one million people every year. To your left is the Gurtenbahn's car park.

The signpost directs to a steeply ascending small road that passes by the car park. The increasing elevation provides a great view of Bern with the tower of the reformed St. Vincent Cathedral and the House of Parliament standing out against the Jura mountains at the horizon.

After 200 meters the route leaves the tarmac road and turns right onto the forested flank of the Gurten mountain. On a gravel trail the route zigzags steeply up through the forest, until you get to a farm and meadow on the first highland plateau. The route climbs more gradually in a southeastern direction over the next 2 km. The forests bordering the highland plateau block all views.

A tarmac farm road through meadows changes to a gravel road, which changes to a narrow trail along the edge of the forest, where two small streams are crossed. The route reaches the elevated outskirts of the town Kehrsatz, from where you have a good view over the Aare River valley and the Bernese Alps at the horizon.

The route descends steeply over 1 km on tarmac roads and footpaths through the residential areas of Kehrsatz. Shortly before main road nr. 221 (*Seftigenstrasse*) the route turns sharply right, going up the hill again. At this location it is worthwhile to make a 1.2 km detour (600 meters to and from) to the church of Kehrsatz. Instead of turning sharp right, continue straight to cross the main road and pass by the Kehrsatz train station. Follow the *Bernstrasse* in the curve to the left, take the *Mättelistrasse* on the right, and you arrive at the Ecumenical Church of Kehrsatz (at km 8.3).

Ecumenical Church, Kehrsatz (Oekumenisches Zentrum) L-37

Mättelistrasse 24, 3122 Kehrsatz

St. Andrew

The Ecumenical center was built in 1975-76 and is used by both the protestant and the catholic parishes of Kehrsatz. This Ecumenical center was a shared project: both parishes contributed to the planning, financing, and construction of the center. The center includes a church named Andrew church (*Andreas Kirche*), a small chapel called Room of Silence (*Raum der Stille*), a small cafeteria, and several class rooms. As Protestants do not use a reference to saints, the word saint was left out of the name of the church.

The church and chapel are used by both the catholic and reformed parishes, and therefore have a neutral interior. This is a unique arrangement: one of only three along the Way of St. James where both Protestants and Catholics have chosen to share the same space for their religious activities, in mutual respect for each other's traditions.

Pope John Paul II visited this Ecumenical center, as part of his trip to Switzerland, on 14 June 1984.

From the church walk back the same 600 meters to the signposted route nr. 4. The route goes steeply up the hill through residential areas, after which it turns into a patch of forest. After 400 meters on a steeply ascending narrow gravel forest trail you continue along meadows where the route becomes less steep, as you reach the second highland plateau. You pass by a retirement and nursing home (*Alters- und Pflegeheim Kühlewil*), in the middle of nowhere, on the *Englisberg*. Their first building was a home for the poor of the city of Bern (*Armenanstalt*), constructed in 1892.

The route continues on gradually ascending tarmac farm roads between agricultural fields for 1.3 km. You pass by fruit trees with plums, pears, and apples. At the road's T-crossing the route goes straight and changes to a hardened footpath in the Kühlewilwald forest. About 1.2 km into the forest the Way of St. James reaches the second high point at 921 meters (at km 13).

The forest trails are broad gravel paths, easy to walk on. For another 500 meters the route follows the edge of the forest, after which the gravel road passes through agricultural fields.

From the highland plateau the views towards the Bernese Alps in the south open up. The route gradually ascends and then descends to the village Niedermuhlern. The Way of St. James passes through the village with the typical Bernese farmhouses and continues in a southern direction. From the village the route starts ascending again, first on tarmac, then on gravel, followed by tarmac. You pass by a Bernese farmhouse with a wood-carving workshop; statues of carved animals stand in its yard. The tarmac road ends and the trail changes to grass, while briefly following the edge of a forest and then crossing through a small patch of forest (Ratteholz). In the middle of the forest a fallen tree blocks the dirt path. A beaten path goes around it; it looks like the tree has been lying there for quite some time.

At the other end of the patch of forest the route reaches another highland plateau, providing wide views over agricultural fields to the Bernese Alps. The route follows a tarmac road and turns right before the parking lot of restaurant Leueberg. In between meadows the gravel path goes steeply up a hill. On your left (east) you overlook the Gürbe and Aare river valleys and the city of Thun, with Lake Thun and the Bernese Alps behind it.

The following 2 km the Way of St. James is in the Taanwald forest. Towards the end of the forest three fallen trees block the path, spread over 50 meters. You can easily climb over the first fallen tree and duck underneath the second one. At the third one a beaten path goes around its upheaved roots; it looks like it has been lying there for quite some time. The route reaches the highest point of the day of 980 meters at km 21, shortly before leaving the forest.

At this location you need to pay attention to the signaling. The main path continues in a western direction, but the signposted route nr. 4 turns south. Coming out of the southern side of the Taanwald forest, you overlook the settlement Mättiwil in the valley below and the Gantrisch mountain range in the south. A tractor trail leads you down the hill to **Mättiwil** and at km 22.2 you reach the location where

stage L5 converges with stage 12 of the Swiss Way of St. James (132 km since the splitting of the route in Brunnen at the start of stage L1). The route nr. 4 signpost stands in front of a Bernese half-timbered farmhouse.

Hiking the Route from the Converge point in Mättiwil (km 22-36)

In case you are a day-hiker, you need to decide what to do next. You can either end in Mättiwil or continue along stage 12 to Schwarzenburg. In case you end in Mättiwil and want to go to the nearest train station, it is easiest to take bus nr. 631 in the direction of Riggisberg (the bus stop is near the hiking signpost on the southern side of the street). The bus goes at 49 minutes past the hour and takes you to *Riggisberg Post* in 11 minutes. Change to bus nr. 320 in the direction of *Thurnen Bahnhof.* This bus leaves at 11 minutes past the hour (12 minutes transfer time; the bus leaves from the same station) and takes you to the train station of Thurnen in 10 minutes (total trip 32 minutes, plus waiting time in Mättiwil for the bus to arrive).

In case you are a thru-hiker (or a day-hiker who wants to continue to Schwarzenburg), continue your pilgrimage to Schwarzenburg. This is an additional 13.5 km and 730 altitude meters, making the day-hike a total of 35.7 km and 2'055 altitude meters. For the details of the subsequent route of stage 12, and the churches, chapels, monasteries, and points of interest, please continue reading the pages 232-242.

APPENDICES

Appendix 1: List of Churches

Appendix 1 lists all churches and chapels along the Way of St. James in Central Switzerland, with references to the locations, stages, and page numbers. The numbering continues from Volume I.
The descriptions of their history and special features are included in the chapters of the respective hiking stages.

Churches from Einsiedeln to Fribourg, via Alpine Lakes route

Nr.	Name	City	Stage	Page
40	St. Joseph Chapel	Einsiedeln	5	37
41	Benedictine Convent Church	Au	5	39
42	St. Stephen Church	Trachslau	5	41
43	St. Apollonia Church	Alpthal	5	42
44	Pilgrim Chapel	Haggenegg Pass	5	44
45	Haggenegg Chapel	Haggenegg Pass	5	46
46	St. Fridolin Chapel	Ried	5	47
47	Jesuit Collegium Church Mary-Help	Schwyz	5	49
48	St. Michael Chapel	Schwyz	5	50
49	Holy Cross Chapel	Schwyz	5	51
50	St. Martin Church	Schwyz	5	51
51	Dominican Convent Church	Schwyz	5	55
52	Capuchin Monastery Church	Schwyz	5	56
53	Sorrowful Mother of God Chapel	Schwyz	5	57
54	Reformed Church	Schwyz	5	57
55	Five Francises Chapel	Ibach	5	58
56	St. Anthony Church	Ibach	5	59
57	Holy Cross Chapel	Ibach	5	60
58	Toothache Chapel	Unterschönenbuch	5	61
59	St. Wendolyn Chapel	Unterschönenbuch	5	62
60	Lourdes Cave	Ingenbohl	5	63
61	Ingenbohl Convent Church	Ingenbohl	5	65
62	Sorrowful Mother of God Chapel	Ingenbohl	5	66
63	St. Leonard Church	Ingenbohl	5	66
64	Reformed Church	Brunnen	6	72
65	Fourteen Holy Helpers Chapel	Brunnen	6	73
66	Federation Chapel	Brunnen	6	73
67	St. Anne Chapel	Volligen	6	76
68	Holy Cross Chapel	Emmetten	6	79
69	St. James and Thérèse Church	Emmetten	6	80
70	St. Anne Chapel	Emmetten	6	81
71	St. Anne Chapel	Beckenried	6	82
72	St. Henry Church	Beckenried	6	83
73	Cemetery Chapel	Beckenried	6	84

Nr.	Name	City	Stage	Page
74	Lourdes Cave	Beckenried	6	84
75	Mary at the Ridli Chapel	Beckenried	6	85
76	Fourteen Holy Helpers Chapel	Buochs	6	87
77	St. Martin Church	Buochs	6	87
78	Sorrowful Mother of God Chapel	Buochs	6	89
79	Loreto Chapel	Ennerberg	6	91
80	St. Anne Chapel	Waltersberg	6	92
81	Mühlimatt Chapel	Oberdorf	6	93
82	St. Henry Chapel	Oberdorf	6	94
83	Capuchin Monastery Church	Stans	6	95
84	Capuchin Convent Church	Stans	6	98
85	Mount of Olives Chapel	Stans	6	100
86	Charnel Chapel	Stans	6	100
87	St. Peter and Paul Church	Stans	6	101
88	Mary under the Stove Chapel	Stans	6	103
89	Mary at the Snow Chapel	Kniri	7	110
90	St. James Church	St. Jakob	7	113
91	Mei Chapel	Wisserlen	7	114
92	St. Catherine Chapel	Wisserlen	7	115
93	St. Anthony Chapel	Halten	7	116
94	Dominican Convent Chapel	St. Niklausen	7	118
95	St. Nicholas Chapel	St. Niklausen	7	119
96	Brother Ulrich Chapel	Mösli	7	121
97	Lower Ranft Chapel	Flüeli-Ranft	7	122
98	Upper Ranft Chapel	Flüeli-Ranft	7	124
99	St. Borromeo Chapel	Flüeli	7	126
100	Open-Air Chapel	Flüeli	7	127
101	Burial Chapel	Sachseln	7	128
102	St. Theodore Church	Sachseln	7	129
103	St. Apollonia Chapel	Ewil	8	137
104	St. Lawrence Church	Giswil	8	139
105	St. Michael Chapel	Giswil	8	140
106	St. Anthony and Wendolyn Chapel	Bürglen	8	143
107	St. Beatus Chapel	Obsee	8	145
108	Sacred Heart of Jesus Church	Lungern	8	146
109	Reformed Church	Brienzwiler	8	152
110	Our Lady Chapel	Brienz	9	161
111	Reformed Church	Brienz	9	162
112	Reformed Church	Oberried	9	166
113	Reformed Castle Church	Ringgenberg	9	169
114	Ruins St. Peter Church	Goldswil	9	172
115	Holy Spirit Church	Interlaken	9	174
116	Reformed Augustinian Monastery Church	Interlaken	9	175
117	Reformed Augustinian Monastery Chapel	Interlaken	9	176
118	Reformed Church	Unterseen	10	186
119	Former St. Beatus Chapel	Sundlauenen	10	191
120	Reformed Church	Merligen	10	195
121	Reformed Castle Church	Spiez	10	196
122	Reformed City Church	Spiez	10	199
123	St. Matthew Chapel	Spiez	10	200
124	Brother Klaus Church	Spiez	10	201

Churches from Luzern to Mättiwil, via Luzern/Bern route

Nr.	Name	City	Stage	Page
L-1	St. Leodegar Church	Luzern	L1	295
L-2	St. Leonard Chapel	Luzern	L1	296
L-3	Reformed Matthew Church	Luzern	L1	298
L-4	St. Peter Chapel	Luzern	L1	299
L-5	Jesuit Collegium Church	Luzern	L1	301
L-6	Franciscan Monastery Church	Luzern	L1	303
L-7	Mary on the Reuss Chapel	Luzern	L1	307
L-8	St. Jost Church	Blatten	L1	310
L-9	Reformed Mirjam Church	Malters	L1	312
L-10	St. Martin Church	Malters	L1	313
L-11	St. Idda Chapel	Malters	L1	314
L-12	Sacred Heart of Jesus Chapel	Schachen	L1	316
L-13	Franciscan Monastery Church	Werthenstein	L1	318
L-14	Countryside Court Chapel	Buholz	L2	326
L-15	St. Gall and Erasmus Chapel	Buholz	L2	327
L-16	St. James Church	Geiss	L2	329
L-17	St. Nicholas Chapel	Willisau	L2	331
L-18	St. Peter and Paul Church	Willisau	L2	334
L-19	Holy Blood Chapel	Willisau	L2	335
L-20	Reformed Church	Willisau	L2	336
L-21	St. John Church	Ufhusen	L2	339
L-22	Reformed Church	Huttwil	L2	341
L-23	Brother Klaus Church	Huttwil	L2	342
L-24	Reformed Church	Dürrenroth	L3	349
L-25	Reformed Bartholomew Chapel	Burgdorf	L3	354
L-26	Reformed Castle Chapel	Burgdorf	L3	359
L-27	Reformed City Church	Burgdorf	L3	360
L-28	Assumption of Mary Church	Burgdorf	L3	361
L-29	Reformed Church	Krauchthal	L4	368
L-30	Reformed Nydegg Church	Bern	L4	378
L-31	St. Peter and Paul Cathedral	Bern	L4	381
L-32	Crypt Church	Bern	L4	382
L-33	Reformed French Church	Bern	L4	383
L-34	Reformed St. Vincent Cathedral	Bern	L4	386
L-35	Reformed Church	Wabern	L5	399
L-36	St. Michael Church	Wabern	L5	400
L-37	Ecumenical Church	Kehrsatz	L5	402

Appendix 2: Biography of Saints

Appendix 2 lists, in alphabetical order, all the names of saints represented along the Way of St. James in Central Switzerland, with references to the church numbers.

A short biography of these saints, in alphabetical order, is provided on the next pages. Their biography should be read in the context of the background of saints and Roman catacomb relics, as described in the chapter Religious Context of the General Introduction to the Swiss Camino in Volume I.

Saints from Einsiedeln to Fribourg (both routes)

Name	Church nr.
10'000 Martyrs	97, L-17
St. Agatha	58
St. Andrew	L-37
St. Anne	45, 67, 70, 71, 80, 90, 142
St. Anthony of Padua	46, 52, 56, 83, 84, 106, L-6
St. Anthony the Hermit	93, 140
St. Apollonia	43, 58, 103, 138
St. Bartholomew	147, L-25
St. Beatus	82, 107, 119, 148
St. Borromeo	83, 84, 99
Brother Klaus	*See St. Nicholas of Flüe*
Brother Ulrich	96
St. Canisius	155, 157
St. Catherine	92, L-7
St. Celestine	L-6
St. Christopher	111, 121, 126, 127, L-4
St. Clare	84
St. Conrad	78
St. Erasmus	L-15
St. Fidelis	83
Four Evangelists	108, 110, L-3, L-27, L-30
Fourteen Holy Helpers	65, 76
St. Francis Borgia	55
St. Francis de Sales	55, 153
St. Francis of Assisi	55
St. Francis of Paola	55
St. Francis Xaver	55, L-5
St. Fridolin	46
St. Gall	90, 107, L-15
St. Helena	L-21
St. Henry	72, 82
Holy Family	40, 79, 83, 91, 108, 120, L-28

Name	Church nr.
St. Idda	L-11
St. Ignatius	156
St. James the Greater	69, 90, 103, 133, 143, 146, L-6, L-16
St. Joachim	45, 90
St. John the Baptist	49, 55, 107, 142, L-21, L-26
St. John the Evangelist	55, L-6
St. Joseph	40, 46, 55, 106, 142
St. Jost	L-8
St. Jucundus	L-10
St. Lawrence	95, 104, 121, L-24
St. Leodegar	L-1
St. Leonard	63, L-2
(Mary-) Lourdes	60, 74, 142
St. Margaret	127
St. Martin	50, 77, 130, 144, L-10
St. Mary	45, 47, 49, 55, 58, 75, 77, 79, 81, 82, 83, 88, 89, 90, 97, 110, 115, 145, 151, 152, L-2, L-6, L-7, L-12, L-13, L-27, L-28
St. Mary Magdalene	49, 94, 97, 127, 132, 133, 137, 154, L-30
St. Matthew	123, L-3
St. Maurice	102, 126, 149, L-1, L-7, L-29
St. Maximilian Kolbe	152
St. Meinrad	45
St. Michael	48, 105, 120, 125, 134, 155, L-34, L-36
Mirjam	L-9
St. Nazarius	50
St. Nepomuk	79
St. Nicholas of Flüe	78, 83, 84, 87, 92, 93, 97, 98, 99, 100, 101, 102, 106, 108, 115, 124, L-5, L-12, L-23, L-28
St. Nicholas (of Myra)	95, 127, 148, 150, L-17
St. Odile	58
Our Lady	*See St. Mary*
St. Paul	87, 111, 131, L-18, L-31, L-33
St. Peter	87, 111, 114, 131, 142, L-4, L-18, L-31, L-33
St. Peter of Verona	51
St. Polycarp	50
St. Prosper	84
St. Remy	87
St. Sebastian	76, 129, 141
St. Silvanus	L-5
Sorrowful Mother of God	53, 62, 78, 146
St. Stephen	42
St. Theodore	102
St. Thérèse of Lisieux	69
Twelve Apostles	97, 121, L-18
St. Victor	149
St. Vincent	L-34
St. Wendolyn	59, 92, 106

Biography of Saints

10'000 Martyrs

Two legends of 10'000 Martyrs exist. One is of allegedly 10'000 soldiers crucified on Mount Ararat, who had refused to renounce Christianity after they were miraculously converted by the voice of an angel. The other legend refers to the large number of Christians, who were killed at the beginning of the persecution of Christians under Roman Emperor Diocletian (around 303).

St. Agatha

St. Agatha (of Sicily) died for her Christian faith around 251. According to legend, she refused to give up her virginity to suitors. One suitor had her arrested out of revenge. She was forced in a brothel, tortured, and her breasts were cut-off. St. Peter visited her in prison and healed her wounds, before she died around the age of 20. She became the patroness Saint of women with breast cancer and victims of sexual abuse.

St. Andrew

St. Andrew was one of the Twelve Apostles and the brother of St. Peter. As his brother, St. Andrew was a fisherman before becoming a follower of Jesus. According to legend, he traveled to Eastern European countries such as Turkey, Ukraine, and Russia to preach and convert pagans to Christianity. He was said to have established the Bishopric of Byzantium (Constantinople or Istanbul) and to have been martyred in Greece. From the middle ages he was said to have been crucified (tied with ropes) to an X-shaped cross, now known as the St. Andrew's Cross. St. Andrew became the patron Saint of many countries and cities, of which several have the X-shaped cross in their flag (e.g. Scotland).

St. Anne

St. Anne was married to St. Joachim and was the mother of Mary and the grandmother of Jesus. She died in 12 AD. She became the patroness Saint of grandmothers and miners. Her womb was considered the source from which silver (representing Mary) was mined, while gold (representing Jesus) was mined from Mary's womb.

St. Anthony of Padua

St. Anthony of Padua was a Portuguese friar (from Lisbon) in the Franciscan Order, well known for his teaching and preaching. He died from an illness in Padua, Italy in 1231. He became the patron Saint of lost souls, lost people, and lost things. A novice stole his psalm book, which was returned to him after he prayed for it to be found.

St. Anthony the Hermit

St. Anthony the Hermit was an Egyptian monk, who was considered to be the first abbot and founder of ascetic monasteries in the 4th century. He was believed to have been the first monk to live an ascetic life as a hermit (in the Egyptian desert). It was said that St. Benedict was influenced by him, when he established the first Benedictine monasteries in the 6th century. St. Anthony the Hermit became the patron Saint of hermits and monks, as well as of the poor and farmers and their animals.

St. Apollonia
St. Apollonia was a martyr who lived in Alexandria, Egypt. During an uprising against Christians she was captured and tortured; all her teeth were pulled. She refused to renounce her Christian faith and upon the threat of getting burned alive, she went into the fire voluntarily and burned to death (249). She became the patroness Saint of dentists and was invoked against tooth problems.

St. Bartholomew
St. Bartholomew was one of the Twelve Apostles. According to legend he went on missions to India and Armenia. He supposedly died for his faith by being skinned alive and beheaded. He became the patron Saint of butchers and leatherworkers.

St. Beatus
According to legend, St. Beatus of Lungern was an Irish monk ordained in Rome by St. Peter the Apostle to become the first missionary to Switzerland in the 1st century. This gave him the name of the (first) Apostle of Switzerland. According to legend, St. Beatus first stayed in, what is now, Canton Aarau where he converted many pagans to Christianity, after which he moved south, where he lived as a hermit in a cave high above lake Thun. Allegedly he died there at the age of 100 in the year 112. According to myth, he slayed a dragon that lived in the caves. This is more likely symbolism for his efforts to convert 1st century Swiss pagans to Christianity.

It is probable that a hermit Beatus indeed lived in the caves in the 6th or 9th century. The legend around this Beatus was created by the Augustinian monastery of Interlaken, who owned the chapel at the cave. In 1511 they asked a Franciscan friar from Basel to rewrite the legend of St. Beatus of Lungern. This monk applied the legend of the 3rd century St. Beatus of Vendome (France) to Switzerland.

St. Borromeo
St. Charles Borromeo came from a noble Italian family north of Milan (his uncle was Pope Pius IV) and was Bishop of Milan in 1564-84. He was one of the leaders of the Roman-Catholic resistance against the Reformation and initiated significant reforms in the Catholic Church. He was known for the 19th Ecumenical Council of Trent (in northern Italy) in 1562-63, which resulted in important Counter-Reformation activities and reforms of Catholic doctrines. The Pope appointed him apostle to Switzerland, for which he made several trips to the Catholic Cantons (Unterwalden, Schwyz, Luzern) to help them strengthen their Counter-Reformation activities and implement the required reforms. During famine and the plague in Milan he organized care and support for the local population and tried to feed more than 50'000 people, after the Authorities had fled the city in 1576. He became the patron Saint against illnesses and the plague. He died in 1584 and was canonized in 1610.

Brother Klaus
See St. Nicholas of Flüe.

Brother Ulrich
Brother Ulrich was a priest from Bavaria, Germany, who joined Brother Klaus in his hermitage in 1469. He settled at a large boulder and cave on the eastern side of the

Ranft gorge, whereas Brother Klaus was on the western side. He died in 1491 and was buried at the parish church in Kerns.

St. Canisius
St. Peter Canisius was a Dutch Jesuit priest, who countered the Reformation and promoted the establishment of catholic boys' schools. He spent much of his life in Germany and Switzerland (Fribourg). He led the Collegium St. Michael in Fribourg from 1582 until his death in 1597. He was canonized in 1925.

St. Catherine
St. Catherine (of Alexandria, Egypt) was imprisoned and tortured, but refused to give up her belief, for which she was beheaded in 305. She became the patroness Saint of the condemned. St. Catherine was one for the Fourteen Holy Helpers and also the patroness Saint of students and educators (she devoted herself to study and was a strong debater).

St. Celestine
St. Celestine I was a Roman Pope in the years 422 to 432. Not much is known of his person, other than that he spent his 10-year papacy fighting ideologies that were not reconcilable with the Church. He sent missionaries to England, Scotland, Ireland, and Gaul (France) to convert pagans and strengthen Christianity in these regions.

St. Christopher
St. Christopher probably lived in the 3rd century. Nothing is known of his life or death, and some historians doubt he really existed. His broad popularity as a Saint originated from legends created in the 6th century. By the 9th century his legends spread through Europe and he became a popular Saint of travelers and children. This despite the fact that he was neither recognized by the Church, nor canonized as a Saint. He was one of the Fourteen Holy Helpers. The name Christopher was derived from 'Christ-bearer', linked to the following legend.

Christopher was a tall and strong man, born in Arabia. He wanted to serve the most fearless King. After he saw that the King was afraid of the devil, he went to search for the devil. He met the head of a bandit gang, who called himself the devil. He started serving him, but soon found out that this bandit was afraid of Christ. Christopher continued to look for Christ, who supposedly was the most fearless person. A hermit advised him to serve Christ by carrying people across a dangerous river, where many had died in the currents. After doing so for a while, a young boy asked him to be carried across. While Christopher was crossing the river, the water level rose and the boy's weight increased to become almost impossible to carry. He asked the boy why he was so heavy. The child responded that he was Christ and carried the weight of the world. Christopher converted to Catholicism and subsequently converted many pagans. He was beheaded upon his refusal to make offerings to pagan Gods.

St. Clare
St. Clare (of Assisi) was one of the first followers of St. Francis of Assisi and established the Order of Saint Clare, or Poor Clares, as the nunnery counterpart of the male Franciscan Order. She wrote a rule book, focusing on poverty, austerity, physical labor, and prayer. She became the patroness Saint of embroiderers and goldsmiths, and was

invoked against eye disease. In 1958 she also became the patroness Saint of television, because on the wall of her room she saw a projection of services, which she could not attend because of illness. St. Clare died in 1253 and was canonized in 1255.

St. Conrad

St. Conrad was a Bishop of Konstanz in 934-975. He shared his wealth with the Church and the poor, and built many churches in his Bishopric. He died in 975 and was canonized in 1123.

St. Erasmus

St. Erasmus (of Formia), also called Saint Elmo, lived in 3rd century Italy and was a Bishop of Formia, before he became a wandering preacher and converted many pagans to Christianity. According to legends, he was captured and tortured multiple times by the Romans for his Christian faith, but each time he miraculously survived. He continued preaching even when lightning struck beside him. He became the patron Saint of sailors, who frequently were in danger from electrical discharges from the masts of their sailing ship during thunderstorms (also called St. Elmo's Fire). Saint Erasmus died around 303, when his stomach was cut open and his intestines were wound up on a winch. He became the patron Saint against abdominal pain and was one of the Fourteen Holy Helpers.

St. Fidelis

St. Fidelis (of Sigmaringen) was a German Capuchin friar who strongly supported the Counter-Reformation in Switzerland and Austria. He was murdered by protestant soldiers in eastern Switzerland in 1622, after he refused to denounce Catholicism. He was canonized in 1746.

Four Evangelists

The Four Evangelists were Matthew, Mark, Luke and John, accredited with writing the four Gospel accounts of the New Testament. Matthew (a former tax collector) and John (a former fisherman) were two of the Twelve Apostles, whereas Mark was a travel companion and interpreter of St. Peter, and Luke was a former physician. Matthew was often symbolized as a winged man, Mark as a winged lion, Luke as a winged ox, and John as an eagle. The four Gospels, probably written in 66-110, gave an account of the life of Jesus.

Fourteen Holy Helpers

The Fourteen Holy Helpers were a group of Saints who were believed to have helped overcome diseases, particularly the Black Plague. This group was formed in the 14th century (around 1347, at the time the plague spread through Europe, after it had arrived in Italy on a merchant ship from Asia). The fourteen Saints were: Agatha, Barbara, Blaise, Catherine of Alexandria, Christopher, Denis, Erasmus, Eustace, George, Giles, Margaret of Antioch, Pantaleon, Syriac, and Vitus.

Each of these Saints was invoked against specific physical diseases and their symptoms. Collectively they were assigned the holy power to overcome even the worst of medieval diseases, the Bubonic Plague. The Plague, transmitted by rats because of the poor hygienic circumstances in which most of the medieval population lived, killed between

40 to 60 percent of the European population in the 14th century, and reoccurred regularly in later centuries.

St. Francis Borgia

Francis Borgia was born in a Spanish noble family where many high-level clergy (Pope, Bishops) came from. He served at the court of the Holy Roman Emperor Charles V and composed many pieces of religious music. After his wife died, he renounced his noble title and joined the Jesuit Order in 1551. He founded several catholic boys' schools in Spain and quickly rose in the ranks of the Jesuit Order. He died in 1572 and was canonized in 1670.

St. Francis de Sales

St. Francis de Sales (pronounce in French) was a Bishop of Geneva in 1602-22, and an important contributor to the Counter-Reformation. Because Geneva was under the control of Calvinists, he resided in Annecy, France (about 45 km south of Geneva). He became the patron Saint of authors (he used books to convert Protestants to Catholicism) and the deaf (he developed a sign language to convert a deaf man).

St. Francis of Assisi

St. Francis of Assisi was an Italian friar, who lived in 1182-1226. He became one of the most well-known religious figures and was canonized in 1228. He became the patron Saint of animals; he prayed to birds and persuaded a wolf not to attack a village. He was the first one to arrange a live nativity (birth) scene (nowadays known as the Christmas manger) in 1223. St. Francis established the Franciscan Order in 1209.

St. Francis of Paola

St. Francis of Paola (Calabria, southern Italy) was a Franciscan friar. He lived as a hermit in a cave in southern Italy for many years. After several other hermits had joined him, they built a chapel dedicated to St. Francis of Assisi, and started a new Order called the Hermits of Saint Francis of Assisi (1436). Because of their ascetic life as hermits, the Order was later renamed to the Order of Minims. He died in 1507 and was canonized in 1519. He became the patron Saint of mariners and sailors. According to legend, he sailed across the sea by tying his cloak to his staff and using it as a sail.

St. Francis Xaver

St. Francis Xaver was co-founder of the Jesuit Order and Jesuit missionary to India and Japan. He established the foundations of the Catholic Church in Japan. He died on a small island off the coast of China, where he was preparing for missions into China in 1552. He was canonized in 1622 and became the patron Saint of missionaries.

St. Fridolin

St. Fridolin (of Säckingen) was an Irish missionary, who made many journeys through France, Germany, and Switzerland (Canton Glarus has an image of this Saint, with walking stick, in their flag). He died in 540 and became the patron Saint of good weather.

St. Gall

St. Gall (or Gallus) was an Irish missionary who followed St. Columbanus to northern Switzerland around the year 610. St. Columbanus continued his travels to Italy, whereas St. Gall remained in Switzerland. Together with several other monks he lived in the isolated forests south of Lake Constance, where they built a small chapel near a waterfall around 612. St. Gall died in Arbon around 645, after which his remains were brought to his former cell in the forest. The City of St. Gallen was named after him and the St. Gallen Abbey Cathedral was built on the site of his cell. The sarcophagus in the cathedral still contains parts of the skull of the Saint. He became the patron Saint of birds. He spoke with animals who helped him survive as a hermit. St. Gall was often depicted with a small bear. According to legend, St. Gall talked a bear into bringing him firewood and accompanying him during his years of hermitage in the dense forests. St. Gall became one of the patron Saints of Switzerland.

St. Helena

St. Helena was the mother of Roman Emperor Constantine the Great and Empress of the Roman Empire. Her husband divorced her for political reasons. In 326-328 she made a pilgrimage to the Holy Land in search of relics of early Christianity. She had several churches constructed and allegedly identified the True Cross. According to legend, she found three crosses and nails under a pagan temple. She had a dying woman touch all three crosses. Her healing upon touching the third cross identified the True Cross. Her son, Emperor Constantine the Great, had the Church of the Holy Sepulcher built on the site of her discovery. She died around the year 330 and became the patroness Saint of divorced women and archaeologists. The Island of St. Helena and several mountains were named after her (e.g. Mount St. Helens, famous for its eruption in 1980).

St. Henry

St. Henry II was a devout Catholic born in the German Otto dynasty. He succeeded his family members by becoming King of Germany (1002), King of Italy (1004), and Roman Emperor (1024). During his reign he maintained close relationships with the Church and Popes. He expanded Catholicism in his growing empire, built several churches, and made many donations to the Church. He died from an illness in 1024 and was canonized in 1147. Because of his religion, he and his wife lived in chastity and left no children. He became the patron Saint of the childless.

Holy Family

The Holy Family consisted of Joseph, Mary, and Jesus.

St. Idda

Saint Idda (also named Ida of Toggenburg) lived in a cell on the site of the present church in Au, before becoming a nun at the Abbey of Fischingen. She became the patroness Saint of pregnancy and was invoked against bodily pains and lost cattle. She died around 1200 and was canonized in 1724.

According to legend, a raven stole her wedding ring. A young man found the ring in the nest and put it on his finger. Under suspicion of adultery her husband (Lord of Toggenburg) cast her out, after which she lived as a hermit in a cave at the foot of the Hörnli mountain (Hörnli translates as horn) close to the Abbey of Fischingen. A deer with 12 lights in its antlers showed her the way through the dark forest when she was going to morning prayers every day. St. Idda was always depicted with a deer or with antlers.

St. Ignatius

St. Ignatius of Loyola was a Spanish catholic priest, who co-founded the Jesuit Order in 1539. He was canonized in 1622 and became the patron Saint of soldiers, because of his years of service in the Spanish army.

St. James the Greater

St. James (the Greater or the Elder) was one of the Twelve Apostles. He was called the Greater (or Elder) to distinguish from James the Lesser, who was also one of the Twelve Apostles and the first Bishop of Jerusalem. St. James the Greater was either taller or older than the other James. King Herod had James (the Greater) beheaded by the sword in Jerusalem in the year 44; he was considered the first apostle who died for his faith in Christ. He became the patron Saint of Spain and pilgrims.

The legend that the remains of St. James were kept in Spain (Santiago de Compostela) arose around 900. According to this legend, St. James was a missionary in Iberia and after his execution in Jerusalem, his remains were miraculously shipped from Jerusalem to Santiago de Compostela. His remains were allegedly discovered in Spain in the 9th century (although he had died in the 1st century). In the 9th century the Spanish hermit Pelagius was said to have had a revelation of the location of the tomb of St. James. The then bishop of the region identified the tomb, the Spanish King Alfonso II had a church built for the relics in Santiago de Compostela, and Pope Leo XIII officially recognized this legend in 1884. Several versions of the legend were told: some said that St. James was an apostle in Spain before going back to Jerusalem (this version surfaced in the 9th century); others said he was never in Spain. It is, however, likely that his remains were spread over several locations in Europe, amongst others Santiago de Compostela.

St. Joachim

St. Joachim was the husband of St. Anne and father of Mary. He came from Nazareth and married St. Anne from Bethlehem. He was usually depicted as a wealthy man. According to legend, he and Anne had difficulties conceiving a child. As penance he spent 40 days fasting in the desert, where angels appeared to promise a child. Mary was born around the year 18 BC. St. Joachim died in the year 15 AD in Jerusalem.

St. John the Baptist

St. John the Baptist was considered a prophet, as he announced the coming of Jesus. He was born around the same time as Jesus: a pregnant Mary visited his pregnant mother Elisabeth, known from the scene of the Mary Visitation. St. John baptized Jesus when He was around 30 years of age. King Herod had St. John beheaded around 28-36, after St. John had criticized the King for divorcing his wife and taking the wife of his brother.

St. John the Evangelist

St. John the Evangelist was one of the Twelve Apostles, also called John the Apostle. He was the younger brother of St. James the Greater. He died of old age around the year 100 and was the only Apostle who was not martyred.

St. Joseph

St. Joseph was married to Mary and was Jesus' foster father. He became the patron Saint of fathers and carpenters (he raised Jesus and was a carpenter).

St. Jost

St. Jost (also called Judoc or Joyce) was born in a noble family in Breton (France) in the 7th century. Around 636 he renounced the family fortune and went on a pilgrimage to Rome, became a priest, established a monastery, and lived as a hermit in northern France until he died in 668. Though he was never canonized, he was considered a Saint. In the middle ages he was an important Saint for pilgrims, together with St. James.

St. Jucundus

St. Jucundus was a Bishop of Aosta, northern Italy, who died while protecting his church against non-believers of the Christian faith in 407.

St. Lawrence

St. Lawrence was born in Spain, but moved to Italy where he became a deacon (a member of clergy responsible for charity) for the Pope in Rome. In 258 Emperor Valerian ordered all Christian Church officials in Rome to be executed, after which Lawrence was imprisoned. As a deacon Lawrence had been responsible for safekeeping the treasures of the church and giving to the poor. Thus, the Roman Authorities asked him to hand over the treasures. According to legend, instead of presenting the treasures, he presented the poor and ill people as the real treasures of the Church. He was executed by being roasted on a metal grating above hot coal. He became the patron Saint of cooks and firefighters.

St. Leodegar

St. Leodegar (of Poitiers), or Leger, was a Bishop of Auton, France, in the 7th century. Around 675 he was captured by a rival King and his Bishops, who drilled out his eyes, scorched his sockets, and cut out his tongue. He was let go, but four years later captured again, and beheaded in 679. He became the patron Saint against blindness and eye problems.

St. Leonard

St. Leonard (of Noblac) was a French nobleman, who was converted to Christianity by St. Remy, Bishop of Reims, together with King Clovis I. Leonard asked the King the right to free prisoners. He became a hermit and founded the Abbey of Noblac, where he died in 559. He became the patron Saint of prisoners. He enabled the release of prisoners and prisoners who prayed to him had their chains miraculously broken.

(Mary-) Lourdes

Mary-Lourdes, or Our Lady of Lourdes, is a title of the Virgin Mary at the location of Lourdes. Lourdes (France) is the site where the Virgin Mary was reported to have appeared 18 times in 1858. The Virgin Mary appeared to a local 14-year-old girl called Bernadette Soubirous, who was canonized in 1933 (Saint Bernadette of Lourdes). The spring water of the Lourdes cave is said to have healing powers and the Catholic Church has officially recognized several dozens of miraculous healings. Every year millions of pilgrims visit the Lourdes cave and drink the spring water.

St. Margaret
St. Margaret (also known as Margaret of Antioch or Margaret the Virgin) was one of the Fourteen Holy Helpers. In 304 she was tortured to death at a young age, after she refused to give up her virginity and Christianity to marry a Roman Governor of Antioch, Turkey. She became the patroness Saint of pregnant women and child birth.

St. Martin
St. Martin (of Tours) was a cavalry soldier in the Roman army, for which he traveled through France and Germany. According to legend, during his army presence in France he cut his army cape in two and gave one half to a barely dressed beggar outside the gates of Amiens (150 km north of Paris) on a cold winter day. Subsequently he dreamt that Jesus wore the half-cape he had given to the beggar. This vision made him convert to Christianity, renounce the fighting, and leave the army. After becoming a monk, traveling, and living as a hermit for a while, he had to be persuaded to become the Bishop of Tours (275 km southwest of Paris) in 371. He established a monastery in Tours (372), but kept traveling through France, converting pagans and freeing prisoners. He died in Tours in 397.

The Abbey of Marmoutier became an important pilgrimage destination during the early middle ages, because of the shrine of St. Martin. According to legend, the half-cape he had kept was a precious relic of this abbey. The location in the abbey where this half-cape was kept was called the Chapelle, or sanctuary for the little cape. The word chapel was derived from the medieval Latin word for little cape, Capella, translated into medieval French as Chapelle. This became Chapel in English and Kapelle in German.

St. Mary
St. Mary was the mother of Jesus and known under many different names, such as Virgin Mary, Our Lady, Mother of God, Madonna, and Queen of Heaven. She was the daughter of St. Joachim and St. Anne, and was born in Nazareth around 18 BC. According to tradition, Jesus was conceived through the Holy Spirit, while she remained a virgin. She was married to Joseph. Besides the adoration of Jesus, the adoration of Mary became the most widespread in Christianity.

St. Mary Magdalene
St. Mary Magdalene was one of the main and closest followers of Jesus in the 1st century. She came from a wealthy family and helped finance the travels of Jesus, while she traveled with him across Galilea. Jesus cured her of a physical disorder (called the cleansing of 'seven demons'). She was present at Jesus' crucifixion and burial, and was the first person who saw Jesus after his resurrection. She was one of the main, and first female, apostles after Jesus' death. She became the patroness Saint of converts and women. There is no reliable history of when, how, and where she died.

The important role attributed to her in the 1st century was quite special, given the male-dominated patriarchal society of that time. However, her image was changed during the middle ages (particularly around the Reformation), when she was (untruly) branded to have been a repentant sinner as a prostitute. This image change was created by the male-dominated celibate monks, who considered women to be sinners for tempting men. She became the patroness Saint of prostitutes.

St. Matthew
St. Matthew was one of the Twelve Apostles, one of the Four Evangelists, and witnessed the resurrection of Jesus. He was a tax collector for the Roman Empire in Galilee in the 1st century and became the patron Saint of bankers.

St. Maurice
St. Maurice was an Egyptian commander of the Theban Legion of the Roman Empire in the 3rd century. According to legend, the Theban Legion was sent to Switzerland to clear the Great St. Bernhard Pass from rebelling Swiss Christians. St. Maurice and his soldiers were ordered to slay fellow Christians, but they refused. As punishment Roman Emperor Maximinus had Maurice and his soldiers executed. The Abbey of St. Maurice in Canton Valais was dedicated to the martyrs of the Theban Legion (and still keeps their relics), as it was believed that the executions took place at that location. The Swiss alpine ski resort St. Moritz was named after him. He became the patron Saint of soldiers.

Other soldiers from the Theban Legion, who became martyrs together with St. Maurice, were St. Victor, St. Felix and Regula, and St. Innocence.

St. Maximilian Kolbe
St. Maximilian Kolbe was a Polish Franciscan friar and founder of a monastery near Warsaw (Poland). In 1930-36 he went on missions to Asia and founded monasteries in Japan, near Nagasaki, and India. In 1941 the Nazis closed his Polish monastery and imprisoned him in concentration camp Auschwitz. The Nazis executed him after he had volunteered to take the place of another man, who was to be executed. St. Kolbe was canonized in 1982.

St. Meinrad
St. Meinrad came from Swabia (southern Germany) and was educated as a monk at the Benedictine Monastery of Reichenau, situated on an island in Lake Constance. He spent some time in a subsidiary abbey east of the Obersee (Benken), before he retreated as a hermit at the Etzel Pass around 828. He brought a statue of the Virgin Mary from Benken to his cell at the pass. Because of the many pilgrims who visited him for advice, he moved his retreat to the remote forests seven kilometers to the south (present location of the Abbey of Einsiedeln) in 835. Although the location was isolated and difficult to reach, he was still frequently visited by pilgrims looking for his advice. There he spent 26 years as a hermit leading an ascetic life, until he was killed by two robbers in the year 861. According to legend, Meinrad had two black ravens who followed his two killers all the way to Zurich. In Zurich the ravens pointed to the location were the killers were hiding, which led to their capture and punishment. To this day two ravens are in the coat-of-arms of the City of Einsiedeln. The Abbey of Einsiedeln was built on the site of his cell. He became the patron Saint of hospitality, based on his hospitality to strangers in the remoteness of the dark forest.

St. Michael
St. Michael was not a saint, though he was called that; he was never canonized. It is unlikely that he existed as a living person. St. Michael was one of the three archangels (together with Gabriel and Raphael); an archangel was the highest-ranking angel, always depicted with wings. He became the patron Saint of soldiers: in The Bible he

was the leader of God's army that protected the Church and defeated Satan (often depicted as a dragon or serpent). For this reason, he was often chosen as the patron Saint of castle churches and chapels.

According to Roman-Catholic scriptures, St. Michael is the angel who is present at the hour of death and accompanies the soul to heaven where he weighs the good vs. bad deeds of the soul in their last judgement (deciding whether the soul goes to heaven or hell). For this reason, he was often chosen as the patron Saint of funeral and cemetery chapels.

Mirjam
Mirjam is Hebrew for Mary and relates to several independent and caring women mentioned in The Bible.

St. Nazarius
St. Nazarius had to flee Rome to escape the persecution of Christians by Roman Emperor Nero. He traveled in Western Europe and preached in Trier, the Alps, and Geneva, converting pagans to Christianity. After returning to Milan he was captured and beheaded for refusing to denounce his faith (around 395).

St. Nepomuk
St. John of Nepomuk was a priest in 14th century Bohemia (nowadays Czech Republic) and confessional of the Queen of Bohemia. In 1393 he was drowned in the Vltava River by the King of Bohemia, when Nepomuk refused to disclose the confessions of the Queen. He became the first martyr of the Confessional Seal and the patron Saint of defamation and bridges, and was invoked against flooding and drowning. He was canonized in 1729.

St. Nicholas of Flüe
St. Nicholas of Flüe (also called Brother Klaus, *Bruder Klaus*, or *Niklaus von Flüe*) was born in 1417 and served in the Swiss Confederate Army of Unterwalden until the age of 37. He subsequently served as a judge and counselor for the Canton. After a vision he retreated from his wife Dorothee and 10 children, and became a hermit in a gorge close to their house. He lived an ascetic life, allegedly living of Eucharist for 20 years. He was sought after for his wisdom and counsel, by pilgrims and Authorities. Many pilgrims visited him in his cell to ask for advice. In 1481 he had a decisive consulting role that prevented a civil war, which would likely have caused a split of the Swiss Confederation. He died in 1487 and was canonized in 1947. He became the patron Saint of Switzerland and the Swiss Guard at the Vatican. He is Switzerland's most well-known medieval hermit, mystic, and counselor.

St. Nicholas (of Myra)
St. Nicholas (of Myra) was a Bishop of Myra (Turkey) in the Roman Empire. He died in 342. Though not much is known of his historical person, there are many legends about him. The most famous legends are: secret gift-giving, such as giving three purses of money as dowry for three neighboring virgin girls (so that they could get married), or secretly leaving coins in shoes; staving off a storm and waves that threatened to sink the ship he was on; and reviving three children that had been killed by a butcher, their

flesh intended to be sold as ham during a time of famine. These legends made him the medieval patron Saint of children, sailors, and fishermen.

The legend of the secret gift-giving has survived nearly 1'700 years, though nowadays it is called Santa Claus (a popularization of the name Saint Nicholas). Santa Claus has its origins in Dutch traditions, where on 5th/6th December, the commemorative day of St. Nicholas' death, Sinterklaas (or Sint Nikolaas; Dutch derived from Saint Nicholas) would leave small presents in the shoes of children. When the Dutch established New Amsterdam (nowadays named New York) in 1625, they continued this tradition. Under the American commercialization of Sint Nikolaas in the 19th century, he was renamed Santa Claus and the timing of the gift-giving shifted to 24th/25th of December.

St. Odile

St. Odile of Alsace was born in a noble family in the Alsace (eastern France). Because she was a girl and born blind, her parents gave her away to peasants. According to legend, she was taken to a monastery when she was twelve. When Bishop St. Erhard of Regensburg baptized her, she was miraculously healed from her blindness. She founded two convents in southwestern Germany and died around 720. She became the patroness Saint of the blind.

Our Lady

Our Lady, see St. Mary. In German *Unser Liebe Frau*, in French *Notre Dame.*

St. Paul

St. Paul was also known as St. Paul the Apostle, though he was not one of the Twelve Apostles. He lived in the first century (5-65). According to legend, he was persecuting followers of Jesus, but was converted to Christianity when a resurrected Jesus appeared to him while he was on the road to Damascus. He started preaching the word of God and traveled extensively through the Roman Empire, where he established churches. According to legend he was decapitated in Rome by order of Emperor Nero. He became the patron Saint of missionaries and authors.

St. Peter

St. Peter (originally named Simon) was one of the Twelve Apostles and the brother of St. Andrew. He was a fisherman before becoming a follower of Jesus. He was the first Pope of Rome and was crucified by Emperor Nero around the year 66. He became the patron Saint of fishermen and clergy. The St. Peter's Basilica in the Vatican was built on the site of the grave of St. Peter. This basilica became one of the most well-known churches of Christianity, after which many other churches chose St. Peter as their patron Saint.

St. Peter of Verona

St. Peter of Verona was a Dominican friar who preached in northern Italy in the first half of the 13th century. He was a strong advocate against heresy and was made Inquisitor in 1234. He was responsible for many heresy trails in northern Italy, as a result of which his enemies tried to kill him. He was killed by assassins in 1252.

St. Polycarp
St. Polycarp was a Bishop of Smyrna (Izmir, Turkey), who was killed by the Romans for his Christian faith around 156. He was to be burned alive, but when the flames did not harm him, he was killed with a dagger.

St. Prosper
St. Prosper of Aquitaine (southwestern France) was a writer who spread the knowledge of St. Augustine's teachings, focusing on grace and predestination (free will) in the period 390-455. He was a secretary of Pope Leo the Great and died around 463.

St. Remy
St. Remy (also called Remigius) was a Bishop of Reims (France) and baptized King Clovis I, resulting in the conversion to Christianity of the entire Frankish population of the 6th century. St. Remy died in 533 and became the patron Saint of meditation, providing the worshipper with a clear mind and openness of their thoughts toward God.

St. Sebastian
St. Sebastian was an Italian captain of the praetorian guards of the Emperor's army in Rome in the 3rd century. He had to hide his Christianity; it was discovered after he had converted others to Christianity. Emperor Diocletian had him tied to a stake and shot dead with many arrows. But he miraculously survived and was nursed back to health. He sought out the Emperor in Rome and publicly accused him of brutalities against Christians. The Emperor had him beaten to death with a spiked club and his remains thrown in the sewer in 288. A woman secretly saved his remains and buried him at a cemetery in Rome. He became the patron Saint of archers, soldiers, and athletes, because of his physical fitness, endurance, and recovery from injuries. He was one of the Fourteen Holy Helpers and medieval patron Saint against the Bubonic Plague.

St. Silvanus
St. Silvanus, more often called Silas, preached together with Saints Peter and Paul, the chief Apostles, in the 1st century. He became the first Bishop of Corinth (Greece).

Sorrowful Mother of God
The Sorrowful Mother of God – also Our Lady of Sorrows, the Suffering Mother of God, Our Lady of the Seven Sorrows – refers to the Virgin Mary and her suffering during her life. Seven events relating to Jesus caused intense suffering to Mary:

(1) when Jesus was presented as a baby to a temple in Jerusalem, Simeon prophesied that Mary would suffer, as her son's life would be one of suffering;
(2) when King Herod ordered all boys below two years killed, she, Joseph, and baby Jesus had to flee and undertake a long journey to Egypt;
(3) when Jesus was 12 years old He went missing for three days, but they found him in a temple in Jerusalem debating with Jewish teachers;
(4) when witnessing Jesus carrying his Cross on his way to Calvary (Golgotha);
(5) when seeing Jesus' Crucifixion;
(6) when Jesus' lifeless body was taken from the Cross and laid in her lap (this is what a Pietà depicts); and
(7) when Jesus' lifeless body was laid in the tomb.

These Seven Sorrows were often depicted as seven swords piercing the heart of Mary.

St. Stephen

St. Stephen was a deacon (a member of clergy responsible for charity) in the early Church in Jerusalem. He was considered the first martyr of Christianity. In the year 34 he was stoned to death after he denounced the Jewish Authorities, who accused him of blasphemy. He became the patron Saint of masons.

St. Theodore

St. Theodore (of Sion), also named Theodul of Sitten, was a Bishop of Martigny (Canton Valais, southern Switzerland) at the end of the 4th century. He built the first chapel for the remains of St. Maurice of the Theban Legion around 380-400. According to legend, upon his visit to Rome the Pope gave him a church bell. Theodore had the devil carry this bell over a mountain pass (now called the Theodul Pass) to bring the bell back to Sion. Small pieces of this bell were smelted together with new bells, which gave them the ability to stave off bad weather when they were rung. He became the patron Saint of bells and was invoked against bad weather. He died around 400.

St. Thérèse of Lisieux

St. Thérèse of Lisieux was a nun (from the age of 15) in the Carmelite Convent of Lisieux, France. She died in 1897 (age 24), after many years of suffering from tuberculosis, and was canonized in 1925. After her death she became well-known for her spiritual writings and memoires, offering simple and practical religious viewpoints from a suffering young girl. This gave her the nickname 'The little Flower (of Jesus)'. She became the patroness Saint of florists and gardeners.

Twelve Apostles

The Twelve Apostles were 12 men chosen by Jesus to be sent out on apostolic missions. Initially they were sent out in pairs. These 12 men were: St. Peter (Simon) and his brother St. Andrew, St. James the Greater and his brother St. John the Evangelist, St. Bartholomew, St. James the Lesser, St. Judas, St. Matthew, St. Philip, St. Simon the Zealot, St. Thaddaeus, and St. Thomas.

St. Victor

St. Victor was a soldier in the Theban Legion of St. Maurice, but escaped the executions at Saint-Maurice and fled to Solothurn (about 40 km north of Bern). St. Victor could not escape the martyr's fate of the Theban Legion: he was tortured and beheaded by Roman executioners in Solothurn in 303.

St. Vincent

St. Vincent (of Saragossa) was a spokesman of the Bishop of Saragossa, Spain (who was speech impaired) and a deacon of the church. When the Romans started persecuting Christians in Spain, he and the Bishop were imprisoned. St. Vincent died, after severe torture, from the shards of broken pottery on the floor of his prison cell (around 303). His body was thrown in the sea, but was later recovered by sailors. He became the patron Saint of masons and sailors.

St. Wendolyn

St. Wendolyn (of Trier) was of Scottish royal origin, but led an ascetic life as a pilgrim in Europe. He became a hermit near Trier (Germany), was a shepherd, and founded a community of hermits from which a Benedictine Abbey was established. He died in 617. He became the patron Saint of shepherds and cattle farmers.

Appendix 3:
History of Monastic Orders

Appendix 3 lists all monasteries and convents along the Way of St. James in Central Switzerland, with references to the locations, stages, and page numbers. The numbering continues from Volume I.
The descriptions of their history and special features are included in the chapters of the respective hiking stages.

A short history of these monastic Orders, in alphabetical order, is provided on the next pages. Their history should be read in the context of the medieval monastic world, as described in the chapter Religious Context of the General Introduction to the Swiss Camino in Volume I.

Monasteries from Einsiedeln to Fribourg, via Alpine Lakes route

Nr.	Name	Location	Stage	Page
5	Benedictine Convent	Au	5	38
6	Former Jesuit Collegium	Schwyz	5	48
7	Dominican Convent St. Peter am Bach	Schwyz	5	54
8	Capuchin Monastery	Schwyz	5	55
9	Convent of Merciful Sisters of the Holy Cross	Ingenbohl	5	64
10	Former Capuchin Monastery and Collegium	Stans	6	94
11	Capuchin Convent St. Clare	Stans	6	97
12	Dominican Convent of Bethany	St. Niklausen	7	117
13	Chemin Neuf Community	St. Niklausen	7	118
14	Former Augustinian Monastery	Interlaken	9	177
15	Former Collegiate St. Maurice	Amsoldingen	11	215
16	Former Cluniac Monastery	Rüeggisberg	12	234
17	Former Commandry of the Knights of St. John	Fribourg	13	268
18	Former Augustinian Monastery	Fribourg	13	270
19	Franciscan Monastery	Fribourg	13	275
20	Convent of Holy Mary Visitation	Fribourg	13	278
21	Capuchin Monastery	Fribourg	13	279
22	Former Jesuit Collegium St. Michael	Fribourg	13	280

Monasteries from Luzern to Mättiwil, via Luzern/Bern route

Nr.	Name	Location	Stage	Page
L-1	Former Benedictine Monastery	Luzern	L1	297
L-2	Former Jesuit Collegium	Luzern	L1	302
L-3	Former Franciscan Monastery	Luzern	L1	304
L-4	Former Franciscan Monastery	Werthenstein	L1	317
L-5	Former Augustinian Monastery	Burgdorf	L3	357
L-6	Former Carthusian Monastery	Krauchthal	L4	369
L-7	Former Dominican Monastery	Bern	L4	384

History of Monastic Orders

Augustinian Order

The Augustinian Order follows the Rule of St. Augustine of Hippo. He was a Roman north-African Bishop, from a region in modern-day Algeria, who lived in 354-430. During his early life he spent considerable time teaching philosophy and theology in Tunisia and Italy (Rome, Milan), after he converted to Christianity in 368. Between 400 and 423 he wrote several documents, which together made up a rule-book outlining key aspects of a Christian religious life. His rules focused on chastity, poverty, obedience, and caring for the ill. In effect his rules established the first standards for Western monasteries.

Inspired by his Rule, many monasteries were established in northern Africa and southern Europe during the following century. In the 6th century the Order and their monasteries were in decline, and basically ceased to exist. St. Benedict established his Rule in 529, borrowing from the Rule of St. Augustine. The Rule of St. Benedict was better adjusted to the times of the mid first-millennium and became the new standard for Christian monastic life. As the first Augustinian Order ceased to exist, the new Benedictine Order flourished from the 6th to the 12th century. By the 12th century the Rule of St. Benedict had become outdated, as a result of intellectual and economical changes in society, increasing urbanization, and shifting power and wealth. This led to a revival of the Rule of St. Augustine, which refocused monastic life on the original ascetic and austere rules.

The old Rule found high acceptance and spread over monasteries in western Europe. New Orders such as the Premonstratensians (Norbertines) and Dominicans applied the Rule. The revived Order of St. Augustine was formally established by joining several local hermit Orders in the Tuscany region of Italy in 1244. This gave them the official name of the Order of Hermits of Saint Augustine. In order to adapt to the changed society, Pope Alexander IV enhanced the original Rule of St. Augustine with the mendicant purpose of bringing Catholicism to the people in the cities. From 1256 the mendicant Augustinian Order established monasteries in developing cities for preaching to and converting of the population, and helping the poor.

Nowadays the Order maintains no presence in Switzerland.

Benedictine Order

The Benedictine Order, also called the Order of Saint Benedict, was founded by Benedict of Nursia in Italy in 529. The Order revolved around prayer and physical labor ('Ora et Labora') under the Rule of St. Benedict. Each Benedictine abbey was independent and governed by their own abbot. A supervising abbot was often appointed by local noblemen, with the assignment to control and protect a monastery's assets. The monasteries were autonomous; there was no mother house that set a policy or appointed the abbots. Monks had to vow to stay within the same community and be obedient to the abbot and the Rule of St. Benedict. This gave the abbot full control over the monks: he set the rules for silence, reading, prayer, meals, sleep, and work. They would spend most of their time in prayer (eight times a day), several hours reading, and working the fields (to be self-sufficient). Application of these foundational rules resulted in tight communities of monks, who stayed in one location their whole (monastic) life. This resulted in stability and productivity; they amassed significant wealth in assets (donations of lands and income by noblemen) and knowledge (from studying and copying handwritten books). Monks were often the few people (apart from noblemen) who could read and write. This enabled them to collect and contain knowledge, often resulting in extensive libraries (for example the libraries of the Abbeys of St. Gallen and Einsiedeln). These monasteries created the first universities that collected and transferred knowledge (though within their Order, not to the public in general).

The Benedictine monasteries flourished and dominated the western monastic landscape until the 12th century. They are considered the foundation of western monastic life. They became wealthy through extensive ownership of lands, towns, and income. The medieval Christian doctrine focused on heaven and hell, in which the monasteries and their churches played a central role. Donations were considered a good way to attain salvation for a person's soul. It was the monastery as a community or institution that received the donations, not the individual monks. So long as the community continued to exist through succession of abbots, the monastery would keep accumulating wealth. After several centuries, these Benedictine monasteries had amassed so much wealth (lands, rights, and knowledge) that they often became the center of power of large territories. Their increasing wealth, knowledge, and land ownership resulted in increasing resistance from monarchs, noblemen, and state governors who saw their own territories and rule undermined.

During the 11th and 12th centuries society was changing and the population increasingly concentrated in towns. This set in the decline of the Benedictine monasteries. The application of the Rule of St. Benedict (already 600 years old) often resulted in inflexibility and isolation from the developing society and cities around them. They became complacent as a result of the wealth they had accumulated over the many centuries, and focused more on earthly than spiritual matters. Other Orders arose, such as the Franciscans and Augustinians, which were better adapted to the changing society, the development of cities, and were based on a vow of poverty (instead of amassing wealth) and care for the ill and poor (instead of staying within their own monastery). The Benedictines stayed in their monasteries, which became isolated from society and cities that developed in new areas and territories, while the new Orders participated in supporting the needy.

Nowadays the Order maintains eight monasteries and 12 convents in Switzerland (of which two and one respectively along the Swiss Way of St. James).

Capuchin Order

The Order of Friars Minor Capuchin is a branch of the Franciscan Order. The Capuchin Order was established by Matteo de Bascio, who sought a stricter reinterpretation of the Rule of St. Francis of Assisi, in Italy in 1525. This entailed a simpler life of austerity and poverty, and preaching to and caring for the poor. The Capuchin Order was a mendicant Order, established during the Counter-Reformation. Since they were a beggar-order, they had to be close to the population. Pastoral care and caring for the elderly, ill, and poor required them to be in the towns. The male members of the Order were called friars instead of monks. They dressed in a brown long pointy hooded habit that was tied around the waste with a white cord with three knots, and wore sandals on their feet. Customarily they had a long untrimmed beard. Their name was derived from the hoods, which were called capuchins (in Italian). The Italian coffee cappuccino was named after the shade of brown of their habit.

Nowadays the Order maintains 11 monasteries in Switzerland (of which three along the Swiss Way of St. James).

Capuchin Order of Poor Clares

The Order of Capuchin Poor Clares is a nun's Order established as counterpart of the male Capuchin Order in 1538 (the male Order was founded in 1525). The Order was started by Maria Longo in Italy at the time of the Reformation and sought a strict reinterpretation of the Rule of St. Clare of Assisi (from 1212). This entailed a simpler life of austerity, poverty, and self-sufficiency in an enclosed community.

Nowadays the Order maintains 12 convents in Switzerland (of which one along the Swiss Way of St. James).

Carthusian Order

The Carthusian Order, also called the Order of Saint Bruno, was founded by Bruno of Cologne, Germany, in 1084. The Order revolved around hermitage; each monk had their own austere (primitive) cell for solitude, prayers, reading, and recitations of The Bible. Their buildings were called charterhouses, where only the church and work places were communal areas. The monks wore long white robes with pointed hoods.

Nowadays the Carthusian Order maintains one charterhouse in Switzerland (not along the Swiss Way of St. James).

Chemin Neuf Community

The Chemin Neuf organization is a catholic ecumenical community that has the goal to evangelize, teach, and be involved in society such as at student residences, retreat centers, health centers, and so forth. They mostly focus on young people. Chemin Neuf is French for 'new roads'. The organization was established in France in 1984, in 1992 became a Clerical Religious Institute, and in 2009 obtained the Pontifical Right. The mother Abbey is in Hautecombe, France.

Nowadays the community maintains three houses in Switzerland (of which one along the Swiss Way of St. James).

Cluniac Order

The Cluniac Order was established by the Duke of Aquitaine in Cluny, France, as an offshoot of the Benedictine Order in 910. The name Cluniac was derived from the French town called Cluny (150 km west of Geneva) that housed the first and mother Abbey. The Order sought a reformation of the 6th century Rule of St. Benedict, which had become out of date. The Order and its monasteries were independent, i.e. freed from oversight by lay noblemen and outside the control of the bishops. The Order applied a stricter interpretation of the Rule of St. Benedict, focusing on the traditional monastic life such as liturgy, prayers, copying of manuscripts, and caring for the poor and pilgrims, instead of on physical labor. As the Order became more popular their possessions grew through donations of lands, rights, and goods by nobility. They became the strongest western monastic reform movement of their time, and had many hundreds of subsidiaries during their peak (950-1130). Typical for the Cluniac Order, they had a strong hierarchy and centralization of decisions, where the mother Abbey of Cluny controlled many aspects of their subsidiary monasteries (e.g. the appointment of priors).

Their churches had very specific architecture with Romanesque features: massive walls; few and tiny windows; the bell tower on top of the crossing of the transept; the clear footprint of a Latin cross; three, five, or more apses to the east (of which the chancel in the middle was the largest); and Lombard bands (decorative blind arcades) on the outer walls of the apses.

By 1100 the Cluniac Order was at its peak and had amassed significant wealth, which changed their focus and positioning to earthly matters. Just like the Benedictine Order had become complacent after several centuries of success, so had the Cluniac Order. The Order's decline set in at the beginning of the 12th century. Their network had become too large to be effectively controlled from the center. Poor leadership and decadence as a result of its important position and wealth led to its downfall. The large organization could not adapt to the changing times, as the Benedictine Order could not either.

The Order was dissolved at the time of the French Revolution in the 1790s.

Collegiate

A Collegiate church was managed by a community (college) of clergy (multiple priests) called canons (in German *Stift*). The community did not belong to a monastic Order, was relatively independent of the Bishopric (the Holy See needed to approve its formation and dissolution), and functioned as a self-governing entity under leadership of a provost. The clergy (canons) were not bound to a religious Order or Rule, and did not have to take vows and give up their private possessions. Strictly speaking, they were not a monastery or monastic Order.

Nowadays three Collegiate churches still exist in Switzerland (of which two along the Swiss Way of St. James: the St. Nicholas Cathedral in Fribourg and the St. Leodegar Church in Luzern).

Dominican Order

The Dominican Order, also called the Order of the Preachers, was established by the Spaniard St. Dominic of Guzman in 1216. He recruited priests, brothers, and nuns to preach the true teachings of Christianity. They were not bound by the usual monastic rules of being assigned to one location for life. With their apostolic missions they went out in the world, following the example of the Twelve Apostles. Their focus on preaching, studying, prayer, and meditation made them a leading force of theological intellect during the middle ages. As mendicant Order the Dominicans preached to the poor in a language they understood (instead of the difficult Latin or liturgical words).

Nowadays the Order maintains three monasteries and 11 convents in Switzerland (of which two convents along the Swiss Way of St. James).

The Congregation of the **Dominican Nuns of Bethany** was established by French Dominican friar Jean-Joseph Lataste in 1866. During his visits to prisons he met women who wanted to dedicate themselves to God. Upon their release, however, none of the existing convents wanted to accept these women, who had spent time in prison. Friar Jean-Joseph Lataste established a convent that accepted women irrespective of their past. He named the congregation after the location where the siblings Mary, Martha, and Lazarus (friends of Jesus) had lived. Bethany is a site just outside of Jerusalem, on the slopes of Mount of Olives. At the time of Jesus, it was a place where the poor and ill were cared for.

Franciscan Order

The Franciscan Order was established by St. Francis of Assisi in 1209. He was an Italian catholic friar, deacon, and preacher. The Rule of St. Francis required its members to live in austerity and poverty, in the image of Jesus' life, while preaching Christianity as He had done. This brought them close to the poor and weak members of society. As a mendicant Order they were also called a beggar or barefoot Order, as a reflection of their vow to poverty. In French the Franciscan friars are called ***Cordeliers***, referring to the white rope (*corde*) with three knots, with which they tie their brown habit around their waste.

Nowadays the Order maintains three monasteries and two convents in Switzerland (of which one monastery along the Swiss Way of St. James).

Jesuit Order

The Jesuit Order, also called the Society of Jesus, was founded by St. Ignatius of Loyola, St. Peter Faber, and St. Francis Xavier in 1539. The Order focused their missionary activities on the higher-level education of boys and caring for the poor. They established many schools, which provided them a new way of evangelizing through the education of boys, including the poor who could not afford education otherwise.

In many European countries the Jesuits accumulated significant wealth and possessions over the centuries, and used their powers to influence politics, the economy, and the educational system. Their independence, influence, and tight connections with the Popes became a problem for many European Monarchs and Governments during the 18th century. After decades of European opposition to the Jesuit Order and their influences, many countries had expelled the Jesuit Order by 1759. In 1769 Pope Clement XIV was elected, who could not withstand the European pressures and gave up his support of the Order. In 1773 he issued a decree that formally dissolved the Jesuit Order. The Cantons in Switzerland followed this decree, expelled all Jesuits and seized their considerable wealth and possessions. Their churches, lands, school buildings, and so forth were all confiscated and became the property of the Cantons.

In 1814 Pope Pius VII re-established the Order, after which many Jesuits returned to their Collegiums to resume their educational tasks.

In Switzerland the Sonderbund War had another devastating impact on the Jesuits. After the conservative catholic Cantons lost a civil war from the progressive protestant

Cantons in 1847, the new Government of the Swiss Confederation declared in the country's constitution a prohibition of the Jesuit Order and their monasteries. All Jesuits were expelled from the country in 1848. This constitutional law was repealed in 1973.

Nowadays the Order only maintains six small communities in Switzerland (of which four in cities along the Swiss Way of St. James).

Knights of St. John Order

The 'Order of Knights of the Hospital of Saint John of Jerusalem' is better known as the Maltese Order or the Hospitaller Order. The Order was established at the time of the Crusades in Jerusalem around 1048. Their task was to build a hospital to care for the ill and wounded pilgrims, and secure their safety at the times of military battles for the Holy Land. It was a military organization made up of Knights of noble background with Christian faith. After Islamic troops conquered Jerusalem, they relocated their base to Cyprus (1291), Rhodes (1310), and finally Malta (1530). This last location gave them their name under which they became more popularly known. The Order was seriously weakened by the Reformation that swept over Europe from the 1520s, and the conquests by Napoleon around 1798. They had to give up many of their commandries, and the Order was disrupted when Napoleon conquered the Island of Malta.

Between 1180 and 1456 the Order of the Knights of St. John maintained 20 commandries in Switzerland, which were situated at strategic locations enabling care for the ill and pilgrims. The Swiss Reformation had a devastating impact on the commandries, causing the closure of many of them between 1523 and 1536. The remaining commandries were closed or secularized from 1798, after Napoleon conquered Switzerland.

Nowadays the Order maintains one commandry in Switzerland (which is not along the Swiss Way of St. James).

Merciful Sisters of the Holy Cross

The Ingenbohl Convent of the Merciful Sisters of the Holy Cross (*Barmherzige Schwestern vom Heiligen Kreuz*), also called the 'Sisters of Ingenbohl' or the 'Sisters of the Cross', is a nunnery with a Franciscan Order orientation. The convent was established by Capuchin friar Florentini and Mother Maria Theresia Scherer in 1856.

The sisters lead the Ingenbohl Institute, an international organization of nuns active socially, religiously, and educationally, with Ingenbohl as its mother house. The Institute was at its peak in 1941, when more than 9'600 nuns were active in the Institute's own schools, hospitals, and retirement homes in more than 18 countries on four continents. Nowadays the Institute is still active in 22 locations in Switzerland, in other European countries, as well as in the USA, Brazil, Uganda, India, and Taiwan.

Visitation Order

The 'Order of the Visitation of Holy Mary' is an enclosed nunnery, also known as the 'Visitation Sisters', the 'Salesian Sisters', or the 'Visitation Order'. The Visitation Order was established by St. Francis de Sales in Annecy, France in 1610. St. Francis de Sales was a Bishop of Geneva in 1602-22. Because Geneva was under control of the Calvinists, he resided in Annecy (about 45 km south of Geneva, nowadays part of France).

The name Holy Mary Visitation originates from The Bible, which described that Mary (pregnant with Jesus) visited her cousin Elisabeth, who was pregnant with John the Baptist. Mary stayed for three months to help Elisabeth with the final stages of the pregnancy and the delivery. The sisters of the Order visited and supported ill and poor women in their surrounding communities. The Order recruited older women with more life experience and did not have the rigid austerity, seclusion, and prayer rules as most of the other sister Orders. There was no sister-superior or centralized governing.

Nowadays the Order maintains two convents in Switzerland (of which one along the Swiss Way of St. James).

Appendix 4: List of Points of Interest

Appendix 4 lists all points of interest along the Way of St. James in Central Switzerland, with references to the locations, stages, and page numbers. The numbering continues from Volume I.

The descriptions of their history and special features are included in the chapters of the respective hiking stages.

Points of Interest from Einsiedeln to Fribourg, via Alpine Lakes route

Nr.	Name	Location	Stage	Page
16	Archive Tower	Schwyz	5	53
17	Rose Castle	Stans	6	104
18	Brother Klaus House	Flüeli	7	125
19	Brother Klaus Museum	Sachseln	7	131
20	Former Castle of Hunwil	Giswil	8	138
21	Ruins Castle of Giswil	Giswil	8	140
22	Dundelbach Waterfalls	Lungern	8	144
23	Former Castle of Brienzwiler	Brienzwiler	8	153
24	Open-Air Museum Ballenberg	Brienzwiler	8	153
25	Side-way moving road bridge	Brienz	9	160
26	Former Castle of Brienz	Brienz	9	163
27	80-meter Suspension Footbridge	Ebligen	9	164
28	Ruins Castle of Schaden	Ringgenberg	9	168
29	Planet Trail	Ringgenberg	9	168
30	Ruins Castle of Ringgenberg	Ringgenberg	9	170
31	Castle of Unterseen	Unterseen	10	187
32	Ruins Castle of Weissenau	Weissenau	10	189
33	St. Beatus Caves	Sundlauenen	10	192
34	Castle of Spiez	Spiez	10	198
35	Former Castle of Strättligen	Zwieselberg	11	211
36	Former Castle of Blumenstein	Blumenstein	11	217
37	Castle of Burgistein	Burgistein	12	228
38	Castle of Riggisberg	Riggisberg	12	229
39	Archive Tower	Rüeggisberg	12	232
40	Castle of Schwarzenburg	Schwarzenburg	12	239
41	Ruins Castle of Grasburg	Schwarzenburg	13	248
42	Castle of Heitenried	Heitenried	13	252
43	Medieval City Fortifications	Fribourg	13	264

Points of Interest from Luzern to Mättiwil, via Luzern/Bern route

Nr.	Name	Location	Stage	Page
L-1	Boat Crossing of Lake Lucerne	Lake Lucerne	L1	293
L-2	Medieval Chapel Bridge	Luzern	L1	300
L-3	Medieval Speuer Bridge	Luzern	L1	306
L-4	Mercy Spring	Werthenstein	L1	319
L-5	Medieval City of Willisau	Willisau	L2	332
L-6	Castle of Willisau	Willisau	L2	332
L-7	Hotel Kreuz	Dürrenroth	L3	350
L-8	Lueg Monument	Lueg	L3	353
L-9	Former Leprosarium	Burgdorf	L3	355
L-10	Medieval distance time-marker	Burgdorf	L3	356
L-11	Wynigen Bridges	Burgdorf	L3	356
L-12	Castle of Burgdorf	Burgdorf	L3	358
L-13	Chateau of Utzigen	Utzigen	L4	372
L-14	Paul Klee Museum	Bern	L4	375
L-15	Bear Park	Bern	L4	375
L-16	Ruins Castle of Bern	Bern	L4	377
L-17	Medieval Figured Fountains	Bern	L4	379
L-18	Medieval Clock Tower	Bern	L4	384
L-19	Albert Einstein Museum	Bern	L4	386
L-20	Cathedral Terrace	Bern	L4	389
L-21	Swiss House of Parliament	Bern	L5	397
L-22	Bern Historical Museum	Bern	L5	398

Bibliography and Copyrights

Icons

Hiking Icon, Boat Icon, Church Icon, Castle Icon, Camera Icon, Angel Icon, Antique Building Icon, Skeleton Icon, Rubber Stamp Icon, Shell Icon, all made by Freepik from www.flaticon.com, 2019

Monastery Icon and Pin Icon made by Smashicons from www.flaticon.com, 2019

Pray Icon made by FJStudio from www.flaticon.com

Flags of Cantons from Swiss Cantonal Authorities, 2019

Photos

Page 2: Beumer Hans. Bild Cover Volume I. Copyright vom Bild Black Madonna bei Kloster Einsiedeln, 2019

Page 200: Steiner, Andreas. Bild Innenseite der Matthäus Kirche, Spiez, 2019

Page 263: Nussbaumer, Erwin. Bild der Innenseite der St. Bartholomäus Kapelle, Schönberg, Fribourg, 2018

Page 314: Pfarramt St. Martin Malters. Bild Innenseite der St. Ida Kapelle, Malters, 2019

Page 354: Volker, Margrit. Bild der Innenseite der Bartholomäus Kapelle, Burgdorf, 2019

Geographical Maps

Pages 21, 24, 35, 70, 108, 134, 157, 182, 205, 225, 245, 290, 293, 323, 346, 365, 376, 395, and cover: Geographical Maps from Swiss Federal Office of Topography, 2019

Biographies of Saints

Catholic Online, 2018, www.catholic.org

Commission on Tourism, Leisure and Pastoral Care for Pilgrims, 2018, www.chkath.ch

Schäfer, Joachim. Ökumenisches Heiligenlexikon, 2018, www.heiligenlexikon.de

Historical Information (in geographical order of the chapters/stages)

Stage 5: Einsiedeln to Ingenbohl

Bezirk Einsiedeln, 2019, http://www.einsiedeln.ch/bezirk/wo-ist-was/josefskapelle

Benediktinerinnenkloster Au, 2019, http://www.kloster-au.ch/entry/die-josephskapelle

Benediktinerinnenkloster Au, 2019, www.kloster-au.ch

Hug, Albert. Einsiedeln (Benediktinerinnenabtei), in: Historisches Lexikon der Schweiz (HLS) 2004, URL: http://www.hls-dhs-dss.ch/textes/d/D11604.php

Meyerhans, Andreas. Trachslau, in: Historisches Lexikon der Schweiz (HLS) 2012, URL: http://www.hls-dhs-dss.ch/textes/d/D7431.php

Genossame Trachslau, 2019, https://www.genossame-trachslau.ch/26-trachslau.php

Pfarrei St. Apollonia, 2019, http://www.st-apollonia.ch/st-apollonia/

Gemeindeverwaltung Alpthal, 2019, http://www.alpthal.ch/geschichte/urgeschichte.html

Meyerhans, Andreas. Alpthal, in: Historisches Lexikon der Schweiz (HLS) 2009, URL: http://www.hls-dhs-dss.ch/textes/d/D725.php

Stiftung Pilgerkapelle Haggenegg, 2019, www.pilgerkapellehaggenegg.ch

Pfarrei St. Martin Schwyz, 2019, https://www.kirchgemeinde-schwyz.ch/pfarrei/schwyz/schwyz-alte-pilgerkapelle auf-der-haggenegg-passhoehe

Pfarrei St. Martin Schwyz, 2019, https://www.kirchgemeinde-schwyz.ch/pfarrei/schwyz/schwyz-kapelle-haggenegg

Auf der Maur, Franz. Haggenegg, in: Historisches Lexikon der Schweiz (HLS) 2008, URL: http://www.hls-dhs-dss.ch/textes/d/D21330.php

Kantonschule Kollegium Schwyz, 2019, https://kks.ch/schule/portraet/geschichte/

Pfarrei St. Martin Schwyz, www.kirchgemeinde-schwyz.ch

Horat, Erwin. Schwyz (Gemeinde), in: Historisches Lexikon der Schweiz (HLS) 2018, URL: http://www.hls-dhs-dss.ch/textes/d/D736.php

Burgenwelt.org, 2015, http://www.burgenwelt.org/schweiz/archivturm_sz/object.php

Horat, Erwin. Muota, in: Historisches Lexikon der Schweiz (HLS) 2009, URL: http://www.hls-dhs-dss.ch/textes/d/D7450.php

Frauenkloster Schwyz, 2019, http://frauenkloster-schwyz.ch/geschichte/frauenkloster/

Provinziale der Schweizer Kapuziner, 2019, https://www.kapuziner.ch/schwyz/

Pfarrei St. Anton Ibach, 2019, www. kirchgemeinde-schwyz.ch

Wiget, Josef. Ibach, in: Historisches Lexikon der Schweiz (HLS) 2005, URL: http://www.hls-dhs-dss.ch/textes/d/D7426.php

Castell, Anton. St. Antonius Kirche Ibach – Zu ihrer Einweihung, Schwyz: Paul Wiget, Papeterie, 1939. S. 12-27

Ming, Hans. Heiligkreuz-Kapelle in der Erlen, 1974
Fässler, Antonia. Diplomarbeit: Die Fünf-Franzen-Kapelle, Ibach
Betschart, Othmar. Von Heiligen und Wetterregeln. Schwyz: Triner Druck, 2013. S. 110
Pfarrei Ingenbohl-Brunnen, 2019, http://pfarrei-ingenbohl.ch/unsere-pfarrei/kirchen-und-kapellen/
Gemeinde Ingenbohl-Brunnen, Kulturweg, 2004, http://www.ingenbohl.ch/fileadmin/twwc/seitenTemplate/redakteur/bilder/kultur/grosserkulturweg.pdf
Venzin, Renata Pia. Ingenbohl (Schwesterninstitut), in: Historisches Lexikon der Schweiz (HLS) 2007, URL: http://www.hls-dhs-dss.ch/textes/d/D12127.php
Kloster Ingenbohl, 2019, www.kloster-ingenbohl.ch
Wiget, Josef. Ingenbohl (Gemeinde), in: Historisches Lexikon der Schweiz (HLS) 2008, URL: http://www.hls-dhs-dss.ch/textes/d/D728.php

<u>Stage 6: Ingenbohl to Stans</u>
Evangelisch-Reformierte Kirchgemeinde Brunnen-Schwyz, 2019, https://www.ref-brunnen-schwyz.ch/kirchengeschichte
Gemeinde Ingenbohl-Brunnen, 2019, https://www.brunnen.ch/portrait/sehenswuerdigkeiten/
Pfarrei St. Michael Seelisberg, 2019, http://www.kirche-seelisberg.ch/index.php/bauwerke/st-anna-volligen.html
Pfarrei Emmetten, 2019, http://www.kirche-emmetten.ch/index.php/bauwerke/heiligkreuz-kapelle.html
Sakrallandschaft Innerschweiz, 2019, https://www.sakrallandschaft-innerschweiz.ch/sakrale-orte/kapellenstiftung-brunnen/kirchgemeinde-emmetten/
Steiner, Peter. Emmetten, in: Historisches Lexikon der Schweiz (HLS) 2005, URL: http://www.hls-dhs-dss.ch/textes/d/D750.php
Gemeinde Emmetten, Gemeinde Broschüre, 2016, http://www.emmetten.ch/dl.php/de/585ba10d1d2a7/Gemeindebroschure_2016.pdf, p. 15-18.
Pfarrei Beckenried, 2019, http://www.pfarrei-beckenried.ch/index.php/kirche-und-kapellen/st-annakapelle
Achermann, Hansjakob. Beckenried, in: Historisches Lexikon der Schweiz (HLS) 2011, URL: http://www.hls-dhs-dss.ch/textes/d/D747.php
Sennhauser, H.R. Zu den Vorgängerbauten der Pfarrkirche von Buochs NW, Schlussbericht über Bodenuntersuchungen anlässlich der Kirchenrenovation des Jahres 1960, 1963, https://www.e-periodica.ch/cntmng?pid=bgn-001:1963:28::138
Achermann, Hansjakob. Buochs, in: Historisches Lexikon der Schweiz (HLS) 2010, URL: http://www.hls-dhs-dss.ch/textes/d/D748.php
Information Tafel beim St. Martin Kirche, 2018
Information Tafel beim Obgass-kapelle, 2018
Information Tafel beim Loreto Kapelle, 2018
Pfarrei St. Martin Buochs, 2019, http://www.pfarreibuochs.ch/#/liegenschaften/
Steiner, Peter. Waltersberg, in: Historisches Lexikon der Schweiz (HLS) 2013, URL: http://www.hls-dhs-dss.ch/textes/d/D7481.php
Gemeinde Oberdorf, 2019, http://www.oberdorf-nw.ch/de/freizeitkultur/freizeit/sehenswuerdigkeiten/
Pfarrei Stans, 2019, http://www.pfarrei-stans.ch/kirche-und-kapellen.html
Verein IG Kapuzinerkloster Stans, 2019, www.kapuzinerkloster-stans.ch
Kollegium St. Fidelis, 2019, https://www.kollegistans.ch/portrait/
Verein Kapuzinerkirche Stans, 2019, http://www.vks-nw.ch/files/kapuzinerkirche_stans_flyer.pdf
Gemeinde Stans, 2019, http://www.stans.ch/de/portrait/geschichte/
Kapuzinerinnen Kloster St. Klara, 2019, www.kloster-st-klara-stans.ch
Verein 400 Jahre Kloster St. Klara, 2019, https://www.400jahre-st-klara.ch/klostergeschichte/
Haller-Dir, Marita. ONZ Obwalden und Nidwalden Zeitung, 2. Juli 2010: Die ersten Schwestern waren unerwünscht, https://www.400jahre-st-klara.ch/files/3613/9687/2891/2010_07_02_400Jahre.pdf
Achermann, Hansjakob. ONZ Obwalden und Nidwalden Zeitung, 3. Juni 2011: Wie das Kloster Stans zum Hausheiligen kam, https://www.400jahre-st-klara.ch/files/9713/9687/3833/2011_06_03_Prosper.pdf
Haller-Dir, Marita. ONZ Obwalden und Nidwalden Zeitung, 12. August 2011: Wachstum des Klosters unter Kontrolle, https://www.400jahre-st-klara.ch/files/3013/9687/3958/2011_08_12_Wachstum_Kloster.pdf
Weber, Emil. Stans, in: Historisches Lexikon der Schweiz (HLS) 2012, URL: http://www.hls-dhs-dss.ch/textes/d/D755.php
Höfli Stiftung, 2019, http://www.hoefli-stiftung.ch/content/Rosenburg/
Pfarrei Stans, 2019, http://www.pfarrei-stans.ch/kirche-und-kapellen.html
Burgenwelt.org, 2019, http://www.burgenwelt.org/schweiz/rosenburg_nw/object.php

Papal Swiss Guards, 2013, http://www.guardiasvizzera.va/content/guardiasvizzera/en/storia.html

Stage 7: Stans to Sachseln

Evangelisch-Reformierte Kirchgemeinde Obwalden, 2019, http://www.refow.ch/h/infos/kirchengebaeude/
Pfarrei Stans, 2019, http://www.pfarrei-stans.ch/kniri-kapelle.html
Informationsblatt beim Kniri Kapelle, 2018
Pfarramt Ennetmoos, 2019, http://kirche-ennetmoos.ch/kirchekapellen/pfarrkirche-st-jakob/
Steiner, Peter. Ennetmoos, in: Historisches Lexikon der Schweiz (HLS) 2005, URL: http://www.hls-dhs-dss.ch/textes/d/D752.php
Pfarramt Kerns, 2019, http://www.kirche-kerns.ch/Kirchen-und-Kapellen/
Kath. Pfarramt Kerns, 2018, Informationsblatt beim Mei Kapelle, Wisserlen
Kath. Pfarramt Kerns, 2018, Informationsblatt beim St. Katharina Kapelle, Wisserlen
Weber, Emil. Wisserlen, in: Historisches Lexikon der Schweiz (HLS) 2013, URL: http://www.hls-dhs-dss.ch/textes/d/D41333.php
Von Flüe, Niklaus. Sankt Niklausen, in: Historisches Lexikon der Schweiz (HLS) 2012, URL: http://www.hls-dhs-dss.ch/textes/d/D7491.php
Durrer, Robert. Die Kapelle St. Niklausen bei Kerns und ihre mittelalterliche Wandgemälde, 1897, https://www.e-periodica.ch/digbib/view?pid=gfr-001:1897:52::428#338
Kulturkommission Kerns, 2018, Kulturgüter in der Gemeinde Kerns, http://www.kerns.ch/dl.php/de/5b97bc6383087/KUKO_Kulturgu776ter_Kerns.pdf
Bruder-Klausen-Stiftung, 2019, https://bruderklaus.com/orte-informationen/weitere-orte/
Kloster Bethanien, 2019, www.kloster-bethanien.ch
Gemeinschaft Chemin Neuf, 2019, www.haus-bethanien.ch
Chemin Neuf, 2019, https://www.chemin-neuf.org/en/home/chemin-neuf-community/
Pfarreiblatt Obwalden, 10/2016, https://www.kirche-obwalden.ch/wp-content/uploads/pfarreiblatt_201610.pdf, S. 2-3
Bruder-Klausen-Stiftung, 2019, https://bruderklaus.com/
Informationsblatt beim Untere Ranftkapelle, 2018
Garovi, Angelo. Flüeli, in: Historisches Lexikon der Schweiz (HLS) 2005, URL: http://www.hls-dhs-dss.ch/textes/d/D7490.php
Informationsblatt beim Geburtshaus und Wohnhaus Bruder Klaus, 2018
Garovi, Angelo. Sachseln, in: Historisches Lexikon der Schweiz (HLS) 2011, URL: http://www.hls-dhs-dss.ch/textes/d/D745.php
Pfarrei Sachseln, 2019, http://www.pfarrei-sachseln.ch/kirchen_kapellen/

Stage 8: Sachseln to Brienzwiler

Pfarrei Sachseln, 2019, http://www.pfarrei-sachseln.ch/kirchen_kapellen/kapelle_ewil_st._apollonia/
Römisch-katholische Pfarrei Giswil, 2019, https://www.pfarrei-giswil.ch/kirchen-und-kapellen/
Informationsblatt bei der Kirche Giswil: Hügel mit der Pfarrkirche (6), 2018
Abächerli, Urs. Giswil, in: Historisches Lexikon der Schweiz (HLS) 2006, URL: http://www.hls-dhs-dss.ch/textes/d/D742.php
Burgenwelt, 2019, http://www.burgenwelt.org/schweiz/hunwil/
Gemeinde Verwaltung Giswil, 2019, http://www.giswil.ch/de/portrait/geschichte/
Burgenwelt, 2019, http://www.burgenwelt.org/schweiz/rudenz_ow/
Pfarrei Herz-Jesu Lugern, 2019, https://www.pfarrei-lungern.ch/bereich/kirchen_kapellen/
Ming, Hans. Bürglen und seine Kapelle, in Aus der Pfarreigeschichte von Lungern: Jubiläumsgabe 250 Jahre 33er-Bruderschaft, Lungern: Betagtenheim Eyhuis, 1994. S. 68-74
Halter, Josef. Lungern, in: Historisches Lexikon der Schweiz (HLS) 2008, URL: http://www.hls-dhs-dss.ch/textes/d/D744.php
Halter, Josef. Informationsblatt bei der St. Beat Kapelle: Die Kapelle St. Beat in Lungern, Obsee, 2018
Wyl von, Edy. Lungernsee, in: Historisches Lexikon der Schweiz (HLS) 2009, URL: http://www.hls-dhs-dss.ch/textes/d/D8676.php
Dubler, Anne-Marie. Brienzwiler, in: Historisches Lexikon der Schweiz (HLS) 2002, URL: http://www.hls-dhs-dss.ch/textes/d/D329.php
Gemeinde Brienzwiler, 2019, http://www.brienzwiler.ch/portrait/geschichte
Ballenberg Freilichtmuseum der Schweiz, 2019, https://www.ballenberg.ch/museum/geschichte/

Stage 9: Brienzwiler to Interlaken

Pfarrei Meiringen Guthirt, 2019, https://www.kathbern.ch/pfarreien-seelsorge/pfarreien/meiringen-guthirt/unsere-kirchen/brienz/
Ref. Kirchgemeinde Brienz, 2018, www.kirchebrienz.ch

Perren, Rudolf und Anton Wyder. Die Kirche von Brienz BE. Kirchgemeinde Brienz, 1996
Dubler, Anne-Marie. Brienz, in: Historisches Lexikon der Schweiz (HLS) 2006, URL: http://www.hls-dhs-dss.ch/textes/d/D328.php
Informationsblatt bei der Ref. Kirche Brienz, 2018
Gemeinde Brienz, 2019, http://www.brienz.ch/de/brienzaktuelles/portrait/geschichte/
Günter, Anne-Marie. Jungfrau Zeitung, 4. November 2011: Wenn seine Seilbrücke abgebaut wird, https://www.jungfrauzeitung.ch/artikel/114875/
Dubler, Anne-Marie. Oberried am Brienzersee, in: Historisches Lexikon der Schweiz (HLS) 2009, URL: http://www.hls-dhs-dss.ch/textes/d/D343.php
Dubler, Anne-Marie. Ringgenberg, in: Historisches Lexikon der Schweiz (HLS) 2013, URL: http://www.hls-dhs-dss.ch/textes/d/D344.php
Information tables at the castle church and castle remains in Ringgenberg, 2018
The Swiss Castles, 2019, http://www.swisscastles.ch/Bern/ringgenberg_d.html
Garovi, Angelo. Ringgenberger Handel, in: Historisches Lexikon der Schweiz (HLS) 2010, URL: http://www.hls-dhs-dss.ch/textes/d/D26838.php
Kirchgemeinde Ringgenberg, 2019, www.kircheringgenberg.ch
Interlaken Tourismus, 2019, https://www.interlaken.ch/de/ruine-schadenburg-ringgenberg.html
Archäologischer Dienst des Kantons Bern, 2019, Bergruine Ringgenberg, https://www.erz.be.ch/erz/de/index/kultur/archaeologie/fundstellen/interlaken_oberhasli/ringgenberg_burgruine.assetref/dam/documents/ERZ/AK/de/Archaeologie/AD_Flyer_Ringgenberg.pdf
Archäologischer Dienst des Kantons Bern, 2019, Kirchenruine Goldswil, https://www.erz.be.ch/erz/de/index/kultur/archaeologie/fundstellen/interlaken_oberhasli/ringgenberg--goldswil--kirchenruine.assetref/dam/documents/ERZ/AK/de/Archaeologie/AD_Flyer_Goldswil.pdf
Dubler, Anne-Marie. Goldswil, in: Historisches Lexikon der Schweiz (HLS) 2005, URL: http://www.hls-dhs-dss.ch/textes/d/D3278.php
Information tables at the church ruins in Goldswil, 2018
Pfarrei Heiliggeist Interlaken, 2019, https://www.kathbern.ch/pfarreien-seelsorge/pfarreien/pfarrblatt/5-kirchen-1-pfarrei/interlaken/
Pfarrei Gsteig Interlaken, 2019, http://www.gsteig-interlaken.ch/interlaken-matten/sonstiges/gebaeude/
Verwaltung Schlosskirche Interlaken, 2019, http://www.schlosskirche.ch/historie/
Information Säule beim Schlosskirche und Schloss Interlaken, 2018
Studer, Barbara. Interlaken (Kloster, Amtsbezirk), in: Historisches Lexikon der Schweiz (HLS) 2018, URL: http://www.hls-dhs-dss.ch/textes/d/D8506.php
Order of Saint Augustine, 2019, https://augustinians.net/index.php?page=history

Stage 10: Interlaken to Spiez

Kirchgemeinde Unterseen, 2019, https://www.kirche-unterseen.ch/unsere-kirche/geschichte/
Einwohnergemeinde Unterseen, 2019, https://www.unterseen.ch/gemeinde-unterseen/geschichte.html
Dubler, Anne-Marie. Unterseen, in: Historisches Lexikon der Schweiz (HLS) 2013, URL: http://www.hls-dhs-dss.ch/textes/d/D347.php
Stedtli-Leist Unterseen, 2019, http://www.stedtlileist.ch/index.php/tafel-schloss-unterseen
Swiss Castles, 2019, http://www.swisscastles.ch/Bern/unterseen.html
Information Säule beim Haberdarre und Dorfplatz in Unterseen, 2018
Archäologischer Dienst des Kantons Bern, 2019, Burgruine Weissenau, https://www.erz.be.ch/erz/de/index/kultur/archaeologie/fundstellen/interlaken_oberhasli/unterseen_burgruineweissenau.assetref/dam/documents/ERZ/AK/de/Archaeologie/adb-unterseen_weissenau_infotaf.pdf
Dubler, Anne-Marie. Weissenau, in: Historisches Lexikon der Schweiz (HLS) 2013, URL: http://www.hls-dhs-dss.ch/textes/d/D8490.php
St. Beatus, 2019, www.beatushoehlen.swiss
Fischer, Rainald. Beatus, in: Historisches Lexikon der Schweiz (HLS) 2004, URL: http://www.hls-dhs-dss.ch/textes/d/D10213.php
Reformierte Kirchgemeinde Sigriswil, 2019, http://www.kirchgemeindesigriswil.ch/kirchgemeinde/gebaeude/46-kirche-merligen.html
Dubler, Anne-Marie. Merligen, in: Historisches Lexikon der Schweiz (HLS) 2009, URL: http://www.hls-dhs-dss.ch/textes/d/D8342.php
Dubler, Anne-Marie. Spiez, in: Historisches Lexikon der Schweiz (HLS) 2013, URL: http://www.hls-dhs-dss.ch/textes/d/D8454.php
Schloss Spiez, 2019, https://www.schloss-spiez.ch/schlossbesuch/kirche/
Kühnrich, A., Broschüre: 1000-jährige Kirchen am Thunersee, Uetendorf, 2013

Reformierte Kirchgemeinde Spiez, 2019, www.refkirche-spiez.ch
Christoph Stalder. Spiez Historisch (2): Die Kirchen in der Gemeinde Spiez, in Spiezinfo, Februar 2007, S. 5-9
Burgenwelt.org, 2019, http://www.burgenwelt.org/schweiz/spiez/object.php
Pfarrei Bruder Klaus Spiez, 2019, https://www.kathbern.ch/pfarreien-seelsorge/pfarreien/pfarrei-bruder-klaus-spiez/historisches/

Stage 11: Spiez to Wattenwil

Dubler, Anne-Marie. Einigen, in: Historisches Lexikon der Schweiz (HLS) 2004, URL: http://www.hls-dhs-dss.ch/textes/d/D8317.php
Heim, Thomas. Die Strättliger Chronik - Einblicke in das bernische Wallfahrtswesen, in: Berner Zeitschrift für Geschichte 3/2009, S. 1-56, https://www.bezg.ch/img/publikation/09_3/heim.pdf
Information Säule bei der Kirche Einigen, 2018
Reusser, Annina. Das Paradies von Einigen und seine sagenumwobenen Töchter, in Jungfrau Zeitung, 23.07.2017
Reformierte Kirche Spiez, 2019, https://www.refkirche-spiez.ch/raeume-mieten/kirche-einigen/
Kühnrich, A. Broschüre: 1000-jährige Kirchen am Thunersee, Uetendorf, 2013
Dubler, Anne-Marie. Strättligen, in: Historisches Lexikon der Schweiz (HLS) 2013, URL: http://www.hls-dhs-dss.ch/textes/d/D3291.php
Stadt Thun, Sanierung und Aufwertung der Burganlage Strättligen, 2014, http://www.thun.ch/stadtverwaltung/abteilungenaemter/amt-fuer-stadtliegenschaften/baumanagement/projekte-ausgefuehrt/burganlage-straettligen.html
Dubler, Anne-Marie. Amsoldingen, in: Historisches Lexikon der Schweiz (HLS) 2016, URL: http://www.hls-dhs-dss.ch/textes/d/D520.php
Evangelisch-reformierte Kirchgemeinde Amsoldingen, 2019, Geschichte der Kirche Amsoldingen, M. Leuenberger, 30.08.2004, https://www.ref.ch/amsoldingen/default/index/index/id/2718
Naturpark Gantrisch, 2017, Broschüre: Kirchen im Naturpark Gantrisch, 2012, https://www.gantrisch.ch/app/uploads/2016/11/WEB_download-Kirchenfuehrer-mit-Karte2017.pdf
Utz Tremp, Kathrin. Amsoldingen (Stift), in: Historisches Lexikon der Schweiz (HLS) 2002, URL: http://www.hls-dhs-dss.ch/textes/d/D12004.php
Die Schweizer Schlösser, 2019, http://www.swisscastles.ch/Bern/amsoldingen.html
Dubler, Anne-Marie. Blumenstein, in: Historisches Lexikon der Schweiz (HLS) 2004, URL: http://www.hls-dhs-dss.ch/textes/d/D521.php
Nissen, U. Broschüre: Die Glasgemälde der Kirche von Blumenstein, Blumenstein: 2018
Evangelisch-reformierte Kirchgemeinde Blumenstein-Pohlern, 2018, http://www.kirche-blumenstein-pohlern.ch/i_kir.html
Gemeindeverwaltung Blumenstein, 2018, http://www.blumenstein.ch/gemeinde/geschichte
Dubler, Anne-Marie. Wattenwil, in: Historisches Lexikon der Schweiz (HLS) 2015, URL: http://www.hls-dhs-dss.ch/textes/d/D509.php
Reformierte Kirchgemeinde Wattenwil-Forst, Festschrift Kirchenjubiläum 1983: 300 Jahre Kirche Wattenwil 1683-1983, https://www.kirche-wattenwil.ch/download/nV8MISDcFjA/Festschrift-Kirchenjubilaeum-1983.pdf

Stage 12: Wattenwil to Schwarzenburg

Dubler, Anne-Marie. Burgistein, in: Historisches Lexikon der Schweiz (HLS) 2005, URL: http://www.hls-dhs-dss.ch/textes/d/D486.php
Gemeindeverwaltung Burgistein, 2019, http://www.burgistein.ch/gemeinde-tourismus/geschichte/schloss/
Dubler, Anne-Marie. Riggisberg, in: Historisches Lexikon der Schweiz (HLS) 2015, URL: http://www.hls-dhs-dss.ch/textes/d/D502.php
Kirchgemeinde Riggisberg, 2019, https://www.kirche-riggisberg.ch/home/geschichte/
Information Blatt bei der Kirche Riggisberg, 2018
Gemeinde Riggisberg, 2019, https://www.riggisberg.ch/de/riggisberg_erleben/geschichte
Die Schweizer Schlösser, 2019, http://www.swisscastles.ch/Bern/riggisberg.html
Dubler, Anne-Marie. Rüeggisberg, in: Historisches Lexikon der Schweiz (HLS) 2012, URL: http://www.hls-dhs-dss.ch/textes/d/D503.php
Kirchgemeinde Rüeggisberg, 2019, https://www.kirche-rueeggisberg.ch/de/martinskirche/
Information Tablet bei der Kirche Rüeggisberg, 2018
Archäologischer Dienst des Kantons Bern, 2019, Rüeggisberg: Ehemaliges Cluniazenser Priorat, https://www.erz.be.ch/erz/de/index/kultur/archaeologie/fundstellen/bern_mittelland/rueeggisberg_cluniazenserpriorat.assetref/dam/documents/ERZ/AK/de/Archaeologie/adb-rueggisberg-flyer2013.pdf

Gemeinde Rüeggisberg, 2019, https://www.rueggisberg.ch/de/unsere_gemeinde/geschichte
Naturpark Gantrisch, 2017, Broschüre «Kirchen im Naturpark Gantrisch, 2012», https://www.gantrisch.ch/app/uploads/2016/11/WEB_download-Kirchenfuehrer-mit-Karte2017.pdf
Information Tafeln bei der Ruine Rüeggisberg, 2018
Dubler, Anne-Marie. Schwarzenburg (Gemeinde), in: Historisches Lexikon der Schweiz (HLS) 2011, URL: http://www.hls-dhs-dss.ch/textes/d/D8370.php
Information Tafel bei der Dorfkapelle Schwarzenburg, 2018
Gemeinde Schwarzenburg, 2019, http://www.schwarzenburg.ch/portraet/geschichte/
Dubler, Anne-Marie. Wahlern, in: Historisches Lexikon der Schweiz (HLS) 2014, URL: http://www.hls-dhs-dss.ch/textes/d/D483.php
Fritz Indermühle. Kirchen Fenster in Wahlern, in: Das Magazin von Schwarzenburg, Ausgabe No 10, Oktober 2012, S 4-8, http://www.schwarzenburg.ch/fileadmin/_migrated/content_uploads/schwarzenburg_10-2012.pdf
Reformierten Kirchen Bern-Jura-Solothurn, Kirchenvisite, 2019, http://kirchenvisite.ch/verzeichnis/?open=66&title=KircheWahlern
Schloss Schwarzenburg, 2019, https://www.schloss-schwarzenburg.ch/schloss/geschichte

Stage 13: Schwarzenburg to Fribourg
Dubler, Anne-Marie. Grasburg, in: Historisches Lexikon der Schweiz (HLS) 2016, URL: http://www.hls-dhs-dss.ch/textes/d/D8443.php
Burgenwelt.org, 2019, http://www.burgenwelt.org/schweiz/grasburg/object.php
Information Tafeln bei der Ruine Grasburg, 2019
Birchler, Ursula. Heitenried, in: Historisches Lexikon der Schweiz (HLS) 2008, URL: http://www.hls-dhs-dss.ch/textes/d/D1028.php
Pfarrei St. Michael, 2018, www.pfarrei-heitenried.ch,
Vereins- und Kulturhaus Heitenried, 2018, http://www.vereinshaus.ch/index.php?id=1_1
Die Schweizer Schlösser, 2019, http://www.swisscastles.ch/Fribourg/heitenried.html
Pfarrei St. Michael, 2018, http://www.pfarrei-heitenried.ch/kapellen/magdalenakapellen.html
Kolly, Franz. Die Magdalenakapelle und die zwei Bethäuschen im Schlosswald Heitenried, 2009
Pfarrei St. Michael, 2018, http://www.pfarrei-heitenried.ch/kapellen/winterlingen.html
Information brochure at the chapel in Winterlingen, 2018
Folini, Christian. Schlacht bei Murten, in: Historisches Lexikon der Schweiz (HLS) 2010, URL: http://www.hls-dhs-dss.ch/textes/d/D8884.php
Pfarramt Reformierte Kirchgemeinde St. Antoni, 2018, www.ref-kirche-stantoni.ch
Kopp, Peter. Sankt Antoni, in: Historisches Lexikon der Schweiz (HLS) 2011, URL: http://www.hls-dhs-dss.ch/textes/d/D1033.php
Pfarrei St. Antoni, 2019, http://www.pfarrei-stantoni.ch/?gebauede_geschichte
Gemeinde St. Antoni, 2019, https://www.stantoni.ch/geschichte/4428
Pfarrei Tafers, 2019, https://www.pfarrei-tafers.ch/ueber-uns/liegenschaften/
Information Tafeln bei Kapelle und Kirche in Tafers, 2018
Catedral de Santo Domingo, 2019, http://catedralsantodomingo.com/patrimonio
Kopp, Peter. Tafers, in: Historisches Lexikon der Schweiz (HLS) 2012, URL: http://www.hls-dhs-dss.ch/textes/d/D1037.php
Pfarrei Düdingen, 2019, https://www.pfarrei-duedingen.ch/hauptseite/gebäude_geschichte/kapellen_einsiedelei.html
Saner, Regula. Freiburger Nachrichten: Schönberg-Kapelle wird restauriert, 04.07.2017, https://www.freiburger-nachrichten.ch/grossfreiburg/schonberg-kapelle-wird-restauriert
Paroisse de St-Nicolas/St-Paul Fribourg, 2019, https://www.stpaul.ch/infrastructure/eglise-st-paul
Nicoulin, Martin. Invitation à la joie éternelle, L'église de l'Auge et ses saints: Paroisse Saint-Maurice, Fribourg, 2016.
Paroisse Saint-Maurice Fribourg, 2018, https://www.stmaurice-fribourg.ch/art-histoire/
Galliker, Michel, 2018, on abbaye1500.ch, http://www.abbaye1500.ch/index.php/lieux-dedies/lieux-dedies-suisse/eglise-saint-maurice-fribourg-fribourg-suisse
Paroisse de St-Nicolas/St-Paul Fribourg, 2019, https://www.stnicolas.ch/cathedrale/histoire
Fribourg Tourisme, 2018, Information Brochure in the church: Fribourg, Cathedral of St. Nicholas
Fribourg Tourisme, 2018, www.fribourgtourisme.ch/en/P20901/notre-dame-basilica;
Fondation de la Basilique Notre Dame, 2019, http://basilique-fribourg.ch/
Fribourg Region, 2019, www.fribourgregion.ch/en/P20905/franciscan-church
Cordeliers/Minoriten, 2019, https://www.cordeliers.ch/kloster/schweiz/freiburg/kloster/geschichte-des-franziskanerklosters/

Franziskanerkloster Freiburg, Information Broschüre in der Kirche, 3. Auflage, 2017
La Visitation de Sainte Marie, 2019, http://www.la-visitation.org/les-monasteres/fribourg/le-monastere
Zbinden, Raphael. Kath.ch: Die Kapuziner sind seit 400 Jahren in Freiburg, 27.10.17, https://www.kath.ch/newsd/die-kapuziner-sind-seit-400-jahren-in-freiburg/
Capucins-fribourg.ch, 2019, https://www.capucins-fribourg.ch/geschichte/
Collegium St. Michael, 2018, http://www.csmfr.ch/www/Notre-college/L-Historique
Schöpfer, Hermann. Freiburg (Gemeinde), in: Historisches Lexikon der Schweiz (HLS) 2010, URL: http://www.hls-dhs- dss.ch/textes/d/D953.php
Fribourg Tourisme et Région, 2019, https://www.fribourgtourisme.ch/de/Z9484/die-stadtmauern;

Stage L1: Luzern to Werthenstein

Welti, Philippe. Zeitpunkt: Die Fast-Reformation in Luzern, 28. Dezember 2017, http://www.zeitpunkt.ch/die-fast-reformation-luzern
Katholische Kirche Luzern, 2018, https://www.kathluzern.ch/st-leodegar-im-hof/ueber-uns.html
City of Luzern, 2018, https://www.luzern.com/en/things-to-do/sights/church-of-st-leodegar/
Wanner, Konrad. Luzern (Gemeinde), in: Historisches Lexikon der Schweiz, (HLS) 2016, URL: http://www.hls-dhs-dss.ch/textes/d/D624.php
Katholische Kirche Luzern, 2018, https://www.kathluzern.ch/tourismus/hofkirche/rundgang-aussen/hotspots-aussen/leonhardskapelle.html
Katholische Kirche Luzern, 2018, Othmar Frei, 1250 Jahre gelebter Glaube im Hof, in Pfarreiblatt 6/2018, Luzern, https://www.kathluzern.ch/fileadmin/user_upload/Files/Dokumente/Pfarreiblatt_2018/Pfarreiblatt_Stadt_Luzern_06_2018.pdf
Reformierte Kirche Luzern, 2018, Geschichte der Matthäuskirche, https://www.reflu.ch/luzern-stadt/ueber-uns/Gebaeude-und-Raeume/Matthaeuskirche-und-Gemeindehaus-Altstadt/Geschichte-der-Matthaeuskirche
Katholische Kirchgemeinde Luzern, 2017, Gesamtsanierung und Neugestaltung Innenraum Peterskapelle, https://www.kathluzern.ch/fileadmin/user_upload/Files/B_A_Peterskapelle_Web.pdf, S. 3-6
City of Lucerne, 2018, https://www.luzern.com/en/highlights/the-city/chapel-bridge-and-water-tower/
All-about-switzerland.info, 2005-2010, http://lucerne.all-about-switzerland.info/lucerne-chapelbridge-watertower.html
Jesuitenkirche Luzern, 2018, http://www.jesuitenkirche-luzern.ch/geschichte.htm
Katholische Kirche Luzern, 2018, https://www.kathluzern.ch/jesuitenkirche.html
Katholische Kirche Luzern, 2018, https://www.kathluzern.ch/tourismus/franziskanerkirche/geschichte.html
Kamber, Peter. Luzern (Kanton), in: Historisches Lexikon der Schweiz, (HLS) 2018, URL: http://www.hls-dhs-dss.ch/textes/d/D7382.php
Lischer, Markus. Luzern (Gemeinde), in: Historisches Lexikon der Schweiz, (HLS) 2016, URL: http://www.hls-dhs-dss.ch/textes/d/D624.php
Hegglin, Clemens und Fritz Glauser. Kloster und Pfarrei zu Franziskanern in Luzern, Geschichte des Konvents (vor 1260 bis 1838) und der Pfarrei (seit 1845), Baugeschichte der Kirche. Luzern/Stuttgart: Rex-Verlag, 1989. S. 130-133, S. 381
All-about-switzerland.info, 2005-2010, http://lucerne.all-about-switzerland.info/lucerne-spreuerbridge-dance-death.html
Moos von, Dorothe. Maria auf der Reuss, Pfarreiblatt Stadt Luzern 09/2011, S. 2
St. Jost.ch, 2018, http://www.st-jost.ch/10_kirche/kirche-fs.html
Reformierte Teilkirchgemeinde Malters, 2015, Festschrift zum 100 Jahr Jubiläum der Mirjamkirche, S. 21.
Pfarrei Malters, Pfarreiblatt 12/2015, http://www.pfarrei-malters.ch/__/frontend/handler/document.php?id=244&type=42, p. 10-11.
Gemeindeverwaltung Malters, 2018, http://www.malters.ch/de/tourismus/sehenswuerdigkeiten/welcome.php?action=showobject&object_id=2119
Hörsch, Waltraud. Malters, in: Historisches Lexikon der Schweiz, (HLS) 2009, URL: http://www.hls-dhs-dss.ch/textes/d/D625.php
Kaiser, Lothar. Blatten – Malters – Schachen, Pfarrkirche und Kapellen, Malters: Kirchenrat Malters, 2004.
Lipp, Tamara. Luzerner Zeitung, 12.11.2014, https://www.luzernerzeitung.ch/zentralschweiz/luzern/kirche-malters-wollte-hoch-hinaus-ld.101342
Gemeindeverwaltung Malters, 2018, http://www.malters.ch/de/tourismus/sehenswuerdigkeiten/
Pfarramt St. Martin Malters, Pfarreiblatt 20/2017, 375 Jahre St-Ida-Kapelle, http://www.pfarrei-malters.ch/__/frontend/handler/document/42/323/Web_20-17_MaltersSchwarzenberg.pdf, S. 4
Pfarramt St. Martin Malters, Pfarreiblatt 16/2014, Die Herz-Jesu-Kapelle strahlt wieder, http://www.pfarrei-malters.ch/__/frontend/handler/document.php?id=217&type=42, S. 4
Pfarrei Werthenstein, 2018, http://www.pfarrei-werthenstein.ch/51081499d20d42306/index.html

Stadler, Matthias. Luzerner Zeitung, 31.05.2016. Kirche Werthenstein: Hier kommt der Politiker ins Schwärmen, https://www.luzernerzeitung.ch/zentralschweiz/luzern/serie-kirche-werthenstein-hier-kommt-der-politiker-ins-schwaermen-ld.99255
Gemeinde Werthenstein, 2013, http://www.werthenstein.ch/wirtschaft-tourismus/kloster-werthenstein/
Mulle, Peter. Werthenstein, in: Historisches Lexikon der Schweiz, (HLS) 2013, URL: http://www.hls-dhs-dss.ch/textes/d/D591.php

Stage L2: Werthenstein to Huttwil
Erni, Lena, and Saphina Kunz. Let's go jogging. Abschluss Projekt 2014, P. 17, http://www.ruswil.ch/dl.php/de/5385d9f8b6dab/Lets_go_jogging.pdf
Pfarrei St. Mauritius Ruswil, 2018, http://www.pfarrei-ruswil.ch/?Kirchgemeinde:Kirchen_und_Kapellen:Kapelle_St._Gallus_und_Erasmus_in_Buholz
Sanktgallus.net, 2018, http://www.sanktgallus.net/die-kirchen/buholz/
Gemeinde Menznau, 2018, Geschichte Geiss, http://www.menznau.ch/xml_1/internet/de/application/d1/f84.cfm
Hörsch, Waltraud. Geiss, in: Historisches Lexikon der Schweiz, (HLS) 2005, URL: http://www.hls-dhs-dss.ch/textes/d/D7515.php
Katholische Kirche Willisau, 2018, https://www.kath-kirche-willisau.ch/unsere-kirchen.html
Burgenwelt.org, 2018, http://www.burgenwelt.org/schweiz/willisau_sm/object.php
Häfliger, Alois. Die Kapelle St. Niklaus auf dem Berg in Willisau. Willisau: Regionales Verkehrsbüro Willisau, 2003
Willisau Tourismus, 2018, www.willisau-tourismus.ch, https://www.willisau-tourismus.ch/fileadmin/user_upload/Willisau_Tourismus/PDF/staedtlifuehrung-willisau_105x210mm_web.pdf
Verkehrsverein Willisau, Kleiner Geschichts- und Kunstführer Willisau, Willisau: 1985
Balli, Susanne. Luzerner Zeitung, 27.01.2015, Willisau: Kirche verbindet alt und neu, https://www.luzernerzeitung.ch/zentralschweiz/luzern/willisau-kirche-verbindet-alt-und-neu-ld.101173
Hörsch, Waltraud. Willisau Stadt, in: Historisches Lexikon der Schweiz, (HLS) 2016, URL: http://www.hls-dhs-dss.ch/textes/d/D688.php
Reformierte Kirche Luzern, 2018, https://www.reflu.ch/willisau-hueswil/ueber-uns/Liegenschaften/Kirchenzentrum-Adlermatte
Kirchenrat Ufhusen, 2018, Profil der Pfarrei St. Johannes Ufhusen, http://www.ufhusen.ch/uploads/media/2018_Pfarreiprofil_Ufhusen.pdf, S. 7
Kneubühler, Anita. Ufhuser Kirche St. Johannes Bapt. und Ihre Kunstschätze. Ufhusen: Pfarrei Ufhusen, 2014.
Hörsch, Waltraud. Ufhusen, in: Historisches Lexikon der Schweiz, (HLS) 2014, URL: http://www.hls-dhs-dss.ch/textes/d/D684.php
Reformierte Kirchen Bern-Jura-Solothurn, 2018 http://kirchenvisite.ch/verzeichnis/?open=62&title=KircheHuttwil
Rettenmund, Jürg. Huttwil, in: Historisches Lexikon der Schweiz, (HLS) 2008, URL: http://www.hls-dhs-dss.ch/textes/d/D550.php
Röm. Kath. Kirchgemeinde Langenthal, 2019, https://kathlangenthal.ch/huttwil/portrait/historisches/
Röm. Kath. Kirchgemeinde Langenthal, 2019, https://kathlangenthal.ch/assets/Huttwil/Bilder/Portrait/Geschichte%20der%20Pfarrei.pdf

Stage L3: Huttwil to Burgdorf
Romantik Hotel Bären, 2018, https://www.baeren-duerrenroth.ch/assets/Uploads/Geschichtliches-und-Historisches.pdf
Tourismus Oberaargau, 2018, http://www.myoberaargau.com/de/freizeit-ausfluge.53/angebote.194/kirche-durrenroth.1004.html
Dubler, Anne-Marie. Dürrenroth, in: Historisches Lexikon der Schweiz, (HLS) 2018, URL: http://www.hls-dhs-dss.ch/textes/d/D548.php
Switzerland Tourism, 2018, https://www.myswitzerland.com/en-ch/lueg-affoltern-im-emmental.html
Reformierte Kirche Burgdorf, 2018, https://www.ref-kirche-burgdorf.ch/kirchgemeinde/gebaeude/bartholomaeuskapelle/
Schweizer, Jürg. Die Kunstdenkmäler des Kantons Bern, Landband 1: Die Stadt Burgdorf. Basel: 1985. S. 447-450
Reformierte Kirche Burgdorf, 2018, https://www.ref-kirche-burgdorf.ch/kirchgemeinde/geschichte/
Reformierte Kirchen Bern-Jura-Solothurn, 2018, http://kirchenvisite.ch/verzeichnis/?open=41&title=StadtkircheBurgdorf
Römisch-Katholische Kirchgemeinde Burgdorf, 2018, https://www.kath-burgdorf.ch/wir.html

Swiss Timber Bridges, 2018, http://www.swiss-timber-bridges.ch/detail/687
Stiftung Schloss Burgdorf, 2018, https://schloss-burgdorf.ch/
The Swiss Castles, 2018, http://www.swisscastles.ch/Bern/burgdorf_d.html
Stadtverwaltung Burgdorf, 2018, https://www.burgdorf.ch/de/leben-wohnen/stadtportrait/geschichte.php
Dubler, Anne-Marie. Burgdorf (Gemeinde), in: Historisches Lexikon der Schweiz, (HLS) 2011, URL: http://www.hls-dhs-dss.ch/textes/d/D241.php
Dubler, Anne-Marie. Burgdorferkrieg, in: Historisches Lexikon der Schweiz, (HLS) 2003, URL: http://www.hls-dhs-dss.ch/textes/d/D8733.php
Dubler, Anne-Marie. Burgdorf (Herrschaft, Amtsbezirk), in: Historisches Lexikon der Schweiz, (HLS) 2003, URL: http://www.hls-dhs-dss.ch/textes/d/D24619.php

Stage L4: Burgdorf to Bern
Reformierte Kirchgemeinde Krauchthal, 2018, http://www.kirche-krauchthal.ch/startseite/portrait/kirche/
Reformierte Kirchen Bern-Jura-Solothurn, 2018, http://kirchenvisite.ch/verzeichnis/?open=60&title=KircheKrauchthal
Dubler, Anne-Marie. Krauchthal, in: Historisches Lexikon der Schweiz, (HLS) 2008, URL: http://www.hls-dhs-dss.ch/textes/d/D251.php
Dubler, Anne-Marie. Thorberg, in: Historisches Lexikon der Schweiz, (HLS) 2012, URL: http://www.hls-dhs-dss.ch/textes/d/D8503.php
Polizei- und Militärdirektion des Kantons Bern, 2018, https://www.pom.be.ch/pom/de/index/freiheitsentzug-betreuung/vollzugseinrichtungen_erwachsene/anstalten_thorberg/portrait/geschichte.html
The Swiss Castles, 2018, http://www.swisscastles.ch/Bern/thorberg.html
Dubler, Anne-Marie. Utzigen, in: Historisches Lexikon der Schweiz, (HLS) 2013, URL: http://www.hls-dhs-dss.ch/textes/d/D8365.php
Stadtgrün Bern, 2018, Broschüre: Der Schosshaldenfriedhof, Ein Spaziergang mit Geschichten.
Switzerland Tourism, 2018, https://www.myswitzerland.com/en-ch/paul-klee-center-bern.html
City of Bern, 2018, https://www.bern.com/en/detail/the-bearpark
Burgenwelt.org, 2018, http://www.burgenwelt.org/schweiz/nydegg/object.php
Reformierte Kirchgemeinde Nydegg, 2018, https://nydegg.refbern.ch/de/-stellt-sich-vor/die-nydeggkirche-98.html
Reformierte Kirchen Bern-Jura-Solothurn, 2018, http://kirchenvisite.ch/verzeichnis/?open=50&title=Nydeggkirche
Mawson, Emily. the local.ch, 30.06.2014, https://www.thelocal.ch/20140630/berns-brimming-fountains-tell-the-capitals-story
Plattform für Kunst Kultur und Gesellschaft, 2018, g26.ch, https://web.archive.org/web/20111009221144/http://g26.ch/berninfo_brunnen.html
Schweizerische Gesellschaft für Kulturgüterschutz, 2012, http://www.sgkgs.ch/de/Kulturgueter-1/Hist-Bauten--Baudenkmäler/Bern/Bern-Historische-Brunnen
Christkatholische Kirchgemeinde Bern, 2018, https://www.christkath-bern.ch/kirche-st-peter-und-paul/
Rutschi, Sandra. Berner Zeitung, 08.12.2014: Der Kirche der etwas anderen Katholiken, https://www.bernerzeitung.ch/region/bern/Die-Kirche-der-etwas-anderen-Katholiken/story/25926699
Evangelisch-reformierte Kirchgemeinde Bern, 2018, https://www.egliserefberne.ch/fr/une-eglise-vivante/un-peu-dhistoire-64.html
Switzerland Tourism, 2018, https://www.myswitzerland.com/en-ch/franzoesische-kirche-french-church-bern.html
Bern Tourist Information, 2018, http://www.zeitglockenturm.ch/
Marti, Markus. 2018, http://www.zytglogge-bern.ch/
Einstein House Bern, 2018, http://www.einstein-bern.ch
Berner Münster, 2013, https://www.bernermuenster.ch/de/berner-muenster/
Zahnd, Urs Martin. Bern (Gemeinde) in: Historisches Lexikon der Schweiz, (HLS) 2016, URL: http://www.hls-dhs-dss.ch/textes/d/D209.php
Junker, Beat, und Anne-Marie Dubler. Bern (Kanton) in: Historisches Lexikon der Schweiz, (HLS) 2018, URL: http://www.hls-dhs-dss.ch/textes/d/D7383.php

Stage L5: Bern to Mättiwil
Tiefbauamt Bern, 2018, https://www.kirchenfeldbruecke.ch
Bernisches Historisches Museum, 2018, https://www.bhm.ch
Das Schweizer Parlament, 2018, https://www.parlament.ch
Evangelisch-reformierte Kirchgemeinde Köniz, 2018, https://www.kg-koeniz.ch/de/meine-kirchgemeinde/portrait/Geschichte/index.php#anchor_241624dd_Accordion-Kirche-Wabern

Pfarrei St. Michael, 2018, 50 Jahre St. Michael – Festschrift 2009, https://www.kathbern.ch/fileadmin/user_upload/Pfarreien/koeniz-wabern/Dokumente/Informationen/Jubilaeum/Festschrift_50_Jahre_St._Michael_scan.pdf
Gurten – Park im Grünen, 2018, https://www.gurtenpark.ch/de-CH/Gurtenbahn
Alters- und Pflegeheim Kühlewil, 2018, https://www.aph-kuehlewil.ch
Oekumenisches Zentrum Kehrsatz, 2013, http://www.oeki.ch/oeki

www.ingramcontent.com/pod-product-compliance
Lightning Source LLC
LaVergne TN
LVHW050914080826
845145LV00001B/77

* 9 7 8 3 9 0 6 8 6 1 3 5 7 *